WINGS
THE CONQUEST OF THE AIR

THE JET AGE

David Jefferis

Illustrated by
Terry Hadler
Ron Jobson and Michael Roffe

Franklin Watts
London New York Toronto Sydney

First published in 1987 by
Franklin Watts
12a Golden Square
London W1R 4BA

First published in the USA
by Franklin Watts Inc.
387 Park Avenue South
New York, N.Y. 10016

First published in Australia
by Franklin Watts
Australia
14 Mars Road
Land Cove, NSW 2066

UK ISBN: 0 86313 522 6
US ISBN: 0-531-10508-3
Library of Congress
Catalog Card No: 87-50779

Technical consultant
Tim Callaway, RAF Museum,
Hendon, London

Designed and produced by
Sunrise Books

Printed in Belgium

WINGS
THE CONQUEST OF THE AIR

THE JET AGE

Contents

Introduction

The jet age dawned on August 27, 1939, when Erich Warsitz test-flew a small, single-seat plane on a short circuit round an air base at Marienhe in Germany. The plane was the Heinkel He 178, the world's first jet aircraft. Other countries had their research programmes too and in Britain, Frank Whittle ran his first working jet engine on April 12, 1937. His company, Power Jets Ltd, was given a contract to build an engine for an experimental plane, the E.28/39. The plane made its first flight in May 1941.

During World War II several jets went into service, but jet fighters were never flown in combat against each other.

Jets have taken over from propellers because, size for size, a jet gives much more power and speed. Propellers give a maximum speed of little more than 885 km/h (550 mph). Jet planes can go nearly four times as fast.

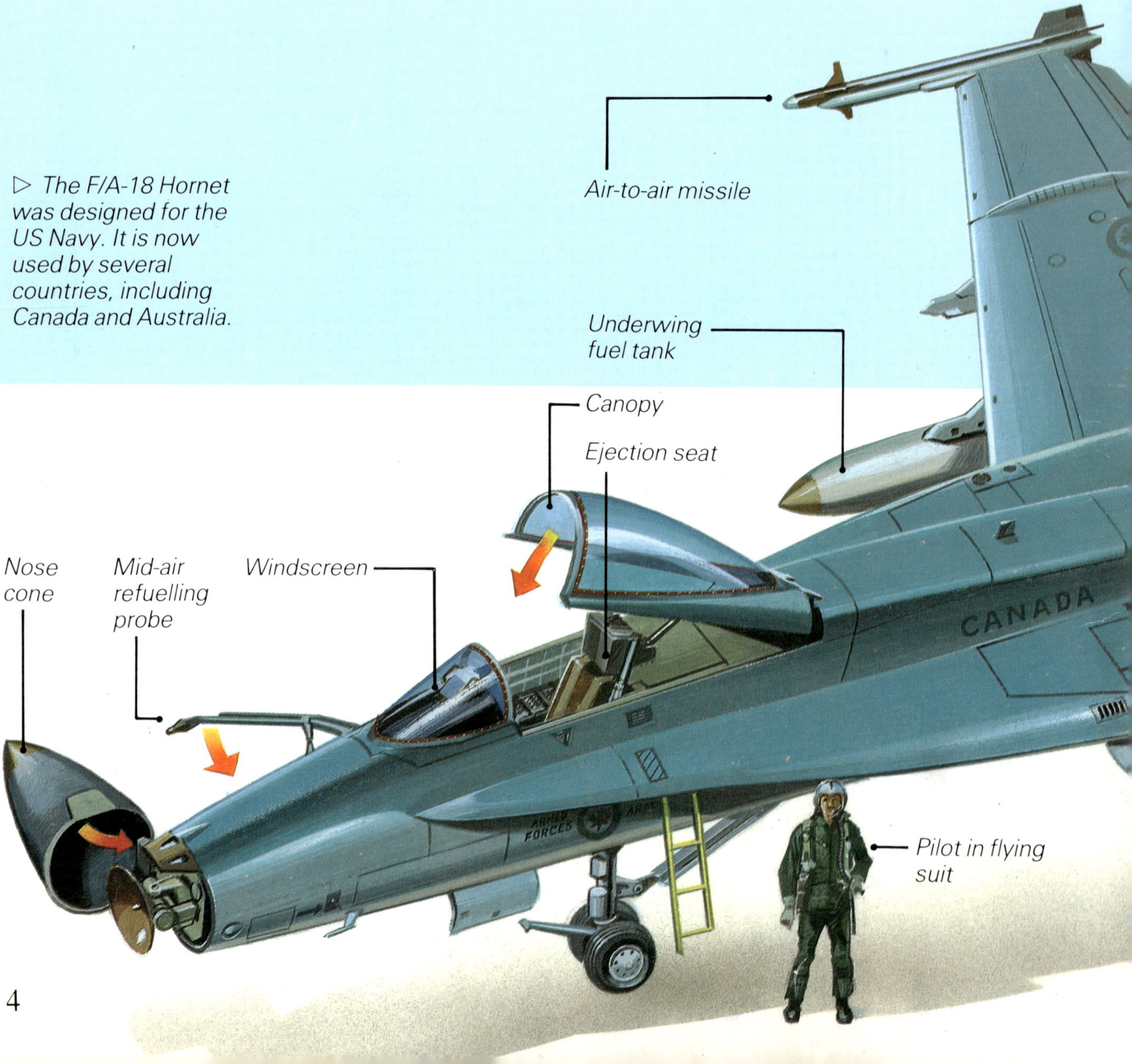

▷ *The F/A-18 Hornet was designed for the US Navy. It is now used by several countries, including Canada and Australia.*

The modern combat jet

Today's fast jets combine many attributes, of which high speed is only one. The fastest jets can fly at over 3,220 km/h (2,000 mph), but often designers put agility and turning ability before top speed. In air combat a missile can be launched to outpace a plane which is using straight-line speed to escape the fight. And a jet flying at very high speeds uses huge amounts of aviation fuel.

A reasonably short takeoff distance and the ability to carry heavy loads are other important design features.

The twin fin F/A-18 Hornet shown here is a typical modern attack fighter. It was designed as a navy plane, for use on aircraft carriers, but it is suitable for ordinary runways too. Its two engines have high power for good acceleration and give the pilot a safety margin in case one of the engines fails – he ought to be able to get home safely on the remaining engine.

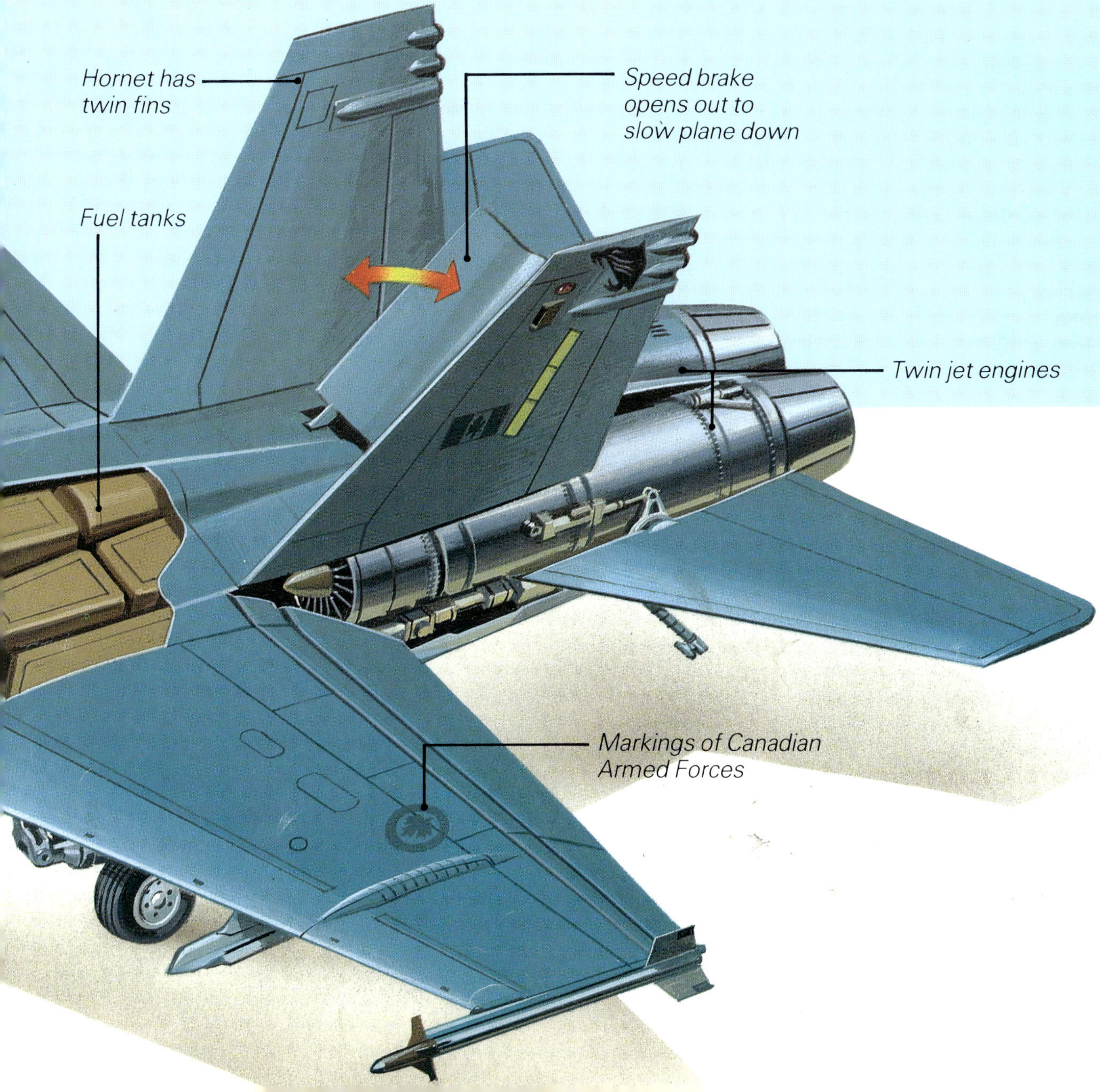

Downing a doodlebug

The British Gloster Meteor was the first jet to be used in an attack against another jet, the unmanned German V-1 flying bomb nicknamed the "doodlebug". V-1s were small robot planes launched against Britain by the Germans from sites in France. The V-1 flew on a pre-set course for up to 200 km (125 miles). Then the engine cut out and it glided down to the ground and exploded.

By late July, 1944, the first Meteor squadron was ready to go hunting for doodlebugs. On August 4 Flying Officer Dean spotted a V-1 flying below him. Dean swung his Meteor into a head-on dive at 724 km/h (450 mph). He lined up on the V-1 and squeezed his gun trigger, but at the last moment the guns jammed and the bomb flew on, unharmed. Dean pulled round in a diving turn and chased the V-1 from behind. With jammed guns, he couldn't shoot the robot down, so he flew just below it and banked sharply, catching the V-1's wing with his own.

The violent disturbance toppled the V-1's sensitive gyro stabilizer and the flying bomb flipped sideways, to crash in open countryside. Twenty-five minutes later, at 4.41 pm, another pilot in Dean's squadron downed a V-1, but this time by cannon fire – the other Meteor's guns didn't jam.

The fastest jet used in the war was the Messerschmitt Me 262. But its engines were unreliable and it came too late to have much effect against the slower but much more numerous Allied aircraft.

Breaking the sound barrier

Mach 1 is the speed of sound, 1,225 km/h (762 mph) at sea level. When a plane nears Mach 1, the air in front is compressed to form pressure waves, rather like the V-shape patterns at the bow and stern of a ship. These are strong enough to cause damage, especially to the wings and tailplane. In the mid-1940s several planes broke up and pilots were killed as they tried to break the "sound barrier". Many people thought it was impossible. But research showed that with thin wings and other design changes, planes might be able to go supersonic. In 1947 American pilot Charles Yeager flew a rocketplane to break the sound barrier for the first time. On September 9, 1948, the British De Havilland DH 108 was flown past Mach 1. Though it had to dive to build up enough speed, the little plane was the first supersonic jet. First fighter to go supersonic in level flight was the Super Sabre, which went into service in 1953.

△ *Dean flew his Meteor just under the V-1's wing to unbalance the bomb. The V-1 had a type of engine known as a pulse jet. It took in rapid gulps of air, which were mixed with fuel and ignited. The blast sputtered back, out of the tailpipe.*

Sabre against MiG

The first combat between swept-wing jet fighters was during the Korean War, in which United Nations troops fought Communist forces who were trying to invade South Korea.

On December 17, 1950, American pilot Bruce Hinton, flying in a group of four swept-wing Sabres, spotted four Chinese Air Force MiG-15s climbing up towards them. The Sabre and the MiG were similar in size, though the MiG was a little faster.

Hinton picked on the number two MiG and dived into the MiG's "6 o'clock" position, directly behind it, Hinton's Sabre bounced and twisted in the MiG's turbulent exhaust, but he closed in to 244 m (800 ft). He took careful aim and fired his guns, sending a long burst of shells straight up the MiG's tailpipe and into its engine. Pieces flew out, smoke filled the tailpipe and a long tongue of flame licked out of the opening.

The MiG slowed down and Hinton closed his throttle and popped out his airbrakes to follow the Chinese plane. The MiG banked left, losing height, and Hinton pulled back to watch the smoking jet. The two planes were alone in the sky, having lost the others during their combat. "OK, I'll finish him!" thought Hinton, and dived in to fire another long burst, this time into the forward fuselage.

The MiG rolled on its back, trailing smoke and flame, Hinton looked down to see it crash into the snow-covered winter ground below.

The Chinese pilot went down with his plane – Hinton saw no parachute.

▷ Before firing a second time, Hinton flew in close to the MiG. MiG is a Soviet aircraft, the letters standing for the design team of Mikoyan and Gurevich. The MiG-15 was their first swept-wing fighter.

Combat manoeuvres

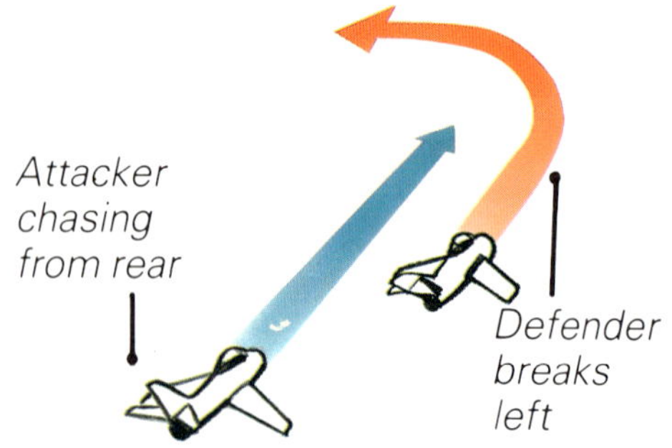

△ Jet combats are similar to those of earlier wars, though fought with more powerful machines. The break is a sharp turn to left or right to avoid an enemy aircraft chasing from the rear.

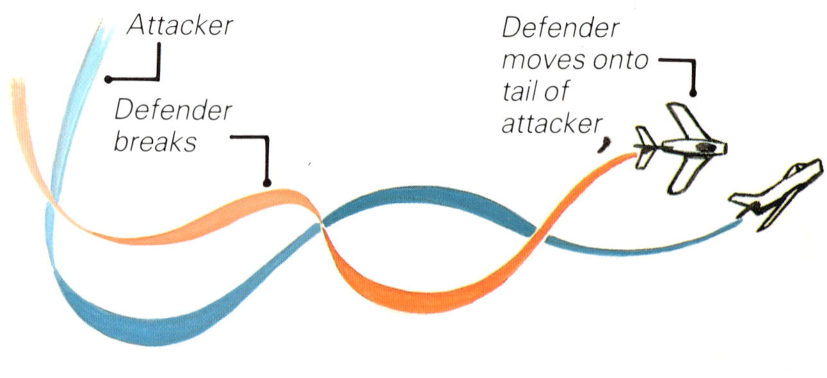

△ Using the scissors is a way to get on the tail of an attacker. A hard break by the defender can make the attacker overshoot. As he turns, the defender cuts across onto his tail. The defender can become the attacker.

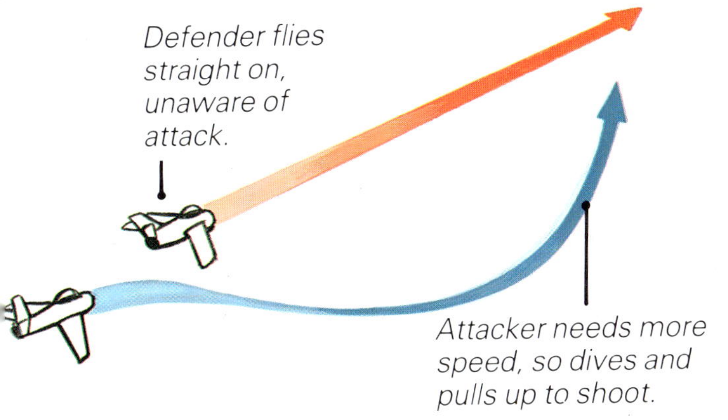

△ There are several types of yo-yo. This one gives an attacker more speed in a chase. He goes into a shallow dive to pick up more speed, then pulls up and shoots into the enemy aircraft's underside.

△ The clock code is used by pilots to indicate the direction of other aircraft. A plane always points to its own 12 o'clock position, so 6 o'clock is behind it, while 9 o'clock is on its left, 3 o'clock on the right.

Eject! Eject!

One of the problems of flying a high-speed jet is getting out in an emergency. The airflow is so powerful that it can trap a pilot inside the plane. Propeller planes flew slower, so pilots didn't have quite such a problem.

In January 1944 a test pilot tried to get out of a Meteor when the engines failed, but he was knocked out cold by the battering ram of the airflow. As the plane went down he was flung out, still unconscious, and was killed.

German aircrew had begun to use ejection seats several years earlier, in 1941. By the end of World War II more than 60 German pilots had made emergency ejections, using compressed gas-powered seats. The problem was that the men were blasted out so quickly they often had severe spine injuries. So future ejection seats had to have a powerful but smooth acceleration.

Many answers to the problems of leaving a high speed plane were suggested, including one that did away with the ejection seat. Instead, the aircraft would disintegrate, leaving the pilot in mid-air, ready to pull his parachute rip-cord!

The ejection seats of today are fully automatic. The pilot simply pulls the firing handle. The seat punches out, the parachute opens automatically and the seat falls away. Even so, back injuries are common after ejection.

On overwater missions, survival equipment includes life jacket, rubber dinghy and radio beacon.

▷ *In the years since their development, ejection seats have saved the lives of thousands of aviators.*

In May 1967, the pilot of this Lightning escaped when the aircraft fell out of control. It eventually crashed into the sea.

How an ejection seat works

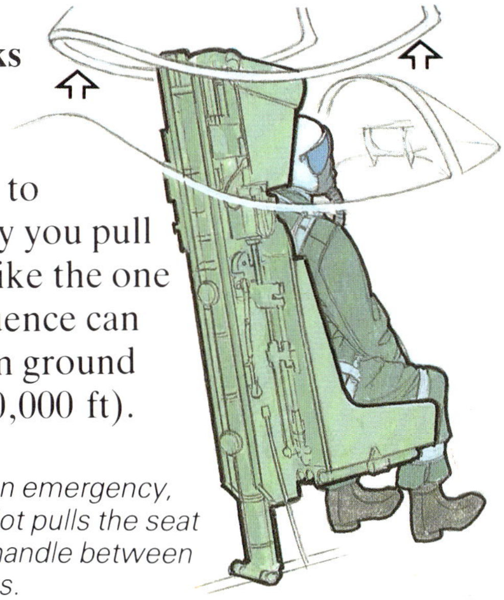

Ejection seats are easy to use – in an emergency you pull the firing handle. A seat like the one shown in this picture sequence can be used at any height from ground level to over 15,000 m (50,000 ft).

▷ In an emergency, this pilot pulls the seat firing handle between his legs.

◁ Rockets blast seat out of the cockpit.

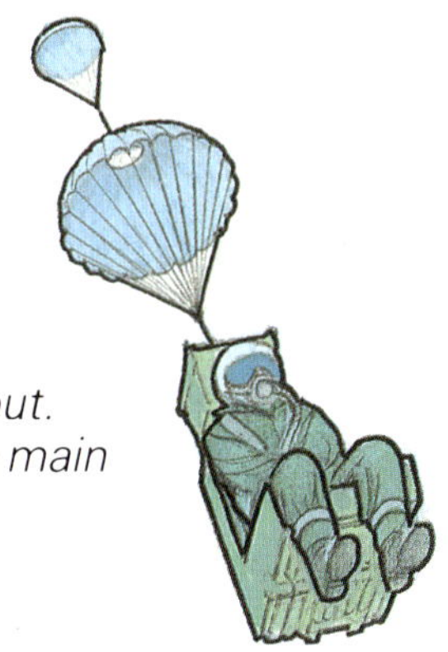

▷ Small drogue parachute pops out. This pulls out the main parachute.

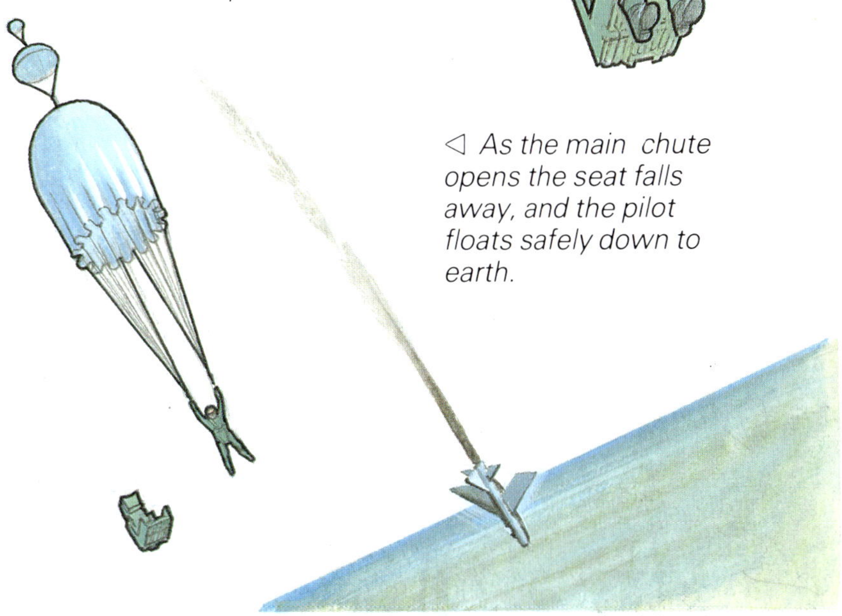

◁ As the main chute opens the seat falls away, and the pilot floats safely down to earth.

Runway busters

Until the end of World War II, all that most fighter planes needed for takeoff was a large, fairly smooth, flat area, but most jets take off at high speed, so they need long runways. The importance of runways was made clear on the first morning of the Arab-Israeli war in 1967.

Just after dawn on June 5 flights of Israeli fighter-bombers took off to cross the Sinai desert at over 900 km/h (600 mph). Their targets were Egyptian air bases. The Israeli planes flew low so they wouldn't be spotted until the last moment. And they were too low and fast for Egyptian anti-aircraft missiles to hit them.

The only Egyptian planes in the air were four trainers, all of which were shot down. The attackers, in four waves, headed straight for the hundreds of planes – fighters, bombers, transports and helicopters – lined up at the various airfields.

But the Israeli jets ignored all those planes and made instead for the runways. As they roared by, they dropped a new kind of bomb, a "concrete dibber". As each bomb was released, rockets slowed it down, a parachute popped out of the tail and the bomb swung down towards the runway. Then booster rockets blasted the bomb straight down onto the

concrete. As the bomb exploded, it blew a hole in the runway surface. A few bomb craters down each runway made it useless, and the Egyptian planes were trapped on the ground.

The next waves of attackers fired guns and missiles at the trapped aircraft. Frantic Arab pilots started up their MiGs, only to find the hot exhausts made perfect targets for Israeli heat-seeking missiles. The wrecked aircraft created yet more havoc on the runways.

By midday 17 airfields had been attacked and only eight MiGs had managed to get off the ground. By the end of the day the Israelis had destroyed about 300 aircraft – most of the Egyptian air force was wrecked, burning and useless.

▽ Mirage fighters were among the attackers. The delta-wing Mirage, made in France, has been sold to many countries as a result of its success in the 1967 war. The Egyptian planes were almost all Soviet designs, including various types of MiG fighter.

Missiles or guns?

In the late 1950s missiles were developed to replace guns. Many experts thought that missile-armed aircraft would not need guns as well.

But in the skies over Vietnam in the 1960s and 1970s, combats between American and North Vietnamese planes were often one-to-one duels, similar to the dogfights of World War I. As a result, pilots needed both missiles and guns to be sure of victory.

There were various tricks to throw a missile off-track. A hard break left or right could make a missile overshoot. A climb toward the sun could fool a missile's heat detectors, which would go for the hottest thing around – the sun – instead of a jet tailpipe.

But missiles were used successfully, and on May 10, 1972, American ace Randy Cunningham, flying a Phantom II with Willie Driscoll, fought with a North Vietnamese ace, Colonel Toon. Toon roared towards the American plane, firing his MiG-17's guns. To avoid the gunfire, Cunningham pulled up into a vertical climb, only to see the enemy pilot watching him from a few metres away and matching the manoeuvre. Seconds later, as they pulled out of the climb, Toon flew his agile MiG-17 into Cunningham's six o'clock position. Cunningham threw him off and the two pilots battled on using scissors manoeuvres, each trying to get into the other's six o'clock long enough to fire a missile or gun.

Then Cunningham cut his engine power, opened out his speedbrakes and swung in right behind Toon's MiG. He was too close to fire a missile without damaging his own plane, so he waited until Toon pulled up. Then Cunningham swung the Phantom's nose at the twisting MiG and gently squeezed the firing trigger.

A missile blasted off and exploded next to the MiG. The damaged plane went down, trailing fire.

▷ Cunningham fired a Sidewinder missile at Toon's MiG-17. The blast from the missile sent the MiG crashing out of control.

Phantoms were faster than MiG-17s, but the slower plane was more agile in combat manoeuvres, especially when flying low.

Inside a dogfighting missile

The Matra Magic is a typical air-to-air missile, similar in appearance to the Sidewinder. Like many other missiles of this type, Magic uses an infra-red system to home on a jet's exhaust heat.
1 *Infra-red heat detector system.*
2 *Computer systems guide the missile.*
3 *Explosive warhead.*
4 *Fuel for rocket motor.*
5 *Rocket nozzle.*

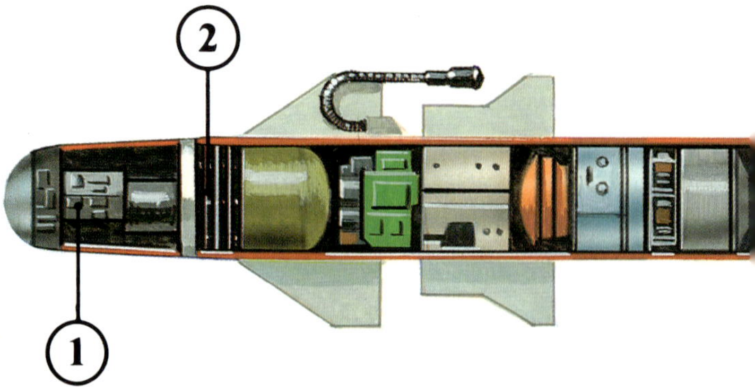

NG
VF-96
NAVY
3
4
5

Catapult takeoff

One way to get a jet into the air quickly is by using a catapult. Steam powered "cats" are used on the aircraft carriers of many navies.

One of the fastest ship-borne planes is the two-jet Grumman F-14 Tomcat which can fly at more than twice the speed of sound. Takeoff is an awesome sight as an F-14 jockeys into position, lining up on the catapult launch track. Steel plates swing up from the carrier deck to deflect the blast of the engines, which can blow a man off the deck into the water. The deck is slippery with spilt jet fuel as the ground crew prepare the F-14 for departure. In a howling gale – the carrier is steaming into wind – and in the roar from the engines the men do their various jobs.

The two men aboard the plane cross their hands over their helmets as a red-jacketed armaments man removes the "safeties" from the missiles. The hands-up position ensures no one in the plane accidentally presses a missile release trigger. Another man links the nosewheels to a hook on the catapult. Then it's launch time. The F-14 pilot lights his afterburners and extra fuel is sprayed into the exhausts to increase thrust. White-hot flames roar out of the jet pipes. The flight director waves his

arms, crossing them over his head, then crouches down, pointing down the catapult track.

"Fire the cat" comes the order. In the ship's bridge the controller presses a red button and the F-14 hurtles down the cat track. In two seconds, the plane is off the deck and clawing into the air, speed 240 km/h (150 mph) and rising. Back on deck steam hisses from the catapult, the deflector plates swing down and another plane moves up for launch.

△ A 30-tonne F-14 roars off the deck of an aircraft carrier. The F-14 has swing-wings. They move straight out for extra lift on takeoff and landing, but at high speeds the wings sweep back to arrow through the air.

Bringing a plane in for the "controlled crash" of a landing is one of the most difficult jobs any navy pilot has to do, especially at night. Then, all that is visible in the midnight-dark sea is the landing lights of the carrier, looking far too small to land on. The lights change if you are too high, too low, or not in line with the deck. In the last ten seconds you concentrate all your energy on getting down in one piece – and that means catching the plane's arrester hook on one of the five wires stretching across the deck of the carrier. If you miss, you apply full power to fly round again for another attempt.

When the Tomcat's arrester hook catches a wire, the jet is yanked from its approach speed of 225 km/h (140 mph) to a standstill in a few metres.

A flight in a sky spy

An essential job for any air force is reconnaissance – finding out what the other side is doing. The very first military planes were used as spotters for army chiefs and modern jets carry out similar jobs. The fastest recce jet is the Lockheed SR-71, named Blackbird for its blue-black finish.

Before an SR-71 mission, the pilot and reconnaissance systems officer (RSO) usually have a steak and eggs meal. This keeps them going on a mission which can last ten hours or more. After eating the two men have a thorough medical check before a final weather and mission briefing. They put on astronaut suits in case they have to eject at high altitude. Then pilot and RSO are driven out to their Blackbird, waiting on the tarmac. On the ground, the SR-71 leaks fuel. Until heated by the friction of high speed flight, the fuel tanks are porous and they "bleed" fuel until they warm up! So the pilot takes off as soon as possible.

The SR-71 climbs to 24,384 m (80,000 ft), nearly three times higher than most airliners. Once at height the plane cruises at around 3,220 km/h (2,000 mph) and its surface heats up to about 300°C (572°F).

While the pilot flies the plane the RSO operates the navigation and other equipment. This includes cameras and radar, which can map the ground even through cloud.

Once the survey is complete the pilot heads for home. After landing the ground crew have to be careful – the SR-71 stays too hot to handle for 30 minutes or more.

△ The two exhaust nozzles of the SR-71 glow white-hot as the plane flies through the upper air, too high and too fast for easy interception. But recent reports have stated that Soviet laser beams have been fired at SR-71s to blind the electronic survey systems and to dazzle the crews.

Intercepting a Bear

Like the ships and aircraft of Western armed forces, the Soviet navy and air force carry out military exercises in the Atlantic Ocean. Their aircraft, including the four-engined Tupolev Bear, often fly into the skies guarded by European air forces.

If an unidentified aircraft is spotted interceptors are sent up to investigate. The latest interceptor is the swing-wing Panavia Tornado F Mk 3 operated by the Royal Air Force.

Each squadron keeps Tornados on QRA (Quick Reaction Alert), ready for takeoff. The Tornado carries a crew of pilot and navigator. Waiting on QRA can be very boring, but often a loudspeaker in the alert room can bark a message, such as, "We have one Zombie, heading south west. We expect to scramble you in 20 minutes".

It is after midnight when, suddenly, all is action as the Tornado crew struggle into their flying suits. They climb into the plane and the pilot twirls his forefinger, a sign to the ground crew that he is ready to start up. In seconds the engines roar into life and the pilot eases the throttles forward.

The Tornado moves from its hangar towards the runway, and as the plane rolls forward pilot and navigator busily complete their pre-flight checks. All is "go": without stopping the pilot steers the Tornado onto the runway, and the jet hurtles into the air.

△ A Tornado closes in on a Bear. Such interceptions sometimes happen several times in a week. Various types of Bear are in service, including missile carriers, bombers and reconnaissance versions. The Tornado is built by aircraft makers in Britain, West Germany and Italy.

The Tornado flies north, climbing to 10,670 m (35,000 ft), guided by ground control or airborne radar planes. High over the North Atlantic pilot and navigator look for the "Zombie" and there, outlined against the glow of dawn, is a Russian Bear.

The Tornado closes in on its left wing, the international interception signal, then flies across so the pilot can inspect it. His navigator holds up a camera to take pictures and now faces can be seen looking through the Bear's portholes. Behind other windows Russian crewmen hold cameras, taking pictures of the Tornado. At mission's end both sides will inspect their photographs to see whether there is anything new in the other side's equipment.

Soon the Bear has passed out of the RAF's airspace and the Tornado is ready to return. This time there were no problems and the crews of the two planes waved to each other. But the Tornado's gun and missiles were armed and ready – and the Bear's guns tracked the RAF plane throughout the interception.

Flight training

In World War I only a few hours of flying lessons were given before pilots were sent off to fly combat missions in France but today's pilots learn to fly on a training course which lasts a year or more. Flying a modern jet aircraft is an extremely complex and demanding job. Different air forces have methods which vary in detail, but a typical course starts after a pupil has finished school or university.

Pupils take exams for intelligence, leadership and physical fitness. Then several weeks are spent on military training which includes drill routines (marching, saluting and other basics) and weapon handling. Then the flying course starts. This involves about 150 hours of flight time.

On graduation, when a pupil has

In a Hawk's cockpit

At first glance the cockpit of the Hawk jet trainer looks very complicated, yet the basic controls are similar to those of a World War I biplane.

A central stick controls side-to-side roll. Moving the stick backwards and forwards pitches the nose up and down. Foot pedals work the rudder. And a throttle controls the thrust produced by the jet engine.

In the Hawk the pupil sits in the front cockpit while the instructor sits in the raised back seat.

△ *This is the T-45A Goshawk, the US Navy's new jet trainer. It is based on the British Aerospace Hawk, a popular single-engined trainer used by several air forces, including those of Britain and Finland.*

learned to fly, he receives his "wings" and is selected for advanced training on transport or combat aircraft.

Combat pilots are taught to fly fast jets, such as the Hawk shown on these pages. Pupils learn high and low-level flying, interceptions, bad weather flying and the use of weapons – guns, missiles and bombs. The last stage of training is to specialize on one type of aircraft, thoroughly learning every part of its systems and performance.

Once this is completed, flying training is over and a pilot is posted to a squadron – and that is when the real job of combat flying starts.

Training jet pilots is very expensive and new training courses use simulators to keep costs down. A simulator has a replica cockpit connected to computers which give a realistic view out of the canopy. The cockpit tilts and moves just like the real thing and all sorts of problems and emergency situations can be run through with no danger to anyone. Once the practice routines have been mastered pupil pilots can go up in real aircraft to polish their skills. McDonnell Douglas, who are in charge of a new training scheme for the US Navy, claim "Everything the pupil does in the air he will do first in the simulator".

Aerobatic displays

Aerobatic teams show precison flying at its most skilful and the pilots who fly the planes are among the very best. Before volunteering to fly in a jet display team a pilot needs several years of experience flying in an air force squadron.

During the summer display season the new pilot flies in the back seat to get the feel of the team and of the air show business. Training proper starts after the display season has finished, at the end of autumn.

The new pilot can already fly close formation and do aerobatics. But display work demands perfection, so from now on it's practice all the time.

At first a new pilot flies in a two-plane formation, flying at medium height with the team leader. Soon they can work on more demanding low-level flying. Other aircraft are added to the two-plane formation, with the "new boy" going further out from the leader.

During a formation display the Team Leader is in complete command, flying the team of planes almost as if it were a single aircraft with the other pilots locked on to his plane, following it through the various manoeuvres. Brief radio orders from the leader tell the other pilots when to change formation.

All positions are finely judged since display jets fly as little as 2–3 m (6–10 ft) apart at speeds of 480–560 km/h (300–350 mph). The slightest error can spoil a formation display.

△ A Big Nine of jets arrive then pull up into a loop. As they climb they change into a Diamond Nine formation.

▽ The planes fly below and behind each other along the runway. They pull up into a Caterpillar Loop.

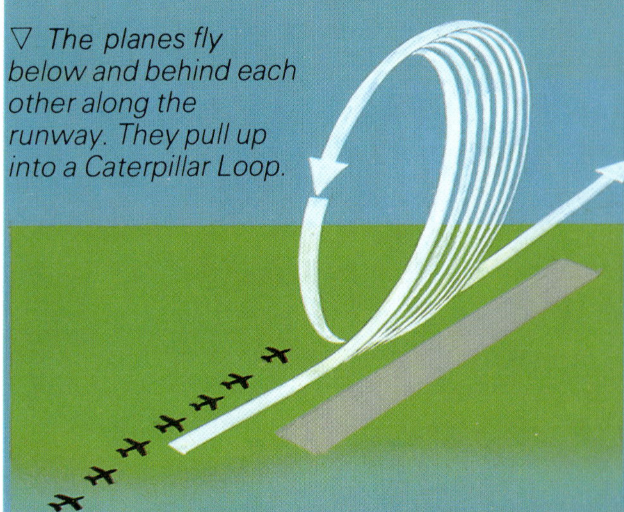

△ The Parasol Break is spectacular to watch, especially if the planes are equipped to trail coloured smoke behind them.

△ A Concorde flypast groups the team in a shape like that of the supersonic jet's wings. They pull round and change into a Feathered Arrow formation to climb and loop.

▽ Many countries have display teams. The US Air Force Thunderbirds are shown on the cover of this book, while below are the display jets of three other famous teams.

Top, Britain's Red Arrows. Middle, Italy's Frecce Tricolori. Bottom, the Patrouille de France.

Bombers

During and after World War II, heavy bombers were mostly flown at high level to keep out of range of ground based anti-aircraft guns and defending fighters.

The first jet bombers continued this tradition, the idea being that their high speed and height would make them invulnerable to defenders. But the missile age changed all that – guided by powerful radars, ground-to-air missiles developed in the 1960s could hit bombers flying at maximum altitude.

The answer was to develop bombers which could fly at low level. Flying fast and low, a bomber can fly under an enemy's radar defences – and by the time the bomber is spotted, it is too late to launch missiles.

The latest anti-bomber fighters fly at medium height and are armed with "look-down, shoot-down" missiles.

△ The Soviet Backfire is a twin-jet bomber. It is very fast and can fly at over Mach 1 at low altitude.

▽ The Tornado was first designed as a bomber. The chunky looking plane has swing-wings.

◁ The Canberra first flew in 1949 and was twice as fast as the propeller bombers in use at the time.

△ The Vulcan "V-bomber" went into service as a high altitude bomber. Later it was used for low level bombing.

△ The B-52 heavy bomber first flew in 1952 and is still in front-line service. It has eight engines.

▷ The F-111 has swing-wings. They sweep straight out for takeoff, then back for cruise.

▽ The B-1B is also a low-level attacker. It is slower than Backfire but can carry heavier loads.

Air data

Here are the main aircraft described in this book shown to scale. Bombers and Bear are in the box. The Bear is powered by turboprops, a type of engine that uses turbine power to turn propellers. Speeds shown are those at high altitude, where jets fly fastest in the thin air. At low altitude most jets give little more than half their high-level performance.

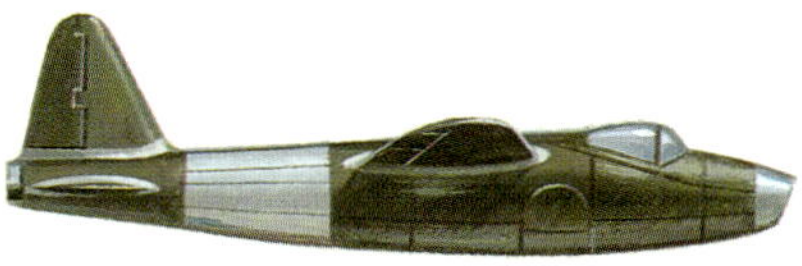

△ **Heinkel He 178**
Wingspan: *7.2 m (23 ft 7½ in)*
Length: *7.48 m (24 ft 6½ in)*
Speed: *700 km/h (435 mph)*

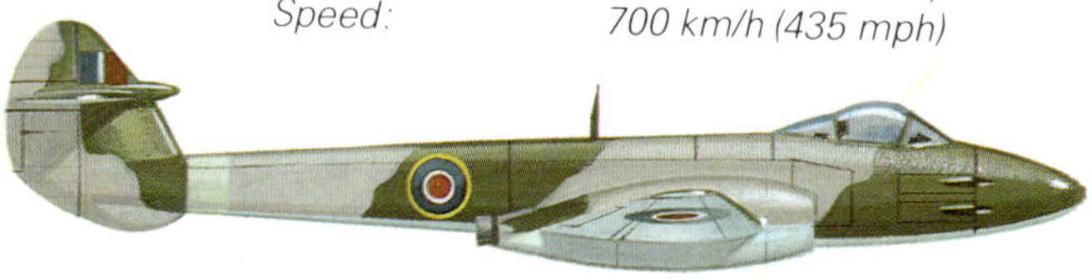

△ **Gloster Meteor 1**
Wingspan: *31.1 m (43 ft)*
Length: *12.57 m (41 ft 3 in)*
Speed: *676 km/h (420 mph)*
A later version set a world speed record of 991 km/h (616 mph) in 1946.

△ **MiG-15**
Wingspan: *10.08m (33 ft 1 in)*
Length: *10.1 m (33 ft 2 in)*
Speed: *1,075 km/h (668 mph)*

▽ **BAC Lightning**
Wingspan: *10.6 m (34 ft 10 in)*
Length: *16.25 m (53 ft 3 in)*
Speed: *2,415 km/h (1,500 mph)*

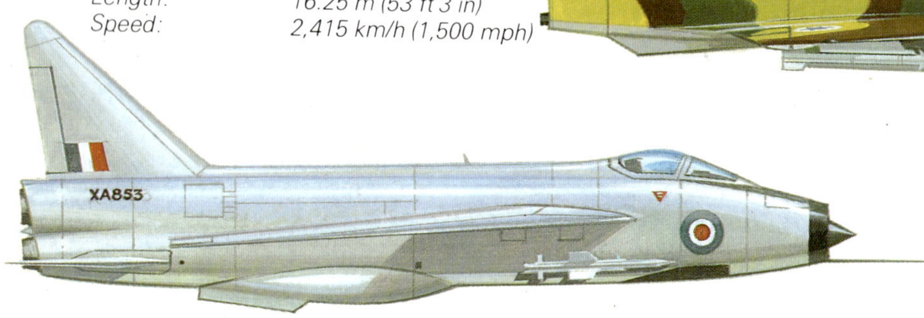

△ **MiG-17**
Wingspan: *9.63 m (31 ft 7 in)*
Length: *11.09 m (36 ft 4½ in)*
Speed: *1,145 km/h (711 mph)*

△ **North American F-86 Sabre**
Wingspan: *11.31 m (37 ft 1 in)*
Length: *11.43 m (37 ft 6 in)*
Speed: *982 km/h (610 mph)*

▽ **Dassault Breguet Mirage III**
Wingspan: *8.22 m (27 ft)*
Length: *15.5 m (50 ft 10 in)*
Speed: *2,350 km/h (1,460 mph)*

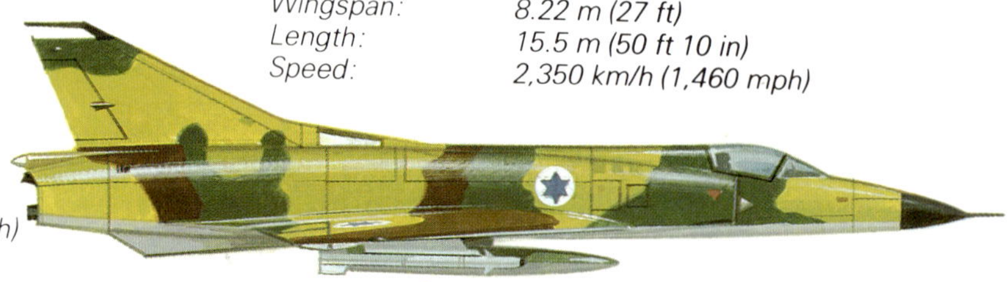

△ **McDonnell Douglas F-4 Phantom II**
Wingspan: 11.7 m (38 ft 5 in)
Length: 17.76 m (58 ft 3 in)
Speed: 2,415 km/h (1,500 mph)

▽ **Grumman F-14 Tomcat**
Wingspan swept: 11.63 m (38 ft 2 in)
Wingspan straight: 19.54 m (64 ft 1½ in)
Length: 19.10 m (62 ft 8 in)
Speed: 2,517 km/h (1,564 mph)

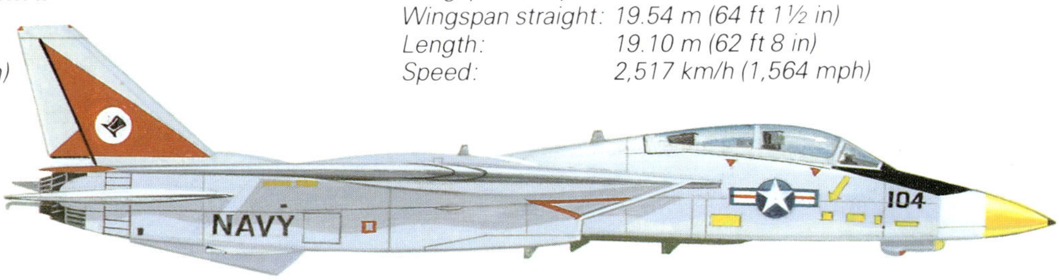

△ **Lockheed SR-71 Blackbird**
Wingspan: 16.94 m (55 ft 7 in)
Length: 32.74 m (107 ft 5 in)
Speed: 3,220+ km/h (2,000+ mph)

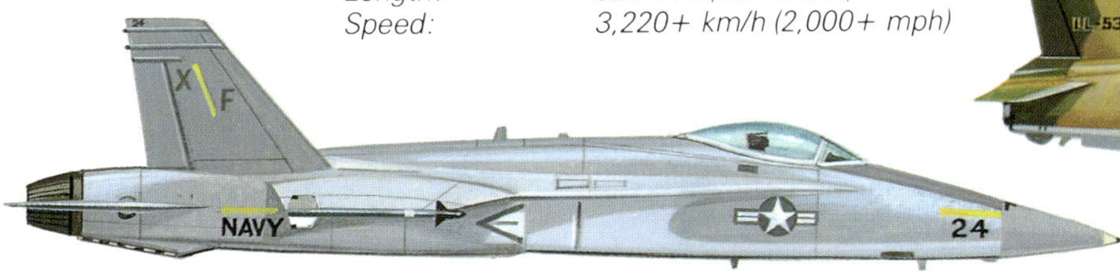

△ **British Aerospace Hawk/ McDonnell Douglas T-45**
Wingspan: 9.39 m (30 ft 10 in)
Length: 11.17 m (36 ft 8 in)
Speed: 1,038 km/h (645 mph)

△ **McDonnell Douglas F/A-18 Hornet**
Wingspan: 11.43 m (37 ft 6 in)
Length: 17.07 m (56 ft)
Speed: 1,940 km/h (1,200 mph)

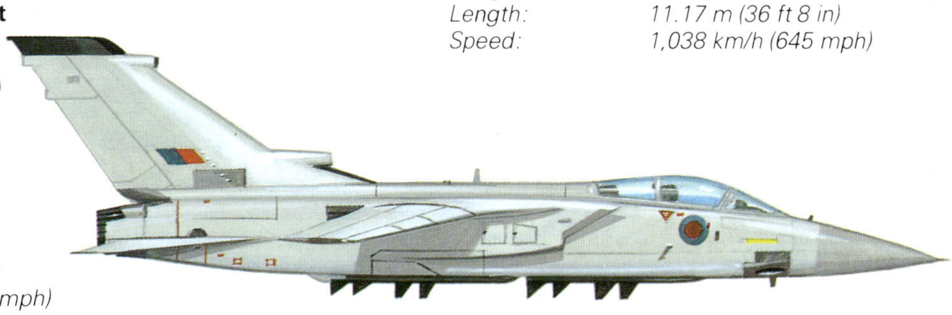

▷ **Panavia Tornado F Mk 3**
Wingspan swept: 8.6 m (28 ft 2½ in)
Wingspan straight: 13.9 m (45 ft 7 in)
Length: 18.06 m (59 ft 3 in)
Speed: 2,415 km/h (1,500 mph)

The Bear and the jet bombers are mostly too big to show with the other planes, so they are shown in this box.

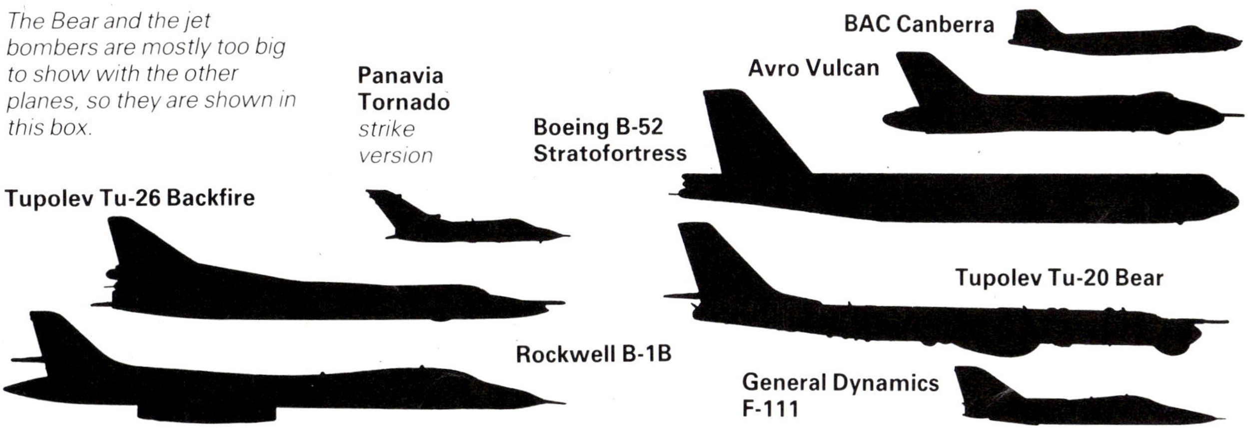

Dressing for flight

Fast jet pilots wear G-suits. In a manoeuvre such as pulling out of a dive, a pilot's weight increases for a few moments. The effect is similar to how you feel when a high-speed lift stops at the ground floor, but much greater. A G-suit inflates tight against the lower body and legs to stop blood pooling low down. Without blood flowing to the brain, a pilot will black out.

1 *Helmet with earphones. The built-in dark visor can be pulled down when required.*
2 *Oxygen mask with built-in microphone. Oxygen is essential at high altitudes, and the microphone is used to talk to control and to other flyers.*
3 *Oxygen hose connects to plane's on-board supply.*
4 *Life preserver, in case of a crash in the sea.*
5 *G-suit bladder. This and the leggings pump up tight during combat manoeuvres.*
6 *Knee pad for making notes.*
7 *Soft gloves.*
8 *G-suit worn over undersuit.*
9 *Zip pocket for equipment.*
10 *Tough boots.*

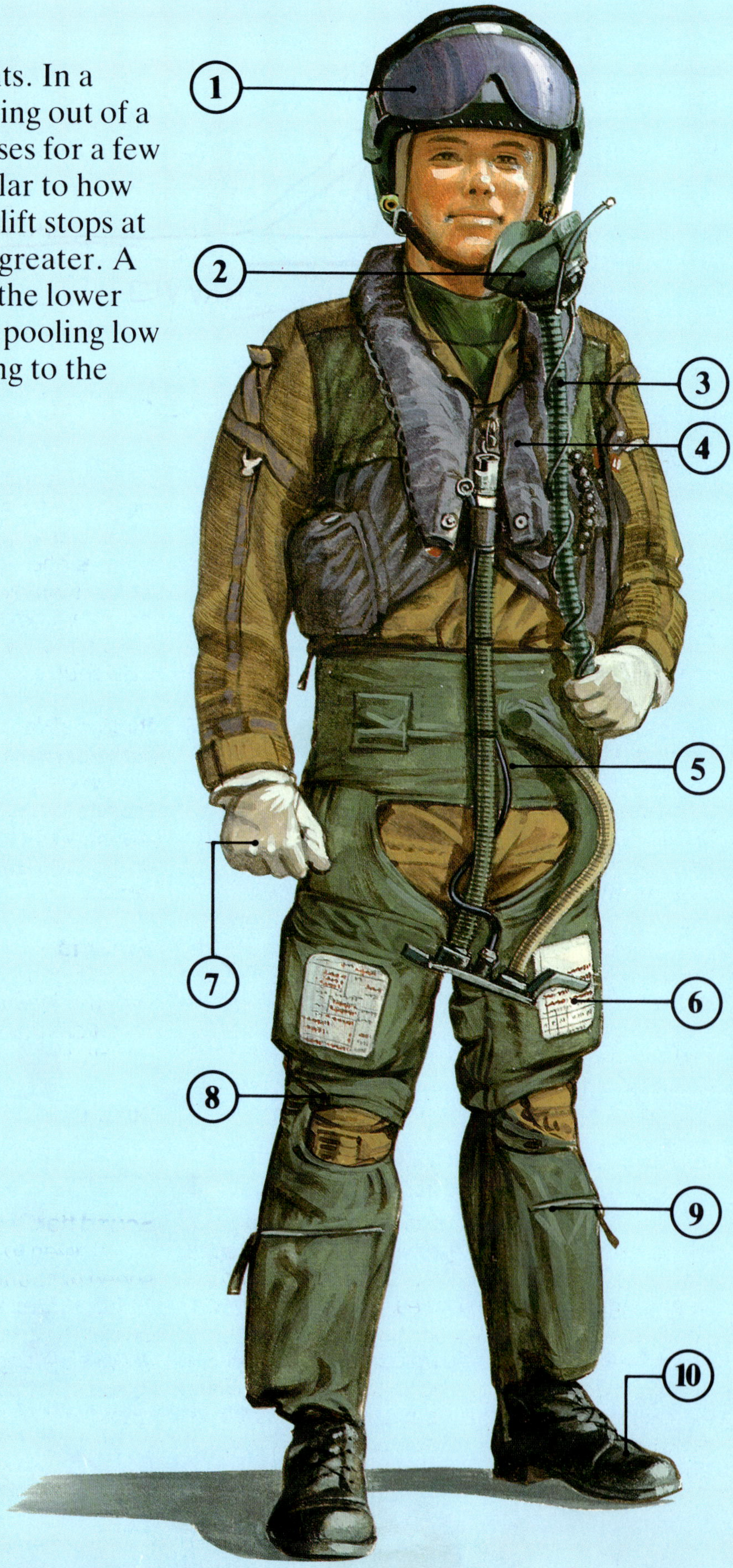

Glossary

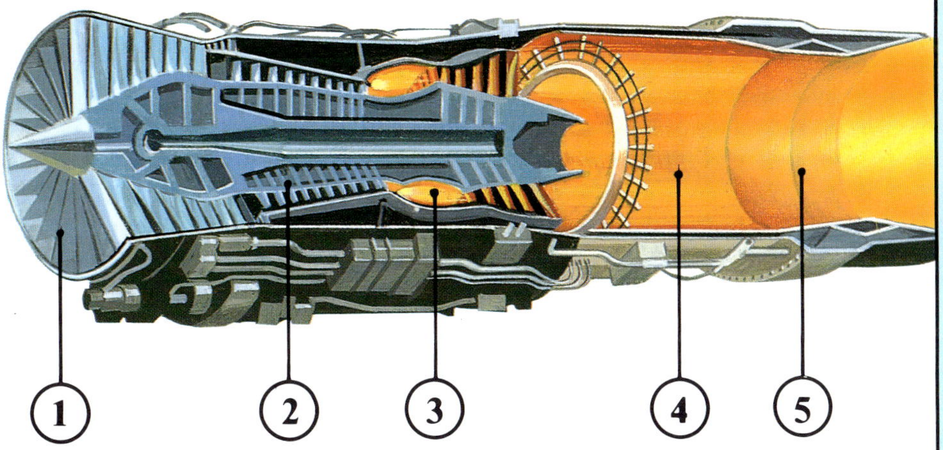

Break
Sharp turn to left or right. Used in combat to throw off a plane attacking from the rear.

Cannon
Gun which fires explosive shells. A modern cannon can fire up to 6,000 shells a minute.

Ejection seat
Sometimes nicknamed a "bang seat", an ejection seat is used to rocket a pilot out of a plane in an emergency.

G-suit
Special suit worn by combat pilots. It helps to stop them blacking out in violent air combat manoeuvres.

Gyro stabilizer
Small mechanism to keep an aircraft at the required angle during flight.

Heat-seeking missile
Missile which detects and homes on the heat from a jet exhaust. Missiles can also be guided by radar.

Jet engine
*Though complex in detail, all jets work on the same simple principles. Air is sucked in through an air intake (**1**) and is compressed by a series of spinning compressor blades (**2**). Fuel is sprayed into the combustion chamber (**3**) and ignited. The hot gases roar out of the exhaust (**4**) and the reaction pushes the jet along. An afterburner (**5**) injects more fuel into the exhaust to increase thrust even more. This is also known as reheat.*

Laser beam
Narrow beam of very intense light.

Pressure suit
Sealed suit which protects a pilot against the low air pressure at height. Without the suit a pilot's blood would boil. Oxygen is also necessary at high altitudes and every high-flying jet has an on-board oxygen system.

Radar
System which sends out a powerful radio beam. When the beam hits a solid object it bounces back to the radar transmitter. The signal is shown on a TV screen as a glowing "blip". Radars are carried aboard most planes to warn of other aircraft nearby and of bad weather. Radar stations on the ground are often extremely large and very powerful.

Retractable undercarriage
The wheels of an aircraft, which fold into the body after takeoff and extend again for landing.

Scissors
Combat manoeuvre in which a defender tries to get on the tail of his attacker.

Scramble
Term for rapid combat takeoff.

Sound barrier
Word given to the speed of sound in the 1940s, when many people thought it was impossible to go faster. At sea level, sonic speed is about 1,225 km/h (762 mph). It slows with height, until above 12 km (7.45 miles), it stays constant at 1,062 km/h (660 mph). The speed of sound is named Mach 1 after Ernst Mach, an Austrian scientist who worked out its value.

Speed brake, air brake
Flat plate which pushes out into the air stream when required, to help slow a plane down.

Swept wing
Wing which is angled to the rear. It allows for faster flight than the straight wings of slower aircraft. The delta, another high-speed wing, is shaped like a triangle.

Wings
A student pilot's certificate of competence to fly.

Yo-yo
Down-and-up combat manoeuvre, used in a rear chase to overtake a faster plane.

Index

Printed in Belgium by proost International Book Production

The Book of
Musicals
from Show Boat to Evita

The Book of Musicals
from Show Boat to Evita

Foreword by Clive Barnes

by Arthur Jackson

Mitchell Beazley
London

A *Webb & Bower* BOOK
Edited, designed and produced for
Mitchell Beazley Limited by
Webb & Bower Limited, Exeter, England

Picture Research by Anne-Marie Ehrlich

First published by Webb & Bower Limited 1977
Revised Edition 1979

ISBN 0 85533 191 7

Set in Monophoto Times

Printed in Great Britain by
Jolly & Barber Limited,
Rugby Warwickshire

Bound by Webb, Son & Company,
London and Wales

Title page: **West Side Story** (1957). Riff (Mickey Calin) and Bernardo (Ken Le Roy) fight to the death in 'The Rumble'.

Contents

Foreword

It is curious, and wonderful, what an enormous amount of pleasure the musical has given all of us over the years. Whether we have called it operetta, light opera (was there ever *heavy* opera? perhaps!), musical comedy (well, certainly there was never musical tragedy) or simply the musical, the form has been a staple of the entertainment theatre for the best part of the century. We have hummed its tunes, adored its ladies, and relished its frequently somewhat naïve jokes. Except rarely, it was never a particularly sophisticated form of theatre. It was not intended to stir deep emotions, but much more a means to while away happily the interregnum between a good dinner and a convivial nightcap.

The interesting thing is how much remarkably good work has been done in this field, how much talent has been invested, how much money won and lost. Also how the form has continually developed – both musically and theatrically. Of course there have been trends, over the years, in the so-called legitimate theatre, but these often seem to have been prompted by the sudden eruption of a dramatic genius, switching, sometimes almost single-handedly (in the case of, say, an Ibsen or even, to take a smaller single hand, an Ionesco), some course of drama, thus creating the shudder of a movement. But the development of the musical theatre—as can be clearly seen in this book—has been much more, at least until recent times, one of evolution.

It is as though drama had been created by its own individual geniuses, whereas the musical has been almost the wish-creation of the ever-changing audience. Of course, certain giant figures – a Cole Porter, a George Gershwin, even a Jacques Offenbach or a Johann Strauss—did seem to have an instinctive advance warning of what its audience needed, but it was still fundamentally a talent to provide what the people wanted rather than what the times demanded.

We have seen many playwrights having to fight for recognition – we have even seen one or two only acquire recognition posthumously. But never writers of musicals. The success is instant and immediate – and usually unrepeatable. Apart from classic operettas, including, of course, Gilbert & Sullivan, the light musical theatre does not lend itself to revivals, as the author of this book very sagely notes. In recent years we have had many examples of musical revivals – all hitched onto the star of nostalgia – but none of them has really succeeded. Years ago, of course, there was the very special exception of *Pal Joey* by Rodgers and Hart (a musical clearly before its time) and there were also the modishly retreaded versions of *No, No, Nanette!* and *Irene* (although the latter unexpectedly lost money on Broadway), but these cannot be considered revivals.

More recently we have seen the comparative failures of such extravagant Broadway revivals as *A Funny Thing Happened on the Way to the Forum*, *Lost in the Stars*, *My Fair Lady*, even to an extent (and I hope this does not sound like sacrilege) Zero Mostel, himself, in *Fiddler on the Roof*, which the second time around by no means proved the indestructible hit everyone expected. Perhaps a case for an exception could be made for Harold Prince's version of Leonard Bernstein's great *Candide*, but here – in one sense like *No, No, Nanette!*, and in another sense as unlike as possible – this was a radically new treatment of an old work. No, we do not have a classic popular music theatre. Perhaps we need one, and perhaps the answer would be to treat old musicals with the same respect, or lack of respect, that we apply to opera, making each new production suitable to its new time. Far too many revivals of musicals are merely slavish copies of the originals, even down to their decoration. Is it any wonder they appear old-fashioned?

The author of this book has very diligently and brightly outlined the origins of the musical and charted its progress. Few will disagree with him when he marks out *Oklahoma!* as a sort of watershed in the history of the musical, and one is delighted to see proper dues paid to Gershwin's *Porgy and Bess*, the semiserious intent of *Show Boat*, and other attempts to broaden the appeal of the musical, such as *Pal Joey*. Yet it was *Oklahoma!* that heralded the golden age – perhaps brief but definitely brilliant – of the Broadway musical.

Notice I say Broadway musical. What happened to Germany, France, even Italy in the period immediately after World War II? And even to the present day? To be sure, there are musical entertainments still presented at the Châtelet in Paris, but they would hardly be exportable, and even the Vienna woods are offering us no more songs – or at least no more popular songs. As for the English musical, it is possible that here our present writer is overgenerous. England today seems as incapable of producing a great musical as of producing a world heavyweight boxing champion, and the days of Leslie Stuart and Bob Fitzsimmons are well and truly over. There have been a few lightweights, a Lionel Bart here, an Anthony Newley and Leslie Bricusse there, even that Joan Littlewood bitter mélange *Oh, What a Lovely War!*, but nothing has flowered on the West End to compare with the luxuriant growths of Broadway.

The author also deals generously and at length with the Hollywood musical, and indeed this was once a superb entertainment form. Now, maybe I have been missing things, but when was the last great Hollywood musical? Come to think of it, what was the last Hollywood musical? Could it have been *Godspell*? As I write we have *A Little Night Music* about to arrive, and it seems that *Hair* is finally going to be given a Hollywood coiffure. But what was the last original Hollywood musical – *Funny Lady*? And not all that original, maybe.

Then perhaps we ought to face the facts about the Broadway musical itself. Really, what kind of condition is this in? There are two very obvious points to be made about the current state of our musical theatre. The first is its cost. The musical can now lose more money in one night than any other activity known to man except roulette and arson. The costs of mounting a Broadway musical are today stupendous – a musical can easily cost a million and a quarter dollars. This book notes that some comparatively minor musicals, the amiable *Promises, Promises*, for example, or surprising show business phenomena such as *Grease*, are running for far longer than did the hit shows of yesteryear, even when those shows were, by any reasonable account, far more distinguished. The reason is simple. It is now more and more difficult for a show to pay off its backers and produce a profit. A splashy musical can run for more than a year on Broadway and still show a loss. These are hard days on the Rialto.

There is a second obvious point to be taken in any consideration of the contemporary musical. At one time – not so long ago, just before Elvis and the Beatles – pop music and theatre music were one and the same thing. Twirl the dial on your car radio (or press those buttons, whichever) and the music you would hear would be the current hits from Broadway and Hollywood musicals, interspersed with a few cabaret ballads and novelty songs. Not so now. We do have a few 'sweet music' stations, and certainly in moments of stress, such as elevators going up or aircraft coming down, one is treated to a predigested form of sweetpop called Musak, which often does derive from show music. But usually the bright young composers are simply writing rock. Not even Lennon and McCartney – two of the pop music giants of the postwar years – produced a stage musical. And why should they? Why should a talented young composer/lyricist go through all the birth-pang agonies of creating a Broadway musical when he can make more money from one single golden disc. For the composer, the musical no longer makes economic sense.

There are loyalists, such as Stephen Sondheim, Cy Coleman, and others. They are producing conceptual musicals such as *Company*, *Follies* or *Pacific Overtures*, or using other kinds of innovations such as the comedic content of *I Love My Wife*. We have ethnic musicals such as *The Wiz*, or musicals that deliberately avoid the issue of a modern sound, such as *Zorba!* or even *Fiddler* itself. And wasn't *My Fair Lady* really more of an operetta than a musical? Of course we have had rock musicals, notably *Hair*, which started as a tourist trip for parents to see what their strange children were doing in the 'sixties, and then suddenly was taken for real, and actually became a youth cult. But the rock musical was a shortlived form.

Interestingly – with a few composer/lyricists apart – the main motive force in the Broadway musical today is, oddly enough, the director. Perhaps it started with Jerome Robbins, but certainly directors such as Bob Fosse and Michael Bennett are more important than the composer of the musicals they are directing. One thinks of Bob Fosse's *Pippin* rather than Stephen Schwarz's *Pippin*, or one thinks of Michael Bennett's *A Chorus Line* rather than Marvin Hamlisch's *A Chorus Line*.

Is this decadence? Is this the end of the line for the musical theatre? Is the book you now hold in your hand fundamentally a memory-guide to nights past rather than any promise of nights future? Perhaps. Theatrical forms do come and go. Yet somehow I feel that there will always be room for the musical. Is our theatre to have no more cakes and ale? No, my own guess is that the musical is at present passing through a stage of transition, a stage where it is not quite sure of its own direction. Yet I am certain it will find that direction and, in time, reach another destination, and continue to give us fun and pleasure on the journey.

Clive Barnes

Introduction

To talk about facts and figures in connection with musicals may at first sight appear to be an anachronism. The music-loving theatre-goer who has spent a few hundred enchanted evenings with Rodgers and Hammerstein, Kern, Gershwin, Porter, Berlin, Arlen, Loesser, Coward or Romberg may wonder what hard statistics can have to do with it all. But this is show *business*, and the box-office thrives on facts and figures. It depends on them. The Dillinghams and Ziegfelds of an earlier era, no less than the Merricks and Princes of today, were great showmen whose names endure in Broadway history. They were also primarily businessmen. They made fortunes, lost them on one unsuccessful venture, but generally managed to recoup their money with the next hit. It is no coincidence that the biggest, most legendary, names in theatrical history are those of the talented people who produced, wrote, composed or starred in musical comedy, generally the most enjoyable and viable form of stage entertainment.

Musicals have always been a great and expensive risk, to be sure. But let the facts speak for themselves. In the history of Broadway, only some 217 shows have run for over 500 performances, although in this respect it is well to remember that, while in the sixties a *Fiddler on the Roof* could notch up 3,242 performances, and even a not too well-remembered musical like *Promises, Promises* had a run of 1,281, such legendary, and for their time epoch-making, musicals as *Anything Goes* (420), *Of Thee I Sing* (441), *Pal Joey* (374 originally, 542 on revival) and *Strike Up the Band* (191) were happy to settle for a fraction of this success. Even a milestone like *Show Boat* ran for only 572 performances at the outset. Nevertheless, ninety-five out of those 217 long-running shows were musicals, as were twenty-six* out of the top forty Broadway shows of all time. The list is worth quoting in full:

Fiddler on the Roof (1964). Zero Mostel as Tevye, the central figure in the Bock-Harnick-Stein adaptation of Sholem Aleichem's stories, which had a record Broadway run of 3,242 performances.

Fiddler on the Roof	3,242
Hello Dolly	2,844
My Fair Lady	2,717
Man of La Mancha	2,328
Oklahoma!	2,212
Grease	2,179
Pippin	1,928
South Pacific	1,925
Hair	1,750
Mame	1,508
The Sound of Music	1,443
How to Succeed in Business . . .	1,417
The Music Man	1,375
Funny Girl	1,348
Promises, Promises	1,281
The Magic Show	1,253
The King and I	1,246
1776	1,217
Guys and Dolls	1,200
Cabaret	1,165
Annie Get Your Gun	1,147
Kiss Me Kate	1,077
Don't Bother Me, I Can't Cope	1,065
The Pajama Game	1,063
Damn Yankees	1,019
Shenandoah	973
The Wiz	972

Even these majestic figures pale beside the 1960 off-Broadway *The Fantasticks* which, by mid-1976, had chalked up a non-stop run of 6,699 performances, while the 1954 revival of Kurt Weill's *Threepenny Opera* (its first showing outside Germany since 1928) filled the off-Broadway Theater De

*See Long Runs on Broadway in the Appendix for the complete listing down to 500 performances.

My Fair Lady (1956). In the Ascot scene Eliza Doolittle (Julie Andrews) exhorts her horse to greater efforts in choicest Cockney, watched anxiously by (to her right) Professor Henry Higgins (Rex Harrison) and Colonel Pickering (Robert Coote).

Lys on 2,707 occasions, and by mid-1976 *Godspell* had notched up 2,100 performances and was still running.

Against these, of course, we must offset the many more shows that never make it. The little, bad shows that meet their fate by the first Saturday night; the big, lush productions that run well enough but never recoup the initial outlay; the mediocrities that produce a handful of hit songs which outlive the show; or the nonentities that produce nothing at all. Yet the musical show has a universal appeal far beyond mere escapism, the excuse generally given, however condescendingly, for the success of this type of entertainment. At its very best, particularly in the post-war years, the musical has been accepted as an art form, no fewer than five having elevated the prestige of the genre by being awarded the Pulitzer Prize for Drama – for the record: *Of Thee I Sing* (1931); *South Pacific* (1949); *Fiorello* (1959); *How to Succeed in Business without Really Trying* (1961) and *A Chorus Line* (1976).

The appeal of the stage musical to a wide cross-section of the public owes not a little to the fact that this is the most eclectic form of stagecraft, adapting to its own needs popular literature and the classics, classical music and rock, jazz and the perennial operetta form, the history of the past and the world of the future. It cannibalizes its own world of show business, absorbing alike the big dramatic play or the venerable Hollywood movie. Whatever it is, let's make a musical out of it! Most importantly, the musical no less than any other form of drama can reflect the contemporary scene and sometimes even manages to make a social comment on the world around it.

It hasn't always been thus. There was a time when the stage musical dwelt in its own Cloud-cuckoo-land of Ruritanian romance or Long Island tennis-parties. When revues with their chorus lines and vaudeville acts were indistinguishable from the sort of 'book' shows where stars of enormous

South Pacific (1949). Ensign Nellie Forbush (Mary Martin) and Luther Billis (Myron McCormick) entertain their fellow-Marines with 'Honey Bun'.

personality and box-office appeal would overwhelm the proceedings. As when Al Jolson's Winter Garden shows with their carefully crafted Romberg scores would gradually be jettisoned by the star interpolating all his own songs, or sending the cast home while he gave a one-man performance. Or when George S. Kaufman, standing in the wings of a Marx Brothers show, received an uncomfortable shock because he thought he had heard one of his own lines! That was sheer entertainment, asking nothing of undemanding and worshipping audiences except their applause. Then the musical stage developed both a sense of artistry and a conscience. It is generally accepted that the metamorphosis began with *Show Boat*, continued with *Of Thee I Sing* and *Strike Up the Band*, Gershwin's political and anti-war satires, and with his *Porgy and Bess*, the first genuine American 'folk opera', and attained a peak with *Pal Joey*, an 'adult musical' so far ahead of its time it had to wait twelve years for acceptance. There were other milestones – *Oklahoma!*, *My Fair Lady*, *West Side Story*, *Man of La Mancha* – until finally *Hair* shattered the barriers between the legitimate theatre and the world of contemporary rock, paving the way for the new generation's comments on its ambience of pseudo-religion, race relations and the drug scene. That's entertainment?

Yet the traditional musical remains. The rock-bound seventies also paid tribute to the backstage story of *A Chorus Line* and the basic operetta concept of *A Little Night Music*, and enormously successful revivals of *No, No, Nanette*, *The Great Waltz*, *Irene*, etc. It seems ungracious to cavil by affirming that the musical theatre no longer abounds in hit songs. But the blame for this does not lie with the integrated musical. Rodgers and Hammerstein were undisputed masters of their craft who integrated book, lyrics and music as no one had ever done before, yet every song from *Oklahoma!*,

Man of La Mancha (1965). Richard Kiley played the dual role of Miguel Cervantes and his fictional creation Don Quixote.

Carousel or *The King and I* is fondly remembered twenty-five to thirty-five years later. In contrast, what is memorable about *Mame* or *Hello Dolly* other than their catchy title tunes? And what have the rock musicals contributed to the standard repertoire? *A Little Night Music* and *A Chorus Line* each produced one popular song, and even the prolific hit-maker Burt Bacharach failed to achieve more than this with *Promises, Promises*. This is just one of the plain facts concerning the shift of emphasis in musicals today (and it should be borne in mind that quality songs are no longer in fashion), from which a general theory might be drawn that a show, particularly one whose run goes into four figures, should be remembered *as* a show rather than as a mere vehicle for hit songs. Certainly the early Gershwin, Rodgers and Hart, and Porter shows are long forgotten (perhaps advisedly) except as the source of some of the world's greatest evergreen songs. A few shows have been individually memorable as well as being chockful of good, durable songs: most of Rodgers and Hammerstein; *My Fair Lady*, *Guys and Dolls*, *Annie Get Your Gun*; even *Rose Marie* and *The Desert Song*. But although Broadway as a source of potent song material is no longer the force it was, it survives. The era of the great Hollywood musical has long since passed by. A $20 million investment on a *Hello Dolly* that nobody goes to see is not the sort of expenditure approved by the new conglomerate ownerships of the big studios.

Hello Dolly (1964). The original show had been running for three years and ten months at the St James Theater when David Merrick produced a second, all-black, version starring Pearl Bailey (1967).

The Broadway musical, on the other hand, is still very much alive in all its various shapes, sizes and modes, and at the time of writing there are probably more musical shows running on and off Broadway than at any time in its history. New writers are constantly appearing, though whether they can ever match the track record of the 'greats' of Broadway's past remains to be seen. And what a past it has been! It is in an endeavour to document, illustrate and generally recall that past that this book has been written. (Not overlooking the London stage which, if not as notable for enchanted evenings, has contributed its own quota of musical memories.) The commencement date of 1919* is quite arbitrary except insofar as a start has to be made somewhere, and the emergence of George Gershwin seems as good a place to begin as any. Both narrative and reference sections are limited to 'book' shows of British or American origin. Operettas of foreign origin have regretfully been omitted, with apologies to Lehár, Straus, Stolz and all the other European masters of melody who gave us so much in their own way. Similarly, it was impracticable to list revues, great as were the attractions of the *Ziegfeld Follies*, *George White's Scandals*, *Earl Carroll's Vanities* and Irving Berlin's *Music Box Revues* in all their various annual editions. The purist may argue that *The Band Wagon*, *Call Me Mister* and a few others were technically revues, but the author remains unrepentant, exercising his prerogative of personal selection.

**See p. 153 for the earliest, pre-1919, recorded musicals.*

1 Overture and Beginners

Babes in Toyland (1903). Although basically a children's entertainment, Victor Herbert's charming operetta became one of the best-loved of American musical productions.

Something strange, unique and altogether wonderful happened during the evening of 27 December 1927 at the Ziegfeld Theater in New York. The occasion was the first night of Jerome Kern's and Oscar Hammerstein's adaptation of Edna Ferber's novel *Show Boat*, a production by the master showman Florenz Ziegfeld whose forte had, until then, been the presentation of glamorous spectaculars whose appeal was hardly cerebral. What happened that night fifty years ago can be expressed quite simply and concisely. The musical came of age. Although musical comedy, as it had been known in the previous two decades, was by no means dead or even moribund – nor would it be for many years, if ever – *Show Boat* added a new dimension to the musical stage and proved that audiences had the right to expect, and demand, something more of a musical than the perennial boy-meets-girl plot with its supporting cast of comedians and speciality dancers and singers. Nor did theatre-goers have to insult their musical senses with interpolated songs that could be added, dropped or switched around at the discretion of director or artists. The result of this musical milestone was that drama, characterization, plot development – even tragedy – and, above all, complete integration of music and libretto, in which songs advanced the story-line as did arias in opera, were to be the norm in the best musicals of the future. The lessons that Broadway learned from Kern and Hammerstein have formed, and are still forming, a vital part in the development of the musical stage.

Comedy would remain an integral part of the plot, but 'musical comedy' as a descriptive term for a genre would soon be *passé* – as were the generic titles allotted to the various forms the musical had taken on its way to the Ziegfeld. What we now recognize and refer to as 'the musical' is an end-product, the final result of a hundred years of honing, shaping and refining of numerous influences. Into the melting-pot of musical progress went such variegated ingredients as ballad opera, Singspiel, opera bouffe, comic opera, minstrel shows, operetta, vaudeville, light opera, burlesque (in its early and original sense of parody or travesty), ragtime, revue, extravaganza and 'straight' drama. From this heterogeneous and thoroughly cosmopolitan ragbag of sources emerged, in due course, that truly original and indigenous product, the American musical, an art form of the twentieth century which reached its apogee with *Show Boat* – not to mention *Porgy and Bess*, *Pal Joey*, *Oklahoma!*, *Carousel*, *South Pacific*, *My Fair Lady*, *Annie Get Your Gun*, *West Side Story*, *The Sound of Music*, *The Most Happy Fella*, *Cabaret*, *A Little Night Music* and *A Chorus Line*! The most heartening factor about it was that these outstanding musical plays achieved their success by a blend of artistry and commercial validity. As the musical had grown to adulthood so had its audience, and no longer did playwrights and composers have to write down to the mass market.

The first American musical *per se* is generally acknowledged to have been *The Black Crook*, a 'musical extravaganza' with book by Charles M. Barras and musical adaptations by Giuseppe Operti. It had the semblance of a plot which served as a basis for spectacular effects that filled the stage for five and a half hours and the auditorium of Niblo's Gardens in New York for 474 performances in 1866–7. It was followed two years later by *Humpty Dumpty*, a pantomime in the literal meaning of the word written by the mime

Opposite above: An original Julius M. Price poster for *The Gay Parisienne*, first produced at the Duke of York's Theatre, London, in 1896.

Opposite below: An original E. P. Kinsella poster for *The Shop Girl*, first produced at the Gaiety Theatre, London, in 1894, with Seymour Hicks and George Grossmith.

Show Boat (1927). Irene Segalla's costume design for a member of the chorus in the London production (1928).

The Belle of Mayfair (1907). Camille Clifford and the Gibson Girls in Charles E. Brookfield and Cosmo Hamilton's musical comedy, with music by Leslie Stuart at the Vaudeville Theatre, London.

The Gay Parisienne

GAIETY THEATRE
Licensed by the Lord Chamberlain to ALFRED BUTT
Managing Director - ALFRED BUTT
The SHOP GIRL

New York's biggest and most expansive theatre, the Hippodrome, was opened in 1905, and although it had a chequered existence it is still remembered for the series of extravaganzas which occupied its mammoth stage for seventeen years.

Left: **Chu Chin Chow** (1916). Two colour posters by Percy Anderson for Oscar Asche's play with music by Frederic Norton, which created a record run of over 2,300 performances at His Majesty's Theatre, London.

artist George L. Fox, which was even more spectacular though its plot was flimsier still. However, the first true musical comedy, with an original musical score by Edward E. Rice, was an 1874 production entitled *Evangeline*.

For the fundamentals of the musical we must look to Europe, and to England in particular, where Allan Ramsay's pastoral drama *The Gentle Shepherd* (1725) and John Gay's more justly famous *The Beggar's Opera* (1728) (which found renewed fame exactly 200 years later as *Die Dreigroschenoper*) established the ballad opera, based mainly on folk music, as a musical form. It was to be 125 years, though, before any positive musical tradition was to be established in the theatre, the breakthrough coming from Jacques Offenbach who, incredible though it seems, wrote no fewer than eighty-nine operettas in the last twenty-seven years of his life, from *Pepito* (1853) to the memorable *Tales of Hoffman*, first produced one year after his death in 1880. The European operetta tradition, begun by this German-born composer's typically French works, continued apace in the late nineteenth and early twentieth centuries with such men as André Messager (*Veronique*, *Monsieur Beaucaire*, etc) and Karl Millocker (*The Dubarry*, etc). Perhaps the most seminal figure was Franz von Suppé who, although better known nowadays for his overtures than for the operettas to which they were the prelude, can be said to have founded the school of Viennese operetta, which was carried over into the present century by such apt practitioners as Franz Lehár, Oskar Straus, Robert Stolz, Emmerich Kalman and Ralph Benatzky, and eventually Americanized by Sigmund Romberg, Rudolf Friml and Victor Herbert.

Probably the closest nineteenth-century counterpart to the present-day musical comedy is the work of Gilbert and Sullivan. The wealth of melody in their work may inspire imaginative followers to refer to them as the Rodgers and Hammerstein of their day. But a truer analogy would be Rodgers and Hart, for W.S. Gilbert's lyrical talent, his gift for satire and wryly humorous comment are more akin to the sophisticated and mordant wit of Lorenz Hart. The Gilbert and Sullivan operettas (to be more precise, they should be described as light operas) are inescapably of their period yet stand constant revivals, and it is worth noting that in the interviews with celebrated lyricists

The Merry Widow (1907). Originally produced in Vienna in 1905, Franz Lehár's colourful operetta came to Daly's Theatre, London, in 1907, and has since become one of the most popular of all the Viennese operettas.

and composers of Broadway, Hollywood and Tin Pan Alley assembled in Max Wilk's book *They're Playing Our Song* so many of today's writers – of the calibre of Sammy Cahn and Johnny Mercer – cite W.S. Gilbert as the fountainhead of all lyric writing and their own prime influence.

Apart from the emergence in America of Victor Herbert with *The Wizard of the Nile* (1895), the development of the light opera took place in England with such composers as Lionel Monckton, whose *The Country Girl* was a hit in 1902 at Daly's Theatre, London, as was Edward German's *Merrie England* and *Tom Jones* (1907), and Leslie Stuart, whose *Floradora* flounced into New York's Casino Theater in November 1900 and introduced Broadway to the British product. With the international success of Lehár's *The Merry Widow* (1907) and Oskar Straus's *A Waltz Dream* (1907) and *The Chocolate Soldier* (1910), allied to Victor Herbert's consolidation as the king of the American product with such shows as *Babes in Toyland* (1903), *It Happened in Nordland* (1904) and *The Red Mill* (1906), the scene was set for the complete integration of the European operetta tradition into the American theatre.

Victor Herbert (1859–1924). The Irish-born cellist turned conductor, who became the father of American operetta.

Vaudeville and burlesque, now in its later accepted sense of knockabout comedy and leg shows, were other, basically American, tributaries which around this time entered the mainstream of musical entertainment, to be absorbed into the embryonic but fast-developing musical comedy tradition-to-be. A series of enlarged vaudeville sketches by Tony Hart and Ed Harrigan, with music by David Braham, were written around a set of characters referred to under the generic name of 'The Mulligan Guards' who embarked in 1879 on a sequence of adventures such as *The Mulligan Guards' Ball*, *The Mulligan Guards' Christmas*, *The Mulligan Guards' Surprise*, etc. Twenty years later at the turn of the century a similar kind of series was masterminded by the author John J. McNally, the lyricist J. Cheever Goodwin and the composer Maurice Levi. They set the real-life Max and Gus Rogers in

The Chocolate Soldier. The entire cast on stage for the second act finale of Oscar Straus's operetta based on George Bernard Shaw's *Arms and the Man*. Originally produced at the Theatre an der Wien, Vienna, in 1908, the English version by Stanislaus Stange opened in New York in 1909 and at the Lyric Theatre, London, in 1910.

Leave it to Jane (1917). Starring Edith Hallor and Robert Pitkin, this was not the first collaboration by Jerome Kern, Guy Bolton and P. G. Wodehouse, but was the first to bring them a success on Broadway proper after the Princess Theater shows.

a series of variously located enterprises – namely *The Rogers Brothers in Central Park*, as well as *in London*, *in Washington*, *in Paris*, and so on. But the Rogers Brothers were, it seems, little more than a carbon copy of the undisputed kings of burlesque, Joe Weber and Lew Fields, erstwhile small-time comics who made the transition to Broadway so successfully that eventually they owned their own Music Hall at which, from 1896 to 1912, they presented a series of 'extravaganzas', mostly starring themselves, with such distinguished guest stars as Lillian Russell, Marie Dressler and Fay Templeton, whose names still ring bells seventy years later. The Weber and Fields shows were in essence revues, but they paved the way for not only the spectacular revues of Florenz Ziegfeld, Earl Carroll, George White and John Murray Anderson, but also for the transition from vaudeville and burlesque to the Broadway stage of such artists as Ed Wynn, Bert Williams, W.C. Fields, Eugene and Willie Howard, Bert Lahr and Eddie Foy.

At this point, when it comes to naming names, it is as well to mention the influence of the minstrel shows. Not great in itself, though it is true that revue and the parody type of burlesque can be said to have stemmed from the minstrel routines, at least one of the stage's greatest artists learned his craft in Lew Dockstadter's Minstrels, and this heritage is apparent in not only the black face but in the whole style of delivery and song projection of Al Jolson, probably the greatest Broadway entertainer of all, whose vivid personality and magnetic appeal were never quite captured on film or record.

At this same time there also emerged from the vaudeville stage an irresistible one-man band of a performer-creator who was to put the final seal on the integration of vaudeville into musical comedy as the modern world came to know it. A part of his family's act, The Four Cohans, from the age of nine, George M. Cohan had ambitions which far outstripped his record to date of sharing a top-of-the-bill spot in the sticks. A natural composer and author,

Amy Mortimer in *Little Johnny Jones* (1904). George M. Cohan's first Broadway hit was the foundation of his long-term producing partnership with Sam H. Harris.

Opposite: One of the many exotic costumes used in *Chu Chin Chow* (1916), the long-running London musical play by Oscar Asche and Frederic Norton.

Cohan introduced himself to New York in 1902 with two unsuccessful productions developed from his vaudeville sketches. But turning producer in partnership with Sam H. Harris he finally made it two years later with *Little Johnny Jones*, the first of a string of hits that were to keep his name on Broadway for decades. As a musician he was no Kern, his lyrics would never bear comparison with a Gershwin or Hammerstein, and his often jingoistic libretti would land with a dull thud on the stage of today. But what Cohan did was to inject the Broadway stage with the vitality and brashness of vaudeville, to emphasize his own gifts as singer, dancer, actor, writer and personality *par excellence*, and, perhaps most important of all in retrospect, to create an audience for the 'book' musical in a musical theatre attuned by habit and environment to extravaganzas and operettas.

Thus, while the London stage was still living in another century with Monckton's *The Arcadians* and *The Quaker Girl*, Sidney Jones's *Gaiety Girl* and *The Geisha*; while Frederic Norton's Chinese musical-melodrama *Chu Chin Chow* filled His Majesty's Theatre for most of World War I; while preposterously uniformed soldiery serenaded princesses and serving wenches in the imaginary Ruritania of continental operetta; while all this was going on outside that small section of Manhattan Island known as The Great White Way, one man was setting the American musical stage on the course it was to take for the remainder of the twentieth century and bringing to the musical that typical indigenous modernity that would finally correlate all those disparate influences into a new and highly individual entity – the Broadway musical.

2 Curtain Up!

The years during and after World War I represented the era of the great showmen. In New York the situation was similar to early Hollywood, where the movie moguls were for the most part European-Jewish immigrants, generally from the rag trade, who made their first American dollars by introducing nickelodeons, following up with the creation and distribution of their own movies. The factor common to the movie moguls and the Broadway barons was their total lack of artistic pretensions. Often uncouth, lacking in personal taste and refinement, they yet had a keen sense of what the public wanted, and a business acumen which prompted them to use the finest artists, composers, designers, musicians, writers and directors. Many became even more legendary than the artists and shows they produced, by giving their names to their own theatres and the shows presented therein.

Autocracy ran roughshod over artistry, yet show-business ideals not only survived but flourished. The great managements were respected for their furtherance of talent and the glamour and success of their productions, but hated and feared by all who had to cope with their dictatorial methods. A performer who fell foul of the Shuberts, or Klaw and Erlanger, could find

Left: **The Greenwich Village Follies** progressed from the original concept of off-Broadway intimate revue (in 1919) to the typical Broadway production with the sort of chorus line featured in this photograph from the 1925 edition at the 46th Street Theater.

Below left: **Ziegfeld Follies** (1925). All the qualities demanded by Florenz Ziegfeld are represented in this 'Ziegfeld Girl' . . . beauty, poise, the revealing yet elegant costume.

Below right: **The Great Ziegfeld** (1936). Hollywood's version of a Ziegfeld costume.

himself blacklisted in every theatre in America. But the world outside the theatre, if it ever knew of these things, ignored them, and judged the product on name value. 'The new Dillingham show' was sufficient word-of-mouth recommendation of a potential box-office hit. And since Charles Dillingham was responsible for the best of late Victor Herbert and early Jerome Kern, his name naturally was synonymous with commercial success and artistic values.

The stock in trade of these producers was spectacle for the tired businessman who could revel in girls, costumes, girls, top comedians, girls, hit songs, girls, luxurious sets, girls – small wonder that the title 'Ziegfeld Girl' denoted not so much a profession as a way of life. The spectacular revues predated and for many years ran concurrently with the 'book' musicals, and of all the many series presented at different theatres by various showmen it is *The Ziegfeld Follies* which is most redolent of that era, even to those not even born then, and the name Florenz Ziegfeld still represents the archetypal Broadway showman. No other producer, after all, had three Hollywood musicals devoted to his art – *The Great Ziegfeld* (1936), *Ziegfeld Girl* (1941)

A popular leading man in early screen musicals, Alexander Gray, although not a member of the original cast of *The Desert Song* (1926) did appear as the Red Shadow later in the run.

and *Ziegfeld Follies* (1944) – as well as being portrayed by many an actor in other show-business biopics. If personally he was a million light years removed from the suave image offered by William Powell on screen, the films at least did justice to his monumental staging.

The *Follies* appeared annually from 1907 to the time of Ziegfeld's death in 1932, after which they were carried on by his widow, the actress Billie Burke. Although 'Ziggy's' concept was first and foremost the exhibition of feminine pulchritude, he was willing to concede the value of musical scores by his semi-regular team of Raymond Hubbell, Dave Stamper, Irving Berlin, Louis Hirsch, Harry Tierney, Victor Herbert, Buddy De Sylva, Rudolf Friml, Walter Donaldson, and many others like Gordon and Revel whose songs were interpolated. To sing the songs he engaged stars of the calibre of Nora Bayes, Eva Tanguay, the Dolly Sisters, Helen Morgan, Jane Froman, Ann Pennington, Marilyn Miller, Ruth Etting, Harry Richman and Ina Claire, and featured the orchestras of Paul Whiteman, George Olsen and Art Hickman. Equally did he recognize the value of comedy, and some of the world's finest comics, whether at the beginning or the peak of their careers, worked in the *Follies*. Among these were Fanny Brice, Leon Errol, Olsen and Johnson, Bert Williams, Ed Wynn, Helen Broderick, W.C. Fields, Eddie Cantor, Will Rogers, Gallagher and Shean, to name but a few. Flo Ziegfeld did everything in the grand manner, even dying a million dollars in debt, but he gave Broadway new standards by which to live. His followers and rivals were legion, and they all kept the music going round and round, and provided stiff opposition for fading operetta and burgeoning musical comedy alike.

George White's Scandals appeared each year from 1919 to 1929 then spasmodically through the thirties, and *Earl Carroll's Vanities* from 1923 to 1932. Insofar as spectacular revues can be literate, White's were more so than those of Carroll, whose motto 'Through These Portals Pass the Most

From 1921 to 1924 composer Irving Berlin and producer Sam H. Harris presented a series of Music Box Revues at their newly opened theatre of that name. Here is a scene from the 1924 edition, illustrating the kind of spectacle audiences could expect.

Beautiful Girls in the World' clearly stated his personal credo. George White, on the other hand, was responsible for introducing George and Ira Gershwin and De Sylva, Brown and Henderson to Broadway, and using such performers as Charles King, Winnie Lightner, Tom Patricola, Willie and Eugene Howard, Rudy Vallee, Ethel Merman, Alice Faye, Ray Bolger, Bert Lahr and Cliff Edwards.

Irving Berlin's *Music Box Revues* presented annually by Sam H. Harris at the composer's own Music Box Theater in the period 1921–4 starred Charlotte Greenwood, Clark and McCullough, Fanny Brice, William Gaxton, the Brox Sisters and Robert Benchley, with Grace Moore introducing Berlin's immortal 'What'll I Do?' and 'All Alone'. In 1925 the Theater Guild staged a one-day revue in their own Guild Theater featuring young players such as Sterling Holloway and Romney Brent, with songs by the comparatively new writers Richard Rodgers and Lorenz Hart, whose only Broadway spots to date had been with songs interpolated in a moderate success, *Poor Little Ritz Girl* (1920), and a flop, *The Melody Man* (1924). Audience and critical acclaim was such that the 'one day' *Garrick Gaieties* ran for 211 performances, followed in 1926 by the second edition. When the third *Gaieties* appeared in 1930 Rodgers and Hart had moved on to bigger things and music was provided by, among others, Vernon Duke, Marc Blitzstein and Aaron Copland.

The *Hitchy-Koo* series, attracting such composers as Victor Herbert and Cole Porter, ran from 1917 to 1922; but the biggest and most ambitiously spectacular spectacles were presented by the Shuberts, and later Dillingham, at the vast Hippodrome every fall from its opening in 1905 to 1922. Far removed from Ziegfeld's notion of what was spectacular, the Hippodrome featured everything from circus to Pavlova, Indian shows to Houdini, the Civil War to John Philip Sousa. Another of the great showmen, John Murray Anderson, was responsible for the inception of *The Greenwich Village Follies* (1919–25 and one more in 1928), based originally on the bohemian life of downtown New York and featuring Fred Allen, Joe E. Brown, Frank Crumit, Martha Graham and the bands of Ted Lewis and Vincent Lopez. Even more intimate in scale and content were Agnes Morgan's *Grand Street Follies* (1922–9), originally advertised as 'A low-brow show for high-grade morons' but in fact specializing in satire of the highest quality, with, in the 1926 edition, the first stage songs to be written by young Arthur Schwartz, and in 1928–9 a young hoofer named James Cagney.

No history of these early years would be complete without mention of the Winter Garden Theater, a stronghold of musicals and revue under the control of the Shuberts. They held the stage from 1912 to 1924 with annual editions of *The Passing Show*, filling in from 1923 to 1925 with *Artists and Models*, with its early exhibitions of nudity on Broadway. Most Shubert shows were written by Harold Atteridge, and they had the services as staff composer of Sigmund Romberg, working in a medium far removed from his own world of operetta and in which he turned out all kinds of hack music that generally went unnoticed in the spectacle. Or which, in the case of Al Jolson's Winter Garden shows, was summarily dismissed by the egomaniac star, who insisted on creating his own hits (on which he would cut himself in as 'co-composer' for the privilege of plugging other writers' songs). This was disheartening for Romberg, perhaps, but he was learning American stagecraft and had his own compensations shortly afterwards with *Maytime* (1917), *Blossom Time* (1921), *The Student Prince* (1924), *The Desert Song* (1926) and *The New Moon* (1928), which were to provide him with royalties for life.

Although the spectaculars were Broadway fixtures for the next decade or so, there were portents of the way musicals were going as early as 1915. The man responsible for a certain degree of integration of music, lyrics and

Opposite: **The Cocoanuts** (1925). Book by George S. Kaufman, songs by Irving Berlin. But with the Marx Brothers rampant (and here is Groucho surrounded by some of his favourite people) both book and songs were liable to go for nought.

Left: **Irene** (1919). One of the first of the 'modern' musical comedies, starring Edith Day, Walter Regan, Bobbie Watson and Adele Rowland, *Irene* was yet another vintage show to be revived with great success in the 1970s.

libretto was the same person who was to give the musical its greatest metamorphosis thirteen years later in *Show Boat*, and the initial Jerome Kern 'Princess Theater Shows' could have afforded no greater contrast to the monster revues. Although the seating capacity of 299 permitted neither expensive staging nor enormous profits *90 in the Shade*, *Nobody Home*, *Oh Joy!*, *Very Good, Eddie* and *Oh, Lady, Lady!* were original enough in presentation if not conception (basically they were the same old variation on the boy-meets-girl theme and marital complications) to establish Kern, Guy Bolton and P.G. Wodehouse as the most formidable team of writers on Broadway. Kern followed up with his first big hits on the larger stage – *Stepping Stones* (1923), a vehicle for the great comedian of the era, Fred Stone and his family, and *Sally* (1920) and *Sunny* (1925), both illuminated by the glowing talent of the immortal Marilyn Miller.

This was something of a transition period, with Romberg serving his time backstage at the Winter Garden, Friml having established himself in 1912 with *The Firefly*, Irving Berlin still writing for *The Ziegfeld Follies* after having contributed six songs in an attempt to modernize Victor Herbert's *The Century Girl* of 1916, and Herbert himself and George M. Cohan nearing the end of their Broadway triumphs. Harry Tierney, another of the *Follies* writers, gave Broadway its longest run to date with *Irene* (670 performances in 1920–1) and one of its biggest hit songs, 'Alice Blue Gown', but the show offered little variation on the traditional shop-girl-rags-to-riches formula that had been staple fare since Victorian times. But there were men waiting in the wings to provide a more modern and sophisticated antidote to the effete music of operetta and the tinsel of the shop-girl romances which were, in essence, but a step removed from operetta themselves. A twenty-year-old publisher's pianist from Brooklyn had already had single songs used in minor shows, but it was not until Al Jolson stopped

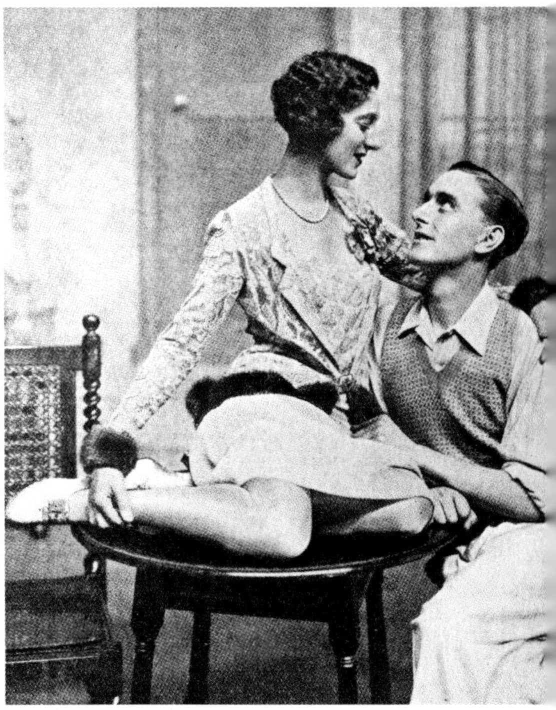

Oh Kay! After completing a 1926–7 Broadway run of 256 performances, Gertrude Lawrence brought yet another Gershwin-Aarons-Freedley show to London. Pictured here is her 'Do, Do, Do,' duet with Harold French, at His Majesty's Theatre.

Funny Face (1927). The combination of producers Alex A. Aarons and Vinton Freedley, composer George Gershwin, and stars Fred and Adele Astaire, was an unbeatable formula on Broadway of the twenties. Their successes were usually repeated in London.

the show with 'Swanee' in *Sinbad* that George Gershwin was seen to be something more than just another songwriter. His first complete score that same year (1919) for *La, La Lucille* earned him a commission from George White to write the next five years' *Scandals*. These and other shows culminated in *Lady Be Good*, produced under the aegis of Alex A. Aarons and Vinton Freedley, who were to present the best of Gershwin over the next few years. There was *Oh Kay!* and *Funny Face* – even two relatively unsuccessful attempts at operetta in collaboration with composers well-versed in the idiom, Herbert Stothart with *Song of the Flame* (1925) and Romberg with *Rosalie* (1928), which proved only that this was not Gershwin's *métier*, even if *Rosalie* did produce 'How Long Has This Been Going On?'.

Bert Kalmar and Harry Ruby made their bow with *Helen of Troy, NY* in 1923, and De Sylva, Brown and Henderson formed their historic partnership after Buddy De Sylva's success as lyricist for Kern, Gershwin and Romberg, having a hit at the very outset with *Good News* (1927). The Marx Brothers erupted on to Broadway with *I'll Say She Is* (1924), *The Cocoanuts* (1925) and *Animal Crackers* (1928) with their own anarchic brand of lunacy which reduced revue or 'book' show alike to a shambles, and while their antics may have infuriated the authors they kept audiences perpetually delighted.

Rodgers and Hart, elevated by the success of *The Garrick Gaieties*, with their friend and librettist Herbert Fields had their first mild success in 1925 with *Dearest Enemy*, based on events real or apocryphal in the War of Independence, followed a year later by *The Girl Friend*. This had only fifteen more performances than its predecessor, yet it remains the more remembered event in show-business annals. *A Connecticut Yankee* came immediately afterwards, and with great songs like 'My Heart Stood Still' and 'Thou Swell', plus a more imaginative plot (by Mark Twain) than most musicals of the time, it made Rodgers and Hart and Fields an unbeatable team. But even they could miss now and again, as with *Chee-Chee*, an off-beat fable of Old China that proved too advanced (or obscure) for 1928.

These, then, were the 'new boys', intent on sending the Broadway musical in a new direction, along with Vincent Youmans, who at this time came up with *No, No, Nanette*, which no one could have dreamt would spark off a whole series of revivals forty-five years later. Suffice it to say that *Nanette* was one of the big hits of the mid-twenties, a period strong in the kind of shows that would prove to be perennials, however dated the operetta style might appear to be on the surface. For within two or three years in the middle of the 'Roaring Twenties' the most outstanding shows were *Rose Marie*, *The Student Prince*, *The Vagabond King* and *The Desert Song*. As will be seen time and time again, innovations and tradition march side by side.

The point is made elsewhere that many of the legendary shows of Kern, Gershwin, Rodgers, Youmans, Porter and others achieved their place in the Hall of Fame more by virtue of their durable scores than for any intrinsic value as musicals. Certainly the libretti rarely withstand close scrutiny today. However, the musical is one theatre form that is not dependent on strength of plot. Other facts must be taken into consideration as being conducive to an evening's entertainment – the visual aspect is paramount with costumes, sets, imaginative lighting, choreography. But the essential

Tip Toes (1925). One of the slighter Gershwin shows of the twenties, *Tip Toes* introduced such songs as 'Looking For a Boy' and 'That Certain Feeling', and what Lorenz Hart was moved to call an utterly charming performance by Queenie Smith, seen here with the elegant chorus.

element of show business is people, the performers – singers, dancers, actors, comedians, and the hard core of featured players who were the backbone of Broadway no less than Hollywood. If, a decade previously, the talking point and selling angle were the name of a producer like Ziegfeld or Dillingham, in the twenties it was the new star system which sold a show. The sweethearts of Broadway were Fred and Adele Astaire, assuming the mantle of Vernon and Irene Castle, the pre-war toasts of the town before Vernon's death in a World War I flying accident. The perfect dancing team since they were children, the Astaires came, were seen, and conquered with their personal dancing style and, strangely enough, Adele's winsome personality rather than Fred's more retiring demeanour. When they broke up on Adele's marriage, the wiseacres cast doubts on Fred's ability to carry on alone! The verdict of a Hollywood casting director on Fred Astaire has passed into show-business folklore, but in case there is some Rip Van Winkle who has never heard it, it is worth repeating: 'Balding. Can't sing. Can't act. Dances a little'.

Marilyn Miller and Jack Donohue, Fanny Brice, Jolson, Vivienne Segal, Victor Moore, Sophie Tucker, as well as stars previously mentioned – these were the names which drew people, the stars for whom shows were written in days when going to the theatre was an event. It was unequivocally a colourful, exciting time, from which an even more exciting pattern was to emerge.

No, No, Nanette (1925). A pretty girl and handsome chorus boys were stock properties of any twenties musical, but *No, No, Nanette* provided more hit songs than most, and was revived successfully forty-five years later.

3 Show Boat and the Great Change

The new era ushered in by *Show Boat* should have begun a year or so earlier, once Jerome Kern and Oscar Hammerstein II had persuaded Flo Ziegfeld to mount this, for him, unusual show at his new Ziegfeld Theater. 'Ziggy' preferred to start with the more conventional *Rio Rita* on 2 February 1927, and it ran for an unexpected 494 performances, tying up the stage and causing the authors, at first self-confident through love for their own creation, severe self-doubts and copious rewriting. Ziegfeld also had doubts, but kept his word and gave *Show Boat* all the expertise of which he was capable.

The point has been made at the outset that this was a new departure in the world of musicals. Not only was this manifested by the musical play itself and the wonderful score, and no less by the fine performances by Charles Winninger, Edna May Oliver, Sammy White and Eva Puck and a magical one by Helen Morgan, whose performance of 'Bill' for ever identified the song with her, but also by what it represented – namely, a blend of music, lyrics and libretto that would serve as a guidepost for the future and an object lesson for all aspiring show-writers. Yet, paradoxically enough, neither Kern nor Hammerstein took advantage of their breakthrough. The massively competent Oscar would do so sixteen years later, and Kern was to create superb film music, but on Broadway they were content to return to the *Mittel-Europa* operetta of *Music in the Air* and the turn-of-the-century

Opposite: **Show Boat** (1927). The *Cotton Blossom* was the show boat, scene of the romance, drama, and music so superbly integrated in Jerome Kern and Oscar Hammerstein's musical adaption of the Edna Ferber novel.

Below: **Rio Rita** (1927). Rio Rita (Ethelind Terry) and Captain Jim (J. Harold Murray) depicting what passed for searing passion in the twenties.

backstage musical in *Sweet Adeline*. *The Cat and the Fiddle*, by Kern and his other long-time collaborator Otto Harbach, dispensed with the trappings of musical comedy but was otherwise an unoriginal classic-versus-popular-music duel between the chief protagonists. Yet from these unstartling shows came some of Jerome Kern's loveliest melodies – 'The Night Was Made for Love', 'She Didn't Say Yes', 'The Song Is You', 'I've Told Every Little Star', and two more creations for the lovely but tragic Helen Morgan, 'Don't Ever Leave Me' and 'Why Was I Born?'.

Elsewhere the metamorphosis was equally unapparent at first. Friml was coming to the end of his run with *The Three Musketeers* (1928), a victim of his own inability to change with the times. Romberg continued with *The New Moon* and *Nina Rosa*, but his 1935 *May Wine*, despite an attempt at integration and a story founded on psychiatry (a subject only to become really commercial with *Lady in the Dark* six years later), was to be his last important work for a decade, by which time he had avoided Friml's error and adapted himself to changing conditions. It was left to George and Ira Gershwin to continue where Kern had left off, and with three Gershwin productions of the early thirties the change was complete. Every conventional 'book' show subsequently produced would seem like a retrogression.

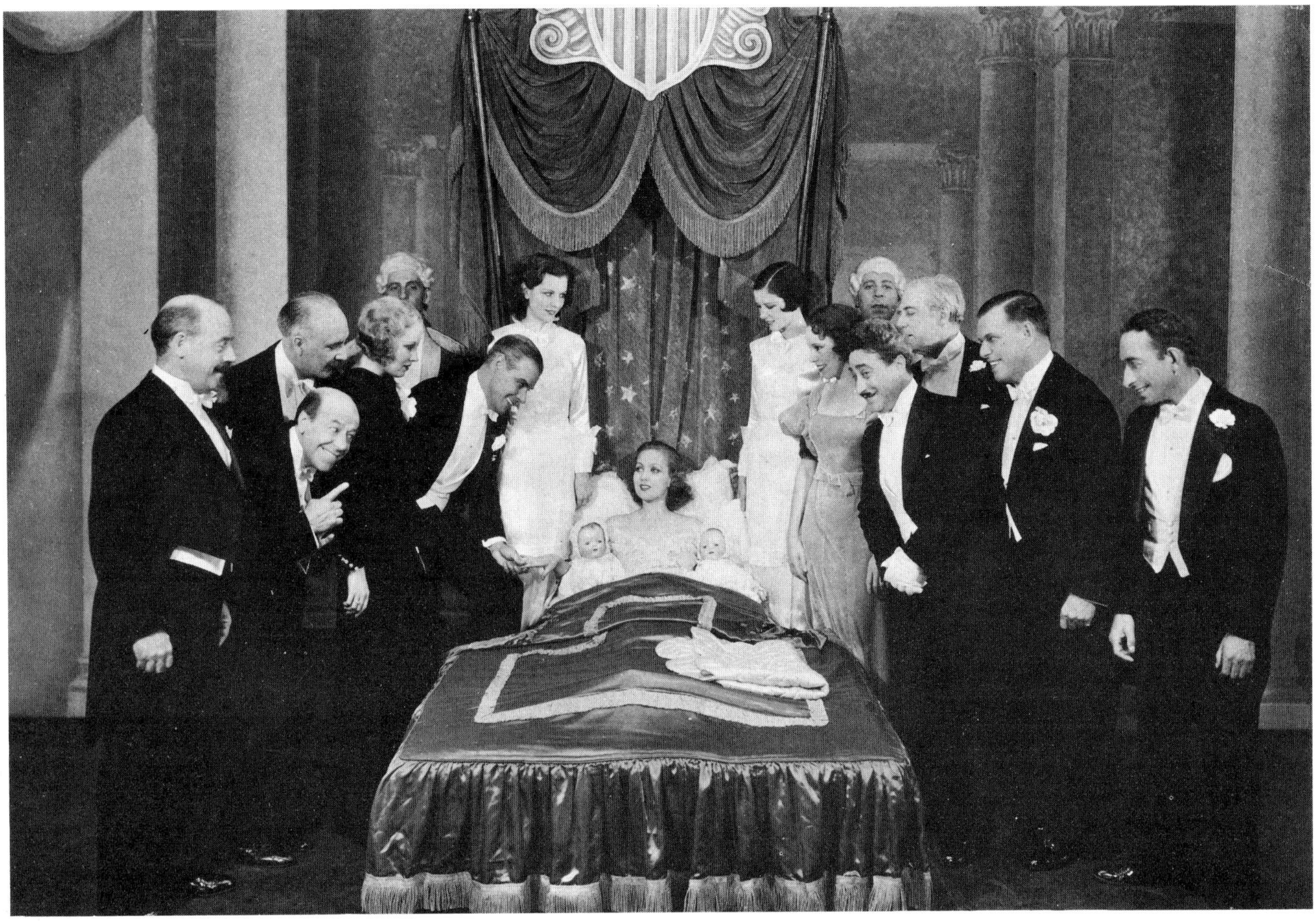

Of Thee I Sing (1931). For the first time the Pulitzer Prize for Drama was awarded to a musical, the Gershwin-Kaufman-Ryskind satire in which all constitutional problems are solved when the President's wife gives birth to twins.

Opposite above: **Gypsy** (1959). One of the glittering chorus ensembles in the original production at the Broadway Theater.

Opposite below: **Kismet.** Joan Diener repeated her Broadway success two years later in the 1955 production at the Stoll Theatre, London.

With author George S. Kaufman they had originally planned *Strike Up the Band* in 1927 and opened it out of town. Critics loved it in New Jersey and Philadelphia, but they couldn't give seats away and crept back to Manhattan to lick their wounds. Edgar Selwyn finally agreed to produce a more commercial version at the Times Square Theater in 1930, and with a more moderate script doctored by Morrie Ryskind it did make its mark. Not with an outstanding run, perhaps, but for an original and still fairly hard-hitting anti-war satire to make any sort of impact was in itself a radical advance. Musically it inspired Gershwin to write a batch of witty 'incidental' themes as well as the hits – 'Soon', 'I've Got a Crush on You' (first used in *Treasure Girl*, 1928) and the title song. The same team followed up with *Of Thee I Sing* the next year, and although success cannot always be repeated, in this instance the blend of anti-political satire garnished with some of Ira's wittiest lyrics and George's musical parodies proved a sure-fire hit with the critics *and* the public who packed the Music Box on 441 occasions. More important for the prestige of the genre was the first-time award of the Pulitzer Prize for Drama to a musical – although not to George Gershwin! The prize went instead to Kaufman, Ryskind and Ira. No precedent having been established, there could be no award for music, a situation that was later changed to honour composer as well as writers.

George S. Kaufman was concerned the same year in *The Band Wagon* which, although basically a revue, has long been hailed as one of the best ever musicals (certainly the 1953 film which tacked an original story on to the songs was one of the all-time great screen musicals). It was the last

10¢
JUMBO
HENRY CLIVE

THEATRE ROYAL
DRURY LANE
Managing Director · PRINCE LITTLER
General Manager · FRANK C. MARSHALL
THE THEATRE GUILD
PRESENTS
OKLAHOMA!
A MUSICAL PLAY
Music by RICHARD RODGERS
Book and Lyrics by OSCAR HAMMERSTEIN II
Production Directed by ROUBEN MAMOULIAN
Choreography by AGNES de MILLE
Settings by
LEMUEL AYERS
Costumes by
MILES WHITE
Production under the supervision of THERESA HELBURN & LAWRENCE LANGNER
Production reproduced by JEROME WHYTE

ALFRED BUTT in conjunction with LEE EPHRAIM presents
The THEATRE ROYAL, DRURY LANE Production
The DESERT SONG
BOOK & LYRICS BY
OTTO HARBACH
OSCAR HAMMERSTEIN 2ND
& FRANK MANDEL
MUSIC BY
SIGMUND ROMBERG
SEPARATE NUMBERS
PRICE
The Desert Song 2/- NET
Romance 2/- "
The Riff Song 2/- "
"It" 2/- "
One Alone 2/- "
One Flower grows alone in Your Garden 2/- "
Piano Selection 2/6 NET
Desert Song Valse 2/- "

Opposite above left: **Jumbo** (1935). As can be seen from this programme Billy Rose's spectacular at the New York Hippodrome offered one of the less cerebral forms of musical entertainment.

Opposite above right: **Oklahoma!** (1947). London's first taste of postwar American musicals.

Opposite below: A typical example of Chappell's sheet music of the twenties. At a time when the average popular song sold for 6d, this publishing company's excerpts from the big shows cost four times as much.

chance Broadwayites would have of seeing Fred and Adele Astaire work together before Adele's irrevocable retirement, and the Astaires joined with Tilly Losch, Frank Morgan and Helen Broderick to give the performance of their lives in honour of Kaufman's witty script, Albertina Rasch's choreography, and some of the best songs Arthur Schwartz and Howard Dietz ever wrote. If for nothing else *The Band Wagon* will be remembered for 'Dancing in the Dark', surely one of the Top Ten tunes of the century. Another of the few revues which qualify for inclusion in any history of the musical was Moss Hart's *As Thousands Cheer* of 1933, with which Sam H. Harris followed *Of Thee I Sing* at Irving Berlin's Music Box Theater. Berlin produced one of his finest scores with Clifton Webb and Marilyn Miller featured in 'Easter Parade' and 'Not for All the Rice in China' and Ethel Waters making her own Broadway success with 'Heat Wave' and the show-stopping 'Supper Time', a sombre but immensely moving song about the aftermath of a lynching. This was unusual material for Berlin, but as he was to show time and again he could adapt himself completely to any theme or circumstance. *Thousands* tilted at more specific targets than the more amiable *Band Wagon*, but together these shows represent the zenith of achievement in their genre.

Hit shows simply rolled off the assembly lines during those early thirties, most of them benefiting in one way or another from an increasing awareness of the value of a good script rather than a vacuous libretto, as well as from

The Band Wagon (1931). Containing one of the most memorable musical scores of Arthur Schwartz and Howard Dietz, this was the swan song of the favourite Broadway team of Fred and Adele Astaire.

the rapidly developing sophistication in popular songwriting. A major factor governing the latter was the advent in 1928 of Cole Porter, whose previous work for Broadway had included the short-lived (fifteen performances) *See America First* in 1916 and several contributions to the *Hitchy-Koo* revues. Born of a well-to-do family, Porter initially wrote as a dilettante in his *milieux* of Paris, Venice and the Riviera, but once accepted as a Broadway composer with *Paris*, *Fifty Million Frenchmen*, *The New Yorkers* and *Wake Up and Dream*, a total of over 750 performances in the period 1928–30, Porter made New York his home base (with an apartment at the Waldorf-Astoria) and settled down to establish himself as one of the few geniuses of both words and music.

The thirties, an era rich in great shows and hundreds of the best popular songs ever written, was Cole Porter's decade. He and his shows typify the growth to adulthood of popular entertainment. *The Gay Divorce* made Fred Astaire a star in 1932 in his first solo performance and gave the world 'Night and Day'. *Anything Goes*, although far from Ethel Merman's début, consolidated her position as a world star and produced 'I Get a Kick Out of You', 'All Through the Night', 'You're the Top' and the unforgettable title song. *Red, Hot and Blue* possessed a formidable comedy trio in Merman, Jimmy Durante and Bob Hope, and *Leave It to Me* was stolen from right under the noses of the stars William Gaxton, Victor Moore and Sophie Tucker by a young redhead from Texas named Mary Martin with the daring (for its period) 'My Heart Belongs to Daddy' (second from the left among the four chorus boys supporting her in Eskimo costume was a young hopeful named Gene Kelly). Even a comparative flop like *Jubilee*, with only 169 per-

Above: **Babes in Arms** (1937). The Rodgers and Hart musical abounded with youthful high spirits and good tunes, and proved a good 'nursery' for such future stars as Duke McHale (left), Mitzi Green (centre) and particularly Alfred Drake (right), who became one of Broadway's dominant figures in *Oklahoma!* and *Kismet*.

Opposite above: **Fifty Million Frenchmen** (1929). A scene from the Cole Porter-Herbert Fields Paris-based musical.

Opposite: **On Your Toes** (1936). A combination of musical comedy and ballet, both classical and jazz (the memorable 'Slaughter On 10th Avenue') starring Ray Bolger and Tamara Geva.

formances in 1935, gave us 'Begin the Beguine' and 'Just One of Those Things'.

Rodgers and Hart hit their peak also. *Jumbo* (1935), one last fling for the Hippodrome, revived memories of the old extravaganzas with master showman Billy Rose's presentation that included a circus, Paul Whiteman's orchestra, Jimmy Durante and an elephant. To show that he too could do things in the grand manner Rose not only got Rodgers and Hart to write 'The Most Beautiful Girl in the World', 'My Romance' and 'Little Girl Blue' but engaged Ben Hecht and Charles MacArthur to write the book. George Abbott joined forces with Rodgers and Hart on the book of *On Your Toes* (1936), bringing culture to the Broadway musical with a ballet story, definitively choreographed by Georges Balanchine, and climaxed by the famous 'Slaughter on Tenth Avenue' portrayed by Ray Bolger and Tamara Geva. 'There's a Small Hotel' didn't do too badly either.

They dispensed with outside help for the book of *Babes in Arms* the following year, a paean to youth which included such future stars as Dan Dailey, Alfred Drake, Mitzi Green, Grace MacDonald, Robert Rounseville and the Nicholas Brothers. This archetypal putting-on-a-show-in-the-barn divertissement was a hit by virtue of the freshness of performers and presentation alike and such 'instant evergreens' as 'Where or When', 'My Funny Valentine', 'The Lady Is a Tramp' and 'I Wish I Were in Love Again'. Seven months after the Babes made their bow Rodgers and Hart teamed up with George S. Kaufman and Moss Hart for *I'd Rather Be Right*, the sort of political satire that would have been impossible to mount before *Of Thee I Sing* broke the ice. The show is chiefly remembered for George M. Cohan's return to the stage he had left so many years before. He gave a fine performance and it was an enjoyable comeback for the audiences. However, as had been proved when he worked with Rodgers and Hart on the film *The Phantom President* some years earlier, Cohan, even in his sixtieth year, was too much of an egotist to work in harmony with composers for whom he had no respect, and the atmosphere backstage was hardly convivial.

Porgy and Bess (1935). George Gershwin's near-operatic setting of DuBose and Dorothy Heyward's play *Porgy* was not an immediate hit, but has since become an important part of the standard musical stage and operatic repertoire.

In more traditional musical comedy style the Gershwins had begun the decade well with *Girl Crazy*. The nineteen-year-old Ginger Rogers introduced two of Gershwin's best-known standards, 'Embraceable You' and 'But Not for Me', but all the honours were stolen by a twenty-one-year-old ex-typist called Ethel Zimmerman who, night after night, stopped the show with a song arrangement she still uses after forty-five years. When she threw her head back and held that high note for half a chorus in the final ride-out of 'I Got Rhythm' Ethel Merman was making the kind of show-business history usually found only in the cornier backstage musical plots, and at the same time creating for herself a reputation as one of the most vital performers ever to tread the boards on Broadway. But to prove that the vagaries of show business are no respecters of persons, the Gershwins fell on their faces in 1933 with *Pardon My English* and *Let 'em Eat Cake*. Even they couldn't win 'em all, but to compensate for these flops The Big One was on its way, one work by which Gershwin will be remembered for a hundred years however much else is forgotten.

How incredible it is that *Porgy and Bess* was originally meant to be written by Jerome Kern for *Al Jolson*! But as adapted by George and Ira Gershwin from Dorothy and DuBose Heyward's play *Porgy* it can be seen as the ultimate experience in the musical theatre to which all the other 'transition' musicals had been merely stepping-stones. *Porgy and Bess* was a creation of the Broadway stage by a Broadway writer, yet at the same time it was a musical of such stature, with its operatic construction and artistry of staging by Rouben Mamoulian, that it has been acknowledged as the first truly indigenous American opera. It is folk opera if you like, whose overall flavour and elements such as the street cries were evidently drawn by Gershwin from his stay in South Carolina in which he tried to absorb the Negro idiom, yet the score is unique and it owes nothing at all to any of Gershwin's previous work. Unfortunately its creator never saw his masterpiece receive the acclaim it merited. Presented by the Theater Guild at the Alvin Theater on 9 October 1935, *Porgy and Bess* was torn to shreds by critics who wilfully or stupidly misunderstood its import, and it closed after 142 performances. And had not the same thing happened to 'Rhapsody in Blue' eleven years before? Musical appreciation had advanced, but there was still a strong tendency to pigeonhole music in supposedly neat categories. Like the 'Rhapsody', *Porgy and Bess* was neither classical, jazz nor 'popular' music. Few people, especially those in responsible critical positions, were smart or unprejudiced enough to accept that George Gershwin was not expressing himself in any one of the conventional idioms; rather, he was combining elements of them all to create his own idea of what American music should be. The result was not a hybrid, but a new entity altogether.

The world eventually caught up with Gershwin. Despite their operatic context the songs from *Porgy* spread far and wide, at first via the 'Original Cast' 78 rpm records by Anne Brown and Todd Duncan and later by their assimilation into the standard repertoire. When *Porgy* was given a second chance in 1942 it was the most successful revival in Broadway history, greeted with the sort of critical acclaim it should have had seven years previously. A world tour in 1952 with Laverne Hutcheson and William Warfield alternating as Porgy, with Leontyne Price as Bess and the former bandleader and scat singer Cab Calloway as a magnificent Sportin' Life, set the seal on its universal acceptance.

It would be tempting to invent some tenous link between *Porgy*, Marc Connolly's *Green Pastures* (1930), with its use of spirituals to illustrate the story of 'de Lawd', and *Cabin in the Sky* (1940), with its Vernon Duke score based on Lynn Root's play. Tenuous it certainly would be, and also spurious, for apart from being all-black productions they have nothing in common. In the latter two one is conscious of an Uncle Tom touch which is never evident in *Porgy*, despite the phonetic spelling and pronunciation of such lyrics as 'Dere's a Boat Dat's Leavin' Soon for New York', a practice that has more in common with *Carmen Jones*, in which Oscar Hammerstein, in his 1943 adaptation of Bizet's *Carmen*, used the original music in a Negro environment. Even before the remarkable change in black attitudes in the second half of the century there was something more than slightly condescending about this kind of interpretation of black music. Or perhaps, even as recently as the mid-forties, a liberal and literate man like Hammerstein still felt bound by the show-business tradition of accepting black actors, singers and musicians only in menial roles.

In documenting so many successful shows it is easy to overlook those which never made it. There were probably many reasons why a show flopped – the main one being, no doubt, because it just wasn't good enough. In 1931, to take one example, we find a musical called *Here Goes the Bride* which opened on 3 November and died after seven performances. Why? It had songs by the famous duo of Johnny Green and Edward Heyman sung by Frances Langford, and starred Broadway's favourite comedy team of Clark and McCullough. Three years later came *Revenge with Music*, a musical play by Arthur Schwartz and Howard Dietz based on Falla's *The Three-Cornered Hat*, which ran for 158 performances. True, it may have been overshadowed by the success of *Anything Goes* which had opened a week earlier, but there must surely have been room for an imaginative musical that starred Charles Winninger, Libby Holman and Georges Metaxa and included 'You and the Night and the Music' and 'If There Is Someone Lovlier than You'. And then there was *Very Warm for May*, notorious as the biggest Kern-Hammerstein flop. Its main song, 'All the Things You Are', has outlived the show by thirty-eight years to date, and yet even with a popular leading man, Jack Whiting, and the up-and-coming stars Eve Arden, Donald Brian and Grace MacDonald (and, tucked away in the chorus line, June Allyson and Vera-Ellen), it lasted for no more than fifty-nine performances. Show business is full of imponderables, and no one can foretell with any precision what will make a hit. One show that did survive, if briefly, against all the odds, was Marc Blitzstein's left-wing musical drama *The Cradle Will Rock*, an Orson Welles Mercury Theater production. Its outspoken anti-capitalism theme was frowned upon by the government, and strings were pulled to have it banned from the state-owned theatre while the audience was assembling for the first night, in June 1937. Thereupon players and spectators alike paraded down the street to the empty Venice Theater, where the show was performed on a bare stage without costumes, accompanied by Blitzstein at the piano narrating the story, a performance that brought so much to the stark quality of the play that the producer Sam H. Grisman took it into the Windsor Theater some months later for an extended run in its improvised form. Revived several times in subsequent decades, *The Cradle Will Rock* has achieved certain fame more for Blitzstein's music than for its now outdated theme. Marc Blitzstein was later to adapt Kurt Weill's *Die Dreigroschenoper* for American consumption, but at the time of his early trials and tribulations Weill was very much a new boy on Broadway. A victim of the Nazi régime in his native Germany, his first attempt at writing for the American stage was *Johnny Johnson* (1936), Paul Green's adaptation of Jaroslav Hašek's novel *The Good Soldier Schweik*, a Group Theater production which foreshadowed the Actors' Studio of the forties and fifties, directed as it was by Lee Strasberg and with a cast including Morris Carnovsky, Lee J. Cobb, Elia Kazan and John Garfield. An anti-war tract at the opposite end of the scale to *Strike Up the Band*, its sixty-one performances represented an honourable failure.

In *Knickerbocker Holiday* two years later Weill's music fitted Maxwell Anderson's book and lyrics like a glove, most notably when Walter Huston sat alone on stage to sing the immortal 'September Song'. This slice of early American history was illustrated graphically by a score which revealed how

Richard Rodgers b. 1902.

Pal Joey (1940). Rodgers and Hart's setting of John O'Hara's story of show-business had to wait many years for universal acceptance, but consolidated Vivienne Segal's position as a durable Broadway star, and provided the best possible springboard for the subsequent career of Gene Kelly.

well the composer had assimilated the American idiom. With his scores for Moss Hart's *Lady in the Dark* (1941) and Ogden Nash's *One Touch of Venus* (1943) his absorption into the Broadway style was complete. Both musicals were sheer fantasy, perhaps the kind of escapism for which audiences were crying out in wartime. *Venus* was the longer-running show, but *Lady* kept going for over a year and gave Gertrude Lawrence her most glamorous role ever. It also introduced Danny Kaye, who promptly stopped the show with the tongue-twisting 'Tchaikovsky and Other Russians'. Ira Gershwin, in his first theatrical venture since George's death, provided words of a quality to match Weill's sparkling music, and although the psychiatric angle, with involved dream sequences, could have warranted criticism, Gertrude Lawrence's virtuoso performance stilled any possible objections. As did that of the ever-improving Mary Martin in *Touch of Venus* with its even more way-out plot.

Whatever may have been happening on Broadway's legitimate stage or elsewhere in show business, no sense of impending doom pervaded the musical stage as the thirties gave way to the forties. The 'fun' shows came thick and fast – *Dubarry Was a Lady*, *Panama Hattie*, *Let's Face It*, *Something for the Boys*, all by the indefatigable team of Cole Porter and Herbert and/or Dorothy Fields; as well as *Yokel Boy*, *Best Foot Forward*, *Hold On to Your Hats* – Jolson's short-lived return to the stage after a long period of idleness; *Louisiana Purchase*; and Mike Todd's ambitious 'popular' versions of the classics in *The Hot Mikado* and *Swingin' the* (Midsummer Night's) *Dream*. All of them were enjoyable, productive of good songs, and featured favourite stars doing what they did best. And all of them were thoroughly inconsequential, in the general scheme of things. But musicals are for entertainment, pure and simple – and if they happen to carry a message or approach the level of Art so much the better.

Pal Joey did not entertain; not at first. Rodgers and Hart had been doing very nicely with *I Married an Angel*, *The Boys from Syracuse*, *Too Many Girls* and *Higher and Higher* when John O'Hara came to them with the idea of turning his book of short stories about the seedier side of show business into a musical. They saw the opportunity to create a new type of 'adult' musical, following the course charted by *Show Boat*, *Of Thee I Sing*, *Porgy and Bess* and *The Cradle Will Rock* but differing from all of them. *Pal Joey* was thick with unsympathetic characters, none more so than Gene Kelly's brilliant Joey, and presented without euphemism the cheap wheeling and dealing of an unlovable small-time heel and his use of a younger (Leila Ernst) and an older (Vivienne Segal) woman to gain his ends. Despite the presence of such (eventual) evergreens as 'Bewitched' and 'I Could Write a Book' – both songs of cynicism and irony before conventional usage changed them into soft-core ballads – *Pal Joey* was far from the stereotype musical. Critical opinion varied, and while audience appreciation took it to 374 performances, still a fairly good run for those days, the show hardly carried the cachet of success.

While public taste was slow in developing, by the early forties the musical had taken large strides from the days of dreaming shop-girls and princesses in disguise. Satire had proved itself a marketable proposition, ballet was an accepted ingredient of musical comedy thanks to the choreography of George Balanchine, Agnes De Mille, Busby Berkeley and Albertina Rasch, musical standards had improved beyond recognition, and staging had become even more professional in the hands of directors such as Rouben Mamoulian, George Abbott, Joshua Logan and Moss Hart. Indeed, the musical had come a long way, but not quite far enough, *Pal Joey* having to wait another twelve years to be accepted as the masterpiece it was. It was this show which was to provide a link of sorts with the next progressive stage of the Broadway musical, one that was to sweep aside the last remaining shreds of convention and open up new vistas.

4 The New Broadway

The curtain rose on an almost empty stage. *Stage left, an old woman churning butter. Off-stage right, the voice of a lone cowboy singing 'Oh What a Beautiful Morning'*. From so restrained a beginning sprang not only the most fabulously successful production in theatrical history but an epoch-making musical play that caused a revolution in the progress of the Broadway musical. The opening scene, a complete departure from convention (even the legendary *Show Boat* had an ensemble opening), hardly seemed auspicious for the success of *Oklahoma!*, linked with its being based on Lynn Riggs's flop play *Green Grow the Lilacs* and its presentation by the Theater Guild with a cast of unknowns. Nor had there been much demand for folksy, 'country' musical shows, much less one written by Richard Rodgers, without Lorenz Hart for the first time in over twenty years, and Oscar Hammerstein II, whose track record for the past decade had been one of unalleviated failure. Indeed, for the sophisticated Rodgers to team up with an older man, firmly grounded in the traditions of operetta and old-style musical comedy, seemed quite incongruous. No wonder backers were hard to find. Those who did invest in the show did so with little hope of seeing any return for their money. Most assuredly they could never have dreamt that, after 2,212 performances in New York, 1,543 in London, thousands more

Above: **Pipe Dream** (1955). Met opera star Helen Traubel made her Broadway début in Rodgers and Hammerstein's musical version of John Steinbeck's *Sweet Thursday*.

Opposite above: **Oklahoma!** Howard (then known as Harold) Keel and Betty Jane Watson ride off in the surrey with the fringe on top in the finale of the 1947 London production at Drury Lane.

on the road and on world tours, and a record-breaking screen version *Oklahoma!* would present its angels with a percentage return on a total of more than $100 million – excluding subsequent revivals and stock performances.

How did it happen? Paradoxically, through all the factors that had at first appeared to militate against its success. The unsuccessful play formed the basis of a new kind of musical plot; the Western location was equally new bringing a breath of fresh air and the wide open spaces to the claustrophobic Broadway stage. And the 'unknown' Theater Guild actors turned out to be Alfred Drake, Celeste Holm, Howard Da Silva, Bambi Lynn, Marc Platt Lee Dixon and Joseph Buloff (though the leading lady Joan Roberts doesn't seem to have been heard of much in later years). However, the principal overriding reason for *Oklahoma!*'s still great reputation was the fortuitous pairing of Rodgers and Hammerstein, and a score in which even the smallest number became a standard song.

After *Pal Joey* Rodgers and Hart had a nice hit with *By Jupiter*, but Larry Hart, whose personal and professional behaviour had always been, to quote Rodgers, 'a source of permanent irritation', became even more erratic and evinced no interest at all in the *Green Grow the Lilacs* project. Although neither man could have known just how near the tragic ending was, they did realize that Rodgers and Hart as a work-force were almost finished. Oscar Hammerstein had always been a friend of Rodgers, they had written songs at Columbia College in 1919, and since Hammerstein himself had originally tried to talk Jerome Kern into making a musical out of the old play it was perhaps inevitable that they should join forces after Hart's defection. Hammerstein saw this as an opportunity to take a stage further the principles of musical and dramatic integration he had inaugurated sixteen years before in *Show Boat*, and in Dick Rodgers he found a partner willing to alter his own style of writing to accommodate the different literary ideas of his new lyricist. To round off the integration by the inclusion of narrative dance they brought in Agnes De Mille as choreographer, her *pièce de résistance* being the principal ballet which carries within it the main thread of the story-line. No less effective than this modern ballet in a stylized period setting was Miss De Mille's handling of numbers like 'The Farmer and the Cowman', a gay colourful routine bursting at the seams with vitality and a perfect combination of music, lyrics, humour and movement.

It is impossible to overestimate the importance of *Oklahoma!* or of Rodgers and Hammerstein themselves, for they went on to write further musical plays which would measure success in terms of ever-longer runs, and musical values in the wealth of songs which, while essential to the stage action, could be taken out of context with no loss of appeal. These in turn rubbed off on what, consequentially, became the other outstanding hits of the post-war years, bringing a whole aura of progress in musical development around shows of the next decade. A new era came into being, in which shows got bigger and better and more successful, many repeating their Broadway success in London, and during which the stage created new stars and every show seemed a veritable cornucopia of song hits. If the thirties were, as previously claimed, *the* decade for durable songs of quality, it was the forties and fifties which had the largest percentage of great shows which have endured *as shows*. And every few years the precursors of this new form of musical theatre themselves turned out another blockbuster to keep Broadway on the right lines and inspire their rivals to even greater efforts. Hammerstein in his dual role of author and lyricist ensured the smooth transition from dialogue to songs, while Rodgers developed a more lush and sweeping style of composing, with certain specific harmonic changes which recurred in score after score, but as a trademark rather than a formula.

It is pertinent at this point to mention the enormous contribution made to many Broadway musicals, but in particular to those of Rodgers and Hammerstein, by Robert Russell Bennett, a master orchestrator who was, in effect, Richard Rodgers's *alter ego*. Possibly it was he, rather than the composer, who introduced the harmonic touches that made a Rodgers score so individual, and listening to one of these shows in its 'Original Cast' or sound-track recording is as much of an experience for the accompaniments as for the songs themselves.

What is the best of Rodgers and Hammerstein? Most of their shows were enormous hits, although they did have inexplicable misses with *Me and Juliet*, *Allegro* and *Pipe Dream*. Their second most successful musical was *South Pacific* (1,925 performances), followed by *The Sound of Music* (1,443), *The King and I* (1,246), *Carousel* (890) and *Flower Drum Song* (600); while in terms of a combination of mammoth London run and motion-picture success *The Sound of Music* must rank as their most profitable post-*Oklahoma!* product. But there is no more fallacious argument in show-business circles than trying to equate commercial and artistic values! What is remarkable is that all but two Rodgers and Hammerstein shows were based on existing plays or books, yet are now so firmly established as original musicals that their origins are all but forgotten.

Opposite: **South Pacific** (1949). Ensign Nellie Forbush in sailor's uniform (Mary Martin) and Luther Billis (Myron McCormick) entertain their fellow-Marines with 'Honey Bun'.

Opposite below: **The King and I** (1951). Rodgers and Hammerstein's charming story of Western manners in an Oriental society proved a welcome debut for Yul Brynner and a sad farewell for Gertrude Lawrence.

Below: **Carousel.** Billy Bigelow (Stephen Douglass) and Julie Jordan (Iva Withers) meet by the carousel of the title in the 1950 London production, again at Drury Lane.

There is charm and beauty in both *Carousel* (1945) and *The King and I* (1951), though they were very different from each other. The combination of English culture and Oriental elegance in *The King and I* inspired a production of taste and delicacy. True, the performances of Yul Brynner and Gertrude Lawrence helped establish its initial success, but even when after eighteen months the apparently indispensable Miss Lawrence died, *The King and I* carried on unimpaired for several years. *Carousel* is most generally regarded as the finest Rodgers and Hammerstein show *qua* show. Based on the Hungarian dramatist Ferenc Molnár's *Liliom* it delves into the realm of fantasy, but is so exquisitely handled that there is no sense of anachronism about it. It is almost inconceivable that the authors of these two musical delights could have been responsible for the ebullient *South Pacific*, which erupted on to the stage of New York's Majestic Theater on 7 April 1949 to become one of the greatest entertainments of all time. Contrasting moments of tenderness ('Younger than Springtime') and joy ('A Wonderful Guy') with the drama of war in the Pacific and the robust plaint of sex-starved Marines ('There Is Nothing Like a Dame'), and daring to introduce the subject of miscegenation and inherent racial prejudice ('Carefully Taught'), *South Pacific* was in a class of its own. Not least of its attractions was the début of the operatic bass Ezio Pinza on the Broadway stage, but what really carried it to greatness in both New York and London was the bubbling, effervescent performance of Mary Martin. Although in her mid-thirties and mature for the role, these handicaps did not show on

stage; that she was definitely too old when the screen version came along nine years later will always be a matter for regret.

That Rodgers and Hammerstein were not going to have it all their own way in the new Broadway they had created became evident in 1944 when Betty Comden and Adolph Green wrote and starred in *On the Town*, their adaptation of the Leonard Bernstein–Jerome Robbins ballet *Fancy Free*. The composer himself proved an adept songwriter with Comden and Green's help, and George Abbott's direction allied to Jerome Robbins's choreography provided an exciting and wholly original musical. Performed with energy and enthusiasm by a talented young cast, *On the Town* was as much a landmark in stage musicals as it was to become five years later in the development of the Hollywood musical.

Notice that what used to be 'dance direction' was now called 'choreography'. This change of terminology derived not so much from any artistic pretensions as from the actual development of interpretive dancing and meaningful ballet sequences which had now come to replace the old chorus and solo routines. After her fine work in *Oklahoma!* Agnes De Mille – with George Balanchine – remained on Broadway with two shows that were running simultaneously with *On the Town*. These were, respectively, Harold Arlen's *Bloomer Girl* and *Song of Norway*, created by Bob Wright and Chet

One of Broadway's monumental and historic performances – Ethel Merman as Annie Oakley in *Annie Get Your Gun* (1946).

Forrest from the works of Edvard Grieg. Either show could have been produced at any time in the previous twenty years, although probably without the success that attended their runs of 654 and 860 performances. The audience was growing, even for more othodox shows like these. *Song of Norway* was quite simply and honestly billed as 'an operetta', proving that this moribund genre could, with the right ingredients, still find a place in the forward-looking forties. Sigmund Romberg's *Up in Central Park* (1945) was far from his old operetta style, and actually antedated such shows of the sixties as *Tenderloin* and *Fiorello* with their basis in New York City politics. It dealt with the notorious Tammany Hall political machine – used, of course, as background to a love story. Musicals couldn't depart *too* much from the norm! After *Bloomer Girl*'s similar subject material (a biography of the women's rights propagandist Amelia Bloomer, whose name achieved wider fame in another connotation), it became apparent that source material for musicals could emanate from a pretty wide spectrum.

Although three years separated *Oklahoma!* and *Annie Get Your Gun* on Broadway, London theatre-goers always link them together, opening as they did within five weeks of each other at Drury Lane and the Coliseum respectively in the spring of 1947. The vanguard of the 'American invasion' of the West End theatre, they were the first American musicals many British people had ever seen – not to say the best that had ever been produced. *Oklahoma!*, starring the then unknown Harold (Howard) Keel, was greeted with the same wild enthusiasm that it had incurred in New York, and *Annie* made just as much of an impact. If we couldn't get Ethel Merman, who was still playing Annie Oakley on Broadway, we did get Dolores Gray who, at the age of twenty-one, took London by storm and proved much more than a mere carbon copy of Merman. *Annie Get Your Gun* broke no new ground in theatrical tradition, tore down no barriers. It told a story with broad humour rather than wit, brought colour to the stage with Buffalo Bill's Wild West Show, and was the sort of 'fun' entertainment a good musical should be. Not least of all it gave the world what must be one of the best all-round scores ever written, certainly the finest of Irving Berlin's long and distinguished career. Other aspects of Berlin's theatre work may be open to discussion, but *Annie Get Your Gun* remains his masterpiece.

If his *Miss Liberty* of 1949 failed, despite a book by Robert Sherwood, choreography by Jerome Robbins and Moss Hart's direction, *Call Me Madam* more than compensated the next year. Once again Irving Berlin had the assistance of Ethel Merman's considerable talent in a role tailor-made for her – as a fictional counterpart of the real-life Perle Mesta, the US Ambassador to Luxembourg, 'The Hostess with the Mostes' ' as she was eloquently described in one of the many attractive songs, which also included 'You're Just in Love', an example of vocal counterpoint that never failed to stop the show.

Indicative of the progressive Broadway stage at this time was the re-emergence of Cole Porter with three of his most important musicals, for not since *Anything Goes* of 1934 had he produced anything other than entertaining *hors d'oeuvres*. Now he came up with a main course. *Kiss Me Kate* was no ordinary musical. True, it had the most phenomenal run of any Cole Porter show, but, more than that, it represented the composer's triumph over

Call me Madam (1950). Irving Berlin wrote some great songs for Ethel Merman, but perhaps none more so than in this lively comedy in which she co-starred with Hollywood veteran Paul Lukas.

adversity. For his death in 1964 at the age of seventy-three was the culmination of twenty-seven years of agony after a riding accident in which he had had both legs crushed. Following this mishap, for more than a third of his life Cole Porter had been a helpless cripple, undergoing dozens of operations until the final ordeal of amputation. That this tortured man, his enormous talent vitiated by constant and excruciating pain and lack of sleep, could write at all was amazing enough. That he could produce, in *Kiss Me Kate*, the wedding *par excellence* of intricate melodies to literate, witty lyrics was a miracle. The fact that it met with an equally literate and witty book from Bella and Samuel Spewack was a bonus, helping to earn it a Perry Award, 1,077 Broadway performances from 1948 to 1951, and as many again round the world and at the London Coliseum where its star, Patricia Morison, took it after it had closed in New York. Every outstanding composer has his masterpiece, and *Kiss Me Kate* was Cole Porter's. Only because it set such high standards did his remaining shows, *Can Can* (1953) and *Silk Stockings* (1955), seem of comparatively minor quality. By any other writer's standards they would have been gems. Abe Burrows wrote the book for both, and the dance direction in *Can Can* was by Michael Kidd, already an old hand on the stage, with his screen career yet to come. It had one infallible show-stopper in 'I Love Paris'; but while there was no such individual hit in *Silk Stockings* it had the better all-round score, one really not far removed from *Kiss Me Kate* in quality.

In the mid-forties there emerged a show-writing team which, while contributing nothing new musically and producing in all less than a handful of great musicals, wrote their names large in latter-day Broadway history. The name of Alan Jay Lerner stands alongside Oscar Hammerstein as a writer of both book and lyrics, his memorable partnership with the Viennese-born Frederick Loewe, after one or two false starts, first getting under way with *Brigadoon*, a show which laid to rest any possible theory that fantasy would

Finian's Rainbow (1947). Finian McLonergan (Albert Sharpe) and his daughter Sharon (Ella Logan) come to Rainbow Valley.

not be acceptable in a modern musical of 1947. In fact it was running side by side with the equally whimsical *Finian's Rainbow* of Burton Lane and Yip Harburg, both shows topping the average Broadway run. Perhaps the inference is that after the war years audiences were more willing to suspend disbelief and accept as real – maybe through wish-fulfilment – the fantasies of a Scottish village that appeared only once every hundred years, or an Irish leprechaun in search of a crock of gold. Disregarding extra-musical whys and wherefores it need only be said that both *Brigadoon* and *Finian's Rainbow* were beautifully presented shows full of good songs, choreographed by the ubiquitous Agnes De Mille and Michael Kidd respectively, and that they are wholly worthy of a place in musical history.

Lerner and Loewe, firm believers in quality rather than quantity, waited four years before returning to the stage with *Paint Your Wagon*, but the Western environment which had worked for *Oklahoma!* and *Annie* failed to achieve a similar success for Lerner's Gold Rush story. There were good songs – 'Wanderin' Star', 'I Talk to the Trees', 'They Call the Wind Maria', 'I Still See Elisa' – which became popular immediately as hits and in the long term as evergreens, particularly when the show was finally filmed eighteen years later with a completely different story. But who can say why one show succeeds and another fails? Jule Styne and Sammy Cahn's Broadway début with *High Button Shoes*, also in 1947, did well for them, although it is not a musical that springs immediately to mind when one recalls the era. Those who saw any of its 727 performances, however, will remember Phil Silvers's typical brash performance as a 1913 civilian version of Sergeant Bilko and Jerome Robbins's Keystone Cops ballet, a magnificent example of immaculate staging with split-second timing.

In the last five years of his life Kurt Weill was active, albeit not too successfully, on Broadway with *The Firebrand of Florence* (1945), *Street Scene* (1947), *Love Life* (1948) and *Lost in the Stars* (1949). But, once again, it may be asked how prestige can be measured in terms of commercial success. In all of these Weill was drawing progressively nearer to the operatic medium in which he had started. The Broadway sophistication of *Lady in the Dark* and *One Touch of Venus* had given way to a dramatic intensity which convinces the onlooker that the opera-house rather than the Broadway stage would have become Weill's natural habitat had he lived beyond the relatively meagre span of fifty years. There is some consolation in the fact that, posthumously in 1954, he received his due when his widow, Lotte Lenya, star of the original *Die Dreigroschenoper* in Berlin in 1928, sponsored and starred in Marc Blitzstein's translation which, as *The Threepenny Opera*, ran and ran without making any concessions to public taste by softening Weill's angular writing.

Where's Charley? was a happy introduction to the New York stage for songwriter Frank Loesser, proving that even a hackneyed old comedy like *Charley's Aunt* could be given a new lease of life with singable songs and a star personality like Ray Bolger. But Loesser's own particular masterpiece came along two years later in 1950 when *Guys and Dolls* was added to the list of all-time Broadway greats. Damon Runyon's stories of Broadway characters were interpreted to perfection by Robert Alda, a Hollywood reject who carved a new career on the strength of it, the archetypal dumb blonde of Vivian Blaine, the sterling character actor Sam Levene and the corpulent Stubby Kaye. There have been many show-stopping moments in musical comedy, but few more thrilling than Kaye's 'Sit Down, You're Rocking the Boat' which was inevitably given the one-more-time treatment. From the busy pantomime opening of a crowded Broadway (which came off, if anything, even better on screen) the direction of George S. Kaufman and Michael Kidd's imaginative dance scenes never flagged. If Loesser was well served by the book by Jo Swerling and Abe Burrows, he did himself equally proud in 1956 with *The Most Happy Fella*, a one-man effort from beginning to end in which he served as composer, author, librettist, publisher and producer (one professional colleague was moved to remark 'I looked in the box-office. It wasn't him!'). This adaptation of Sidney Howard's *They Knew What They Wanted* came as near to opera in terms of popular music as any musical in the history of the stage. Although the songs themselves were pure Broadway their use throughout the show, often with musical links and bridges in place of dialogue, approached, without overstepping, the bounds of operatic tradition.

This was an era when a favourite star could work wonders for even a second-rate show, a fact of life as true as it had been in the days of Al Jolson and the Winter Garden series. But why only female stars? There were talented leading men galore, but the *big* big attractions were the Ethel Mermans, Mary Martins, Gertrude Lawrences just as previously they had been the Vivienne Segals, Helen Morgans, Sophie Tuckers, Bea Lillies and Marilyn Millers. Now, in the fifties, three names new to Broadway musicals made instant reputations by virtuoso performances in shows that were good anyway, but just that much better for their presence. The riotous Carol Channing may have proved too idiosyncratic for the cinema screen, but, larger than life as she was, her style was just right for the big stage, and in

The Pajama Game (1954). Although Janis Paige was outstanding as Babe Williams in 1,063 Broadway performances opposite John Raitt, her role in the screen version went to the more 'commercial' Doris Day.

Gentlemen Prefer Blondes (1949) she was the perfect Lorelei Lee, as in later years she would be the perfect Dolly Levi. Shirley Booth, more renowned for dramatic roles, was the making of *A Tree Grows in Brooklyn* (1951), a more downbeat subject than usual for a musical but one that gained from the score by Arthur Schwartz and Dorothy Fields. But for sheer force of personality the supreme accolade should be accorded to Rosalind Russell, who took *Wonderful Town* (1953) firmly in both hands and created her own personal triumph. Never a singer *per se* (in the film *Gypsy* her songs were dubbed by Lisa Kirk), she found an empathy with Leonard Bernstein's music and the lyrics of Betty Comden and Adolph Green that made a minor classic of a musical which was to be revived on several occasions in later years, always with the same enthusiastic reaction.

The final star performance came from a girl who had stolen every scene in which she appeared in a minor role in *Can Can*, and who was to captivate theatre-goers again and again in years to come. The show was *Damn Yankees* (1955), with songs by Richard Adler and Jerry Ross, written and directed by George Abbott, with choreography by Bob Fosse – the same

Opposite: **Damn Yankees** (1955). 'Whatever Lola wants . . .' Gwen Verdon gave a magnetic performance that carried her to Broadway stardom.

team which had made a hit the previous year with *The Pajama Game*. The vital redhead who proved the catalyst for all these talents was Gwen Verdon, little known outside America but one of the more recent personalities, skilled in singing and dancing, who can illuminate any theatre by her presence alone. These two shows represented a complete departure from musical comedy tradition, involving, respectively, the Faust legend in the context of a baseball team and union troubles in a pajama factory, and were personal triumphs for all the creative talents common to both. Not least of all, they were successful enough to launch on his production career Harold Prince, one of the two Broadway impresarios who were to become as powerful in the next two decades as had been Ziegfeld and Dillingham in days gone by.

Around this time a seemingly corny little English musical in twenties style which had had a surprising (and to some, inexplicable) success in London arrived in New York with a young English singer-actress in the lead. She was not a star then, but *The Boy Friend* gave her the experience and reputation to go on to other things. Her name was Julie Andrews.

5 From the Book

Julie Andrews . . . Lerner and Loewe . . . *My Fair Lady* – another milestone. But there was no change of direction this time, except perhaps in one respect which we shall come to later. *My Fair Lady* was a show in the mainstream of musical comedy as we had come to know it since it came of age. It was the combination of its individual assets that set it apart from other musicals: it had a classic story, a wonderful score, a fine production and a magnificent cast. Then there was Moss Hart's direction, Oliver Smith's sets and, especially, Cecil Beaton's costumes. Most important of all, George Bernard Shaw's *Pygmalion*, the play from which it was adapted, and a model of writing and stagecraft, was left virtually intact, being enhanced rather than marred by Alan Jay Lerner's integration of the now famous songs. (The spurious happy ending, of which Shaw most certainly disapproved, had been added to the Gabriel Pascal film of *Pygmalion*, on which interpretation the show was based.) One original aspect was that it presented a non-singing actor in the lead, the first notable occasion for this to have occurred, and Rex Harrison's brilliant *Sprechgesang* performance of some extremely difficult songs could not have been equalled by a more academic rendering. Julie Andrews, a star in London at the age of twelve, now became, at twenty-one, the darling of Broadway. How ironic that when Warner Brothers filmed *My Fair Lady* eight years later they had no confidence in her drawing power and substituted Audrey Hepburn's physical and Marni Nixon's vocal presence. Miss Andrews's consolation prizes from other studios turned out to be *Mary Poppins* and *The Sound of Music*, and had the film of *My Fair Lady* not been so successful the brothers Warner may well have been left with the proverbial egg on their collective faces. It need only be said that *My Fair Lady* has been, along with *Oklahoma!* and *The Sound of Music*, one of the most prodigious financial successes in the musical theatre.

The same team of Lerner, Loewe, Hart, Smith and Andrews emerged again in 1960 with *Camelot*, adapted from T.H. White's *The Once and Future King*, and if the success was neither as immediate nor lasting it did run for 837 performances, a more than respectable total even in those days of ever-increasing runs. With Robert Goulet as a virile Lancelot, Richard Burton emulating the Harrison form of non-singing, and Julie Andrews being Julie Andrews, *Camelot* was a thoroughly professional show, being handsomely mounted and a delight to eye and ear, but it lacked the compactness, the theatrical magic of *My Fair Lady*. As it transpired, it was a last fling on Broadway for Julie Andrews, for Lerner and Loewe (other than the *Gigi* of 1973 with a revised score for Broadway), and for Moss Hart, who died midway through the run.

Below: Illustration from Playbill cover for the 1976 revival of *Candide*.

Opposite: Poster of the original London production of *My Fair Lady* (1956).

Left: **Happy Hunting** (1956). Ethel Merman and friend.

Below: **Mr Wonderful** (1956). Sammy Davis Jnr's first Broadway hit in a type-cast role as a many-faceted entertainer.

Whether or not it was directly attributable to the success of *My Fair Lady*, producers and writers suddenly began scouring the world of literature – both classic and modern – for stories adaptable to musical treatment. Some most unlikely subjects came to light: Oscar Wilde's *The Importance of Being Earnest*, Eugene O'Neill's *Ah, Wilderness* and *Anna Christie*, Sean O'Casey's *Juno and the Paycock*, Terence Rattigan's *The Sleeping Prince*, Christopher Isherwood and John Van Druten's *I Am a Camera*, Edna Ferber's *Saratoga Trunk*, Thornton Wilder's *The Matchmaker*, James Hilton's *Lost Horizon*, N. Richard Nash's *The Rainmaker*, Jane Austen's *Pride and Prejudice*, Elmer Rice's *Dream Girl*, Hans Andersen's *The Princess and the Pea* and *Thumbelina*, Miguel de Cervantes's *Don Quixote*, Miklos Laszlo's *Parfumerie*, Herman Melville's *Billy Budd*, Patrick Dennis's *Auntie Mame*, Noël Coward's *Blithe Spirit*, Aristophanes' *Lysistrata*, Shakespeare's *Romeo and Juliet*, Voltaire's *Candide*, James Thurber's *The Secret Life of Walter Mitty*, Budd Schulberg's *What Makes Sammy Run?*, Jerome Weidman's *I Can Get It for You Wholesale* and Shepherd Mead's *How to Succeed in Business without Really Trying*. This goodly collection of literary gems from past and present all appeared as Broadway musicals in the late fifties and early sixties, some with outstanding success, others with higher hopes than actual achievement. Only the last five were produced musically under their original titles. The rest were presented as, respectively: *Ernest in Love* (1960), *Take Me Along* (1959), *New Girl in Town* (1957), *Juno* (1959), *The Girl Who Came to Supper* (1963), *Cabaret* (1966), *Saratoga* (1959), *Hello Dolly* (1964), *Shangri-La* (1956), *110 in the Shade* (1963), *First Impressions* (1959), *Skyscraper* (1965), *Once Upon a Mattress* (1959), *Have I Got One for You?* (1968), *Man of La Mancha* (1965), *She Loves Me* (1963), *Billy* (1969), *Mame* (1966), *High Spirits* (1964), *The Happiest Girl in the World* (1961) and *West Side Story* (1957). In addition, a melange of Sherlock Holmes stories was put together under the title *Baker Street* (1965), which can only have infuriated Conan Doyle devotees by casting the arch-villainess Irene Adler as Holmes's 'lady friend' and collaborator!

Perhaps we can stretch a point and include comic strips among the literary sources, since they are in a sense an offshoot of twentieth-century culture. Among these were *Li'l Abner*, *It's a Bird . . . It's a Plane . . . It's Superman!* and *You're a Good Man, Charlie Brown*. The apparently impossible attempt in 1967 to interpret Charles Schultz's 'Peanuts' characters in terms of adult actors finally resulted in *Charlie Brown* being the ninth most successful musical ever to play on or off Broadway. Norman Panama and Melvin Frank's adaptation of Al Capp's *Li'l Abner* (1956) with music by Gene De Paul and Johnny Mercer was a surprisingly adult performance, a hilarious satire on the American way of life with sparkling ballet sequences by Michael Kidd, but *Superman* of 1966 lasted all of 75 performances.

This particular period was rich in highly successful and musically memorable shows. There seemed to be no in betweens; there were either great hits or dismal flops. Some of the latter were undeserved, as was Lillian Hellman's stage version of *Candide*, which despite Leonard Bernstein's magnificent score survived a mere 73 performances in 1956; or John Latouche's *Golden Apple* of 1954 which, with a Jerome Moross score that included 'Lazy Afternoon', one of the best songs for years, received two awards as Best Musical yet went under after 125 showings. The same year the Schwartz-Fields *By the Beautiful Sea* was no more successful than their previous *A Tree Grows in Brooklyn* (with same star, Shirley Booth). Even Frank Loesser suffered a small reverse with the failure of the charming small-town saga *Greenwillow* (1960), but he made up for it the next year with a big hit which even outshone *Guys and Dolls* commercially if not musically. Leaving others to write the book for *How to Succeed in Business without Really Trying*,

You're a Good Man, Charlie Brown (1967). Gary Burghoff starred as the hapless Charlie Brown in the Clark Gesner-John Gordon musical adaptation of Charles M. Schultz's 'Peanuts' strip cartoon.

How to Succeed in Business Without Really Trying (1961). Robert Morse illustrates how *not* to in this shot from the Broadway production.

Loesser reverted to his more accustomed role of songwriter and collected awards galore, including the Pulitzer Prize.

In contrast to these shows, which were distinguished and honourable failures, came some of the most fantastically successful productions ever seen on the Great White Way. One towered above them all, in terms of novelty of stagecraft allied to musical brilliance. On stage and screen (this was one of the few occasions when a film version did more than justice to a top Broadway show) *West Side Story* was an unforgettable experience, appealing to both head and heart. The spirited young cast lent a special vitality to the inspired work of Jerome Robbins, in the dual role of director and choreographer. Only one man could have handled both these functions, since every movement in each scene was choreographed rather than directed, each dramatic situation having its own underlying musical *motif* expressed in the movements of the participants. The principal asset was the music of Leonard Bernstein, whose love of jazz added to his classical knowledge and experience created a form of music that expressed to perfection the emotional and physical turmoil of racial hatred and forbidden love in New York's 'Hell's Kitchen'. Artistically, *West Side Story* represented integration at its highest level. Everything worked interdependently, and however much Stephen Sondheim may now repudiate some of his lyrics (and some of the ballads are, admittedly, on the old musical comedy level),

both show and film stand up to analysis as well now as they did in 1957 and 1961 respectively. *West Side Story* stands alone, the perfect entity.

Rodgers and Hammerstein came almost to the end of their road together with *Flower Drum Song* (1958). This amiable evocation of the battle of the sexes, set in San Francisco's Chinatown, offered some equally amiable but minor song hits, though nothing worthy of Rodgers and Hammerstein's past successes. Some of the songs could well have been leftovers from *The King and I*, suggesting that perhaps Rodgers had written himself out – an impression that *The Sound of Music* did little to correct the following year. However, it was an enjoyable enough show providing wholesome family entertainment – and even if it smacked of operetta Hammerstein had left behind in the thirties it produced for all concerned greater financial rewards than almost any other of their productions. Sadly, Oscar Hammerstein never lived to know what a world-wide success it became. Nine months after the show opened, and before it ever reached London, this great man, truly one of the giants of the American musical theatre, died of cancer. His career had spanned the years from old-style musical comedy in 1920, through operetta, through all the highs and lows of personal effort and success, to the most important developments in music. Twice he changed the direction of the American musical, with *Show Boat* and *Oklahoma!*, and he left the whole world singing his latest songs. No man could have had a finer epitaph.

West Side Story (1957). Riff (Mickey Calin) and Bernardo (Ken Le Roy) fight to the death in 'The Rumble'.

Left: **Flower Drum Song** (1958). A charming scene from Rodgers and Hammerstein's Oriental musical set in San Francisco's Chinatown.

Below: **Bye Bye Birdie** (1960). The set devised by director/choreographer Gower Champion for the 'Telephone Hour' number.

Left: **Destry Rides again** (1959). Dolores Gray and Andy Griffith in the Harold Rome–Leonard Gershe musical version of a popular screen Western.

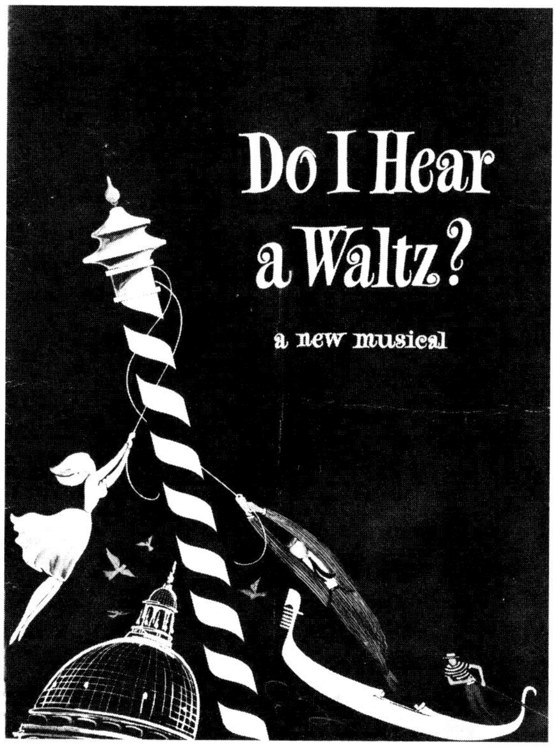

Following Hammerstein's death, for the first time in forty years Richard Rodgers was alone. He wrote his own lyrics for *No Strings* (1962), a Tony Award winner notable for its treatment of a black-white love affair without reference to the colour problem and also for the presence of a stringless orchestra on stage, often participating in the action. Then for *Do I Hear a Waltz?* (1965) he collaborated with the up-and-coming Stephen Sondheim in a show which is memorable only for its title tune and the lowest box-office returns he had known since the early days with Lorenz Hart.

Broadway now belonged to the newer generation of show-writers and producers, who came into the business at a time when one show could furnish greater rewards than their predecessors achieved with five or six. If it were the right show at the right time, that is. Flops were still just as likely to happen, and even a name like Irving Berlin was no talisman against failure. Such was the fate of *Mr President*, which made a sad farewell in 1962 to the Grand Old Man of American music. But in 1964 *Fiddler on the Roof* and *Hello Dolly* made their entrance on the stages of the Imperial and St James Theaters, which they were to occupy for many years to come. These were the musicals which made the producers Harold Prince and David Merrick the most powerful men in show business today, and firmly established the reputations of Bock and Harnick and Jerry Herman as composers. Jerry Bock and Sheldon Harnick had done well with *Fiorello!* (1959), a biography of Mayor La Guardia which reaped many rewards, including a Pulitzer Prize for Drama; with *Tenderloin* (1960), a similar slice of New York history about the cleaning up of the city's 'red light' district; and with *She Loves Me* (1963), a charming version of the film known as *The Shop around the Corner*. All of these were produced by Harold Prince. *Fiddler on the Roof*, a musical adaptation of Sholem Aleichem's stories of a Jewish community in pre-revolution Russia, was something else again. Despite Jerome Robbins's customary expert staging of Joseph Stein's book no one, least of all the composers, expected it to do much more than break even, a feeling that out-of-town notices did nothing to dispel. A generally drab story about the persecution of the Jews, despite such lighter moments as 'Tradition' and 'If I Were a Rich Man' and the beautiful presentation of 'Sunrise, Sunset', based firmly on Jewish traditions and music, here was no obvious hit show. But by

the time *Fiddler on the Roof* had won numerous awards, become the longest-running show in the history of the theatre, and reaped a harvest of something over $30 million, somebody must finally have been convinced they'd done something right.

Jerry Herman's *Hello Dolly* and its follow-up *Mame* (1966) were in the basic musical comedy tradition – they were pure, unadulterated entertainment, star vehicles for Carol Channing and Angela Lansbury but without a memorable song between them except for the corny, sing-along title tunes at which Herman was so adept. Perhaps that isn't fair criticism, though it should be said that while his songs worked well enough in the shows themselves, generally they failed to survive beyond the exit doors. *Dolly* and *Mame* were star vehicles and never pretended to be any more than ingenuous showbiz hokum. They deserved their success on both stage and screen.

Opposite: **Mr President** (1962). Described by *Time* as 'the worst musical on Broadway' and by *Life* as 'an enjoyable old-fashioned show'. Irving Berlin's farewell to the musical stage starred Robert Ryan and Nanette Fabray.

After *On the Town* the brilliant writing team of Betty Comden and Adolph Green settled in Hollywood to write books and lyrics of the highest order for many of MGM's finest musicals, but with the screen musical a dying art they had returned to New York to work almost permanently with Jule Styne, another émigré from Tinsel Town. With *Bells Are Ringing* (1956) they were

Hello Dolly. Pearl Bailey starred as Dolly Levi and Cab Calloway as Horace Vandergelder in David Merrick's all-black production which shared the Broadway stage with the original version from 1967.

reunited with their old revue partner from the late thirties, Judy Holliday, whose superb talent enabled her to give a performance (and definitive renderings of songs like 'Just in Time' and 'The Party's Over') that made *Bells* one of the most likeable of musical comedies. *Say Darling* (1958) was a brave try by Abe Burrows, and Richard and Marian Bissell, to document in musical comedy form how they came to write and produce *The Pajama Game*, real-life characters being portrayed by Vivian Blaine, Robert Morse, Johnny Desmond and David Wayne. It should have done well, but either the subject was too esoteric for the general public or the show just wasn't as successful as it might have been. *Subways Are for Sleeping* (1961) and *Fade In – Fade Out* (1964), the latter a *tour de force* for Carol Burnett, were so-so, and the partnership's next-best effort was *Do-Re-Mi* (1960). Written and directed by Garson Kanin, the vigorous performances of Phil Silvers and Nancy Walker enabled the show to chalk up another credit-mark in David Merrick's production career.

Despite his great reputation in the profession as one of the top six composers and a Hollywood career that took him to the top of the tree, Harold Arlen had little luck on Broadway. After starting well with *Bloomer Girl* (1944) he tried again twice, collaborating with Johnny Mercer in *St*

Jennie (1963). Mary Martin (right) returned to Broadway in 1963, but neither she nor an Arthur Schwartz-Howard Dietz score could rescue this biography of old-time actress Laurette Taylor. George Wallace is on the left.

Opposite: **My Fair Lady** (1956). One of the musical stage's favourite double acts – Professor Henry Higgins (Rex Harrison) and Eliza Doolittle (Julie Andrews) in the original production at the Mark Hellinger Theater, New York.

Louis Woman (1946) (revived disastrously in 1959 as *Free and Easy*) and Truman Capote in *House of Flowers* (1954), both starring Pearl Bailey, but on both occasions the unorthodox subject matter kept the crowds away. In 1957 he set up shop again in New York with his old lyricist partner Yip Harburg, and this time he got it right. Under the aegis of David Merrick and with Lena Horne and Ricardo Montalban heading the cast, the colourful *Jamaica* finally gave Arlen the hit he deserved. Merrick also had good fortune in producing *Gypsy* (1959), in which he reunited the *West Side Story* team of author Arthur Laurents, lyricist Stephen Sondheim and director/choreographer Jerome Robbins. Amalgamating their talents with those of the composer Jule Styne and the earth-shaking Ethel Merman – a natural for the role of Gypsy Rose Lee's loud-mouthed, fast-talking and utterly domineering 'stage mother' – was a stroke of genius. Styne produced some of his best-ever show tunes, and with 'Everything's Coming Up Roses' and 'Rose's Turn' Merman was able to repeat her show-stopping form.

Show-business biographies being the 'in' thing, Arthur Schwartz and Howard Dietz tried in 1963 with *Jennie*, the story of the old-time star Laurette Taylor. But apparently she was too long forgotten, and this time even Mary Martin couldn't save the day. Fanny Brice was much more fondly remembered, and a show devoted to her life would probably have been a winner anyway. As it was, a newcomer – Barbra Streisand – played the lead in *Funny Girl* (1964). Whether the show made the star or vice versa is a moot point, but the finished product was a triumph for Streisand, who played Fanny Brice in New York, in London two years later and in Hollywood two years after that. It was a vindication of the faith David Merrick had in her when he took her out of the Blue Angel night club for a small part in *I Can Get It for You Wholesale* (1962) – which she promptly proceeded to steal with her one song, 'Miss Marmelstein'.

All of these had been fairly conventional musicals by latter-day standards. The ever-increasing awareness on the parts of producers and public alike of what a good musical should be had continued to raise the standard of even the most average show until it reached a plateau – higher than before, it is true, but with few peaks such as *West Side Story*. No one was breaking new ground because, within the self-imposed limits of the musical stage as it was then, there was quite simply no new ground to break. Nor would there be until the late sixties and the advent of the rock generation. But interesting, and sometimes highly profitable, experiments there certainly were. *A Funny Thing Happened on the Way to the Forum* (1962) was a burlesque treatment of some of the plays of Plautus which won a Best Musical of the Year Award, Harold Prince's production being directed by George Abbott and choreographed by Jack Cole, another ex-Hollywoodite operating on Broadway after the demise of the screen musical. For the first time Stephen Sondheim contributed his own music as well as lyrics, though he later regretted the combination of his more sophisticated lyrics with what was in essence little more than broad, bawdy farce. But 964 performances speak for themselves.

Even more unlikely, on the face of it, was the idea of a musical set in a prison dungeon and combining the stories of Don Quixote and his creator Cervantes – even less promising material to work on, it would seem, than *Fiddler on the Roof*. But *Man of La Mancha* was the surprise hit of 1965, and, like *Fiddler*, it wound up eventually in the Top Ten of Broadway musicals after an extended run. If its only song to grace the list of evergreens was 'The Impossible Dream', that at least was something of a godsend to concert baritones tired of ending their act with 'Climb Ev'ry Mountain'!

The year 1966 saw the advent of two musical plays which, more than any others, typified the new spirit of artistic freedom about to sweep Broadway. At the beginning of the year that experienced leading lady Gwen Verdon, whose propensity for stealing scenes and shows alike has already been

mentioned, walked off with *Sweet Charity*, with no little help from her husband Bob Fosse as director/choreographer. The Fosses between them kept the show in a state of perpetual movement, and they were by no means inhibited either by Neil Simon's book or Cy Coleman's music. The music was more astringent than the Broadway norm, big and brassy and defiant as befitted the story of dance-hall girls trying without much luck to fight their way out of their depressing environment; and Dorothy Fields, far from the sweetness and gentility of her Jerome Kern days, called on her forty years in the business to write the kind of lyrics suited to the modern stage.

Towards the end of the year came Harold Prince's production of *Cabaret*. This show completed the departure from all established traditions: it was an unpleasant tale of unpleasant people in pre-war Berlin – none more so than the grotesque, sleazy little cabaret compère portrayed with such genius by Joel Grey. It had started as a book of semi-autobiographical stories by Christopher Isherwood, was turned into a play, *I Am a Camera* (1951), by John Van Druten, which had now been rewritten by Joe Masteroff. The period covered by the play-with-music (it was hardly a musical in the modern sense, the musical numbers being part of the on-stage cabaret rather than integrated in the plot) was that in which Kurt Weill was active in Berlin with *Die Dreigroschenoper*, *Happy End* and *Rise and Fall of the City of Mahagonny* and it cannot have been coincidental that the score by John Kander and Fred Ebb reflected this musical idiom to a certain extent. Moreover, Weill's widow, Lotte Lenya, star of those German productions, had a

Opposite: **Kiss Me Kate.** A scene from a London Coliseum revival of Cole Porter's most successful show with Emile Belcourt in the foreground, and Ann Howard standing in the background.

A Funny Thing Happened on the Way to the Forum (1962). Jack Gilford and Zero Mostel brought all their comedy talents to bear in this burlesque treatment of Ancient Rome.

Little Me (1962). Sid Caesar (right) gave a brilliant performance in a variety of roles in Neil Simon's version of the Patrick Dennis novel. He is seen here with Adnia Rice (left) and Virginia Martin (centre).

leading role in *Cabaret*. Perhaps more than any other musical in the history of the American theatre, *Cabaret* was very much an acquired taste, but enough theatre-goers acquired it to make it a solid hit.

No history of the Broadway stage would be complete without a tribute to Meredith Willson's *The Music Man*, which entered the Majestic Theater on 13 December 1957 and stayed till it was time to make the film version four and a half years later. A period piece with some enchantingly original musical vignettes composed by Willson (in this, his first-ever stage show at the age of fifty-five, he wrote the music, book and lyrics), *Music Man* scored heavily with a lusty, vibrant, virtuoso performance by the former Hollywood actor Robert Preston in his musical début. No one who saw Preston encircling the stage with his loping stride in 'Ya Got Trouble' and '76 Trombones' will ever forget him. If *The Unsinkable Molly Brown* (1960) and *Here's Love* (1963) paled in comparison with the monumental *Music Man*, they still represented minor triumphs for this 'new' composer.

Hitherto we have been concerned with what is generally known as the Broadway stage, although only a proportion of theatres were actually located on the Great White Way itself. Nevertheless, the area in midtown Manhattan situated roughly between Broadway and Fifth Avenue and bounded approximately by 42nd Street to the south and 50th Street to the north has always been known colloquially in theatre parlance as Broadway. This is the main theatre district, and any playhouses, barns, cellars, lofts,

clubs, converted cinemas, any form of auditorium in fact, outside this parochial area (parochial in more than the physical and geographical sense, one might add) is referred to as off-Broadway. The latter was not very important in the general scheme of things except as a nursery for new talent. But suddenly in the sixties off-Broadway began to take on airs and graces hardly befitting a poor relation, mounting shows, legitimate and musical, which actually dared to compete with the establishment products of the Merricks and Princes. There was *Little Mary Sunshine*, for instance, which opened at the Orpheum Theater in 1959 and stole the patrons of the Broadway houses for 1,143 performances. A one-man effort by Rick Besoyan, it was a relentless satire on operetta of all types, sending up everything from *Music in the Air* to *Rose Marie* with what may even have been a dig at George M. Cohan's flag-waving in the finale. Once in a while the Broadway entrepreneurs would cash in on an obviously commercially sound off-Broadway production, but for some reason they left *The Fantasticks* alone in the tiny Sullivan Street Theater from its opening in 1960 to its final performance some time well into the seventies. However, it made the names of its producer Lorenzo Noto and its composers Harvey Schmidt and Tom Jones – with songs such as 'Try to Remember' and 'Soon It's Gonna Rain' – offering what was, strictly speaking, neither a revue nor a 'book' musical but primarily a new kind of entertainment. This was just one of the new ingredients that off-Broadway was to add to the story of the musical.

6 The New Wave

West Side Story may not have directly influenced the course of the musical, but it had repercussions via inspiring greater dramatic realism. Its projection of the tensions and hostilities existing in the lower environs of contemporary New York encouraged writers of the late sixties and seventies to hold a mirror up to life and expose its seamier side. Nothing was omitted, be it racial problems, drug usage, nudity, permissiveness, or merely the freakishness of youth in general. At the same time there came a complete metamorphosis in musical styles as rock took over in the theatre as it had in other entertainment media. Composers' credits revealed a succession of new names, and in place of Gershwin, Berlin, Porter and Arlen of earlier days there were Hal Hester and Danny Apolinar, Galt MacDermott, Jerome Ragni, James Rado, Nancy Ford and Gretchen Cryer, John Sebastian, Peter Link, Al Carmines, Sam Shepard, Peter Udell, Barry Manilow, Tim Rice, Andrew Lloyd Webber, Gary William Friedman, Stephen Schwartz, Melvin Van Peebles, Mel Shapiro, Eve Merriam, Helen Miller, Micki

A Chorus Line (1976). The British cast which took over this Pulitzer Prize-winning musical at London's Drury Lane.

Hair (1968). A scene from the 'American Tribal Love-Rock Musical' whose iconoclastic approach to life, sex, drugs and rock music established a new pattern for musicals of the late sixties and early seventies.

Grant, Richard O'Brien. How many such names will have endured, how many have met their just fate, by the time this book appears in print can only be a matter for conjecture, but all of them made some sort of impact on or off Broadway during the period under discussion.

The prototype of the genre was *Hair* (MacDermott-Ragni-Rado), in 1968, billed as 'The American Tribal Love-Rock Musical'. For an anti-establishment (anti-everything, in fact) show it made a very establishment-type profit and lasted longer than most conventional musicals. By the time it ended its run of 1,750 performances at the Biltmore Theater *Hair* had itself become almost conventional compared with what was going on elsewhere and was regarded as the Establishment of rock musicals. After all, it had accrued $7 million in just over two years! *Hair* was performed all over the United States and in many world capitals, each edition having so many local references that it became virtually a new show each time it was performed. The London run was even longer than that in New York, an attempt to reach 2,000 performances only failing when the theatre roof fell in after the 1999th presentation.

Right: **Two Gentlemen of Verona** (1971). A scene from Galt McDermott's rock–Shakespeare.

Your Own Thing (Hester-Apolinar) predated *Hair* by three months and ran about half as long, but it made quite a reputation as one of the more literate rock musicals. Based on *Twelfth Night* its literacy may be assumed, although, updated as it was to the rock era and with considerable play being made on the sexual complications of the original, it had retained little of the Bard. Shakespeare was again modernized in 1971 when Galt MacDermott's *Two Gentlemen of Verona* made a reasonable hit in New York and London; and the same year Peter Link, Gretchen Cryer and Doug Dyer went even further back in time for their source material, adapting *The Wedding of Iphigenia* from Euripides. While the locale of Greece and Troy was retained, the music was played by a rock band, and no fewer than twelve actresses played Iphigenia in the course of one performance. In the same period, Link collaborated with Michael Cacoyannis in a musical version of Aristophanes' *Lysistrata* (1972), but even with the magnetic Melina Mercouri in the lead it closed in a week.

Inner City (1971) opened on as opposed to off Broadway, and its meagre ninety-seven performances at the Ethel Barrymore Theater may have reflected a more mature audience's reaction to the interpretation of Mother Goose nursery rhymes in terms of unwed mothers, drug-taking, prostitution and the self-pity of dwellers in big city slums. Nancy Ford and Gretchen Cryer had little success with *Grass Roots* (1968), and *Shelter* (1973) fared no better than thirty-three performances, but between these two misses they had a good critical and audience reaction to *The Last Sweet Days of Isaac* (1970). A two-part play with music, combining philosophy and a suggestion of sci-fi of the future, it had the smart set beating a path to East 74th Street to see the well-acclaimed performances of Austin Pendleton and Fredericka Weber.

Generally speaking, off-Broadway was where much of the off-Broadway material belonged. It was a place for experimentation rather than for financial rewards and public acclain. No theme was too esoteric for it, and the principal ingredient it attracted was self-indulgence, as if some of the would-be theatre people were deliberately turning their backs not only on the establishment but on the very audiences they hoped to attract. On the other hand the description 'off-Broadway' could be applied to any production, wherever presented, which possessed certain hallmarks and characteristics – for instance unwillingness to compromise, originality of theme, and a bright, fresh approach that offered a genuine surprise to jaded palates. Once in a while genuine talent emerged – in the shape of a writer, a performer, or a show that combined off-Broadway innovation with Broadway expertise. Such was the case with two black musicals which appeared *on* Broadway in 1970 with the kind of success usually reserved for the more orthodox product. *Purlie* went direct into the Winter Garden. Starring Cleavon Little and Melba Moore, it was a deliberate satire by its black author Ossie Davis on the *Green Pastures/Cabin in the Sky* view of life in the Deep South, with an intentional Uncle Tom approach that in reality showed how far the world had come in its understanding since the days of Stepin Fetchit and the stereotyped Negro caricature. And how ironic that this should be played at the theatre where generations before Al Jolson had blacked-up to draw the crowds! *Purlie* and its attitudes brought more honour and respect to black artists and writers than the chip-on-the-shoulder approach of so many others. *The Me Nobody Knows* was, on the other hand, a more serious view of black, white and Puerto Rican problems, devised by Herb Schapiro from the writings of and quotations taken from New York schoolchildren. With music and lyrics by Gary William Friedman and Will Holt, it illustrated the frustrations of black youth, and where *Purlie* viewed similar problems with the saving grace of humour, *The Me Nobody Knows* did so without rancour and with a great deal of hope. It fulfilled the ambitions of the genuinely dedicated off-Broadway company by playing at the Orpheum to such good houses that after seven months it moved uptown to the Helen Hayes Theater for another nine months and finally into the Longacre for the remainder of its run of 587 performances.

Rock-religion, or 'Jesus Rock' to give it its trade name, was a popular theme at one time, though it was sometimes difficult to ascertain whether it cloaked an iconoclastic view of religion or was a sincere attempt to convey the message in terms that the younger generation would understand. *Salvation* (1969) posed no such problems. It was strongly anti-religious, although set in the form of a gospel revival meeting complete with psychedelic light show. To the authors, Peter Link and C.C. Courtney, salvation lay in sex and drugs. The definitive 'Jesus Rock' shows came in 1971 with the opening of *Godspell* (Schwartz) off-Broadway and *Jesus Christ Superstar* (Rice-Lloyd Webber) as a major Broadway production. The former depicted Christ and the disciples as clowns, yet despite the trappings of rock music, outlandish settings and an air of cheerful irreverence, both presented what was basically a straightforward Bible story. Despite, or because of, opposition from religious bodies, the two shows established communication

Grease (1972). An off-Broadway production which took an affectionate look at the early days of rock and roll and wound up with a long run at the Broadhurst Theater.

with the youth of the seventies, but whether for the rock music alone or for any kind of religious inspiration one cannot be certain. Late in 1976 the genre was briefly revived with *Your Arm's Too Short to Box with God* which, like *Godspell* and *Superstar*, was based on the Book of Matthew.

Stephen (*Godspell*) Schwartz was back the next year with *Pippin*, a historical romp in the court of the Emperor Charlemagne which earned Tony Awards all round, not the least important of which went to Bob Fosse for his imaginative and inventive direction and choreography. What was apparently a straightforward story was in reality a world of make-believe, controlled by former *Jesus Christ Superstar* actor/singer Ben Vereen, playing a type of master of ceremonies who created, and finally removed, the settings by magic tricks.

Rock musicals abounded in every shape and form on and off Broadway, some receiving no more than their just deserts, but the above were prime examples of those which tried to interpret other stories, other times, or specific messages, in the contemporary idiom. *Grease* (1972) and *The Rocky Horror Show* (1974) were comparatively unpretentious pop-music shows taking a backward look at the heyday of rock and roll. Whether or not their idiom was to one's own taste they did at least denote a return to the 'fun'

The Rocky Horror Show (1974). Philip Sayer in Richard O'Brien's successful satire on horror movies, transvestism and rock.

musical. The preoccupation with drugs, sex and intolerance, the desire to shock for the sake of it, had somehow managed to obscure the theory that the theatre is basically a place of entertainment. That so many of the experimental shows failed to make any impact other than in their own small circle (sometimes not even there) perhaps indicates that even a supposedly rebellious younger generation was still in the main seeking simple enjoyment.

The influx of new writers as well as those who had emerged in the sixties ensured a continuance of the more conventional musical. Few of the older writers were still active, but Richard Rodgers, collaborating with the lyricist Martin Charnin in 1970, returned with *Two by Two*, a musical version of Clifford Odet's *The Flowering Peach* starring Danny Kaye as Noah. Audience reaction was enough to keep it going for a year or so, but Rodgers was less than ecstatic about Kaye's predilection for taking liberties with the

Two by Two (1970). Danny Kaye's return to Broadway as Noah in a latter-day Richard Rodgers musical. Joan Copeland is on the right.

script. In 1976 he collaborated with Sheldon Harnick on *Rex*, but even with the presence of Nicol Williamson it failed. Harvey Schmidt and Tom Jones tried to repeat the success of *The Fantasticks* with the equally offbeat *Celebration* (1969), in which the chorus appeared in masks throughout and the music was provided by an orchestra of nine percussionists on stage. Despite acclaim from the trendier critics it was not another *Fantasticks* and the Ambassador Theater fell vacant again after 109 performances.

This is the period which is referred to briefly in Chapter 8 as one in which a principal source of musical material was the classic old film script, some remakes proving very successful, others less so. Neil Simon's 1968 adaptation of Billy Wilder's and I.A.L. Diamond's *The Apartment*, well garnished with a score by the hit songwriters Burt Bacharach and Hal David, was entitled *Promises, Promises*. The promise was realized with 1,281 performances at the Shubert, critics as well as audiences being delighted with

Opposite: **Company** (1970). Aided by Stephen Sondheim's superbly integrated music and lyrics *Company* emerged as one of the most original musicals of 1970. Elaine Stritch (at back) and Dean Jones headed a cast that included Charles Braswell, Barbara Barrie, Charles Kimbrough, Merle Louise, John Cunningham, Teri Ralston, George Coe, Beth Howland, Steve Elmore, Donna McKechnie, Pamela Myers and Susan Browning.

Simon's witty script, the unobtrusive integration of dialogue and songs, and especially with the performance of the former *Fantasticks* star Jerry Orbach. Equally successful as an adaptation of a classic film was the script turned out by Betty Comden and Adolph Green for *Applause* (1970), a Best Musical award winner. Lauren Bacall, neither a singer nor an experienced stage actress, walked off with the show as Bette Davis had done with the film *All About Eve* twenty years earlier, and if the score by Charles Strouse and Lee Adams produced no hits it was a praiseworthy blend of words and music that worked well within the context of the show.

Ilya Darling (1967) placed Melina Mercouri firmly on the stage of the Mark Hellinger Theater to repeat her *Never on Sunday* screen success, with Jules Dassin again in charge as writer/director. Manos Hadjidakis added other songs to the famous title tune, with lyrics by Joe Darion. A Wilder-Diamond film contemporary with *The Apartment* was *Some Like It Hot*, now revised by Jule Styne and Bob Merrill as *Sugar* (1972), starring Robert Morse, and the same year Harold Rome did a musical version of *Gone with the Wind*. From the Frank Sinatra film *A Hole in the Head* came the musical *Golden Rainbow* (1968), with an Ernest Kinoy script which sacrificed the well-paced dialogue and human relationships of the film for a mini-revue set in Las Vegas. It was purely a showcase for the husband-and-wife singing team of Steve Lawrence and Eydie Gorme, and out of some fifteen songs by Walter Marks only 'I've Got to Be Me' ever meant anything out of context.

This lack of hit songs, symptomatic of the musicals of the last decade or so, was indicative of the sort of true integration which had by now taken place in stage musicals. If composer and lyricist no longer looked for Hit Parade success they could derive satisfaction from the part their songs played in the development of a musical story – not overlooking the fact that a best-selling 'Original Cast' LP would eventually bring greater financial rewards than hit-or-miss single records. Even *Coco* (1969), with book and lyrics by the perennial Alan Jay Lerner and music by André Previn, yielded no individual songs of note. However, the story of the fashion designer Coco Chanel brought Katherine Hepburn back to the New York stage in her first musical role and proved that a big, spectacular musical with a lady who really merits the title of 'superstar' was still what the public wanted. As a production *Coco* was an expensive fashion parade of Cecil Beaton designs, enlivened only by Miss Hepburn's virtuosity, but it did recapture some of the past glamour of Broadway at the height of the sweatshirt-and-jeans mode.

Jerry Bock and Sheldon Harnick had done well in 1966 with *The Apple Tree*, a trilogy of one-act plays by Mark Twain, Frank R. Stockton and Jules Feiffer adapted by Harnick and Jerome Coopersmith as a vehicle for Barbara Harris, who enraptured the critics. They did even better with *The Rothschilds* (1970) under Michael Kidd's direction, while Cy Coleman and Dorothy Fields, in what was sadly her last assignment, did a musical version of William Gibson's *Two for the Seesaw*, already a solid success as play and film. The musical, called simply *Seesaw* (1973), was another in the mainstream of the Broadway musical which proved that the old and the new could still coexist happily.

One of the surprise hits was *1776* (1969), in which Peter Stone's book illustrated, however fancifully, events of that notable year in American history with the words and music of Sherman Edwards. It might have been produced to even greater advantage seven years later for the bi-centenary, but despite the unpromising basis for a musical its 1,217 performances at the 46th Street Theater put it well up in the list of record-breaking shows. But then this was a time of nostalgia. Without going into any psychological or sociological reasons why people should prefer to look back to happier, more uncomplicated times, let it be reported that revivals of what one would have thought to be dated shows such as *No, No, Nanette* and *The Great Waltz*

Above: **A Little Night Music** (1973). Judy Kahan (left), Glynis Johns (centre) and Hermione Gingold (right) take a bow after one of the many musical numbers in Stephen Sondheim's outstanding modernisation of the traditional operetta format.

Left: **Zorba** (1968). Herschel Bernardi (centre) took the Anthony Quinn screen role in the Kander-Ebb musical version of *Zorba the Greek*, a Harold Prince production.

Opposite: **Fiddler on the Roof** (1964). The longest running musical of all, it opened at the Imperial Theater, New York on 22 September 1964 and played for 3,242 performances. The lead role of Tevye changed hands several times. Ken LeRoy (right), Rae Allen (centre), and Harry Goz (left).

found favour with Broadway audiences. There was, too, a deliberate re-creation of the formative years of the musical in the runaway success of the off-Broadway *Dames at Sea*, in which a cast of six with minimal musical accompaniment attempted to recapture the sights and sounds of the Busby Berkeley-Ruby Keeler-Dick Powell era of the movies. It was satire at its most gentle, valiantly performing in reality what it set out to satirize. The same year (1968) the Palace Theater, a New York landmark from the vaudeville era, was the scene of another attempt to recapture former glories with *George M.*, a biography of the great George M. Cohan that resuscitated not only his best-known songs from the early part of the century but many previously unheard treasures from his songbook. Joel Grey, a star in *Cabaret* after many years in the small-time, played Cohan for all he was worth and, since there can have been few in the audiences who remembered Cohan in his heyday, his performance, imitative or not, can only have consolidated his own position as a great entertainer of today.

The comparatively new team of John Kander and Fred Ebb, fresh from their *Cabaret* success which had happily erased all memory of their first 1965 flop, *Flora, the Red Menace*, were now well into their stride as representatives of the new generation of Broadway writers. It is significant that the majority of their work now involved rewriting past stage and film hits. Was Broadway really so barren of new ideas, or was it following a play-it-safe policy? Kander and Ebb had no monumental hits, but with 285 performances *The Happy Time* (1968) was far from being a failure. Robert Goulet and David Wayne received plaudits, but all the honours went to the former Hollywood dancer Gower Champion, whose staging included ballet and the integration of film sequences. This was yet another David Merrick production, but their next, *Zorba* (1968), was for Harold Prince. This musical adaptation of Nikos Kazantzakis's novel *Zorba the Greek* had a certain amount of authentic atmosphere, both in Ronald Field's choreography and Kander's music which suggested the Grecian musical idiom as had his *Cabaret* been redolent of Kurt Weill's Germany. Their *70 Girls 70* (1971) brought back such Hollywood old-timers as Mildred Natwick, Hans Conreid, Lillian Roth and Gil Lamb in a musical based on the play *Breath of Spring*, about a gang of geriatric shoplifters, of which the British film version had been entitled *Make Mine Mink*. In *Chicago* (1975), a remake of an old Ginger Rogers movie, the director, Bob Fosse, by now an even bigger name than he had been in Hollywood, took advantage of the considerable talents and vital personality of Gwen Verdon as Roxie Hart. The latest Kander-Ebb show, *2 by 5*, opened off-Broadway in 1976.

Without doubt the most successful and talented writer on the Broadway scene today is Stephen Sondheim, and he occupies as exalted a position as any of the older generation of music masters. In great demand as a lyricist by composers of the calibre of Leonard Bernstein, Jule Styne and Richard Rodgers, he saw himself primarily as a composer with the facility for writing his own lyrics, a claim borne out by his record to date. Of his one-man shows, *A Funny Thing Happened on the Way to the Forum* (1962) was his first big hit, while *Anyone Can Whistle* (1964) had a mere nine performances, notwithstanding the presence of Angela Lansbury. In the seventies he provided a succession of musicals, each varying from the other musically, but all indicative of a rich vein of talent that augurs well for the future of the Broadway musical. *Company* was voted the best musical of 1970, a sophisticated, thoroughly urban drama about marriage relationships, which Sondheim defended in a television interview as being a highly moral and pro-marriage play despite the quirkiness of the characters involved. The following year Harold Prince produced and directed *Follies* at the Winter Garden, using the historic associations of that theatre to conjure up ghosts of the past in the minds of a group of former Follies stars assembled for a reunion. Described by various critics as 'monumental theatre' and 'astonishingly

futuristic', *Follies* may in the long term prove to have been one of *the* great Broadway musicals. In 1973 Sondheim took what appeared to be a retrograde step into the world of operetta with *A Little Night Music*, based on the Ingmar Bergman film *Smiles of a Summer Night*. However, any resemblance to the operettas of Friml and Romberg was in name only, for Sondheim's score possessed a firm sense of musical purpose, a hard core of reality, as opposed to the vapid romanticism of its precursors. Music critics made comparisons with Mahler and Schubert, but whatever influences may subconsciously have swayed Sondheim, the music was his own rather than a deliberate pastiche. The haunting quality of 'Night Waltz' is not the work of a hack, while the lyrical originality and melodic invention of 'Send in the Clowns' proved a challenge to the world's greatest recording artists. Yet the song remains the property of Glynis Johns, whose odd little non-singing voice added the true heartbreak quality called for in the context of the story. Stephen Sondheim followed this up in 1976 with *Pacific Overtures*, with an Oriental cast and a score far removed from the blandishments of *Flower Drum Song*.

One final masterpiece, to prove that Broadway could still deliver a backstage musical comparable with anything it had achieved in the past, was *A Chorus Line* (1976). Already enshrined in legend, Michael Bennett's conception as realized in book form by Nicholas Dante and James Kirkwood, was no starry-eyed variation on the 'You're going out there a youngster and coming back a star' Ruby Keeler cliché. It was a hard-hitting *exposé* of Broadway auditions for chorus boys and girls which had its counterpart in real life. It all came true in a sense when the American company which went to London's Drury Lane in 1977 became involved in off-stage hassles and Equity problems, and the British press was quick to draw a parallel between the dramatized events and Michael Bennett's actual treatment of the artists auditioning for the replacement British cast. Nevertheless, with its fine score by Hollywood's Marvin Hamlisch and the lyricist Edward Kleban, that included an excellent ballad, 'What I Did for Love', and 'One', the most infectiously corny chorus song since 'Hello Dolly', and expert staging, *A Chorus Line* was assured of West End success.

Here, then, is the musical stage three-quarters of the way through the twentieth century. It has experienced sweeping changes in terms of musical development, literacy, choreography and visual presentation of imaginative, sometimes outrageously bold, conceptions. It has achieved its object of complete integration of songs and text, broadened its horizons and, in welcoming new blood and new ideas, has rejected the ephemeral and absorbed the durable. And now it has come full circle, by the same process of assimilation from other sources as brought musical comedy into being in the first place. Yet the difference between Broadway of today and yesterday seems to be one chiefly of degree. Yesterday the power was in the hands of the Ziegfelds and Shuberts; today it is with the Merricks and Princes. Fifty years ago *The Grand Street Follies* were the epitome of off-Broadway satire; now the off-Broadway houses are still the nursery for satire and new ideas. The star system still operates, and the big successes of the 1970s remain, however sophisticated their development, operetta, backstage musical, and spectacular respectively. In December 1976 five of the top attractions on the New York stage were *My Fair Lady*, *Guys and Dolls*, *Porgy and Bess*, *The Threepenny Opera* and *Fiddler on the Roof*, a fitting enough postscript surely to the American musical.

Opposite: **The Sound of Music** (1959). Although the children changed during the run of 1,442 performances at the Lunt-Fontanne Theater, Mary Martin as Maria von Trapp was one constant and dominating factor in the show's success.

7 Glamorous Nights

As was established in Chapter 1, British and American musical comedy shared the same genesis, and only after World War I did their paths diverge. From that point onwards they had little in common, for as the Broadway musical began straight away to progress, its British counterpart showed little inclination to move out of the conventional rut. Nevertheless, the West End stage has ever been a thriving industry, generally dependent on the imported American product for its blockbusters but at the same time producing a quota of shows sufficient to meet its own demands. Overall, however, British musical comedy contributed little to the repertoire of evergreen songs and even less in the way of historic shows. Even twenty years after *Show Boat* the British 'book' show was still, in the main, offering the same fare to which American theatre-goers had been subjected prior to that breakthrough – but undoubtedly there was a public for it. This helps explain why a somewhat limp little confection called *Salad Days* – some would say a masterpiece of banality – ran for 2,329 performances at the Vaudeville Theatre in London while *Pal Joey*, *Can Can*, *Wonderful Town*, *Kismet*, *The Pajama Game*, *The Threepenny Opera*, *Fanny* and *Damn Yankees* came and went.

The British musical cannot, in the light of its conservative parochialism, be measured by the criteria applied to Broadway, although within its own limitations there have been highlights, big musicals or good little shows, which have proved memorable, and many talented and well-loved performers, some of whom went on to other things with great distinction. The early years were devoted primarily to costume pieces like the long-running *Chu*

Opposite: A glamour girl prepares to go on stage. A photograph taken in the late 1930s.

Right: **Mr Cinders** (1929). A familiar legend was reversed in Vivian Ellis's Adelphi hit, with Bobby Howes as a male Cinderella, and his inevitable co-star Binnie Hale.

Chin Chow (1916), *The Maid of the Mountains* (1917), *A Southern Maid* (1920) and *The Rebel Maid* (1921), all basically adhering to the operetta format. They were written by such indigenous composers as Harold Fraser-Simpson, Frederic Norton, Nat D. Ayer, Montague Phillips, G.H. Clutsam and others. The early musicals were self-contained works, and if not integrated in the sense in which we came to understand the term in later years, provided pleasant enough evenings of make-believe, and produced songs which eventually turned up on the parlour piano in sheet-music form. There were oddities like C.B. Cochran's production *Afgar*, which opened at the London Pavilion in 1919 with Alice Delysia, Harry Welchman, Lupino Lane and Marie Burke. Originally with a score by Charles Cuvillier and Douglas Furber, *Afgar* finally included in its credits the names of Harry Tierney, Irving Berlin, James V. Monaco, Irving Bibo and Joseph McCarthy, though many of their songs may have been interpolated when the show went to New York in 1920 for a two-year run.

It was common practice in the early years for London impresarios to commission musicals from the great American composers specifically for the West End, hence the appearance in their credits of shows unknown to New York theatre-goers, such as George Gershwin's *Rainbow* (1923) and *Primrose* (1924); Rodgers and Hart's *Lido Lady* (1926) and *Evergreen* (1930); Jerome Kern's *The Cabaret Girl* (1922), *The Beauty Prize* (1923) and *Blue Eyes* (1928); and the Schwartz-Dietz *Here Comes the Bride* (1930). Vernon Duke, on his arrival from Russia via Paris, composed the score for *The Yellow Mask* (1928), a musical play by Edgar Wallace starring Phyllis

Dare and Bobby Howes. He also wrote *Yvonne* for London in 1928. *The Lady of the Rose*, a 1922 musical by Jean Gilbert with book and lyrics by Frederick Lonsdale and Harry Graham, was one British show which had a rapid transfer to Broadway, even though in the Atlantic crossing it somehow managed to turn into *Lady in Ermine* with a new score by Sigmund Romberg, Al Goodman and Cyrus Wood. Conversely, *Stop Flirting*, with a London run of 418 performances in 1923, was principally by George Gershwin among other composers. *For Goodness' Sake*, the American production, had played on Broadway the previous year for only 103 performances. The all-British supporting cast was headed by Fred and Adele Astaire, and Gershwin introduced the famous 'I'll Build a Stairway to Paradise' in the London production, although it had originally been written for the *George White Scandals of 1922*. *Princess Charming* (1926) travelled from London to Broadway in 1929, but the first British show really to make an impact in America was Noël Coward's *Bitter Sweet*, which established Coward in America. After four months of its 697-day run at His Majesty's Theatre from mid-1929, a second company opened at the Ziegfeld Theater headed by Evelyn Laye and Gerald Nodin. It had less success in America, but as Coward's first 'book' show it made his name known to a wider audience than the West End. Noël Coward, a man of many parts, was for years one of the few British musical playwrights to make any sort of a name outside his own country. He did not write specifically for Broadway until around 1960, but his revues like *This Year of Grace* and *Words and Music* (*Set to Music* in the USA) in the thirties added to the reputation he had gained with *Bitter Sweet*, followed by *Conversation Piece* in 1934.

London was the first to see Cole Porter's famous *Wake Up and Dream*, the show that introduced 'What Is This Thing Called Love?' and 'Let's Do It', produced by C.B. Cochran at the London Pavilion in March 1929. It moved to the Selwyn Theater in New York in December, taking with it the stars Jessie Matthews and Tilly Losch, with Jack Buchanan replacing Sonnie Hale. Jessie Matthews and Jack Buchanan were but two of the British artists who were as much at home on Broadway as in London, Buchanan of course having starred with Jeanette MacDonald in Hollywood. Cole Porter also wrote *Nymph Errant* for Cochran to produce at the Adelphi in 1933, with Gertrude Lawrence in one of her most enchanting roles singing one of her best-remembered songs, 'The Physician'. Others were 'Experiment', 'How Could We Be Wrong?' and 'Solomon' – unforgettably sung by Elizabeth Welch.

Wonder Bar stopped off at the Savoy *en route* from Germany to Broadway, having a moderate success with the Danish star Carl Brisson and songs like 'Tell Me I'm Forgiven', but not even the magic of Al Jolson could save it from collapsing after seventy-six performances at the Nora Bayes Theater.

The thirties were a peak period for the atypical British musical comedy, little of which remain as reminders of the prolific work of such composers as Noël Gay, Jack Strachey and Phil Charig, lyricists like Clifford Grey, Desmond Carter, Douglas Furber, Harry Graham and Eric Machwitz, and librettists such as Fred Thompson, Guy Bolton and P.G. Wodehouse who, although active on Broadway, found time to write several British musicals. One busy local team was comprised of the composers Jack Waller and Joseph Tunbridge, and the authors/lyricists R.P. Weston and Bert Lee. They wrote *For the Love of Mike* (1931), *Tell Her the Truth* (1932), *He Wanted Adventure* (1933), *Yes, Madam?* (1934) and *Please Teacher* (1935), all for Bobby Howes, then at his peak as a comedy actor and leading man of elfin charm.

Two names were to become prominent in the mid-thirties, and more than any others they are truly representative of the period. One of these, Vivian Ellis, had his first big success with *Mr Cinders* (1929), in which Binnie Hale introduced 'Spread a Little Happiness'. *Follow a Star* (1930) featured Jack

No, No, Nanette had many teething troubles during the out-of-town run, and in fact Binnie Hale and George Grossmith starred at the Palace Theatre, London, in May 1925, some months before the American version reached Broadway.

Wonder Bar (1930). Carl Brisson and Dorothy Dickson shared the spotlight at the Savoy Theatre, London, some months before the former German musical arrived on Broadway as a vehicle for Al Jolson.

Jack Buchanan and Elsie Randolph were a familiar duo on the London musical stage for many years, and must have posed for many photographs such as this. This one is from *Mr Whittington* (1933).

Jill Darling (1934). One of Vivian Ellis's many musical hits of the thirties starred Arthur Riscoe and Frances Day, one of London's favourite American stars of the period.

and Claude Hulbert with a guest appearance by Sophie Tucker; and the next big one was *Jill Darling* (1934), an early starring role for the actor John Mills, who sang 'I'm on a Seesaw' and worked with the American actress Frances Day, at that time resident in London. *Hide and Seek* (1937) introduced Ellis's best-known song, 'She's My Lovely', eternally associated with Bobby Howes. The American writers Sammy Lerner, Al Goodhart and Al Hoffman were working in British films at the time and contributed to *Hide and Seek* and, the same year, *Going Greek*, a vehicle for three of London's outstanding stage comics, Leslie Henson, Fred Emney and Richard Hearne.

The other name, one written large in the annals of British stage music, is that of Ivor Novello, matinée idol of a predominantly feminine audience. A handsome leading man (though, except for a few bars in *Careless Rapture*, *The Dancing Years* and *Perchance to Dream*, he never sang a note in any of his own musicals), he wrote a series of consistently successful and sumptuously mounted neo-operettas possessed of a style and flair that held the stage of Drury Lane from 1935 until the outbreak of war. An actor of repute on stage and screen, he wrote 'Keep the Home Fires Burning' in World War I, but it was not until 1935, when he was forty-two years old, that Novello took London by storm with *Glamorous Night*, the first of his memorable Rur-

Above: **Conversation Piece** (1934). Playwright-composer-lyricist-director-actor Noel Coward with Yvonne Printemps, both looking rather exhausted by the gruelling pace of a His Majesty's Theatre performance.

Above right: **The Dancing Years** (1939). Ivor Novello and Roma Beaumont with Mary Ellis on the stairs. Possibly Novello's best known and most successful show. *The Dancing Years* had to move from Drury Lane on the outbreak of war, but transferred to the Adelphi for a most successful run.

itanian romances. The same names occur throughout the cast lists of the Novello shows – Mary Ellis, Peter Graves, Olive Gilbert, Roma Beaumont, Robert Andrews, Zena Dare, Elizabeth Welch – and give or take a show or two they all followed their leader, bringing a sense of continuity to the productions and of familiarity to the faithful audiences. Whether it was *Careless Rapture* (1936), *Crest of the Wave* (1937), *The Dancing Years* (1939), *Arc de Triomphe* (1943), *Perchance to Dream* (1945) or *King's Rhapsody* (1949), the Novello formula was box-office magic. None of his shows was ever produced in America, and of all the dozens of songs he wrote in collaboration with Christopher Hassall only 'We'll Gather Lilacs' is known there, the lyrics for which were written by Novello himself. When Ivor Novello died one night in 1951 after a performance of *King's Rhapsody* an era came to an end.

Meanwhile, just before Christmas 1936, *Balalaika*, a Cossack romance by George Posford and Bernard Grun with book and lyrics by Eric Maschwitz, opened at the Adelphi. Six weeks later it moved to His Majesty's, where it ran for a year. It was filmed by MGM in 1939 as a vehicle for Nelson Eddy and Ilona Massey but with a much-altered score. The next year MGM reunited Eddy with Jeanette MacDonald in *Bitter Sweet*, a film much more faithful to the original. In 1937 came *Me and My Girl*, one of the longest running British musicals. Starring Lupino Lane, it stayed at the Victoria Palace till the outbreak of war in 1939. With music by Noël Gay, lyrics by Douglas Furber, who wrote the book with Arthur Rose, it was a cheerful bit of Cockney nonsense giving rise to a famous scene when 'Nip' Lane and a coster chorus sang 'The Lambeth Walk', one of the most infectious songs ever to come from a London musical.

In the early war years 'book' musicals took a back seat as intimate revue flourished at the Comedy and other theatres, and the more grandiose variety at the Palladium, Holborn Empire (bombed in 1940) and Prince of Wales, where the great Sid Field became a star 'overnight' in *Strike a New Note* (1943) after years of slogging round the provinces. As wartime conditions became accepted as a way of life musicals came back into favour, and in 1942 *Wild Rose* starred Jessie Matthews (it was actually Jerome Kern's *Sally* under a new name). Richard Tauber was in yet another version of *Blossom Time*, with Schubert's music adapted by G.H. Clutsam; and early in 1943 he wrote, produced and starred in his own *Old Chelsea*, the sort of period piece the British public tended to take to its heart. *The Lisbon Story* was a popular show the same year, combining intrigue and romance with a score by Harry Parr-Davies and Harold Purcell that yielded the perennial 'Pedro the Fisherman'.

The best American shows had always found a home on the London stage, from *Sally* and the Friml and Romberg operettas up to *On Your Toes*. Now, in the midst of a war, the procedure recommenced with West End productions of Cole Porter's *Dubarry Was a Lady*, *Let's Face It* and *Panama Hattie*. Yet the greatest musical thrill for wartime London was the appearance of Irving Berlin and his *This Is the Army* company at the Palladium in 1943 *en route* to entertain the US forces in Europe. The superb production, to quote the London *Daily Herald*, 'knocked London sideways', and it raised a great deal of money for British servicemen's charities. More important, it gave London a taste of the kind of Broadway professionalism it would see in just a few years, when the floodgates would be opened to the products of the New Broadway.

After the war Lupino Lane returned to the Victoria Palace in another Noël Gay show, *Sweetheart Mine* – which was not another *Me and My Girl*. Vivian Ellis also returned to work with the lyricist/author A.P. Herbert on a series of musicals for C.B. Cochran at the Adelphi. *Big Ben* (1946), with Lizbeth Webb and Trefor Jones, and *Tough at the Top* (1949), with George Tozzi, were good enough, but it was *Bless the Bride* in 1947 that provided one of the most successful post-war shows. Lizbeth Webb and Georges Guétary starred, and thirty years later the original recordings of 'This Is My Lovely Day' and 'La Belle Marguerite' are still familiar. The three shows formed a fine tribute to C.B. Cochran who died soon afterwards: he was a man who made mistakes of judgment, who won a few and lost a few, yet whose flair and enthusiasm gave London some of its finest musical entertainment – and many of whose dancers, dubbed 'Cochran's Young Ladies', were to become stars in later years.

In December 1946 Noël Coward presented his first 'book' musical for many years at Drury Lane. But not even Mary Martin could save *Pacific 1860* and within four months the stage of London's most prestigious theatre was ready for a repetition of Broadway history, when Howard Keel walked on from the wings singing 'Oh What a Beautiful Morning' and the American invasion had begun in earnest. There is little point in detailing here the West End productions of the musicals discussed in previous chapters. In many cases the original Broadway stars came over, or replacements of similar calibre. Edmund Hockridge, a Canadian resident in London since the war, was in demand as leading man in *Can Can* and *The Pajama Game*, and other North American expatriates could always find a place in the supporting casts, which at least spared us the agony of watching British casts struggling with

Opposite: **Under Your Hat** (1938). Jack Hulbert and Cicely Courtneidge were a popular husband and wife comedy team who starred in many British stage and screen musical comedies of the twenties and thirties.

Above: **Me and My Girl** (1937). As Bill Snibson, Lupino Lane illustrates the 'Oi' thumb movement from the memorable 'Lambeth Walk', the song that enabled this show to fill the Victoria Palace, London, for 1,046 performances.

Opposite: **Big Ben** (1946). C. B. Cochran's first post-war production at the Adelphi Theatre, the first of several with music by Vivian Ellis and words by A. P. Herbert, Lizbeth Webb (centre, standing) starred.

Left: **Perchance to Dream** (1945). Ivor Novello and Roma Beaumont in a most successful (1,022 performances) variation on the typical Novello theme of love and intrigue in high places.

Below: **Gay's the Word** (1951). In Ivor Novello's last stage score. Cicely Courtneidge had a real show-stopper in 'Vitality'.

unconvincing accents as Broadwayites or mid-West types. While the Broadway baritone Bill Johnson was starring as Frank Butler in *Annie Get Your Gun* his wife Shirl Conway had the lead in the Hans May-Eric Maschwitz *Carissima* at the Palace; but the latter, along with such variegated pieces as *Belinda Fair* and *Her Excellency* (1949), *Blue for a Boy* and *Dear Miss Phoebe* (1950), was distressingly reminiscent of pre-war operetta and vapid musical comedy to raise much of a cheer from audiences now accustomed to *Brigadoon*, *Carousel*, *Kiss Me Kate* and *South Pacific*.

One that did do well was *Love from Judy* (1953), Eric Maschwitz's reworking of *Daddy Long Legs* with a score by Hugh Martin and Timothy Grey. It introduced Jean Carson, who became Jeannie Carson in America, and pop singer Johnny Brandon, who developed in the sixties as a prolific off-Broadway composer. Noël Coward tried to recapture some of his former glory with *Ace of Clubs* (1950) and a musical version of Wilde's *Lady Windermere's Fan* called *After the Ball* (1954), but a period piece like this, even in the hands of The Master, now seemed sadly *démodé*. If the more sophisticated observer felt that *Dear Miss Phoebe*'s 'I Leave My Heart in an English Garden' lacked just a little something compared with the 'Soliloquy' from *Carousel* or Frank Loesser's 'Fugue for Tinhorns', then a still greater

Opposite: The King and I came to London's Drury Lane on 8 October 1953, with Herbert Lom as the King and Valerie Hobson as Anna Leonowens.

Left: **Ace of Clubs** (1950). (Left to right) Graham Payn, Pat Kirkwood and Elwyn Brook-Jones in a Noel Coward show that attempted to depict the seamy side of post-war Soho.

shock was in store. Sandy Wilson, a performer and writer on the 'little theatre' circuit, was obsessed by the twenties, and in April 1953 the Players Theatre put on a modest yet subtle little pastiche of the flapper era, a one-man effort by him called *The Boy Friend*. It became a cult and on transferring via Swiss Cottage to Wyndham's Theatre nine months later it ran for 2,078 performances. This was almost as impressive as Julian Slade's equally 'camp' *Salad Days* mentioned earlier, and it achieved equal success in New York – though for its American presentation the whole emphasis was exaggerated far beyond Sandy Wilson's original conception, much to his personal dismay. Both proved virtually sole successes for their authors, whose subsequent shows joined the many others that fell by the wayside. After the advent of the long-playing record it was a regular occurrence for a West End musical to have been and gone before its 'Original Cast' album reached the record shops, and the fifties in particular are littered with the débris of shows that never made it beyond the first month.

Among those which succeeded to a certain extent, *Summer Song* (1956) was a counterpart of the kind of classically based piece Wright and Forrest had been turning out on Broadway for years, this one being based on themes by Dvorak and decorated vocally by Sally Ann Howes and David Hughes. But the first indication that the musical stage was alive to developments in

The Boy Friend (1954). Sandy Wilson's first and biggest hit had a run of 2,078 performances in the West End and 485 on Broadway, and was followed by a full-scale screen version.

contemporary music was a Wolf Mankowitz story with a score by David Heneker, Monty Norman and Julian More. *Expresso Bongo* (1958) capitalized on the interest in pop music, with James Kenney as a 'coffee-bar cowboy' and Paul Schofield as a wily promoter. Heneker, More and Norman had a big hit three months later with their adaptation of Marguerite Monnot's *Irma la Douce*, and this tale of a Parisian *poule* and her protective *flic* was also a far cry from the traditional British musical.

For the first time the complacency of the theatrical establishment was about to be challenged. The Theatre Royal, Stratford, in London's East End, was run by Joan Littlewood, a fireball woman producer formerly of the left-wing Unity Theatre. In February 1959 she presented a musical play by an ex-convict called Frank Norman with songs by Lionel Bart, an East-ender who had been writing for the then rock star Tommy Steele. *Fings Ain't Wot They Used t' Be* was a new kind of musical – brash, irreverent and 100 per cent working-class English. A year later it went to the Garrick Theatre, where it ran for two more years. *Make Me an Offer*, another slice of East End life, story by Mankowitz, music by Heneker, also made it to the West End. Bart couldn't stop working, and after writing the lyrics for *Lock Up Your Daughters* (to Laurie Johnson's music), a 1959 Mermaid Theatre production of Henry Fielding's *Rape Upon Rape*, he became composer and author also, for what was to be his own personal success. Turning Charles Dickens's *Oliver Twist* into a musical was no more inconceivable than any

Opposite: **Valmouth** (1958). A scene from the original production at the Lyric Theatre, Hammersmith, London, with Fenella Fielding (in stripes) and Peter Gilmore (second from right).

Oh What a Lovely War! Richard Attenborough directs Maggie Smith in the 1969 screen version of Joan Littlewood's anti-war satire from the Theatre Royal, Stratford, East London.

Paint Your Wagon. A scene from the 1953 production at His Majesty's Theatre, London.

other literary adaptation, but no one could have foreseen that when *Oliver!* opened at the New Theatre in 1960 it would have a phenomenal run of 2,618 performances in London, 774 on Broadway, and become an Academy Award winning film. It was Lionel Bart's last big hit, and succeeding shows were an anti-climax until the final disaster of *Twang!* (1965), a musical Robin Hood that failed to hit the bull's-eye.

The other big show emanating from Joan Littlewood's Stratford Theatre was *Oh What a Lovely War!* (1963). Hardly a musical as such, it utilized World War I songs to illustrate a hard-hitting satire on the folly of war.

Although the incidence of flops was as great as ever, more British musicals were now appearing with the hallmark of quality, as a new generation of writers less hidebound by musical comedy traditions of the past put their talents to work. Leslie Bricusse and Anthony Newley had imagination and style, and *Stop the World, I Want to Get Off* (1961) pursued an unconventional theme, with Newley as a little man in clown's guise eternally defeated by circumstances – 'What Kind of Fool Am I?' being his *cri de coeur*. This song, together with 'Gonna Build a Mountain' and 'Once in a

Half a Sixpence (Paramount 1967). Tommy Steele has been serenading leading lady Julia Foster in this production still from the film of the musical version of H. G. Wells's *Kipps*.

Lifetime', became world hits, *Stop the World* having an even greater success on Broadway than some of the American shows of the time. Truly the scene was changing. The follow-up was *The Roar of the Greasepaint, the Smell of the Crowd*, which never got to London after a provincial tour in 1964 but went straight to New York. This, too, produced evergreens in 'Who Can I Turn To?' and 'A Wonderful Day Like Today'.

In 1963 *Pickwick* and *Half a Sixpence*, based on Dickens's *Pickwick Papers* and H.G. Wells's *Kipps*, confirmed that while such British musicals were hardly radical departures in stagecraft they were now backed by a solid core of musicianship and professional expertise too long lacking in the home-grown product. These also made the transatlantic crossing to equal acclaim. The world of literature continued to yield rich pickings for authors of musicals, some successful, some less so. Rudolf Besier's play *The Barretts of Wimpole Street* became *Robert and Elizabeth* (1964), and the same year James Barrie's *The Admirable Crichton* became *Our Man Crichton* with Kenneth More and Millicent Martin. *The Four Musketeers* gave Harry Secombe a chance to prove that his success in *Pickwick* was no fluke,

The Black Mikado (1975). The Gilbert and Sullivan comic opera has appeared in many guises over the years, including both 'Hot' and 'Cool'. In the liberated seventies Derek Griffiths was a Black Mikado, seen here with Anita Tucker.

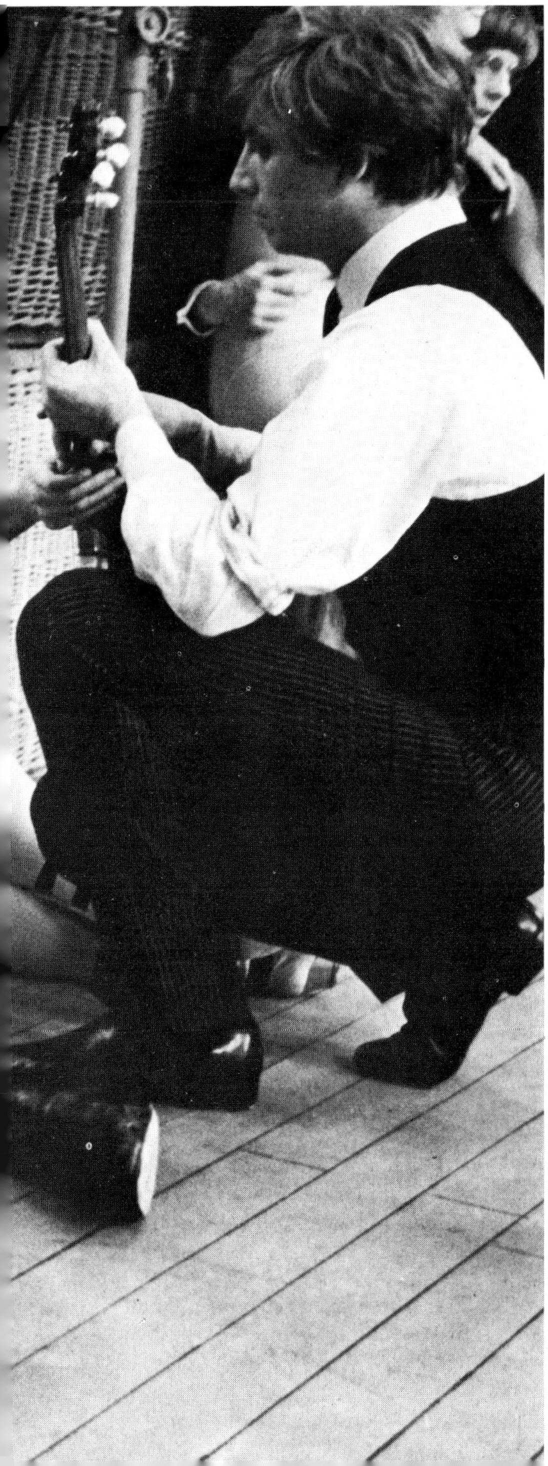

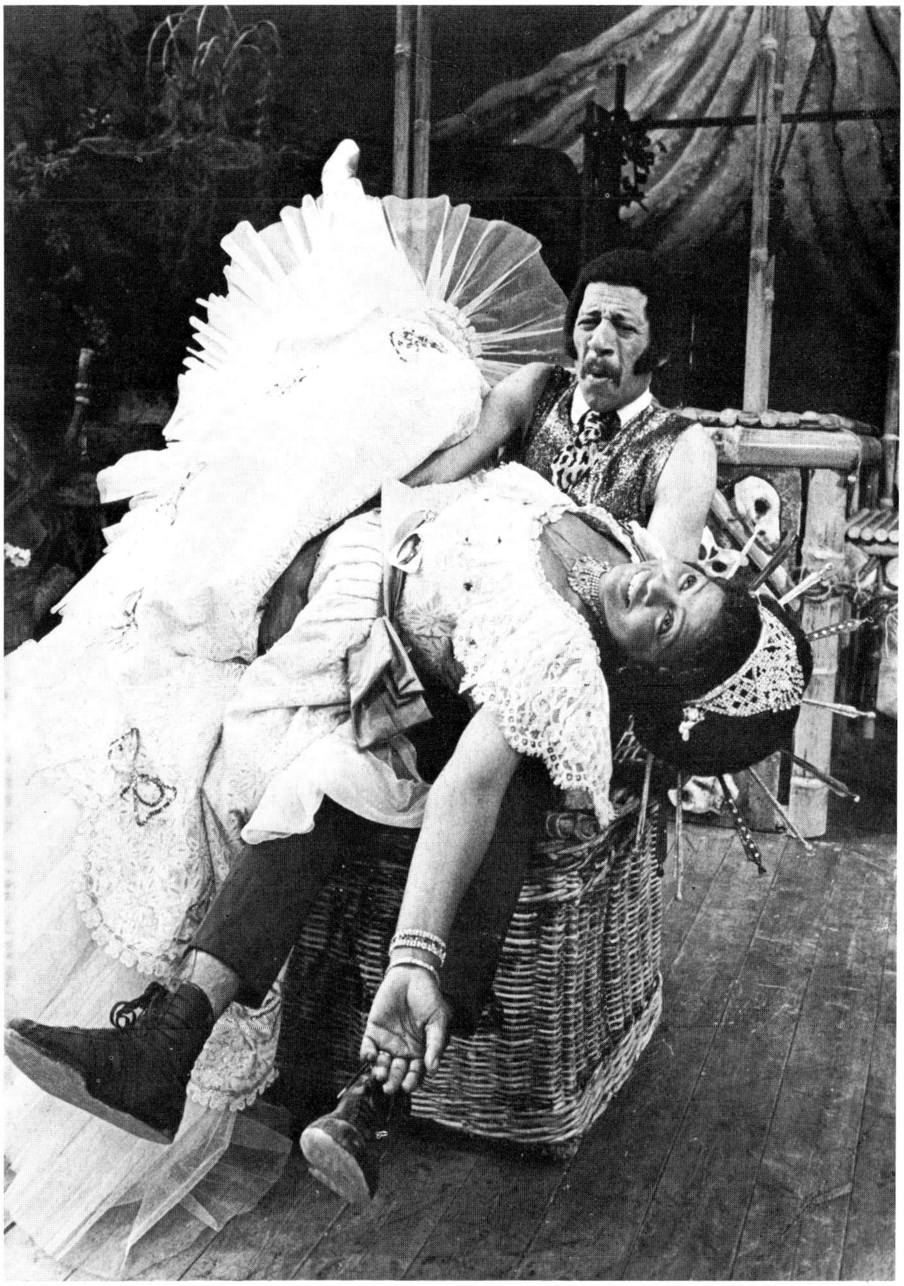

The Good Companions (1974). Judi Dench co-starred with John Mills and Christopher Gable in Ronald Harwood's new version of the J. B. Priestley story, with songs by André Previn and Johnny Mercer.

though its stay at Drury Lane was shorter than the theatre was used to. To the Palace in 1969 came another Dickens adaptation – *Two Cities* with Edward Woodward as Sidney Carton. It was not a good year for musicals, and saw the failure of *Anne of Green Gables* and H.G. Wells's *Ann Veronica*; and while Ginger Rogers was packing Drury Lane as *Mame* Betty Grable failed at the Palace in *Belle Starr*.

The runaway hit of the sixties was an original, not an adaptation, thoroughly English in conception and treatment, and great for the charabanc trade. The veteran star Anna Neagle worked in perfect harmony with younger performers like Joe Brown, Stuart Damon and Derek Nimmo in David Heneker's *Charlie Girl*, which had almost a complete change of cast before it completed its run of 2,202 performances at the Adelphi.

The London stage was trying everything; now it was biographies. Barbara Windsor played the music-hall star Marie Lloyd in *Sing a Rude Song*, which went from the suburban Greenwich Theatre to the Garrick in 1970, and the Scots comedian Stanley Baxter played the Irish songwriter Percy French in *Phil the Fluter*, the third musical to play the Palace in 1969. *I and Albert* (1972), the story of Queen Victoria and her consort, had a score by Broadway's Charles Strouse and Lee Adams, but that did not save it. It seemed that the sense of purpose which had taken hold in the West End musical stage just a few years previously had evaporated; but salvation came at the end of 1972 when Leslie Bricusse and Anthony Newley reunited to give London a solid year's entertainment with *The Good Old, Bad Old Days* at the Prince of Wales. They made more concessions to commerce than in their previous two shows, but still managed to produce an entertainment in every sense of the word that was different without trying too hard.

There was little attempt in the London theatre to reflect the off-Broadway preoccupation with rock shows and social conscience. *Jesus Christ Superstar* was, after all, a British musical first produced on records, but it had to come back to the London stage (the Palace finally had a hit) from Broadway. *Hair* had settled in London, and in the mid-seventies *The Rocky Horror Show* put in an appearance. Tim Rice and Andrew Lloyd Webber, the writers of *Superstar*, did their *Joseph and the Technicoloured Dreamcoat* at the Albery in 1973, but Lloyd Webber's *Jeeves*, based on the P.G. Wodehouse character, failed dismally in 1975. In 1976 there came two shows based on pop music, rather than rock musicals as such, called *Teeth 'n' Smiles* and *Leave Him to Heaven*, but they barely survived. Very little has survived in recent years, though *The Black Mikado* (1975), surprisingly faithful to Gilbert and Sullivan, did well. A new version of J.B. Priestley's *The Good Companions* (1974), by the distinguished partnership of André Previn and Johnny Mercer, had a good score and deserved more success than it achieved. But really the only outstandingly successful British musical has been *Billy*, a spectacular developed around the fantasies of Waterhouse and Hall's *Billy Liar*. It occupied Drury Lane for two years from 1974, yet it was the virtuoso performance of Michael Crawford which drew the crowds – following his television fame – rather than any expertise in musical production.

The new musicals come and go with alarming rapidity, indicating a considerable state of flux in a profession which does not seem to know where to turn for its next hit. The dilemma of the British musical is perhaps best summed up by the fact that at the time of writing the only successful 'book' musicals in London are Jerome Kern's *Very Good, Eddie* of 1915 and the 1919 *Irene*.

Irene. b. 1919 and still going strong in the seventies with Jon Pertwee and Jessie Evans at the Adelphi Theatre, London.

8 Broadway to Hollywood... and Back

The relationship of Broadway with Hollywood has ever been a love-hate affair between two kindred arts that have much in common on the surface yet are fundamentally worlds apart. On the one hand there is the true theatrical, with his mistrust of pictures and picture people and his scorn of screen acting; and on the other there is the film man, with his whole-hearted involvement in his own medium and dislike of the 'tedium' of repetitive theatre work. They are strange opposites indeed in what is basically the same profession – that of entertainment. Yet stage and screen are interdependent, relying on each other as sources of material and revenue alike.

The film capital has never been completely autonomous. It supports a self-contained industry certainly, and one whose most prestigious products have been pure cinema, but is this a truly indigenous art? Did not the writers imported on the advent of sound emanate from New York and London – people like F. Scott Fitzgerald, Robert Benchley, Donald Ogden Stewart, Dorothy Parker, Marc Connolly and the other literary giants, who moved the Algonquin Round Table *en bloc* to the Garden of Allah, attracted by the Californian sunshine and the apparently bottomless purses of the movie moguls? Perhaps more than any other art form, the cinema has always been a hybrid, born of and feeding on the other modern arts of drama, literature and music.

Life was so much less complicated when movies merely moved and Mack Sennett could make a blockbusting comedy by taking his actors and props into the Los Angeles streets and improvising on the events of the day. Or when four silent dramas could be filmed simultaneously in adjacent booths. The slogan 'All-Talking, All-Singing, All-Dancing' gave a new impetus to the industry; yet it also introduced a new headache by making it try to live up to this delirious slogan. *The Jazz Singer* and subsequent Al Jolson vehicles apart, the initial product was the all-star revue, which called for little in the way of creative writing, and merely offered a glorified vaudeville show spotlighting the talents of each individual studio's contract artists. *Paramount on Parade*, MGM's *Broadway Melody* and *Hollywood Revue*,

Left: **The King of Jazz** (Universal, 1930). Chorus line in one of the earliest all-star screen musical revues, and certainly the first in colour.

Below: **The Gold Diggers of 1933** (Warner). A chorus 'playing' violins outlined in neon – merely *one* of Busby Berkeley's presentation ideas for the famous 'Shadow Waltz' sequence.

Right: **Rio Rita** (Radio, 1929). MGM's 1942 version with Abbott and Costello was considerably less faithful to the original Broadway show than this early talkie version starring Bebe Daniels and John Boles.

Below: **Whoopee** (Goldwyn/United Artists. 1930). Goldwyn signed Busby Berkeley to repeat his dance routines from the Broadway musical, and this still shows one of the prototypes of the kind of chorus presentation that was to become the Berkeley trademark.

Universal's *The King of Jazz* and the Warner-Vitaphone *On with the Show* and *Golddiggers of Broadway* were among the photographed stage shows which served to introduce the musical to cinema audiences. But these were no more than a stopgap, a formula upon which the studios relied initially, but the variations on it were strictly limited and soon they were wondering what to do next.

The immediate solution was to present screen adaptations of the established stage hits which had been filling theatres in the previous decade, in the belief that what had been a success in one medium would find equal favour in another. Hence the earliest film musicals of the 1929–30 period were such tried and trusted favourites as *Sunny*, *Rio Rita*, *Sally*, *The Desert Song*, *The Vagabond King*, *Hit the Deck*, *Good News*, *Paris*, *Whoopee*, *Hold Everything*, *The New Moon* and *Manhattan Mary*, which was filmed as *Follow the Leader*. This was to be a familiar pattern in years to come.

Even at this early stage there was a portent of the somewhat arbitrary attitude Hollywood has maintained towards the Broadway musical. For instance, having bought the rights to *No, No, Nanette* and Cole Porter's *Fifty Million Frenchmen*, the studios immediately filmed these shows, but devoid of the music which had presumably attracted them in the first instance. We shall see exactly how this syndrome evolved, and the often quite ridiculous lengths to which Hollywood went in adapting successful stage shows which were assumably commercially viable propositions in no need of improvement to repeat their success.

It would not have been surprising if Broadway, as represented by its eminent and successful producers, directors, composers, lyricists, librettists and choreographers, craftsmen thoroughly schooled in their art, had evinced some resentment at this high-handed disposal of their creations, for which Hollywood had paid so handsomely. But artistic judgment was necessarily tempered with business acumen, for the rewards accruing from the sale of the screen rights of one musical kept the wheels turning by financing the production of the next one. Suffice it to say that Broadway learned to compromise, and for years afterwards those who were its acknowledged craftsmen sought more direct rewards by heading west to sell their individual talents to the dreaded rival. Yet, while the producers Dwight Deere Wiman and Tom Weatherly may have been well pleased with the sale of *The Gay Divorce* to RKO once it had completed its run of 248 performances at the Ethel Barrymore Theater in New York, one is led to wonder how Cole Porter, fresh from the shock of *Fifty Million Frenchmen*, reacted to the complete omission of his beloved score (with one exception) and the substitution of other songs by Conrad and Magidson and Gordon and Revel. Did he find any consolation in the fact that Con Conrad's 'The Continental' became the first film song to win an Academy Award? Perhaps personal satisfaction reached him later, when his one remaining song, 'Night and Day', became one of the most popular songs ever written.

Over ensuing decades Porter must surely have taken a philosophical (or fatalistic) view of Hollywood's cavalier treatment of his scores, although he was by no means the only composer to suffer. Throughout cinema history it has become commonplace for huge sums of money to change hands in order to secure screen rights to a best-selling title, and more often than not it has been the title alone that was used in the finished product – of which, on the non-musical side, Daphne du Maurier's *The Birds* is a prime example. Cole Porter's own *Wake Up and Dream* (1929), *Red, Hot and Blue* (1936) and *Let's Face It* (1941) all lent their titles to films of the forties which bore little or no resemblance, dramatically or musically, to the originals, while his *Mexican Hayride* of 1944 ended up a few years later as a concoction featuring Abbott and Costello.

It is possible to understand, even to justify, this treatment in some instances, since – as has been pointed out – the average stage musical of the

Top left: **Naughty Marietta** (MGM, 1935). A production still of Jeanette MacDonald and Nelson Eddy on set in the first of the filmed operettas that made them universal favourites.

Left: **On the Town** (MGM, 1949). Not only one of the most influential, but one of the most enjoyable of film musicals. This magical moment occurs when (left to right) Betty Garret and Frank Sinatra, Ann Miller and Jules Munshin, Vera Ellen and Gene Kelly stride out of the Empire State Building elevator to the tune of the title song.

Above: **A Connecticut Yankee at King Arthur's Court** (Paramount 1948). An unusual pre-production still which shows Paramount star Gail Russell testing for the role which eventually went to Rhonda Fleming.

twenties and thirties was a flimsy boy-meets-girl affair, affording an excuse for the purely social function of going to the theatre in New York or London but hardly being suited to the earthier demands of people of the Mid-West or provincial Britain. This dichotomy illustrates the essential differences between the art of the theatre, which depends upon an air of unreality heightened by spectacular stage sets and dramatic lighting effects, and that of the cinema. The latter, even in its early stages, was identifiable with reality, with its greater scope for natural settings and, in close-up particularly, an infinitely more restrained and naturalistic type of acting and singing.

No name was too distinguished to escape the ruthless treatment meted out to Cole Porter's musicals. Not even George Gershwin was sacrosanct. When *Lady Be Good* was finally filmed seventeen years after its 1924 run on Broadway, only a fragment of the original score survived, the original story-line had vanished, and the song that won an Academy Award was the interpolated 'The Last Time I Saw Paris' by Jerome Kern. Gershwin's anti-war *Strike Up the Band* of 1930 reached the screen ten years later as a Mickey Rooney-Judy Garland 'let's put on a show' romp with – the title tune apart – a score by Roger Edens; and by some mysterious alchemy Gershwin's *Rosalie* of 1928 became Cole Porter's *Rosalie* in 1937, with Eleanor Powell and Nelson Eddy replacing Marilyn Miller and Jack Donahue. MGM was the company responsible for all three travesties, and it was not until Para-

Left: **Fanny.** Initially based on a Marcel Pagnol trilogy of films about the Marseilles waterfront, *Fanny* became a successful 1954 Broadway musical. When filmed with Leslie Caron (right) seven years later it reverted to a purely dramatic presentation, only Harold Rome's title song being used as background music.

Right: **The Desert Song** (Warner, 1943). Warner Brothers filmed the Romberg success three times. The 1943 version starred Dennis Morgan as The Red Shadow and Irene Manning as Margot.

mount turned *Funny Face* into a screen classic in 1956, with Fred Astaire repeating his stage triumph of thirty years earlier, that a Gershwin show was accorded respectful treatment, which may even have been an improvement on the original. It is worthy of note that even here the old story was thrown out, the score being doctored by Roger Edens and Leonard Gershe who added their own (excellent, as it happens) original material to the basic Gershwin songs.

Rodgers and Hart's *A Connecticut Yankee* reached the screen – very pleasantly in 1948, starring Bing Crosby – with a complete score by Van Heusen and Burke, the original score having been purchased by MGM for their film biography of Rodgers and Hart. The 1940 Rodgers and Hart stage hit *Higher and Higher* was purchased by RKO to introduce Frank Sinatra, but only one Rodgers song was retained in an otherwise new Jimmy McHugh-Harold Adamson score. Lest it be thought that this substitution process was a temporary aberration born of the film capital's growing pains, it is as well to recall that what is now acknowledged as one of the great milestones of film musicals, *On the Town*, achieved its eminence by virtue of the brilliant direction of Stanley Donen and Gene Kelly which translated a stage-bound show into pure cinema. Vital and alive, shot largely on location with the then revolutionary method of advancing the songs' progress by fast cutting and montages, it also scored in the stellar performances and in Betty Comden and Adolph Green's smooth adaptation of their stage libretto. But of Leonard Bernstein's original music, born of his ballet *Fancy Free* which in turn became the 1944 stage musical, little remained; and once again Roger Edens, that little-known but tremendously talented man-about-music at MGM, provided a new score. But how strange that this most epochal of musicals in either medium provided posterity with neither instant hits nor evergreens!

But at least it became a screen musical. *Fanny*, Joshua Logan and S.N. Behrman's Broadway version of Marcel Pagnol's trilogy of films about the Marseilles waterfront, achieved a run of 888 performances at New York's Majestic Theater in the mid-fifties. This respectable success owed itself more than anything to the singing of Ezio Pinza and to Harold Rome's well-integrated score of sixteen songs. Which makes it all the more inexplicable that the film reverted to a purely dramatic presentation, retaining only the title song as background music. Another paradox is that Logan himself directed it! *Irma la Douce* suffered a similar fate. Born in Paris in 1956, nurtured in London in 1958, acclaimed in New York in 1960, the musical Irma died of malnutrition in Hollywood in 1962, in the shape of a Billy Wilder comedy devoid of music.

In general, however, film versions of stage musicals were faithful to the originals, musically if not always dramatically, and these were the more notable exceptions. One favourite Hollywood ploy was to provide additional songs in attempts to update the scores. In some instances (Cole Porter's *Can Can*, Arthur Schwartz's *The Band Wagon*, Rodgers and Hart's *Jumbo* and *Pal Joey*) other songs from old shows by the same composers were cannibalized, while lesser stage numbers were discarded. In others, studio contract writers were assigned the chore of doctoring the original scores (*vide Higher and Higher*, Roger Eden's activities, etc). To add to Cole Porter's tribulations, the bare bones of his most memorable score for *Anything Goes* were included in both screen treatments, but the 1956 revival included a batch of songs by Van Heusen and Cahn, while the 1936 film used but four of the thirteen songs that were still entertaining packed houses at the Alvin Theater as the show was being filmed 3,000 miles away. What was shown on the credits as 'Cole Porter's *Anything Goes*' was in fact 60 per cent Hoagy Carmichael's, Frederick Hollander's, Richard Whiting's and Leo Robin's.

Seven years later, in 1943, *Dubarry Was a Lady*, a hit for Ethel Merman

Above: **The Student Prince** (MGM, 1954). Ann Blyth and Edmund Purdom, whose acting as the Student Prince was supported by the sound-tracked voice of Mario Lanza.

Opposite, above: **Hello Dolly.** Walter Matthau and Barbra Streisand recreated the roles of Horace Vandergelder and Mrs Dolly Levi in 20th Century Fox's 1968 screen version of the ernormously successful Broadway musical.

Opposite: **Kiss me Kate** (MGM, 1953). A production still from the screen version of Cole Porter's long-running show with (left to right) Willard Parker, Howard Keel, Kathryn Grayson, Keenan Wynn and James Whitmore.

on Broadway and Frances Day in London, became an MGM wartime musical for Lucille Ball and Gene Kelly, with only two Porter songs held over and buried in a mass of replacements by Burton Lane, Ralph Freed, Lew Brown, Yip Harburg and Roger Edens, not one of which has survived the years. In fairness, however, it must be admitted that little of Porter's stage score is remembered either, although 'Well, Did You Evah?' finally made its mark a decade and a half later when Porter dug it out of the archives for *High Society*. Possibly the Tierney-McCarthy *Rio Rita* songs which served well enough for Bebe Daniels, John Boles and Wheeler and Woolsey in the early talkie version were considered *passé* by 1942. Be that as it may, the MGM version, which substituted Kathryn Grayson, John Carroll and Abbott and Costello, kept only two of them and interpolated others by for instance Harold Arlen and Yip Harburg. And the mid-fifties films of *Rose Marie*, *The Vagabond King*, *The Student Prince* and *The Desert Song*, while keeping the best known of the Friml and Romberg operetta songs, also utilized updated lyrics by staff writers.

Post-World War II musicals were bowdlerized much less – whether this was because of the higher standard of writing, an increasing respect among movie-makers for the original article, or to a greater control over their work by modern writers, it is hard to say. Probably more credit should be accorded the shows themselves. In the old type of musical comedy songs were used as stopgaps when the dialogue faltered. There may or may not

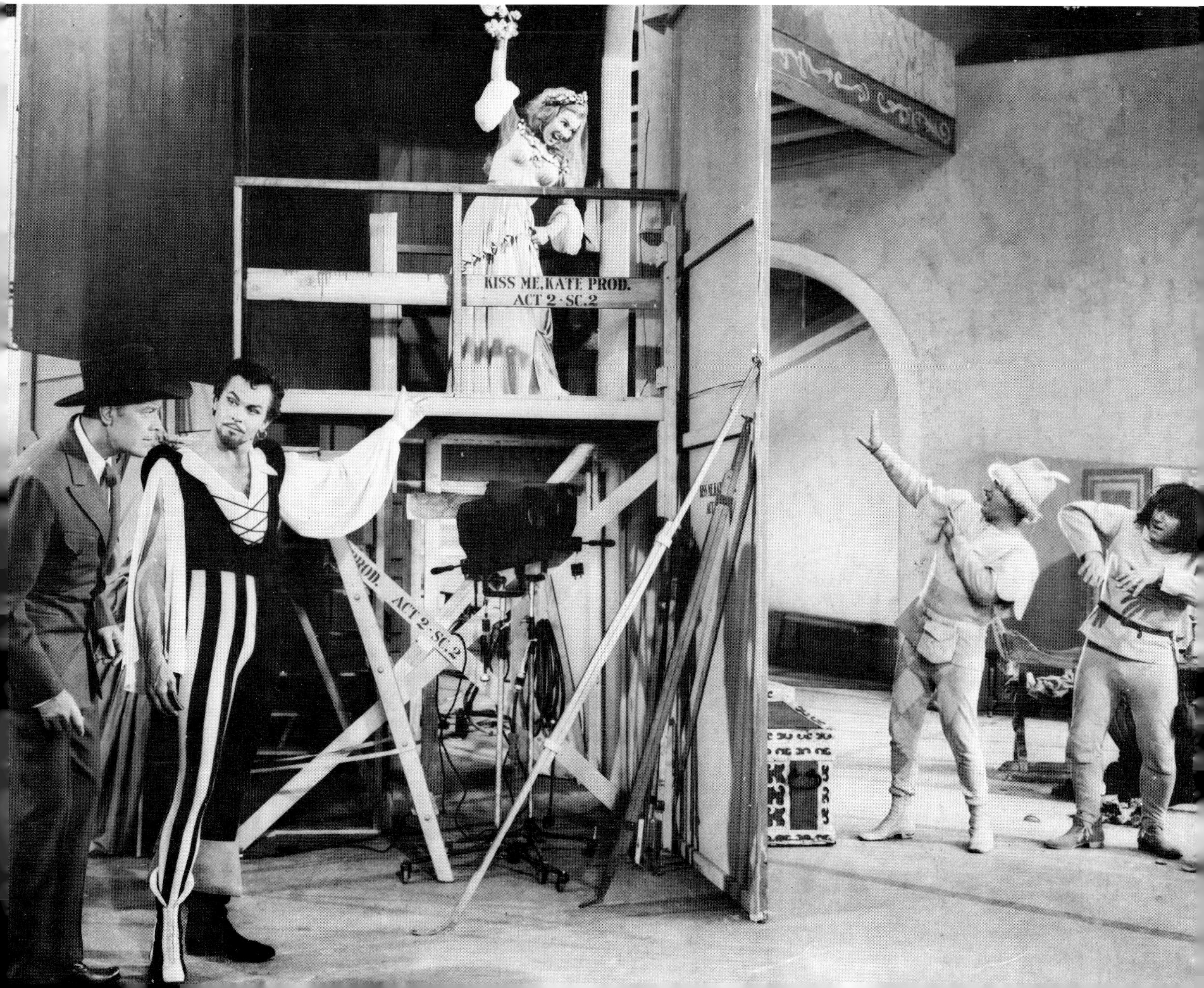

Left: **Oklahoma!** (Magna/Todd AO, 1955). Laurie (Shirley Jones) and Curly (Gordon Macrae) take that long-promised ride in 'The Surrey with the Fringe on Top'.

Below: **South Pacific** (Magna/20th Century Fox, 1958) Mitzi Gaynor as Ensign Nellie Forbush.

have been a cue for song. If one song didn't go down well with the audience, another took its place. The post-war shows, however, were increasingly sophisticated developments of the 'integrated musical', in which each song fulfilled a specific function in developing the story-line almost in the operatic tradition. This blending of plot and music transformed the erstwhile 'musical comedy' into the 'musical play', the far from subtle difference between which can be seen by comparing the cheerful and inconsequential nonsense of, say, *Lady Be Good* with the spectacular and dramatic magnificence of *The King and I* or *Camelot*, *The Most Happy Fella* or *A Little Night Music*. Certainly the composers themselves were more demanding. Even among the older school no one had ever taken liberties with an Irving Berlin song, and a lyricist would have taken his life in his hands to suggest that Jerome Kern alter the metre of a phrase to accommodate a difficult lyric. There were no additions or amendments to a Rodgers and Hammerstein score other than those effected by the writers themselves, while Frank Loesser shows such as *Where's Charley?* and *Guys and Dolls* were filmed as individual entities. Obviously, with a stage score of anything up to twenty numbers, many of an introductory, narrative, or entr'acte nature, something may have had to go in the transition from stage to screen. But however much a score was truncated, augmented or paraphrased to create a polished end-product, it was only logical – and commercially desirable – that the hit numbers should be retained. It is all the more curious, then, that the big love ballads from *Guys and Dolls* ('I've Never Been in Love Before') and *Bells Are Ringing* ('Long Before I Knew You') were omitted from the screen versions.

If it should appear that Hollywood has on occasion treated Broadway with scant respect, it should be pointed out, to redress the balance, that on the whole the stage musical has had a fair deal over the years. Until the 1960s it had been a reasonably held assumption that any show achieving a modest success on the stage would make an equally successful screen product, varying in artistic merit according to the studio, director, writers and actors involved. There were exceptions. Only those intimately involved could explain why such successful and/or musically artistic shows as *Bloomer Girl*, *St Louis Woman*, *High Button Shoes*, *Allegro*, *Miss Liberty*, *Wish You Were Here*, *House of Flowers*, *Me and Juliet*, *By the Beautiful Sea*, *Pipe Dream*, *Plain and Fancy*, *The Most Happy Fella*, *Candide*, *Mr Wonderful*, *Jamaica*,

Paint Your Wagon (Paramount 1969). Harve Presnell, playing a secondary role, had one of the score's biggest songs. 'They Call the Wind Maria'.

Brigadoon (MGM, 1955). Cyd Charisse and Gene Kelly in 'The Heather on the Hill', one of the most beautiful scenes in a screen musical which failed to hide its stage origins.

West Side Story (Mirisch-Seven Arts/United Artists, 1961) Ghost-singer Betty Wand supplied the voice, while Rita Moreno lacked nothing in personality in her visual interpretation of the showstopping 'America' in the rooftop scene.

Say Darling, *Fiorello*, *Little Mary Sunshine*, *Redhead*, *Greenwillow*, *Do-Re-Mi*, *Wildcat*, *Mr President*, *No Strings*, *Little Me*, *Do I Hear a Waltz?*, *I Do, I Do*, *Hair*, *Your Own Thing*, *Company*, *Applause* and *Follies* never had a chance to reach the cinema-going millions. However, as regards those which did reach the screen, it seems there was little standardization in the timing of their presentation. Ideally, the filming of a hit show should take place while it is still a 'hot property' and the songs are still fresh in the public mind; that is, either coincident with or immediately following the stage run, which was the normal procedure. Occasionally contractual obligations precluded the release of a film until the stage version was withdrawn, as when 20th Century Fox, after investing $20 million in *Hello Dolly*, were compelled to keep it under wraps until the Broadway producer David Merrick gave the go-ahead for its release. When he did, the show was five years old, the audience for musicals had gone and Fox went into the red. There may have been some poetic justice in the fact that a major Fox stockholder was David Merrick himself! A similar problem arose with *Kiss Me Kate*, whose seemingly never-ending run extended to 1,077 performances before MGM could recoup their investment on what had originally been a 3-D blockbuster. Unfortunately the 3-D process had died at the box-office while MGM were still biting their nails and *Kate* was finally released 'flat'.

Carmen Jones (20th Century Fox, 1954). Carmen (Dorothy Dandridge) and Joe (Harry Belafonte) in a tranquil moment during their torrid and tragic romance. Off-screen voices were provided by Marilyn Horne and LaVerne Hutcherson respectively.

So far from songs becoming stale after a show's initial impact, the high quality of composition which has been a feature of Broadway shows meant that the best songs very quickly became 'standards', and familiarity with a score enhanced rather than detracted from the appeal of the screen version, whenever it appeared. A time-lag of two or three years never affected the outcome one way or the other. It is surprising, though, just how many potentially cinematically successful shows were shelved by the film companies, not re-emerging until the arrival of a completely new generation. Even the great Rodgers and Hammerstein shows were put into cold storage. *Oklahoma!*, a pace-maker and a monumental hit, took twelve years to reach the screen, *Carousel* eleven years, *South Pacific* nine years, and *The King and I* five years. *Flower Drum Song*, playing on Broadway through 1959 and 1960, came to the screen only a year later; but *The Sound of Music*, which ran concurrently with it on the stage, had to wait six years till *its* run was over (except for London, where both stage and screen versions ran simultaneously). It is hard, too, to understand why *My Fair Lady* had to wait in the wings for eight years, as did *Oliver!*, *Camelot* and *Brigadoon*. The original 1951 production of *Paint Your Wagon* was a long-forgotten event when it finally reached the wide screen in 1969; though, on the other hand, the underlying racial theme of *Finian's Rainbow* was perhaps even more

Gentlemen Prefer Blondes (20th Century Fox, 1953). Dorothy Shaw (Jane Russell) and Lorelei Lee (Marilyn Monroe) meditate on the unhappy consequences 'When Love Goes Wrong'.

Opposite: **Mame.** Ginger Rogers brought Hollywood star quality to London's Drury Lane Theatre in the 1969 production.

topical in 1968 than it had been twenty-one years before. And it may well have been the need for the emergence of a socially aware cinema-going audience that delayed Gershwin's American folk opera *Porgy and Bess* for twenty-four years, rather than its being a case of having to develop screen techniques in order to handle it effectively, for Otto Preminger's direction was as stage-bound as the original theatre production of 1935 (for his innovatory work on which Rouben Mamoulian had been acclaimed). But if we are looking for some sort of record in tardiness, the supreme accolade must go to *Song of Norway*, performed by stock companies, amateur operatic societies and in full-scale professional revivals for twenty-six years before being taken up, by way of a last fling with the genre, in 1970; and to Billy Rose's *Jumbo*, whose progress from the New York Hippodrome to Culver City took twenty-seven years!

In the process of filming an established stage success, the tendency would often be to play safe with a straightforward adaptation (the early Marx Brothers *Cocoanuts* and *Animal Crackers* were clearly little more than photographed stage performances complete with blackouts and Chico-Harpo sketches played before an obvious backdrop), and even as late as 1964 George Cukor's *My Fair Lady* proved to be identical with the stage version. Admittedly, it was a beautiful filmic record of an enchanting experience, but it owed and contributed nothing to the art of the cinema.

The resources of the cinema nevertheless offered every opportunity to broaden the scope of musicals with stage origins, and this has indeed happened on many memorable occasions. Consider, for example, the panoramic opening of *The Sound of Music*, the vitality of the 'Once-a-Year-Day' sequence in *The Pajama Game*, the superb helicopter tracking shots of 'Don't Rain On My Parade' that closed the first half of *Funny Girl*, the colour and depth of '76 Trombones' in *The Music Man*, the magnificent scenery in *Song of Norway* and *Paint Your Wagon*, and above all, the stunning vista of New York in the first fifteen minutes of *West Side Story*. Such moments added a dimension to even the most mundane musical that no stage could ever capture. There were others, many of them, but in general terms it is safe to say that the screen adaptation – even in those shows not deliberately limited by the archetypal backstage story – remained a studio product with the stage as a frame.

This was understandable in the case of the Marx Brothers films mentioned above and other early musicals, when studio facilities were limited, sound and movement techniques still undeveloped, and location shooting by second units but a far-off dream. And also at a time when film presentation of established operetta hits closely paralleled that of the stage, which provided much of the staple diet of the late twenties and early thirties. But just imagine how much more effective Stanley Donen's original and excellent screen musical of 1954, *Seven Brides for Seven Brothers*, would have been had this lusty Western not been shot against a backcloth of plastic fields and cardboard mountains. This penny-pinching (for what else can it have been?) seems all the more extraordinary when considered beside the same studio's remake that same year of the tired old celluloid veteran *Rose Marie*, in which a much higher level of realism was attained. That particular production illustrates Hollywood's affection for stage plots and music of an earlier era and its willingness to repeat them *ad nauseam* as its techniques and resources developed over the years. *Rose Marie* (1937, 1954), *The Desert Song* (1929, 1943, 1952), *No, No, Nanette* (1930, 1940; 1950 as *Tea for Two*), *Show Boat* (1929, 1936, 1951); *Hit the Deck* (1929, 1955), *The Vagabond King* (1930, 1956), *Good News* (1930, 1947), *Rio Rita* (1929, 1942), *The New Moon* (1930, 1940), *Anything Goes* (1936, 1956), *Girl Crazy* (1932, 1943, 1966 as *When the Boys Meet the Girls*) and *Roberta* (1934; 1952 as *Lovely to Look At*) all served the screen well, even into the fifties with wide screens and stereophonic sound.

GRENLAW
CHILI
DRUGS – SODA
CUT RATE DRUGS
COSMETICS
MENS

It was particularly fortuitous that MGM, having the screen rights to so many of the principal operettas, also found Jeanette MacDonald and Nelson Eddy to portray the traditional operetta characters of fluttering heroine and stolid hero. Their syrupy warbling and wooden attitudes now seem faintly ludicrous, but from the moment the two were brought together in a permanently antipathetic personal relationship in 1935 for *Naughty Marietta*, they could do no wrong in the eyes of Louis B. Mayer and the patrons of the cinema. Although both appeared with other partners in 1937, she with Allan Jones in *The Firefly*, he with Eleanor Powell in *Rosalie*, it was together that they possessed the Midas touch – for instance in such period pieces as *Maytime* and *Bitter Sweet*. When finally they essayed modern satire in *I Married an Angel* (1942) their public deserted them and the partnership broke up. Eddy's duets with Rise Stevens in *The Chocolate Soldier* and Ilona Massey in *Balalaika* and *Northwest Outpost* were less well received.

Thus ended the attempts to translate the completely artificial style of traditional operetta into screen terms, apart from those endless remakes of the perennial favourites, and such later shows as *Kismet*, *The Sound of Music*, *Song of Norway*, *Man of La Mancha*, and *The King and I*, which were rooted in the fundamental characteristics of operetta in style if not necessarily in content. In view of the enormous success of *The Sound of Music* (1,443 Broadway performances and still running at the Palace Theatre in London when the film opened in 1965), it may seem contradictory to claim that there was no public demand for operetta. After all, the film was the biggest box-office hit since *Gone with the Wind*. But this was flukish, a one-off hit that scored partly because of the topical appeal of Julie Andrews, partly because of the familiar score, partly because of the gorgeous settings and – perhaps most of all – on account of an unfulfilled demand for family entertainment.

Once in a while a stroke of boldness and imagination brought a new perspective to the screen musical. Directors like Vincente Minelli, Bob Fosse, Gene Kelly, Stanley Donen, Rouben Mamoulian, Joshua Logan and Busby Berkeley could put their own stamp of individuality on a musical whatever the source, while journeyman directors like George Sidney, Mark Sandrich, Michael Curtiz and Norman Z. MacLeod could be relied on to bring in a safe, competent and successful product. But it took a special kind of nerve to hand the filming of the epoch-making *Oklahoma!* to Fred Zinneman, whose high spots to date had been *High Noon* and *From Here to Eternity*, or to cast Otto Preminger as the guiding force behind *Carmen Jones* and *Porgy and Bess*. The dramatically charged content of the two operas made the choice of Preminger less anachronistic than it might seem at first, though it cannot be said that his lethargic treatment of Jerome Kern's *Centennial Summer* showed any natural affinity for this type of quiet, charming, period musical. Howard Hawks was another inspired choice for the 1953 screen adaptation of *Gentlemen Prefer Blondes*, in which he fully captured the mood of the Loos comedy and handled the musical set-pieces with unexpected flair.

As musicals declined in importance in more recent years it was not unheard of for fledgling directors to be assigned to them, and while George Roy Hill's *Thoroughly Modern Millie* (1967) gave the genre a temporary reprieve, Francis Ford Coppola's self-indulgent treatment of *Finian's Rainbow* made it patently obvious that contemporary camera tricks, of whatever era, are no substitute for musical expertise. With the exception of the sixty-nine-year-old Fred Astaire and the choreography of his long-time *alter ego* Hermes Pan, the general lack of talent in the production sealed the fate of this long-awaited (twenty-one years, if you recall) film of one of the Broadway stage's most whimsically charming musical plays. But then over-production and the subsequent massive budgets turned most of the later Broadway-to-Hollywood ventures into top-heavy, often leaden creations,

Opposite: **Guys and Dolls** (Goldwyn/MGM 1955). In this star-studded finale, Regis Toomey conducts a double wedding for Frank Sinatra and Vivian Blaine, Jean Simmons and Marlon Brando, with such Runyonesque guests as (l to r) Benny Southstreet (Johnny Silver), Laverne (Veda Ann Borg), Lt Brannigan (Robert Keith), Big Jule (B. S. Pully), Louie (John Indrisano), Rusty Charlie (Dan Dayton) and Society Max (George E. Stone) with, at front, a 'converted' Nicely-Nicely Johnson (Stubby Kaye).

overwhelming audiences by sheer weight of numbers, like *Fiddler on the Roof*, which plodded on for *hours*. They lacked on the one hand the directness and comparative simplicity of the Broadway stage play, and on the other the freedom and lightness of touch that the screen musical had shown it could possess in those halcyon days of the fifties when MGM had led the way.

The failure of *Hello Dolly* was undeserved, for in some ways it was the best musical of the last decade. For one thing, it was based on a hit play (Thornton Wilder's *The Matchmaker*) and a world-wide hit on stage (earning the New York Drama Critics' Award and no less than ten Tony Awards); while for another, it was produced for the screen by Roger Edens, directed by Gene Kelly, choreographed by Michael Kidd, and scored by Lennie Hayton, each and every one a veteran of those same MGM musicals. And although she was miscast in the role of Dolly Levi, Barbra Streisand was still vibrant. *Hello Dolly* demonstrated at least that star talent and behind-the-camera experience were still the prerequisites for a classic Hollywood musical.

The point was completely overlooked with such subsequent adaptations as *Man of La Mancha*, *Mame*, *A Funny Thing Happened on the Way to the Forum*, and *Camelot*. Technical considerations apart, the musical talents which could, and should, have been an invaluable crutch for such essentially *musical* productions were missing, and the lead roles, even for such a demanding score as *La Mancha*, were handed to non-singing actors. Admittedly *Carmen Jones*, *West Side Story* and *Porgy and Bess* had laid similar emphasis on actors *per se*, but skilful vocal dubbing for most of the leads created musical entities that preserved the illusion, as had the more publicized dubbing of Giorgio Tozzi's voice for Rossano Brazzi in *South Pacific*. Not to mention the ghosting by uncredited studio singers for such non-

Can Can (20th Century Fox 1960). Repeating their 'Gigi' partnership of two years before, Louis Jourdan and Maurice Chevalier sing 'Live and Let Live', one of the few songs retained from Cole Porter's stage score.

singing dancers as Cyd Charisse, Rita Hayworth, Vera-Ellen and Leslie Caron in many an important musical movie. The case of Larry Parks and Al Jolson hardly comes into this category but does show how dubbing can be brought to a fine art.

It seems merely elementary that a musical film or show should be in the hands of musical performers, but the fact appears far from obvious to the moguls. Of course there have been successful paradoxes – Rex Harrison in *My Fair Lady*, Katherine Hepburn in *Coco*, Lauren Bacall in *Applause*, Yul Brynner in *The King and I*, Richard Burton in *Camelot*, Glynis Johns in *A Little Night Music*, Robert Preston in *The Music Man*, Judy Holliday in *Bells Are Ringing* and Rosalind Russell in *Wonderful Town*. Actors and actresses of stature like these brought to their roles a brand of 'star quality' that compensated for any lack of academic musical technique, which was ably camouflaged by co-operative composers and lyricists. What these stars did, despite their musical insufficiency, was to create *the* definitive roles against which all who followed have been measured.

These were the exceptions, the rugged individualists whose success is one of those intangible factors that has always made show business so unpredictable and fascinating. But in the long term the musical stage and screen have depended for their very existence upon their musical stars, whose names are relics of what is now a bygone era. The days when performers such as Marilyn Miller, Al Jolson, George M. Cohan, Ethel Merman, Fred and Adele Astaire, and Gertrude Lawrence could fill a theatre regardless of what was being staged. When Mary Martin, Ray Bolger, Gwen Verdon, Carol Burnett, Clifton Webb, Jack Cassidy, Jack Whiting, Richard Kiley, Alfred Drake, Carol Channing, Vivienne Segal and a host of others made Broadway *their* world and established standards of performance that virtually guaranteed a good investment for potential backers. Or when the names of Bing Crosby, Frank Sinatra, Judy Garland, Gene Kelly, Alice Faye, Betty Grable, Howard Keel, Maurice Chevalier, Ruby Keeler, Dick Powell, Deanna Durbin, Kathryn Grayson, Gordon Macrae, Donald O'Connor, Eleanor Powell, Nelson Eddy and Jeanette MacDonald outside a cinema guaranteed full houses inside. But their styles and talents are no longer in vogue. They themselves grew old or rich, died or retired. Some went on into middle age recreating past glories for adoring or apathetic audiences. Some turned to character acting and gave themselves a second career in television or modern films.

Gypsy (Warner, 1962). Rosalind Russell took over from Ethel Merman as the ebullient Rose Hovick when the Styne-Sondheim-Laurents version of Gypsy Rose Lee's biography was filmed.

Indisputably show business still needs talents like these, and how much better would some of the latter-day musicals have been with them. The tragedy is that when legitimate musicals are written and produced (it still happens; the era that spawned *Hair* and *Grease* also gave birth to *A Little Night Music*, *Seesaw* and *A Chorus Line*; for every rock writer there's a Stephen Sondheim), they can attract artists of ability, but there are no longer the same Broadway or Hollywood superstars to make them memorable as in the halcyon years.

When it became evident that the 'new' Hollywood was incapable of producing musicals on the grand scale of former years (or unwilling to do so) the one-way traffic in talent, in terms of both personnel and basic material, went into reverse. In the initial exodus from the film capital were MGM's great team of dancer-choreographer-directors, personified by Gene Kelly, Bob Fosse, Michael Kidd and Gower Champion, who brought their considerable flair to the task of Broadway direction, proving as successful as they had been in their own *milieux*.

The stage also became a haven for many of the stars whose careers had suffered as a result of the decline in screen musicals, certain of Broadway's plum roles providing a great incentive for many of Hollywood's former leading ladies to polish up their old dancing shoes. A role that was particularly sought after was that of Dolly Levi during the phenomenal run of

Hello Dolly, and, following Carol Channing's original portrayal, Dolly was played variously, on Broadway and tour, by such luminaries as Mary Martin, Ginger Rogers, Martha Raye, Betty Grable and Ethel Merman, with Pearl Bailey starring in a 'black' version of the show. Mary Martin performed the part in London, where she proved she still had everything that West End audiences had come to expect when they took her to their hearts in *South Pacific* fourteen years previously. London had its first view of the legendary Ginger Rogers in *Mame* and Betty Grable in *Belle Starr*, although not even Miss Grable's reputation could stave off a disaster. Angela Lansbury climaxed her years of screen fame with the leads in *Anyone Can Whistle*, *Dear World* and *Mame*, and crossed the Atlantic to enchant London theatre-goers in the British début of *Gypsy* fourteen years after the New York opening.

Still the film stars turned their backs on a Hollywood which no longer wanted them, and found a niche in stage musicals: Janis Paige and Craig Stevens in *Here's Love*; Vivien Leigh and Jean Pierre Aumont in *Tovarich*; Katherine Hepburn in *Coco*; Shelley Winters in *Minnie's Boys* as the mother of the Marx Brothers; Lauren Bacall in *Applause*; Danny Kaye making his return to Broadway in *Two by Two*; Howard Keel and Danielle Darrieux in *Ambassador* (all nineteen performances) and Melina Mercouri in the even shorter-lived musical version of Aristophanes' *Lysistrata*; and Christopher Plummer as a musical *Cyrano*. Plus, of course, *Follies* which, in dealing with the subject of a group of ex-stars who reassemble after many years, could be said to have done a bit of typecasting with Gene Nelson, Alexis Smith, Yvonne de Carlo, Fifi d'Orsay, Ethel Shutta and Jan Clayton. Hardly in the same category but still worthy of note is the fact that even Bing Crosby, the sprightliest seventy-five-year-old in the business, made his Broadway début in his one-man show after refusing stage offers for fifty years.

Truly can it be said that Hollywood's debt to Broadway was being repaid in its entirety. Also that the New York stage, having been systematically milked of its finest product over the years, finally began to turn the tables and select (some often quite surprising) dramatic screenplays as a source of material. This was far from a new gambit, of course, but many of the films previously adapted to the musical stage had stemmed from literary sources in the first instance – for example, *My Fair Lady/Pygmalion, Where's Charley?/Charley's Aunt, Man of La Mancha/Don Quixote, Kiss Me Kate/The Taming of the Shrew, West Side Story/Romeo and Juliet, Oklahoma!/Green Grow the Lilacs, Cabaret/I Am a Camera, The Most Happy Fella/They Knew What They Wanted, Regina/The Little Foxes, Through the Years/Smiling Thru, Take Me Along/Ah, Wilderness, Kismet* and *Gentlemen Prefer Blondes*.

Now stage managements found a new ploy to entice the errant cinema audience away from all those old movies on television. The answer was quite simple: give them old movie stories on the stage, complete with new words and music. No matter how old or recent the screen hit, be it the beloved *Nothing Sacred* of the thirties or *Breakfast at Tiffany's* of the sixties, if the plot lent itself to musical treatment (even if it didn't) it duly made its appearance on Broadway. In these cases the former was transformed by Jule Styne into *Hazel Flagg*, then turned back into a film as *Living It Up* (with Jerry Lewis in a modified version of the Carole Lombard part), and the much bowdlerized screen version of Truman Capote's odd little story was staged musically under the name of its equally odd little heroine, *Holly Golightly*, failing to achieve even a fraction of the film's success. MGM's charming *Lili*, a vehicle for Leslie Caron, was a 1961 hit for Anna Maria Alberghetti as *Carnival*, while more recently the ubiquitous team of Kander and Ebb remade the early forties movie *Roxie Hart* as *Chicago* for Gwen Verdon. Musical versions of *A Tree Grows in Brooklyn, The Secret Life of Walter Mitty, Golden Boy, Gone with the Wind, The Yearling, Destry Rides*

Again and *Seventh Heaven* made the Broadway marquees resemble nothing so much as a festival of film revivals.

No movie, even of foreign origin, was so obscure that it was safe from the 'musicalizers'. The man in the street had probably never heard of Federico Fellini or *Nights of Cabiria*, but after 1966 he most certainly knew about *Sweet Charity*. And while Ingmar Bergman's *Smiles of a Summer Night* may never have played anywhere outside small art houses, the addition of Stephen Sondheim songs, especially the justly acclaimed 'Send In the Clowns', made *A Little Night Music* a stage and screen landmark. Heaven alone knows how Leon Uris's sprawling epic *Exodus* reached the stage of the Mark Hellinger Theater as *Ari* – or why. But as Uris himself adapted his book and screenplay and wrote the lyrics to Walt Smith's music, we must assume the result to be definitive. *Zorba the Greek* became just *Zorba*, *Georgy Girl* became *Georgy*, *Billy Liar* over in London was plain *Billy*, and *Auntie Mame* was familiarized into *Mame*.

Even Garbo's screen classics were not sacrosanct. *Anna Christie* was given a new look by Bob Merrill and George Abbott as the *New Girl in Town* with Gwen Verdon bringing to the role a dimension never dreamed of by Garbo, and Hildegarde Neff became the pliable Soviet heroine of *Silk Stockings*, the musical result of an assault on *Ninotchka* by Cole Porter, George S. Kaufman, Abe Burrows and Leueen McGrath. Billy Wilder's film comedies of the late fifties, *The Apartment* and *Some Like It Hot*, were so perfect in their original form that the addition of words and music by Burt Bacharach and Hal David (*Promises, Promises*) and Jule Styne and Bob Merrill (*Sugar*) respectively can only be said to have gilded the lily. It is equally speculative to say that *Applause* was better as a musical play than *All About Eve* was as a film of high-powered drama.

The list is endless, but with *Having Wonderful Time* revived in 1952 as *Wish You Were Here*, *The Fourposter* in 1966 as *I Do, I Do*, Noël Coward's *Blithe Spirit* given a new lease of life in 1964 as Hugh Martin's *High Spirits*, *The Rainmaker* in 1963 as *110 in the Shade*, *La Ronde* in 1969 as *Rondelay*, and that perennial Christmas television attraction *Miracle on 44th Street* becoming an equally sentimental *Here's Love* in 1963, the idea begins to form that Broadway was indeed turning the tables on Hollywood and proving that the film capital was far from unique in its propensity for borrowing material from another edition. A subconscious form of revenge, perhaps? The same feeling the film moguls had had decades previously that good entertainment would survive the transition between media? Or just acute business sense in attracting to New York stories and stars from the past in order to bring 'new' life to the stage? Who knows?

Big business some of these may have been, but the feeling of *déjà vu* was unmistakable, especially at a time when off-Broadway companies and theatres were experimenting with new sights and sounds – never mind how badly they may have been doing so. There must, naturally enough, always be a blend of the old and the new in whatever field of the popular arts one happens to be engaged. The tyros, novices and embryo Broadwayites should and must learn their craft alongside those of greater experience who, in turn, can prove receptive to new ideas. But when all is said and done, Theatre remains the most ephemeral of the arts. Millions who never saw *She Loves Me*, or even those thousands who did, will remember its cinematic origins with James Stewart and Margaret Sullavan in *The Shop around the Corner* or Judy Garland and Van Johnson in *In the Good Old Summertime*. Thanks to television's revival of the cinema's vintage products they will have more opportunity to remember, at least until such time as Broadway shows are filmed *in situ* so that the rest of the world may know just what a big stage musical is all about. It did happen once, when *Top Banana* was reaching the end of its run in 1953, but as described by Phil Silvers in *The Man Who Was Bilko* it was the kind of experience over which it is best to draw a veil.

9
Hollywood Original

The emphasis in this book has been on the stage rather than the more profusely documented screen musical, which the author for one has already covered in a previous work. Nevertheless, having dealt at some length with Hollywood's treatment of stage material, some attention, however brief, should be paid to the original screen musical as a tribute to the achievement of Hollywood in creating a form of entertainment that not only reaped great financial rewards but occasionally achieved the status of an art form. Despite what may have appeared to be hair-splitting in the previous chapter with regard to screen versions of the big stage musicals which, even though inviting criticism, did not necessarily affect one's enjoyment of the end-product, there remained the masterpieces. *West Side Story*, *Kiss Me Kate*, *The Sound of Music*, *Funny Face*, *On the Town*, *The Band Wagon*, *South Pacific*, *The Pajama Game*, *Bells Are Ringing* – these are just some of the Broadway-based shows whose screenings were all that could be desired in the way of a successful transfer to another medium. Yet the most notable of musical films, those we remember with nostalgia and affection, were conceived and presented in purely cinematic terms. Very seldom has there been a musical in which one could not find *something* to enjoy and remember, be it

Opposite: **Some Like it Hot** (Ashton-Mirisch/United Artists, 1959). Marilyn Monroe sings 'I'm thru' with love' – a genuinely affecting moment in one of the craziest of screen musical comedies.

Sitting Pretty (Paramount, 1933). The mirrors reveal what the fans conceal in Paramount's answer to Busby Berkeley, conceived jointly by director Harry Joe Brown and dance director Larry Ceballos.

Above: **The Golddiggers of 1935** (Warner 1935). Busby Berkeley's setting for 'The Words Are in My Heart'. The girls sat while the pianos 'danced' – a new idea for choreography!

Left: **Golddiggers in Paris** (Warner 1938). Busby Berkeley sets up one of his famous routines.

an isolated song, or dance routine, or some scene of visual splendour or beauty. In the years since the screen found its voice the original musical has taken numerous forms – subdivisions of a genre, if you like: the biopics, all-star variety shows, swing-music novelties, backstage musicals, the Busby Berkeley spectaculars, the 'star' series – Crosby, Durbin, Astaire-Rogers, Eddy-MacDonald, Faye-Grable-Ameche. They went in cycles, but as was the case with stage productions there was always the mainstream of popular entertainment and the 'standard' musical.

We have already dealt with the all-star revues which followed the introduction of sound. The first studio to use cinema as a medium for the expression of individual ideas was Warner Brothers; and the first individual to use the camera as an instrument of expression was an ex-Broadway hoofer and dance director named Busby Berkeley. Initially brought to Hollywood by Sam Goldwyn to work on Eddie Cantor's early movies, Berkeley went to Warners for *42nd Street* and *Golddiggers of 1933*, staying to mastermind a completely new concept of musical cinema and lending his name to a whole era. Except for isolated instances, dancing as such was seldom a feature of Berkeley's work. Rather, he was intrigued by formalized patterns achieved by shooting his ensembles from unorthodox camera angles; yet only rarely in the early days did he perform the role of director, being brought in purely as dance director. Suffice it to say that when the old Warner musicals surface on television screens nowadays the viewer has to endure an hour of dated trash and atrocious acting before reaching the final fifteen or twenty minutes of 'the show'. This is just how unbalanced the films were, how far from the integrated musical of later years.

While Berkeley was finding his feet at Burbank, Ernst Lubitsch was directing a sophisticated brand of musical comedy at Paramount, with

Top Hat (RKO, 1935). Fred Astaire's justly famous routine in the title song – reprised (in essence) eleven years later in *Blue Skies*.

Follow the Fleet (RKO, 1935). Fred Astaire swops his familiar tails for a sailor-suit.

Jeanette MacDonald sparkling with Maurice Chevalier in a way she was never able to do with the more stolid Nelson Eddy in the pedestrian operettas of MGM a few years later. More importantly for the future of screen musicals, at RKO Ginger Rogers and Fred Astaire came together in supporting roles in *Flying Down to Rio*. Between them they stole the film from the principals Gene Raymond and Dolores Del Rio, and in doing so established a formula for success, at the same time setting a standard for screen song and dance rarely equalled. Perhaps the story-lines of *Top Hat*, *Follow the Fleet* and others were no stronger than those of any other musical of the period, but the potency of the Astaire-Rogers partnership and the magnificent songs concocted for them by Berlin, Kern and Gershwin gave them an irresistible appeal which has not diminished with the years.

In the mid-thirties the emergence of such juvenile stars as Shirley Temple, Deanna Durbin and Judy Garland had their respective studios searching for original vehicles for projecting their talents. Temple's and Durbin's respective cuteness and sweetness failed to survive beyond puberty, and it was left to Judy Garland to become a major adult star, a commercial 'property' eventually destroyed by her own success, but one whose star quality shone in some of the finest screen musicals of all.

Many popular musicals of the thirties were built around the warm personality and persuasive singing of Bing Crosby, who introduced in them some of the best popular songs of the time. These movies enabled him to learn the art of acting and projection, which later reaped rewards in partnership with Bob Hope and Fred Astaire in some of Paramount's happiest musicals. One thinks instinctively of *Birth of the Blues* (1941), *Holiday Inn* (1942) and *Blue Skies* (1946) which, although perhaps no more than adequate as screen art, had everything a musical should have in the way of providing thoroughly enjoyable entertainment.

Wartime, and the subsequent need for escapist entertainment, brought to the screen two new variations on a theme. At 20th Century Fox an almost permanent repertory company, made up of Alice Faye and/or Betty Grable, Don Ameche and/or John Payne and/or Cesar Romero, and (always) Carmen Miranda, was employed in a succession of gay, colourful, and generally mindless confections that provided everything a war-torn populace could desire to help 'get away from it all'. And in every studio there was a recurrence of the all-star variety syndrome. Be it Warners' *Thank Your Lucky Stars* and *Hollywood Canteen*, MGM's *Thousands Cheer*, Paramount's *Star-Spangled Rhythm* and *Variety Girl*, United Artists' *Stage Door Canteen* or Universal's *Follow the Boys*, almost every one without fail ended with a flag-waving, morale-boosting finale. Here again story-lines existed only to introduce Hollywood's greatest stars doing their bit for

Follow the Fleet (RKO, 1935). Montage of Fred Astaire rehearsal shots.

Uncle Sam, and such films were less embarrassing in the context of their period and purpose than they appear now.

Biographies of famous songwriters were yet another excuse to assemble on the one hand a roster of contract stars, on the other a couple of dozen of the best-known songs of George Gershwin (*Rhapsody in Blue*, 1945), Cole Porter (*Night and Day*, 1945), Jerome Kern (*Till the Clouds Roll By*, 1946), Rodgers and Hart (*Words and Music*, 1948), Kalmar and Ruby (*Three Little Words*, 1950) Sigmund Romberg (*Deep in My Heart*, 1954), or De Sylva, Brown and Henderson (*The Best Things in Life Are Free*, 1955). The fact that the 'biographies' were almost entirely fictional did not detract from the fun; the consolation was that biopics of the classical composers were even more unintentionally hilarious. When the Hollywood scenarists turned to the life stories of performers the inaccuracies were equally glaring, but two at least are still landmarks in Hollywood musical production. These are *The Jolson Story* (1946) and *Yankee Doodle Dandy* (1942) – never mind how wildly incorrect they are concerning various personal and domestic details relating to their subjects.

A newer generation of musical stars – Frank Sinatra, Danny Kaye, Doris Day, Cyd Charisse – emerged during or shortly after the war to join the

A Star is Born (Warner, 1954). Judy Garland's rendering of Harold Arlen and Ira Gershwin's 'The Man That Got Away', one of the greatest, and last, highlights of a distinguished career.

Seven Brides for Seven Brothers (MGM, 1954). Matt Mattox rises to the occasion in the 'Barn-Raising Ballet'.

ranks of Bing Crosby, Fred Astaire and Gene Kelly in the hierarchy of great film entertainers. However ill-served by their material they may have been on occasion (and all too often even stars of this calibre, under the studio contract system, had to do their best with what they were given), they inevitably gave of their talents to the utmost, a star performance by a star being the minimum the musical enthusiast could expect.

Once in a while the musical exceeded the audience's expectations of mere enjoyment, and Entertainment became Art. Not too often, perhaps, and then mainly in the hands of Vincente Minnelli, Stanley Donen and Gene Kelly, all of whom, working for MGM under the aegis of the knowledgeable and sympathetic Arthur Freed and Roger Edens, created some of the most durable of musical films, Minnelli with his eye for colour and beauty, Donen and Kelly with their intense feeling for movement and unerring instinct for interpretating musicals in terms of the dance. *Singin' in the Rain* (1952) is generally accepted as the apogee of screen musical art, a virtually faultless film by any standards, but this does not invalidate claims which may be made on behalf of *Cover Girl*, *A Star Is Born*, *An American in Paris*, *The Pirate*, *It's Always Fair Weather*, *Some Like It Hot* or *Seven Brides for Seven Brothers*. Since the subject of this chapter is the original screen musical we must omit *On the Town* and *West Side Story*, strong contenders as they are in the overall Hollywood scene.

With films like these Hollywood can meet Broadway on its own terms as a source of great musicals. Certainly, if the true test of art as opposed to ephemeral entertainment is its ability to withstand criticism and endure in an era other than that in which it is created, then such films surely qualify. The point has been made that the theatre is the most ephemeral of arts. We must rely on our memory or at best an 'Original Cast' album or on the written word to help recapture past glories. Screen entertainment, on the other hand, can be kept encapsulated in film reels indefinitely, keeping alive hundreds of singers, dancers and others who have brought us pleasure, and enabling them to do so again . . . and again.

Above: **An American in Paris** (MGM, 1951). Directed by Vincente Minnelli and choreographed by Gene Kelly, this winner of many Academy Awards featured exclusively the music of George Gershwin. Seen here are Gene Kelly and Leslie Caron in the title ballet based on Gershwin's famous tone poem.

Who's Who of Show and Film Music

Below and on the pages following is a checklist of the careers and output of the most prolific and important writers and composers concerned in stage and screen musicals in New York, Hollywood and London. The index of each writer's works includes only 'book' musicals (both complete scores and interpolated songs), but does not preclude mention being made in the text of revues or other work.

ABBOTT, George Author, director, producer, b. 25 June 1889, Forestville, NY. Abbott received his BA in 1911 and made his Broadway début as an actor in 1913. A few years later he began writing and directing, and after establishing himself as one of the great all-round talents of the American theatre he did some of his finest work in musicals. Directed and produced many musicals, in addition to those which he wrote. Directed and/or wrote: *On Your Toes* (36); *The Boys from Syracuse* (38); *High Button Shoes* (47); *Where's Charley?* (48); *A Tree Grows in Brooklyn* (51); *The Pajama Game** (54); *Damn Yankees** (55); *New Girl in Town* (57); *Fiorello* (59); *Tenderloin* (60); *Flora the Red Menace* (65); *Music Is* (76).
*Also wrote and directed the film versions.

ADLER and ROSS Composers, lyricists. RICHARD ADLER (b. 3 Aug 1921, New York), ex-naval officer and writer of commercials, met JERRY ROSS (b. 3 Sept 1926, New York), ex-child actor with the Yiddish Theater, in 1950, and they began writing special material and popular songs. Their first stage work was for the 1953 edition of *John Murray Anderson's Almanac*, and after *The Pajama Game* (54) and *Damn Yankees* (55) they were the new white hopes of Broadway until Ross's death on 11 Nov 1955. Adler returned to television, and executive duties in Washington, his only subsequent show being *Kwamina* (61) until he returned to New York with *Music Is* (76).

ARLEN, Harold (Hyman Arluck) Composer, b. 15 Feb 1905, Buffalo, NY. Son of a cantor, Arlen was a night-club pianist at fifteen and bandleader a few years later. He worked as pianist-singer-arranger in New York bands and the orchestra for George White's *Scandals* (28). While rehearsal pianist on *Great Day* (29) he began writing songs for Earl Carroll, George White and the Cotton Club revues, progressing to his own shows. He went to Hollywood where he wrote for many films, his finest screen scores including: *The Wizard of Oz* (39); *Blues in the Night* (41); *Cabin in the Sky* (42); *Star Spangled Rhythm* (42); *The Sky's the Limit* (43); *Up in Arms* (44); *Here Come the Waves* (45); *Out of This World* (45); *Casbah* (48); *The Country Girl* (54); *A Star Is Born* (54); *Gay Purr-ee* (62). A richly melodic and inventive writer, he is often regarded as next in line outside the 'Big Five', and his occasional Broadway ventures have been artistic, if not always commercial, successes. Stage scores: *You Said It* (31); *Hooray for What?* (37); *Bloomer Girl* (44); *St Louis Woman* (46); *House of Flowers* (54); *Jamaica* (57); *Saratoga* (59).

BART, Lionel Composer, lyricist, author, b. 1 Aug 1930, London. Was working with Tommy Steele's backing group, and writing for Steele and Cliff Richard, when signed by Joan Littlewood to write for the Theatre Workshop at Stratford, East London. His first three shows were successful but his career has since followed a consistent downward curve. Wrote and composed the music for: *Fings Ain't Wot They Used t' Be* (59); *Lock Up Your Daughters* (lyrics only) (59); *Oliver!* (60); *Blitz* (62); *Maggie May* (64); *Twang!* (65); *Costa Packet* (72).

Irving Berlin (b. 1888).

BERLIN, Irving (Israel Baline) b. 11 May 1888, Temun, Siberia, USSR. The four-year-old Jewish boy whose family fled Russia started as a singing waiter and song-plugger, achieved international honours, decorations and degrees, and is probably the outstanding American songwriter of the twentieth century. Despite lack of musical knowledge, his natural instinct for words and music, and a feeling for harmony which he was able to impart to his amanuenses, enabled him to create more hits than any other writer. He contributed prolifically to Broadway shows and revues before and during World War I, and in the twenties created valuable scores for *Ziegfeld Follies* (19, 20, 27) and his own *Music Box Revues* (21, 22, 23, 24), yet he was approaching his sixties before creating the first of his greatest 'book' shows. His film scores are arguably more memorable on the whole, including: *Mammy* (30); *Puttin' On the Ritz* (30); *Follow the Fleet* (35); *Top Hat* (35); *On the Avenue* (37); *Carefree* (38); *Second Fiddle* (39); *Holiday Inn* (42), and the handful of 'specials' which drew on his enormous back catalogue for their scores – *Alexander's Ragtime Band* (39); *Blue Skies* (46); *Easter Parade* (48); *There's No Business Like Show Business* (54); *White Christmas* (54). Some of his stage shows have been less durable, but the highlights are beacons indeed in Broadway history. Stage musicals: *Watch Your Step* (14); *Stop, Look, Listen* (15); *The Century Girl* (16); *Follow the Crowd* (16); *Yip, Yip, Yaphank* (18); *The Cocoanuts* (25); *Face the Music* (32); *As Thousands Cheer* (33); *Louisiana Purchase* (40); *This Is the Army* (42); *Annie Get Your Gun* (46); *Miss Liberty* (49); *Call Me Madam* (50); *Mr President* (62).

BERNSTEIN, Leonard Composer, conductor, b. 25 Aug 1918, Lawrence, Mass. A youthful prodigy who became the all-round genius of American music. Assistant to Koussevitsky at twenty-four, the following year he was assistant conductor of the New York Philharmonic, which later became his 'own' orchestra. A prolific composer in the classical field, his love of jazz and popular music is revealed in his rare, but memorable, excursions into Broadway and Hollywood music. Stage musicals: *On the Town* (based on his *Fancy Free* ballet) (44); *Wonderful Town* (53); *Peter Pan* (54); *Candide* (56); *West Side Story* (57).

BLITZSTEIN, Marc Composer, lyricist, author, b. 2 March 1905, Phildelphia, Pa; d. 22 Jan 1964. Piano soloist with the Philadelphia Orchestra at fifteen, Blitzstein studied in Europe with Siloti, Scalero, Boulanger and Schoenberg, later disseminating his knowledge as lecturer and tutor at American colleges. He has written many film scores and classical works, plus background music for Broadway plays, but was best known initially for his left-wing *The Cradle Will Rock*, and later for his translation of the Brecht text of Kurt Weill's (qv) *Dreigroschenoper* (28). Musical shows: *The Cradle Will Rock* (37); *No for an Answer* (41); *Regina* (49); *The Threepenny Opera* (54); *Juno* (59).

BOCK and HARNICK JERRY BOCK, composer, b. 23 Nov 1928, New York. SHELDON HARNICK, lyricist, b. 27 Dec 1924, Chicago, Ill. The most successful show-writing team of the sixties began independently a decade earlier, both writing revue numbers and special material for well-known artists, before collaborating with others on Broadway shows. After Bock had written *Mr Wonderful* (56) with Larry Holofcenor and George Weiss, they began their association, which started unpromisingly with *Body Beautiful* (57), but took off with: *Fiorello* (59); *Tenderloin* (60); *She Loves Me* (63); *Fiddler on the Roof* (64); *The Rothschilds* (70). Harnick has since worked with Burton Lane (qv) on *Heaven Help Us* and with Richard Rodgers (qv) on *Rex* (76).

BOLTON, Guy Author, b. 23 Nov 1884, Broxbourne, Herts. Probably the most prolific librettist of the period from World War I to the thirties, this former architect, educated in Brooklyn and Paris, is best remembered for his association with P.G. Wodehouse and Jerome Kern (qqv), with whom he wrote the early Princess Theater shows. Musicals include: *Nobody Home* (15); *Very Good, Eddie* (15); *Have a Heart* (17); *Leave It to Jane* (17); *Miss 1917* (17); *Oh, Boy!* (17); *The Girl behind the Gun* (18); *Oh, Lady, Lady!* (18); *Oh, My Dear!* (18); *The Riviera Girl* (18); *Kissing Time* (19); *Sally* (20); *Tangerine* (21); *Lady Be Good* (24); *Primrose* (24); *Tip Toes* (25); *Lido Lady* (26); *Oh Kay!* (26); *The Ramblers* (26); *The Five O'Clock Girl* (27); *The Nightingale* (27); *Rio Rita* (27); *Blue Eyes* (28); *Rosalie* (28); *She's My Baby* (28); *Top Speed* (29); *Girl Crazy* (30); *Simple Simon* (30); *Song of the Drum* (31); *Give Me a Ring* (32); *Swing Along* (*c.* 32/3); *Anything Goes* (34); *Going Greek* (37); *Hide and Seek* (37); *Hold On to Your Hats* (40); *Follow the Girls* (44). Film musicals: *The Love Parade* (29); *Delicious* (31).

BRICUSSE and NEWLEY LESLIE BRICUSSE, composer, lyricist, author, b. 1933, London. ANTHONY NEWLEY, lyricist, b. 1934, London. A talented combination whose shows starring Newley were generally less successful than their originality warranted, but which produced some of the best British 'evergreen' songs. Stage scores: *Stop the World, I Want to Get Off* (61); *The Roar of the Greasepaint, the Smell of the Crowd* (65); *The Good Old Bad Old Days* (73); *The Travelling Music Show* (78). Film score: *Willie Wonka and the Chocolate Factory* (71). Bricusse only: *Pickwick* (with Cyril Ornadel) (63); *Kings and Clowns, Beyond the Rainbow* (78); and films: *Doctor Dolittle* (67); *Goodbye Mr Chips* (69); *Scrooge* (70).

BROWN, Nacio Herb Composer, b. 22 Feb 1896, Deming, N. Mexico; d. 28 Sept 1964. Brown was a former tailor and real-estate agent who achieved fame through his collaboration with Arthur Freed (qv) on MGM film scores from the earliest days of sound, many of which were anthologized in *Singin' in the Rain* (52). Only stage score was *Take a Chance* (32), but over thirty films included: *Broadway Melody* (29, 36, 38); *Hollywood Revue* (29); *Lord Byron of Broadway* (29); *Good News* (30); *Whoopee* (30); *Going Hollywood* (33); *Take a Chance* (33); *A Night at the Opera* (35); *San Francisco* (36); *Babes in Arms* (39); *Little Nellie Kelly* (40); *Ziegfeld Girl* (41); *Born to Sing* (42); *Greenwich Village* (44); *The Kissing Bandit* (48); *Pagan Love Song* (50).

BURROWS, Abe Author, director, composer, b. 18 Dec 1910, Brooklyn, NY. Originally a radio scriptwriter (*Duffy's Tavern*, etc), then a featured singer on television, radio and the cabaret circuit, Burrows came to Broadway in 1950 and had a smash hit with his first show, *Guys and Dolls*. A Pulitzer Prize winner for *How to Succeed in Business*, he directed his own shows as well as other musicals and plays. Directed only: *Two on the Aisle* (51); *Happy Hunting* (56); *What Makes Sammy Run* (64). Wrote *Guys and Dolls* (50); *Make a Wish* (51). Wrote and directed: *Can Can* (53); *Silk Stockings* (55); *Happy Hunting* (56); *Say Darling* (58); *First Impressions* (59); *How to Succeed in Business without Really Trying* (61).

CAESAR, Irving Composer, lyricist, b. 4 July 1895, New York. Caesar was with Ford Motors when his lyric for George Gershwin's (qv) 'Swanee' brought him to Broadway and some of the highest honours in the music business. He graduated through the *Follies* and *Scandals* to writing songs for 'book' shows including: *Dere Mabel* (19); *Good Morning Judge* (19); *Kissing Time* (19); *La, La Lucille* (19); *Dancing Girl* (23); *Betty Lee* (24); *The Bamboula* (25); *Mercenary Mary* (25); *No, No, Nanette* (25); *Betsy* (26); *Hit the Deck* (27); *Yes, Yes, Yvette* (27); *Here's Howe* (28); *Nina Rosa* (30); *Wonder Bar* (31); *Melody* (33).

CAHN, Sammy (Samuel Cohen) Lyricist, b. 18 June 1913, New York. One of the most prodigious writers of our times, Cahn has worked mainly in films and on the production of hit songs (Frank Sinatra has been his greatest sponsor). His work has been principally in collaboration with Saul Chaplin (qv), whom he met when they were dance-band musicians together (1933–43), Jule Styne (qv) (43–50), Nicholas Brodszky (50–6), Jimmy Van Heusen (qv) (56 to date). Principal screen musicals: *Anchors Aweigh* (44); *Step Lively* (44); *Tonight and Every Night* (44); *It Happened in Brooklyn* (46); *Tars and Spars* (46); *Romance on the High Seas* (48); *The Toast of New Orleans* (50); *Because You're Mine* (51); *Rich, Young and Pretty* (51); *April in Paris* (52); *Peter Pan* (53); *Pete Kelly's Blues* (55); *Serenade* (55); *Anything Goes* (56); *Say One for Me* (59); *Let's Make Love* (60); *The Road to Hong Kong* (62); *Robin and the Seven Hoods* (64); *Thoroughly Modern Mille* (67). Broadway scores: *High Button Shoes* (47); *Skyscraper* (65); *Walking Happy* (66); *Look to the Lilies* (70).

CHAPLIN, Saul (Saul Kaplan) Composer, musical director, b. 19 Feb 1912, Brooklyn, NY. Since arriving in Hollywood in 1941 to write songs with Sammy Cahn (qv) for Columbia 'B' pictures, Chaplin has been strictly a film man. As a man-about-music his duties have been those of arranger, vocal coach, musical supervisor, conductor, associate producer and producer (in various permutations) on classic screen musicals such as: *Cover Girl* (44); *The Jolson Story* (46); *Summer Stock* (50); *An American in Paris* (51); *Everything I Have Is Yours* (52); *Lovely to Look At* (52); *Give a Girl a Break* (53); *Kiss Me Kate* (53); *Seven Brides for Seven Brothers* (54); *High Society* (56); *Les Girls* (57); *Can Can* (60); *West Side Story* (61); *The Sound of Music* (65); *Star!* (68); *Man of La Mancha* (72).

COHAN, George M. Composer, author, actor, producer, director, b. 3 July 1878, Providence, RI; d. 5 Nov 1942. The original 'Yankee Doodle Boy', Cohan was the outstanding figure in the American theatre in the early part of the century and possibly its greatest all-round talent of all time. He started as a child in the family act, The Four Cohans, one of whose sketches he turned into his first stage production, *The Governor's Son*, in 1901. Henceforth his name was in lights on Broadway every year for the next quarter of a century, and even after retirement he came back to star in Rodgers and Hart's (qqv) *I'd Rather Be Right* (37). Warner Brothers filmed his biography, *Yankee Doodle Dandy* (42), but he never lived to see it. Overt patriotism and flag-waving make his shows period pieces unsuitable for revival, but he occupies an individual place in show-business history. Very much a one-man band, he wrote, composed, produced, directed and starred in dozens of revues, plays and the musicals, which include: *Little Johnny Jones* (04); *45 Minutes from Broadway* (06); *George Washington Jnr* (06); *The Honeymooners* (07); *The Talk of New York* (07); *Fifty Miles from Boston* (08); *The Yankee Prince* (08); *The Man Who Owns Broadway* (09); *The Little Millionaire* (11); *Hello Broadway* (14); *The Royal Vagabond* (19); *Little Nellie Kelly* (22); *The Merry Malones* (27); *Billie* (28). A biography, *George M* (68), used many of his old hits.

Noel Coward supervises a costume fitting for Mary Martin during the pre-production period of *Pacific 1860* (1946).

COLEMAN, Cy Composer, b. 14 June 1929, New York. A night-club pianist who was playing classical concerts at the age of six, Coleman began songwriting in the fifties and graduated to Broadway with scores for: *Wildcat* (60); *Little Me* (62); *Sweet Charity* (65); *Seesaw* (73); *I Love My Wife* (77).

COMDEN and GREEN Authors, lyricists. BETTY COMDEN, b. 3 May 1918, New York. ADOLPH GREEN, b. 2 Dec 1915. Working together since they met at New York University, Comden and Green, with Judy Holliday, formed 'The Revuers', a successful pre-war club act greatly admired by their friend and contemporary Leonard Bernstein (qv), who engaged them to turn his *Fancy Free* ballet into *On the Town*. Since then they have alternated between Broadway and Hollywood, providing original and inventive scripts and songs of unsurpassed wit and sophistication. Original screen musicals: *Good News* (47); *The Barkleys of Broadway* (48); *Take Me Out to the Ball Game* (48); *Singin' in the Rain* (52); *The Band Wagon* (53); *It's Always Fair Weather* (55). Broadway musicals: *On the Town* (44); *Billion Dollar Baby* (45); *Two on the Aisle* (51); *Wonderful Town* (53); *Peter Pan* (54); *Bells Are Ringing* (56); *Say Darling* (58); *Do-Re-Mi* (60); *Subways Are for Sleeping* (61); *Fade Out – Fade In* (64); *Hallelujah Baby* (67); *Applause* (70).

COWARD, Noël Composer, lyricist, author, actor, director, b. 16 Dec 1899,

Opposite above: **Sweet Charity** (Universal 1968). Shirley Maclaine shouts it from the rooftops that 'I'm a brass band'.

Opposite below: **Catch my Soul** (1971). Othello deals in traditional manner with Desdemona in the Prince of Wales Theatre, London, production of the rock *Othello* with Jack Good and Sharon Gurney.

Teddington, Middx; d. 26 March 1973. Probably Britain's premier theatrical talent, 'The Master' began his distinguished career as a ten-year-old actor, produced and directed his first play at twelve, wrote his first songs at fifteen and his first book at sixteen. He conquered stage and screen as an actor and author in all genres, and his many musicals and revues have contributed more 'evergreens' than those of any other British writer. As a singer he made his greatest mark with the sophisticated, highly individual delivery of his witty comedy songs. Musicals: *Bitter Sweet* (29); *Conversation Piece* (34); *Operette* (38); *Pacific 1860* (46); *Ace of Clubs* (50); *After the Ball* (54); *Sail Away* (61); *The Girl Who Came to Supper* (63); *Mr and Mrs* (68). *High Spirits* (64) was based on his own play *Blithe Spirit* (41).

DE SYLVA, BROWN and HENDERSON Songwriters, producers. B.G. 'BUDDY' DE SYLVA, b. 27 Jan 1895, New York; d. 11 July 1950. RAY HENDERSON, b. 1 Dec 1896, Buffalo, NY; d. 31 Dec 1970. LEW BROWN (Louis Brownstein), b. 10 Dec 1883, Odessa, Ukrainian SSR, USSR; d. 5 Feb 1958. All three men worked with others before and after their collaboration, and their reputation as a legendary musical team rests on the period 1925–30 when they scored several editions of George White's *Scandals* and their own shows and films, from which came their best-known songs. On stage: *Good News* (27); *Manhattan Mary* (27); *Hold Everything* (28); *Follow Thru* (29); *Flying High* (30). On screen: *The Singing Fool* (28); *Say It with Songs* (29); *Sunny Side Up* (29); *The Big Pond* (30); *Follow the Leader* (30); *Just Imagine* (30). Individual members' shows: BROWN AND HENDERSON – *Hot-Cha* (32); *Strike Me Pink* (33). HENDERSON – *Say When* (with Ted Koehler) (34). BROWN – *Yokel Boy* (with Charles Tobias and Sam Stept) (39). DE SYLVA, who went on to become producer at 20th Century Fox and Paramount, and founder of Capitol Records, wrote songs and scores for: *Sinbad* (18); *La, La Lucille* (19); *Sally* (20); *Bombo* (21); *The Broadway Whirl* (21); *The French Doll* (22); *Orange Blossoms* (22); *Sweet Little Devil* (24); *Big Boy* (25); *Captain Jinks* (25); *Tell Me More* (25); *Queen High* (26); *Take a Chance* (32); *Dubarry Was a Lady* (39); *Louisiana Purchase* (40); *Panama Hattie* (40).

DIETZ, Howard Lyricist, author, b. 8 Sept 1896, New York. A contemporary of Oscar Hammerstein II and Lorenz Hart (qqv) at Columbia University, Dietz began his career as a freelance writer in the newspaper and advertising fields. His name is imperishably linked with that of Arthur Schwartz (qv), yet Dietz, although whole-heartedly committed to the theatre, was never in the strictest sense a full-time author, his main vocation being an executive with Goldwyn and MGM, later vice-president of Loew's Inc. But even this limited activity made him responsible for more good shows and memorable songs than most. Musicals: *Poppy* (23); *Dear Sir* (24); *Oh Kay!* (26); *Queen High* (26); *Here Comes the Bride* (30); *Three's a Crowd* (30); *The Band Wagon* (31); *Flying Colors* (32); *Revenge with Music* (34); *Between the Devil* (38); *Keep Off the Grass* (40); *Jackpot* (44); *Sadie Thompson* (44); *The Gay Life* (61); *Jennie* (63).

DONNELLY, Dorothy Lyricist, author, b. 28 Jan 1880, New York; d. 3 Jan 1928. As an actress Donnelly played title roles in original performances of *Candida* and *Madame X* before turning to writing, generally in collaboration with Sigmund Romberg (qv). Musicals: *Blossom Time* (21); *Poppy* (23); *The Student Prince* (24); *My Maryland* (27); *My Princess* (27).

DUKE, Vernon (Vladimir Dukelsky) Composer, b. 10 Oct 1903, Parafianovo, USSR; d. 10 Jan 1969. Like Bernstein and Weill (qqv), Duke brought classical training and experience to bear on American popular music and thereby enriched it. Studied with Gliere and Dombrovsky at Kiev, and when his family left Russia after the revolution he settled in London and composed for Diaghilev's Ballet Russe. On arrival in New York he received his Broadway baptism via revues (*Ziegfeld Follies*, *Garrick Gaieties*, etc) and received his greatest professional boost when he completed the film score of *The Goldwyn Follies* (38) after Gershwin's (qv) death. He always led a dual existence, writing symphonies, concertos, suites, chamber music and so forth under his real name, and making Vernon Duke a hallowed stage name, although few of his shows were commercial hits. Stage shows: *The Yellow Mask* (28); *Cabin in the Sky* (40); *Banjo Eyes* (41); *The Lady Comes Across* (42); *Jackpot* (44); *Sadie Thompson* (44).

EDENS, Roger Composer, lyricist, musical director, b. 9 Nov 1905, Hillsboro, Texas; d. July 1970. Little known to the general public, Edens was probably the most influential figure in MGM musicals for thirty years. With no specific brief except to assist producer Arthur Freed (qv), he formulated musical policy, arranged, coached singers, wrote special material, adapted stage scores for the screen and eventually functioned as producer himself. Among the dozens of musicals with which he was connected in one or other, or all, of these functions, were: *Born to Dance* (36); *Broadway Melody* (36, 38, 40); *A Day at the Races* (37); *At the Circus* (39); *Babes in Arms* (39); *Little Nellie Kelly* (40); *Babes on Broadway* (41); *Lady Be Good* (41); *Ziegfeld Girl* (41); *Cabin in the Sky* (42); *For*

HOTEL MANHATTAN
"there's a girl in my soup"
NINTH FEDERAL SAVINGS

CPT. ANDY
WELCOMES
TO HIS
FLOATING
COTTON BLOSSOM

Me and My Gal (42); *Panama Hattie* (42); *Dubarry Was a Lady* (43); *Girl Crazy* (43); *Thousands Cheer* (43); *Meet Me in St Louis* (44); *Ziegfeld Follies* (44); *Good News* (47); *Easter Parade* (48); *Take Me Out to the Ball Game* (48); *Annie Get Your Gun* (49); *On the Town* (49); *The Belle of New York* (52); *The Band Wagon* (53); *Deep in My Heart* (54); *Funny Face* (56); *Jumbo* (62); *The Unsinkable Molly Brown* (64); *Hello Dolly* (69).

Opposite: **Show Boat.** One of the colourful ensemble numbers from the seventies revival at the Adelphi Theatre, London, of this much revived and much loved Kern-Hammerstein musical show.

ELLIS, Vivian Composer, lyricist, b. 29 Oct 1904, London. Possibly the outstanding British show-writer of the thirties, the erstwhile concert pianist brought charm and craftsmanship to his songs for revues and 'book' shows alike, and also wrote many light music pieces. He had a brief renaissance in the late forties with his old librettist, A.P. Herbert, under the aegis of C.B. Cochran, and when his style of music went out of vogue he turned to authorship with considerable success. Musicals: *Mercenary Mary* (25); *My Son John* (26); *Mr Cinders* (29); *Follow a Star* (30); *Little Tommy Tucker* (30); *Blue Roses* (31); *The Song of the Drum* (31); *Out of the Bottle* (32); *Jill Darling* (34); *Hide and Seek* (37); *Under Your Hat* (38); *Big Ben* (46); *Bless the Bride* (47); *Tough at the Top* (49); *And so to Bed* (51); *The Water Gipsies* (54).

FIELDS, Dorothy and Herbert Lyricists, authors. DOROTHY FIELDS, b. 15 July 1905, Allenhurst, NJ; d. 28 March 1974. HERBERT FIELDS, b. 26 July 1897, New York; d. 24 March 1958. Son and daughter of the comic Lew Fields, of Weber and Fields, Dorothy and Herbert pursued individual careers after their initial collaboration on *Hello Daddy* (28), reuniting in the forties to work with Cole Porter (qv) on *Let's Face It* (41), *Something for the Boys* (43) and *Mexican Hayride* (44). They also worked together on: *Up in Central Park* (45); *Annie Get Your Gun* (46); *Arms and the Girl* (50); *By the Beautiful Sea* (54); *Redhead* (59). Herbert was a boyhood friend of Rodgers and Hart (qqv) and after trying his luck as an actor he worked consistently with them on: *Melody Man* (24); *Dearest Enemy* (25); *The Girl Friend* (26); *Peggy Ann* (26); *A Connecticut Yankee* (27); *Chee-Chee* (28); *Present Arms* (28); *America's Sweetheart* (31). After writing libretti for Youmans (qv), *Hit the Deck* (27), and Gershwin (qv), *Pardon My English* (33), he established a solid working relationship with Cole Porter (qv) on: *Fifty Million Frenchmen* (29); *The New Yorkers* (30); *Dubarry Was a Lady* (39); *Panama Hattie* (40). Dorothy's partnership with Jimmy McHugh (qv) produced some of the best film songs of the early thirties, but she is best known for her screen partnership with Jerome Kern (qv) in: *Roberta* (34); *I Dream Too Much* (35); *Swing Time* (36); *The Joy of Living* (38); *One Night in the Tropics* (40). She continued to work on Broadway until just before her death on such shows as: *Stars in Your Eyes* (39); *A Tree Grows in Brooklyn* (51); *Sweet Charity* (65); *Seesaw* (73). Their elder brother, Joseph Fields (b. 21 Feb 1885, New York), was more successful as a playwright, but did contribute the books to such musicals as: *Gentlemen Prefer Blondes* (49); *Wonderful Town* (53); *The Girl in Pink Tights* (54); *Flower Drum Song* (58).

Rudolf Friml (1879–1972).

FRASER-SIMPSON, Harold Composer, b. 15 Aug 1878, London; d. 19 Jan 1944. British light music composer (usually in collaboration with lyricist Harry Graham), little of whose output has survived other than his settings of A.A. Milne poems and his score for *The Maid of the Mountains* (17). Other musicals: *Bonita* (11); *A Southern Maid* (20); *Head Over Heels* (23); *The Street Singer* (24); *Betty in Mayfair* (25); *Toad of Toad Hall* (29).

FREED, Arthur Lyricist, producer, b. 9 Sept 1894, Charleston, SC; d. 12 Apr 1973. He gained early experience in vaudeville with Gus Edwards and Louis Silvers, and while a sergeant in World War I produced army shows. In post-war years he managed a Los Angeles theatre and began writing songs with Nacio Herb Brown (qv for credits), resulting in an MGM contract for early talkie scores. He became a producer in 1939 and, single-handed, reshaped the entire form and structure of the Hollywood musical by signing up the finest talent available on all levels of production, creating a 'family' atmosphere and a regular production unit and, most important, through his belief that creative artists should be allowed to create without administrative interference. The results can be seen in the MGM musicals which, under his aegis, made the studio supreme in the genre: *Babes in Arms* (39); *The Wizard of Oz* (39); *Little Nellie Kelly* (40); *Strike Up the Band* (40); *Babes on Broadway* (41); *Lady Be Good* (41); *Born to Sing* (42); *Cabin in the Sky* (42); *For Me and My Gal* (42); *Panama Hattie* (42); *Best Foot Forward* (43); *Dubarry Was a Lady* (43); *Girl Crazy* (43); *Meet Me in St Louis* (44); *Ziegfeld Follies* (44); *The Harvey Girls* (45); *Yolande and the Thief* (45); *Summer Holiday* (46); *Till the Clouds Roll By* (46); *Good News* (47); *The Pirate* (47); *The Barkleys of Broadway* (48); *Easter Parade* (48); *Take Me Out to the Ball Game* (48); *Words and Music* (48); *Annie Get Your Gun* (49); *On the Town* (49); *An American in Paris* (51); *Royal Wedding* (51); *Show Boat* (51); *The Belle of New York* (52); *Lovely to Look At* (52); *Singin' in the Rain* (52); *The Band Wagon* (53); *Brigadoon* (55); *It's Always Fair Weather* (55); *Kismet* (55); *Silk Stockings* (56); *Gigi* (58); *Bells Are Ringing* (60).

FRIML, Rudolf Composer, b. 7 Dec 1879, Prague, Czechoslovakia; d. 12 Nov 1972. Coming between Herbert and Romberg (qqv), chronologically, in the production of European-influenced American operetta, Friml occupied the Broadway stage for twenty years until he found he could not adapt to changing fashion. He had studied at Prague Conservatoire under Dvorak and Jiranek and came to America as accompanist to the violinist Jan Kubelik, remaining to work as a concert pianist. He was a success with his first show, *The Firefly* (12), and continued to write consistently, if not brilliantly, in his own *métier*, with at least two outstanding shows – still performed in stock and by amateur societies. Other musicals include: *High Jinks* (13); *Katinka* (15); *The Peasant Girl* (15); *Kitty Darlin'* (17); *You're in Love* (17); *Sometime* (18); *Tumble Inn* (19); *The Blue Kitten* (22); *Rose Marie* (24); *The Vagabond King* (25); *Wild Rose* (26); *The Three Musketeers* (28); *Luana* (30).

GERSHWIN, George (Jacob Gershovitz) Composer, b. 26 Sept 1898, Brooklyn, NY; d. 11 June 1937. Gershwin may have been misunderstood and maligned by both jazz and classical factions, but in show music he was the outstanding composer (certainly the most legendary) of the twentieth century in a career that lasted only twenty years. He was dead at thirty-eight but used to say he had more tunes in his head than he could write in a hundred years. From his first song, 'Since I Found You', written when aged fifteen, to the climax of *Porgy and Bess*, the only authentic American opera, and his very last song, 'Love Is Here to Stay', Gershwin produced music that was 100 per cent American. If classicists deride the orchestral works, 'Rhapsody in Blue', 'Concerto in F', 'Cuban Overture' and 'Second Rhapsody', as hybrids, this is the way Gershwin, a first generation Russian-Jewish immigrant, saw America itself – and its music. He never followed other trends and influences, he created them. Broadway shows: *Ladies First* (18); *Dere Mabel* (19); *Good Morning Judge* (19); *Lady in Red* (19); *Dancing Girl* (22) (interpolated songs). Complete scores for: *La, La Lucille* (19); *A Dangerous Maid* (21); *Our Nell* (22); *The Rainbow* (23); *Lady Be Good* (24); *Primrose* (24); *Sweet Little Devil* (24); *Song of the Flame* (25); *Tell Me More* (25); *Tip Toes* (25); *Oh Kay!* (26); *Funny Face* (27); *Rosalie* (27); *Treasure Girl* (28); *Show Girl* (29); *Strike Up the Band* (29); *Girl Crazy* (30); *Of Thee I Sing* (31); *Let 'em Eat Cake* (33); *Pardon My English* (33); *Porgy and Bess* (35). Films: *Delicious* (31); *Shall We Dance?* (37); *A Damsel in Distress* (37); *Goldwyn Follies* (38). Posthumous use of Gershwin songs in: *Rhapsody in Blue* (biography) (45); *The Shocking Miss Pilgrim* (47); *An American in Paris* (51); *Kiss Me Stupid* (65).

GERSHWIN, Ira (Israel Gershovitz) Lyricist, b. 6 Dec 1896, New York. Although he wrote lyrics for other composers in the twenties, Ira's main concern was with his brother George's (qv) music, and once they collaborated in 1924 neither worked with any other writer. One of the four greatest lyricists of our times, Ira's audacious rhymes and play on words surely contributed as much as George's music to their perennial success. His work after George's death was extremely selective, and he worked only with such composers as Arlen, Kern, Warren and Weill (qqv), yet produced just as many great songs. Stage musicals, as for George Gershwin from 1924, plus: *Two Little Girls in Blue* (21); *Molly Darling* (22); *Be Yourself* (24); *Firebrand* (24); *Top Hole* (24); *Captain Jinks* (25); *That's a Good Girl* (28); *Lady in the Dark* (41); *The Firebrand of Florence* (45); *Park Avenue* (46). Films: *Cover Girl* (44); *Where Do We Go from Here?* (45); *The Barkleys of Broadway* (48); *Give a Girl a Break* (53); *The Country Girl* (54); *A Star Is Born* (54).

GREEN, John W. ('Johnny') Composer, musical director, b. 10 Oct 1908, New York. Leaving Harvard at nineteen with an economics degree Green went to work in Wall Street. Preferring music he started arranging for Guy Lombardo, going on to Paramount as arranger/conductor, and returning to the stage as accompanist to stars. He led his own dance band through the thirties, at which time he wrote his only stage scores, *Here Goes the Bride* (33) and *Mr Whittington* (34). He joined MGM in 1940 as conductor, becoming head of music in 1949. He was musical director on many films, including: *Broadway Rhythm* (43); *It Happened in Brooklyn* (46); *Something in the Wind* (also wrote songs) (47); *Easter Parade* (48); *Up in Central Park* (48); *Summer Stock* (50); *The Toast of New Orleans* (50); *An American in Paris* (51); *Royal Wedding* (51); *Lili* (also wrote songs) (53); *Brigadoon* (55); *High Society* (56); *Silk Stockings* (56); *Pepe* (60); *West Side Story* (61); *Bye Bye Birdie* (63); *Oliver!* (68).

HAMMERSTEIN, Oscar II Lyricist, author, b. 12 July 1895, New York; d. 23 Aug 1960. Descendant of a prominent theatrical family, Hammerstein remained the dominant figure of the Broadway stage through decades of changing fashions in music. Like many other writers he was intended for the law, but while studying during World War I he wrote Columbia University's varsity shows, then began his collaboration with his fellow writer Otto Harbach (qv), and such operetta composers as Friml, Romberg and Stothart (qqv), before commencing his memorable partnership with Jerome Kern (qv). After a barren spell in the late thirties and early forties he joined forces with Richard Rodgers (qv) on the death of Lorenz Hart (qv), and produced the most successful shows of their joint careers. His work was poetic, sometimes homely, rather than witty or 'clever', but he was always the supreme craftsman and a well-loved man. Stage scores: *Always You* (20); *Jimmie* (20); *Tickle Me* (20); *Daffy Dill* (22); *Queen o'Hearts* (22); *Mary Jane McKane* (23); *Wildflower* (23); *Rose Marie* (24); *Sunny* (25); *Song of the Flame* (25); *The Desert Song* (26); *Wild Rose* (26); *Golden Dawn* (27); *Show Boat* (27); *Good Boy* (28); *The New Moon* (28); *Rainbow* (28); *Sweet Adeline* (29); *Ballyhoo* (30); *Free for All, East Wind* (31); *Music in the Air* (32); *Three Sisters* (34); *May Wine* (35); *Very Warm for May* (39); *Sunny River* (41); *Carmen Jones* (43); *Oklahoma!* (43); *Carousel* (45); *Allegro* (47); *South Pacific* (49); *The King and I* (51); *Me and Juliet* (53); *Pipe Dream* (55); *Cinderella* (58); *Flower Drum Song* (58); *The Sound of Music* (59). Films include: *Viennese Nights* (30); *The Night is Young* (34); *High, Wide and Handsome* (37); *One Night in the Tropics* (40); *State Fair* (45); *Centennial Summer* (46).

HARBACH, Otto Author, lyricist, b. 18 Aug 1873, Salt Lake City, Utah; d. 24 Jan 1963. A former college professor, newspaper writer and advertising man, Harbach began writing for the stage while in the last job. During his collaborations with composers Friml, Gershwin, Kern, Romberg, Stothart, Youmans (qqv), and others (especially with Oscar Hammerstein II [qv], his most regular *alter ego*) he divided his interest equally between writing lyrics and libretti for: *The Firefly* (12); *High Jinks* (13); *The Crinoline Girl* (14); *Katinka* (15); *Going Up* (17); *Kitty Darlin'* (17); *You're in Love* (17); *Tumble Inn* (19); *Mary* (20); *Tickle Me* (20); *The Blue Kitten* (22); *Molly Darling* (22); *Kid Boots* (23); *Wildflower* (23); *Rose Marie* (24); *Sunny* (25); *Song of the Flame* (25); *No, No, Nanette* (25); *Criss Cross* (26); *The Desert Song* (26); *Oh, Please* (26); *Wild Rose* (26); *The Golden Dawn* (27); *Good Boy* (28); *Nina Rosa* (30); *The Cat and the Fiddle* (31); *Roberta* (33), etc.

HARBURG, E.Y. ('Yip') Lyricist, author, b. 8 April 1898, New York. Harburg started writing poetry at New York City College, but it was still a mere sideline when, having become a BSc, he started his own electrical business. On its failure he began writing lyrics and was soon a regular contributor to Ziegfeld and Earl Carroll revues, a stepping-stone to Hollywood where his famous partnership with Harold Arlen (qv) began. His many film scores include: *Take a Chance* (33); *The Singing Kid* (36); *Golddiggers of 1937* (37); *At the Circus* (39); *Babes in Arms* (39); *The Wizard of Oz* (39); *Cabin in the Sky* (42); *Ship Ahoy* (42); *Dubarry Was a Lady* (43); *Thousands Cheer* (43); *Can't Help Singing* (45); *April in Paris* (52); *Gay Purr-ee* (62). Stage musicals: *Ballyhoo* (30); *Hooray for What?* (37); *Hold On to Your Hats* (40); *Bloomer Girl* (44); *Finian's Rainbow* (47); *Flahooley* (51); *Jamaica* (57); *The Happiest Girl in the World* (61).

HART, Lorenz Lyricist, author, b. 2 May 1895, New York; d. 22 Nov 1943. Arguably the greatest lyricist of all, Hart, in his long-term partnership with Richard Rodgers (qv) (his *only* partner), produced some of Broadway's greatest shows. Even those which were not up to his highest standards had their quota of songs that have long survived their original rendering. An erudite and literate man, he was working as a linguist when he met Rodgers. Hart was a moody genius and unstable personality, yet any of his lyrics could stand today as a model for aspiring writers. There could be no greater contrast to his scintillating, acerbic wit than the warm philosophy of Oscar Hammerstein (qv), and when Hart died Rodgers's new partner caused a complete change in his own musical style. For credits see RICHARD RODGERS.

HART, Moss Author, director, b. 24 Oct 1904, New York; d. 20 Dec 1961. Hart was one of America's premier playwrights, and although he specialized in comedies rather than musicals, his partnership with George S. Kaufman (qv) producing some of Broadway's wittiest plays, his experience in this field was generally happy, with: *Face the Music* (32); *As Thousands Cheer* (33); *The Great Waltz* (34); *Jubilee* (35); *I'd Rather Be Right* (37); *Lady in the Dark* (41); *Winged Victory* (43); *Seven Lively Arts* (44). He directed *Miss Liberty* (49); *My Fair Lady* (56) and *Camelot* (60).

HERBERT, Victor Composer, b. 1 Feb 1859, Dublin, Eire; d. 26 May 1924. Herbert was the founder of the American operetta, though his work was very much in the European tradition. He began as a cellist, having studied in Stuttgart, and played with continental orchestras until he moved to New York in 1886 for a post in the Metropolitan Opera Orchestra. Appearing as a soloist with principal orchestras he was appointed conductor of the Pittsburgh Symphony, holding the post even after his first Broadway successes, and then leading his own orchestra. It may be difficult, more than half a century after his death, to appreciate his unique position in American theatrical history. Suffice it to say that he paved the way for acceptance of Friml, Romberg and, eventually, Kern (qqv), and the number of his songs which have transcended subsequent changes in musical styles is evidence of their basic and timeless quality. Musicals include: *Prince Ananias* (94); *The Wizard of the Nile* (95); *The Idol's Eye* (96); *Serenade* (97); *The Fortune Teller* (98); *Babes in Toyland* (03); *Babette* (04); *It Happened in Nordland* (04); *Mlle Modiste* (05); *The Red Mill* (06); *Rose of Algeria* (08); *Naughty Marietta* (10); *The*

Enchantress (11); *The Lady of the Slipper* (12); *Sweethearts* (13); *The Madcap Duchess* (14); *The Only Girl* (14); *Princess Pat* (15); *The Century Girl* (16); *Miss 1917* (17); *Eileen* (17); *The Velvet Lady* (19); *Angel Face* (20); *My Golden Girl* (20); *The Girl in the Spotlight* (21); *Orange Blossom* (22); *The Dream Girl* (24).

HERMAN, Jerry Composer, lyricist, b. 10 July 1933, New York. A former art student and BA, Herman started writing for night clubs and off-Broadway productions, entering Broadway in the sixties with three hit shows. Herman writes in traditional musical comedy style but, apart from catchy title tunes (*vide* 'Hello Dolly' and 'Mame'), his scores have hardly proved as memorable as the shows themselves – *Milk and Honey* (61); *Hello Dolly* (64); *Mame* (66); *Dear World* (69).

KAHN, Gus Lyricist, b. 6 Nov 1886, Coblenz, West Germany; d. 8 Oct 1941. One of the music world's most successful songwriters, Kahn began by writing special material for vaudeville artists, but working with composers Egbert Van Alstyne and Walter Donaldson put him in the big time and he worked with many of the finest composers thereafter. Many film scores include: *The Jazz Singer* (27); *Flying Down to Rio* (33); *One Night of Love* (34); *Thanks a Million* (35); *San Francisco* (36); *A Day at the Races* (37); *Go West* (40); *Ziegfeld Girl* (41). Broadway shows: *Sinbad* (18); *Whoopee* (28); *Show Girl* (29).

KALMAR and RUBY BERT KALMAR, composer, author, b. 16 Feb 1884, New York; d. 18 Sept 1947. HARRY RUBY, lyricist, author, b. 27 Jan 1895, New York; d. 23 Feb 1974. Both were in vaudeville when they teamed up to write and publish their own songs. After many single hits they began writing for the Broadway stage, including an early Marx Brothers show, which, when filmed, took them to Hollywood. Kalmar and Ruby were happy to stay there and work on many comedies-with-music by the Marx Brothers and Wheeler and Woolsey, but their most memorable work was behind them on Broadway with the scores and books for: *Helen of Troy, NY* (23); *No Other Girl* (24); *Lido Lady* (26); *The Ramblers* (26); *The Five O'Clock Girl* (27); *Animal Crackers* (28); *Good Boy* (28); *She's My Baby* (28); *Top Speed* (29); returning to New York for *High Kickers* (41). After Kalmar's death Ruby did screenplays for: *Look for the Silver Lining* (49); *Lovely to Look At* (52).

KANDER and EBB JOHN KANDER, composer, b. 18 March 1927, Kansas City, Mo. FRED EBB, lyricist, b. 8 Apr 1932, New York. Broadway's latest show-writers, they are also known for special material for among others Barbra Streisand and Liza Minnelli. Kander's first score was with James and William Goldman for *Family Affair* (62), then he and Ebb made a discouraging start with *Flora, the Red Menace* (65), a failure more than compensated for by the success of *Cabaret* (66). Subsequent musicals: *The Happy Time* (68); *Zorba* (69); *70 Girls 70* (71); *Chicago* (75); *2 by 5* (76) and the film score for *Funny Lady* (75).

KAUFMAN, George S. Author, b. 16 Nov 1889, Pittsburgh, Pa.; d. 2 June 1961. A master of comedy writing, Kaufman was a double Pulitzer Prize winner and the biggest playwright on Broadway for many years, often working with Morrie Ryskind and Moss Hart (qv). For a man who reputedly detested music in any form he wrote a surprising number of great musicals, complaining all the while because the songs interrupted his dialogue. Musicals: *Helen of Troy, NY* (23); *Be Yourself* (24); *The Cocoanuts* (25); *Animal Crackers* (28); *Strike Up the Band* (30); *The Band Wagon* (31); *Of Thee I Sing* (31); *Let 'em Eat Cake* (33); *I'd Rather Be Right* (37); *Seven Lively Arts* (44); *Park Avenue* (46); *Silk Stockings* (55).

KERN, Jerome Composer, b. 27 Jan 1885, New York; d. 11 Nov 1945. Kern was the first master of the indigenous American musical, regarded by Gershwin, Berlin (qqv) and other masters as the greatest of all. He was, in a sense, the bridge between traditional, European-based, operetta and the integrated musical, beginning in the former genre and, achieving, in *Show Boat*, the apotheosis of the latter, though some of his earlier shows had moved towards this ideal more than their contemporaries. After studying at the New York College of Music he went to London and did his first stage work, revising the score of *Mr Wix of Wickham* (04). Most of his earlier work consisted of interpolations in other writers' shows, but he finally made his mark in New York with the series of Princess Theatre musicals, written with Guy Bolton and P.G. Wodehouse (qqv). *Show Boat*, with Oscar Hammerstein (qv), was a milestone in the musical theatre, and Kern followed it up with some of his most melodious scores before going to Hollywood where he remained, returning to New York only a week or so before his death to write a proposed new show called *Annie Get Your Gun*. Musicals include: *The Red Petticoat* (12); *The Girl from Utah* (13); *90 in the Shade* (14); *Nobody Home* (15); *Tonight's the Night* (15); *Very Good, Eddie* (15); *Miss Springtime* (16); *Theodore & Co* (16); *Have a Heart* (17); *Hoop-la* (17); *Leave It to Jane* (17); *Love o'Mike* (17); *Miss 1917* (17); *Oh, Boy!* (17); *Head Over Heels* (18);

Oh, Lady, Lady! (18); *Rockabye Baby* (18); *Toot Toot* (18); *She's a Good Fellow* (19); *The Night Boat* (20); *Sally* (20); *Good Morning Dearie* (21); *The Bunch and Judy* (22); *The Cabaret Girl* (22); *The Beauty Prize* (23); *Stepping Stones* (23); *Dear Sir* (24); *Sunny* (25); *Criss Cross* (26); *Show Boat* (27); *Blue Eyes* (28); *Sweet Adeline* (29); *The Cat and the Fiddle* (31); *Music in the Air* (32); *Roberta* (33); *Three Sisters* (34); *Very Warm for May* (39). Original screen musicals: *I Dream Too Much* (35); *Swing Time* (36); *High, Wide and Handsome* (37); *Joy of Living* (38); *One Night in the Tropics* (40); *You Were Never Lovelier* (42); *Cover Girl* (44); *Can't Help Singing* (45); *Centennial Summer* (46). Many of his best songs were featured in his biography *Till the Clouds Roll By* (46).

LANE, Burton Composer, b. 2 Feb 1912, New York. Lane followed a familiar pattern by preferring music to a life in commerce and starting as a song-plugger, contributing songs to revues including *Three's a Crowd* (30) and Earl Carroll's *Vanities*, etc. At the outset Hollywood, rather than Broadway, held his interest and he contributed to many musical films including: *Dancing Lady* (33); *Kid Millions* (34); *Folies Bergère* (35); *Artists and Models* (37); *Coconut Grove* (38); *Some Like It Hot* (39); *Babes on Broadway* (41); *Presenting Lily Mars* (42); *Ship Ahoy* (42); *Dubarry Was a Lady* (43); *Thousands Cheer* (43); *Royal Wedding* (51); *The Belle of New York* (52); *Give a Girl a Break* (53). Stage musicals: *Hold On to Your Hats* (40); *Finian's Rainbow* (47); *On a Clear Day You Can See Forever* (65).

LATOUCHE, John Lyricist, author, b. 13 Nov 1917, Richmond, Va; d. 7 Aug 1956. Latouche started writing at Columbia University, where he won literary prizes and wrote a varsity show. He contributed to the pre-war revues *Pins and Needles* (37) and *Sing for Your Supper* (39), and had a Broadway hit with his first complete score, *Cabin in the Sky* (40). This was followed by: *Banjo Eyes* (41); *The Lady Comes Across* (42); *Rhapsody* (44); *Polonaise* (45); *Beggars' Holiday* (46); *The Golden Apple* (54); *The Vamp* (55); *Candide* (56).

LAURENTS, Arthur Author, b. 14 July 1918, New York. Initially a dramatist, who had his first hit in 1945, Laurents proved equally adept at musicals, his first being the great *West Side Story* (57), followed by the equally successful *Gypsy* (59). His early play *The Time of the Cuckoo*, filmed as *Summertime in Venice*, had a new lease of life with Richard Rodgers's (qv) music as *Do I Hear a Waltz?* (65), the same year as a drastic flop, *Anyone Can Whistle*. His last musical was *Hallelujah Baby* (67).

LERNER, Alan Jay Lyricist, author, b. 31 Aug 1918, New York. Half the team of Lerner and Loewe, he has his own place as an individual writer of considerable talent. Born of a well-to-do family, he studied music at Juilliard and left Harvard a BSc. Having written Harvard's 'Hasty Pudding' shows, he began his career as a radio scriptwriter, teaming up with Frederick Loewe (qv) in 1942. Since they broke up on account of Loewe's ill-health he has been active both as writer and producer. In Hollywood, apart from adaptations of his own stage shows, he wrote: *An American in Paris* (51); *Royal Wedding* (51); *The Belle of New York* (52); *Gigi* (58); *The Little Prince* (75). On Broadway: *What's Up?* (43); *The Day Before Spring* (45); *Brigadoon* (47); *Love Life* (48); *Paint Your Wagon* (51); *My Fair Lady* (56); *Camelot* (60); *On a Clear Day You Can See Forever* (65); *Coco* (69).

LINDSAY and CROUSE Authors. HOWARD LINDSAY, b. 29 March 1889, Waterford, NY; d. 11 Feb 1968. RUSSELL CROUSE, b. 20 Feb 1893, Findlay, Ohio; d. 3 Apr 1966. The best-known regular working partnership in American drama also contributed the book for a number of outstanding musical successes including: *Anything Goes* (34); *Red, Hot and Blue* (36); *Hooray for What?* (37); *Call Me Madam* (50); *Happy Hunting* (56); *The Sound of Music* (59); *Mr President* (62).

LIVINGSTONE and EVANS Songwriters. JAY LIVINGSTONE, composer, b. 28 March 1915, McDonald, Pa. RAY EVANS, lyricist, b. 4 Feb 1915, Salamanca, NY. Fellow musicians who met in a college dance band, they wrote their first songs for one of the many editions of *Hellzapoppin'*. They became contract writers for Paramount in the mid-forties, writing title themes and songs for dozens of films including *Monsieur Beaucaire* (46); *Pale Face* (48); *My Friend Irma* (49); *Fancy Pants* (50); *Aaron Slick from Punkin Crick* (51); *Here Comes the Groom* (51); *Son of Paleface* (52); *Red Garters* (54) and many others for Crosby, Hope, Martin and Lewis *et al*, collecting a few Oscars along the way. After their Hollywood sojourn they wrote two Broadway shows: *Oh Captain* (58); *Let It Ride* (61).

LOESSER, Frank Composer, lyricist, author, b. 29 June 1910, New York; d. 28 July 1969. A prolific and successful lyricist in partnership with other composers, Loesser came to Broadway fairly late in life, establishing himself as a great all-round talent, writing music to match the flair he had always shown for lyrics, finally writing his own libretti and producing not only his own but other top musicals. After a variety of non-musical jobs he started writing at twenty-one, and in 1938 became a Paramount contract writer. Much of his work was in 'B' pictures, but many great evergreens emerged therefrom, and he occasionally did such main features as: *Coconut Grove* (38); *Thanks for the Memory* (38); *Some Like It Hot* (39); *Kiss the Boys Goodbye* (41); *Thank Your Lucky Stars* (43); *The Perils of Pauline* (47); *Neptune's Daughter* (49); *Red, Hot and Blue* (49); *Hans Christian Andersen* (52). Stage musicals: *Where's Charley?* (48); *Guys and Dolls* (50); *The Most Happy Fella* (56); *Greenwillow* (60); *How to Succeed in Business without Really Trying* (61).

LOEWE, Frederick Composer, b. 10 June 1904, Vienna, Austria. The other half of Lerner and Loewe, he did virtually no work outside the partnership, and after a heart attack during the production of *Camelot* decided to retire on what must be more than merely substantial royalties. Wrote his first musical when he was aged nine, and four years later he played solo piano with the Berlin Symphony Orchestra. On arrival in the United States in 1924 he was night-club pianist, prizefighter, lumberjack and gold-miner, then came back to music in the thirties, writing his first show, *Great Lady* (35) with Earle Crooker, a fiasco that drove him back to piano playing. He met Alan Jay Lerner (qv) in 1942 and redid *Great Lady* as *Life of the Party*, which opened and closed in Detroit. At the age of forty-three he finally became a successful composer – and the rest is history. Stage musicals: *What's Up?* (43); *The Day Before Spring* (45); *Brigadoon* (47); *Paint Your Wagon* (51); *My Fair Lady* (56); *Camelot* (60). Films: *Gigi* (58); *The Little Prince* (75).

LOGAN, Joshua Author, b. 5 Oct 1908, Texarkana, Tex. A successful playwright and director, his few musicals were generally notable. Apart from directing *I Married an Angel* (38); *Annie Get Your Gun* (46) and film versions of *Camelot* (67) and *Paint Your Wagon* (69), Logan also wrote: *Higher and Higher* (40); *South Pacific* (49); *Wish You Were Here* (52); *Fanny* (54).

MARTIN, Hugh Composer, lyricist, b. 11 Aug 1914, Birmingham, Ala. Martin was yet another youthful prodigy, and was studying the piano at five. He was appearing as a singer in *Hooray for What?* (39), for which, among other shows, he did vocal arrangements, when he met Ralph Blane, with whom he wrote for the next twenty years on such screen musicals as: *Broadway Rhythm* (43); *Thousands Cheer* (43); *Meet Me in St Louis* (44); *Ziegfeld Follies* (44); *Good News* (47); *Athena* (54); *The Girl Rush* (55); *The Girl Most Likely* (57). Stage musicals: *Best Foot Forward* (41); *Look Ma, I'm Dancing* (48); *Make a Wish* (51); *Love from Judy* (53); *High Spirits* (64).

McHUGH, Jimmy Composer, b. 10 July 1894, Boston, Mass; d. 23 May 1969. One of the all-time greats of popular music, McHugh started out as pianist at Boston Opera House, a more unusual approach to the inevitable experience as a song-plugger. Wrote his first Broadway songs for *Hello Daddy* (28), but despite his early work on *Blackbirds of 1928* and the *Cotton Club* revues he found Hollywood more congenial and returned only occasionally to New York, for: *Keep Off the Grass* (40); *As the Girls Go* (48); *Strip for Action* (55). Something like forty film scores included the more memorable: *Cuban Love Song* (31); *Dancing Lady* (33); *Every Night at Eight* (35); *King of Burlesque* (36); *You're a Sweetheart* (37); *Happy-Go-Lucky* (42); *Higher and Higher* (43); *Doll Face* (45); *Nob Hill* (45); *Do You Love Me?* (46); *A Date with Judy* (48). Even when the films were less than memorable his songs never were.

MERCER, Johnny Composer, lyricist, b. 18 Nov 1909, Savannah, Ga; d. 25 June 1976. A good composer, and a superlative lyricist, daring and imaginative, Mercer did more than anyone except Hart, Porter and Gershwin (qqv) to raise the standard of literacy in popular songwriting. A more than adequate singer with Paul Whiteman and Benny Goodman and later on records with the Capitol Record Company he helped to found, he was an inimitable interpreter of his own songs, which were featured by the world's top singers. He moved with the times right up to his death and his words to Henry Mancini film-title themes gave us the best songs of the sixties. Writing for more films than can be listed here, he did some of his best work with Jerome Kern (qv) on *You Were Never Lovelier* (42); *Centennial Summer* (46); Gene de Paul on *Seven Brides for Seven Brothers* (54); and Harold Arlen on *Blues in the Night* (41); *Star Spangled Rhythm* (42); *Here Come the Waves* (45); *Out of This World* (45). Broadway scores: *St Louis Woman* (46); *Texas Li'l Darling* (49); *Top Banana* (51); *Li'l Abner* (56); *Saratoga* (59); *Foxy* (64); *The Good Companions* (74).

MERRILL, Robert ('Bob') (Henry Lavan) Composer, lyricist, b. 17 May 1921, Atlantic City, NJ. Merrill took a more unusual route to Broadway fame, as a boy actor, then Columbia film director, joining CBS-TV as casting director in 1948, graduating to television producer. It was all part of his scheme to learn the business thoroughly, and in songwriting he showed the same devious approach, churning out all Guy Mitchell's novelty hits of the early fifties. Finally he reached Broadway with: *New Girl in Town* (57); *Take Me Along* (59); *Carnival* (61); *Funny Girl* (64); *Henry, Sweet Henry* (67); *Sugar* (72).

NOVELLO, Ivor (David Ivor Davies) Composer, actor, author, b. 15 Jan 1893, Cardiff, Glamorgan; d. 6 March 1951. Britain's leading matinée idol of the thirties and forties, Novello shared with Noël Coward (qv) the distinction of being one of the country's principal actor-composer-librettists, though he seldom wrote his own lyrics, usually working with Christopher Hassall. His first big song was the World War I hit 'Keep the Home Fires Burning', and although in the next five years he contributed songs to revues and musical plays he was more interested in acting on stage and screen, and it was not until 1935 that he began his series of legendary Drury Lane musicals. Rich in melody, they dwelt constantly in the Ruritania of earlier days with the theme of unrequited love amid the crowned heads, and a permanent repertory company of leading players served them well. Musicals: *Theodore & Co* (16); *Seesaw* (16); *Arlette* (17); *Who's Hooper?* (19); *A Southern Maid* (20); *The Golden Moth* (21); *Glamorous Night* (35); *Careless Rapture* (36); *Crest of the Wave* (37); *The Dancing Years* (39); *Arc de Triomphe* (43); *Perchance to Dream* (45); *King's Rhapsody* (49); *Gay's the Word* (51).

Cole Porter (1891–1964).

PORTER, Cole Composer, lyricist, b. 9 June 1891, Peru, Ind; d. 15 Oct 1964. It was fortunate indeed for the world of entertainment that Porter, son of a rich family, who had no need to write for a living, did so. His shows were written on the sands of the Riviera and in Venetian *palazzi*, and although his world of 'gay young things' may have sometimes been reflected in world-weary lyricism, his magnificent craftsmanship and gift for melody and harmony brought a welcome air of sophistication to popular music. He wrote his first published piece at the age of twelve, and while studying law at Yale wrote many university shows. When his first Broadway show sank after fifteen performances he enlisted in the Foreign Legion, but returned after World War I to write songs for the *Hitchy-Koo* revues. Crippled in a riding accident in 1937, and suffering constant pain until an amputation twenty-one years later, he continued to write some of his most successful shows. The greatest tribute that can be paid to Cole Porter is that, although he lacked the common touch, his songs included some of the most enduring and appealing among all classes of people. Stage scores: *See America First* (16); *A Night Out* (20); *Paris* (28); *Fifty Million Frenchmen* (29); *Wake Up and Dream* (29); *The New Yorkers* (30); *The Gay Divorce* (32); *Nymph Errant* (33); *Anything Goes* (34); *Jubilee* (35); *Red, Hot and Blue* (36); *Leave It to Me* (38); *You Never Know* (38); *Dubarry Was a Lady* (39); *Panama Hattie* (40); *Let's Face It* (41); *Something for the Boys* (43); *Mexican Hayride* (44); *Seven Lively Arts* (44); *Around the World in Eighty Days* (46); *Kiss Me Kate* (48); *Out of This World* (50); *Can Can* (53); *Silk Stockings* (55); *Aladdin* (59). Original screen musicals: *The Battle of Paris* (29); *Born to Dance* (36); *Rosalie* (37); *Broadway Melody of 1940* (40); *You'll Never Get Rich* (41); *Something to Shout About* (43); *The Pirate* (47); *High Society* (56); *Les Girls* (57).

POSFORD, George Composer, b. 1906, Folkestone, Kent; d. 24 April 1976. British light music composer who wrote (often in collaboration with the author/lyricist Eric Maschwitz) a number of run-of-the-mill British musical comedies including: *Balalaika* (36); *Magyar Melody* (39); *Full Swing* (42); *Masquerade* (48); *Zip Goes a Million* (51); *Happy Holiday* (54).

RAINGER, Ralph Composer, b. 7 Oct 1901, New York; d. 23 Oct 1942. After studying law Rainger played the piano for New York shows, but eventually moved to Hollywood, where long-term contracts with Paramount and 20th Century Fox gave him and the lyricist Leo Robin (qv) a great reputation, mostly as writers of the biggest hits from Bing Crosby's earlier movies. His more prominent film scores include: *Be Yourself* (30); *The Big Broadcast* (32, 36, 37, 38); *She Done Him Wrong* (33); *Here Is My Heart* (34); *Artists and Models* (37); *Waikiki Wedding* (37); *Thanks for the Memory* (38); *Gulliver's Travels* (39); *Moon Over Miami* (41); *Footlight Serenade* (42); *My Gal Sal* (42); *Coney Island* (43).

REVEL, Harry Composer, b. 21 Dec 1905, London; d. 3 Nov 1958. The team of Mack Gordon and Harry Revel provided many film scores and song hits from 1933 to 1939, yet until Revel went to America in 1929 he was better known throughout Europe as a pianist first and composer second. *En route* to Hollywood he stayed in New York long enough to do several revue scores, only returning briefly in 1945 for *Are You with It?*. Gordon and Revel did as many Crosby film scores as Robin and Rainger (qqv), and their screen musicals include: *College Rhythm* (34); *The Gay Divorce* (34); *We're Not Dressing* (34); *Love in Bloom* (35); *Paris in the Spring* (35); *The Big Broadcast of 1936* (36); *Stowaway* (36); *Love and Hisses* (37); *Sally, Irene and Mary* (37); *You Can't Have Everything* (37); *Wake Up and Live* (37); *Rose of Washington Square* (39).

ROBIN, Leo Lyricist, b. 6 Apr 1900, Pittsburgh, Pa. A consistently efficient and tasteful writer, Robin worked with all the leading composers in show business after coming to music via the familiar route of law studies and newspaper work. The best known of his early songs were written with Ralph Rainger (qv for credits), his other notable film scores being: *Monte Carlo* (30); *Paramount on Parade* (30); *The Vagabond King* (30); *One Hour with You* (32); *Take a Chance* (33); *Anything Goes* (36); *The Gang's All Here* (43); *Centennial Summer* (46); *The Time, the Place and the Girl* (46); *Casbah* (48); *Just for You* (52); *My Sister Eileen* (55). He worked sparingly but effectively on Broadway with: *Hit the Deck* (27); *Gentlemen Prefer Blondes* (49); *The Girl in Pink Tights* (54).

Left to right: composer Richard Rodgers, choreographer Agnes de Mille and lyricist/librettist Oscar Hammerstein, a formidable trio responsible for *Oklahoma!* (1943), *Carousel* (1945) and *Allegro* (1947).

RODGERS, Richard Composer, b. 28 June 1902, New York. Until recent years, when he either wrote his own lyrics or worked with Stephen Sondheim (qv), Rodgers had only two permanent collaborators, both of whom influenced his composing style to such effect that shows by Rodgers and Hart and Rodgers and Hammerstein are worlds apart. For the urbane, witty Lorenz Hart (qv) he wrote with sophistication and wit from 1920 to 1942; in fact their *Pal Joey* (40) was as great a milestone in musical history as *Show Boat* had been. The first 'adult' musical, it inspired one critic to muse on the impossibility of drawing sweet water from a foul well. Yet three years later, after Hart's death, the first Oscar Hammerstein (qv) collaboration, *Oklahoma!*, brought a breath of fresh air and wide open spaces to the Broadway stage, succeeding musicals of theirs showing little diminution of charm and warmth. Both collaborations were right for their period, the earlier 'book' shows and the later 'integrated' musicals producing their own host of hits and evergreens, though in box-office terms Rodgers and Hammerstein were infinitely more successful. Stage musicals: *Poor Little Ritz Girl* (20); *The Melody Man* (24); *Dearest Enemy* (25); *Betsy* (26); *The Girl Friend* (26); *Lido Lady* (26); *Peggy-Ann* (26); *A Connecticut Yankee* (27); *Lady Luck* (27); *Chee-Chee* (28); *Present Arms* (28); *She's My Baby* (28); *Heads Up* (29); *Spring Is Here* (29); *Evergreen* (30); *Simple Simon* (30); *America's Sweetheart* (31); *Jumbo* (35); *On Your Toes* (36); *Babes in Arms* (37); *I'd Rather Be Right* (37); *The Boys from Syracuse* (38); *I Married an Angel* (38); *Too Many Girls* (39); *Higher and Higher* (40); *Pal Joey* (40); *By Jupiter* (42); *Oklahoma!* (43); *Carousel* (45); *Allegro* (47); *South Pacific* (49); *The King and I* (51); *Me and Juliet* (53); *Pipe Dream* (55); *Cinderella* (58); *Flower Drum Song* (58); *The Sound of Music* (59); *No Strings* (62); *Do I Hear a Waltz?* (65); *Two by Two* (70); *Rex* (76). Original film scores: *Love Me Tonight* (32); *The Phantom President* (32); *Hallelujah I'm a Bum* (33); *Mississippi* (35); *State Fair* (45, 62). Many Rodgers and Hart songs are featured in their biography, *Words and Music* (48).

ROMBERG, Sigmund Composer, b. 29 July 1887, Nagy Kaniza, Hungary; d. 10 Nov 1951. Although Romberg originally intended to be an engineer, his studies in Vienna were in the theatre rather than college, and he acquired a knowledge of operetta which he took to New York when he was twenty-two. After working in restaurants as a pianist and conductor, he became a hack writer for the Shuberts, scoring Al Jolson's Winter Garden shows among others. Finally he vied with Friml (qv) in bringing the European operetta tradition to Broadway and Hollywood, and the best known of his shows have survived in numerous revivals and amateur productions. For the screen he wrote: *Viennese Nights* (30); *Children of Dreams* (31); *The Night Is Young* (34); *Girl of the Golden West* (38); *Let Freedom Ring* (39); and he was 'honoured' with an MGM biography, *Deep in My Heart* (54). Stage scores include: *Dancing Around* (14); *Whirl of the World* (14); *Ruggles of Red Gap* (15); *The Blue Paradise* (15); *The Girl from Brazil* (16); *Robinson Crusoe Jnr* (16); *Maytime* (17); *The Melting of Molly* (17); *My Lady's Glove* (17); *Over the Top* (17); *Sinbad* (18); *Poor Little Ritz Girl* (20); *Blossom Time* (21); *Bombo* (21); *Lady in Ermine* (22); *Dancing Girl* (23); *Annie Dear* (24); *Louie the XIV* (24); *The Student Prince* (24); *Princess Flavia* (25); *The Desert Song* (26); *My Maryland* (27); *My Princess* (27); *The New Moon* (28); *Rosalie* (28); *Nina Rosa* (30); *Melody* (33); *May Wine* (35); *Forbidden Melody* (36); *Sunny River* (41); *Up in Central Park* (45); *My Romance* (48); *The Girl in Pink Tights (54)*.

ROME, Harold Composer, lyricist, b. 27 May 1908, Hartford, Conn. Rome studied law at Yale, where playing the piano with the university orchestra gave him a taste for music. His first break was writing songs for the revue *Pins and Needles* (37), which was followed by others; but the war intervened and his initial Broadway success was *Call Me Mister* (46), based on his own and others' army demobilization. He continued writing revues and finally emerged into full-scale musicals with: *Wish You Were Here* (52); *Fanny* (54); *Destry Rides Again* (59); *I Can Get It for You Wholesale* (62); *The Zulu and the Zayda* (65); *Gone with the Wind* (72).

SCHERTZINGER, Victor Composer, film director, b. 8 Apr 1890, Mahanoy City, Pa; d. 26 Oct 1941. Although he conducted Broadway musicals in his early days Schertzinger was strictly a Hollywood musician, and wrote one of the first musical scores for a silent film. Originally a violin soloist he played with Victor Herbert's (qv) orchestra at the age of eight and studied in Brussels, giving concerts in Europe and on his return home. He directed many films and wrote scores for these among other musicals: *The Love Parade* (29); *Heads Up* (30); *One Night of Love* (34); *Love Me Forever* (35); *Something to Sing About* (37); *The Road to Singapore* (40); *Rhythm on the River* (40); *Kiss the Boys Goodbye* (41); *The Fleet's In* (42).

SCHMIDT and JONES HARVEY SCHMIDT, composer, b. 12 Sept 1929, Dallas, Tex. TOM JONES, lyricist, b. 17 Feb 1928, Littlefield, Tex. Meeting at the University of Texas, Schmidt and Jones wrote college shows, graduating to night-club revues and special material for stage and cabaret performers. Their first New York show was *The Fantasticks* (60), an off-Broadway production which set new records for durability, its run extending to the mid-seventies. This was followed by: *110 in the Shade* (63); *I Do, I Do* (68); *Celebration* (69).

SCHWARTZ, Arthur Composer, b. 25 Nov 1900, Brooklyn, NY. Unlike many other writers who studied law *en route* to show business, Schwartz actually practised for four years, until spare-time work as an accompanist to silent movies, and the interpolation of individual songs in *Poppy* (23), *Dear Sir* (24) and *Grand Street Follies* (25), turned the lawyer into a full-time composer. He and lyricist Howard Dietz (qv) started with revues but soon graduated to 'book' shows and radio's *Gibson Family* serial. The team split up in the late thirties and thereafter Schwartz added stage and screen producing to his activities, writing many film scores until his return to Broadway in the fifties. Stage scores: *Here Comes the Bride* (30); *Three's a Crowd* (30); *The Band Wagon* (31); *Flying Colors* (32); *Revenge with Music* (34); *Virginia* (37); *Between the Devil* (38); *Stars in Your Eyes* (39); *Park Avenue* (46); *A Tree Grows in Brooklyn* (51); *By the Beautiful Sea* (54); *The Gay Life* (61); *Jennie* (63). In films, he produced: *Cover Girl* (44); *Night and Day* (45); and he wrote scores for, among others: *Follow the Leader* (30); *Under Your Spell* (36); *Thank Your Lucky Stars* (also prod.) (43); *The Time, the Place and the Girl* (46); *Dancing in the Dark* (49); *Excuse My Dust* (51).

SHERMAN, Richard M. and Robert B. Songwriters. RICHARD M., b. 12 June 1928. ROBERT B., b. 19 Dec 1925, New York. Their father was Al Sherman, who wrote many songs for Ziegfeld's *Follies*, George White's *Scandals*, and Earl Carroll's *Vanities*, so their musical heritage was never in doubt. They have been the principal composers of film songs in the sixties and seventies, initially under contract to Disney. Films: *In Search of the Castaways* (63); *Summer Magic* (63); *Mary Poppins* (64); *The Happiest Millionaire* (67); *Jungle Book* (67); *Chitty Chitty Bang Bang* (68); *The One and Only Genuine Original Family Band* (68); *The Aristocats* (70); *Bedknobs and Broomsticks* (71); *Charlotte's Web* (73); *Tom Sawyer* (73); *Huckleberry Finn* (74); *The Slipper and the Rose* (76).

SLADE, Julian Composer, b. 28 May 1930, London. Slade began writing musicals at Cambridge, and while musical director at the Bristol Old Vic he composed incidental music for various plays, also original musicals, one of which, *Salad Days*, came to the West End with a success (2,283 performances and numerous revivals) surprising for a show so obviously dated in theme and musical content. Subsequent musicals (many written with the actress Dorothy Reynolds, b. 1913) have followed a similar pattern. Musicals: *Salad Days* (54); *The Duenna* (54); *Fresh as Air* (57); *Follow That Girl* (60); *Hooray for Daisy* (60); *Wildest Dreams* (61); *Trelawney* (72).

SONDHEIM, Stephen Composer, lyricist, author, b. 22 March 1930, New York. Sondheim wrote his first musical at the age of fifteen and showed it to Oscar Hammerstein (qv). From then until his death Hammerstein encouraged the boy with advice, giving him a job in his office when he was seventeen, and there Sondheim learned the business. As a television scriptwriter he wrote the 'Topper' series, then a meeting with Arthur Laurents (qv) in search of a lyricist for *West Side Story* brought him both a collaborator and a Broadway career. In great demand as a lyricist he prefers to write his own music, but still works with other top composers given sufficient incentive. Stage scores: *West Side Story* (57); *Gypsy* (62); *A Funny Thing Happened on the Way to the Forum* (62); *Anyone Can Whistle* (64); *Do I Hear a Waltz?* (65); *Company* (70); *Follies* (71); *A Little Night Music* (73); *Pacific Overtures* (76).

STOTHART, Herbert Composer, musical director, b. 11 Sept 1885, Milwaukee, Wis; d. 1 Feb 1949. After studying music in Europe Stothart taught it at the University of Wisconsin, before becoming a Broadway conductor. He also wrote songs for: *Katinka* (15); *Somebody's Sweetheart* (18); *Always You* (20); *Tickle Me* (20); *Daffy Dill* (22); *Mary Jane McKane* (23); *Wildflower* (23); *Rose Marie* (24); *Song of the Flame* (25); *Golden Dawn* (27); *Good Boy* (28). He then went to Hollywood on an MGM contract and was the composer of many dramatic scores, writer of songs for the musicals *Cuban Love Song* (30) and *A Lady's Morals* (30), and musical director of Eddy-MacDonald and other operetta-type musicals.

STROUSE and ADAMS CHARLES STROUSE, composer, b. 7 June 1929, New York. LEE ADAMS, lyricist, b. 14 Aug 1924. Mansfield, Ohio. Strouse studied at Tanglewood with Aaron Copland and in Paris with Nadia Boulanger, while Adams graduated from the Columbia School of Journalism. They met in 1950 and began writing popular songs and summer-resort shows, special material for night-club acts and, finally, off-Broadway revues. They wrote one screen musical: *The Night They Raided Minsky's* (68); and, on Broadway: *Bye Bye Birdie* (60); *All-American* (62); *Golden Boy* (64); *It's a Bird, It's a Plane, It's Superman* (66); *Applause* (70); *Six* (71); *I and Albert* (72); Strouse only: *Annie* (W. Martin Charnin) (77).

STYNE, Jule Composer, b. 31 Dec 1905, London. One of the most prolific of Broadway and Hollywood writers, Styne was yet another child prodigy, performing as piano soloist with the Chicago and Detroit Symphony Orchestras before reaching his teens, and going on to win the Mozart Award at the Chicago College of Music. A bandleader at twenty-six, he joined 20th Century Fox as musical associate, moving to Republic, where he churned out 'B' movie scores before teaming up with lyricist Sammy Cahn (qv). Thereafter his standard of employment rose considerably, involving such major film scores as: *Step Lively* (44); *Anchors Aweigh* (44); *It Happened in Brooklyn* (46); *The Kid from Brooklyn* (46); *Romance on the High Seas* (48); *It's a Great Feeling* (49); *West Point Story* (50); and many Sinatra record hits. He turned to Broadway late in the forties and thereafter concentrated on the stage as composer and producer, often in collaboration with Comden and Green (qv). Broadway scores: *High Button Shoes* (47); *Gentlemen Prefer Blondes* (49); *Hazel Flagg* (53); *Peter Pan* (54); *Bells Are Ringing* (56); *Say Darling* (58); *Gypsy* (59); *Do-Re-Mi* (60); *Subways Are for Sleeping* (61); *Fade Out – Fade In* (64); *Funny Girl* (64); *Hallelujah Baby* (67); *Look to the Lilies* (70); *Sugar* (72); *Bar Mitzvah Boy* (78).

TIERNEY, Harry Composer, b. 21 May 1895, Perth Amboy, NJ; d. 22 March 1965. A former concert pianist and publisher's staff writer, Tierney began contributing to revues in London and New York, and was then signed up by Ziegfeld to write songs for his *Follies* and complete musical scores. After supervising two of his film scores in Hollywood he returned to find Ziegfeld in a decline and that his music was considered dated. Stage scores: *Afgar* (19); *Irene* (19); *The Royal Vagabond* (19); *The Broadway Whirl* (21); *Up She Goes* (22); *Glory* (22); *Kid Boots* (23); *Rio Rita* (27); *Cross My Heart* (28).

VAN HEUSEN, Jimmy (Edward Chester Babcock) Composer, b. 26 Jan 1913, Syracuse, NY. With the lyricist Johnny Burke Van Heusen wrote most of Bing Crosby's best songs of the period 1940–52, and with Sammy Cahn (qv) most of Frank Sinatra's in subsequent years, two fruitful collaborations which have accounted for most of his career. This started at sixteen, when he worked as a radio announcer and entertainer, then as a pianist and staff writer at Remick's with Eddie De Lange, winding up in Hollywood with Paramount for which he scored such musicals as the Crosby-Hope *Road* series, and: *Love Thy Neighbour* (40); *Dixie* (43); *Lady in the Dark* (43); *And the Angels Sing* (44); *Belle of the Yukon* (44); *Going My Way* (44); *The Bells of St Mary's* (45); *Welcome Stranger* (47); *A Connecticut Yankee* (48); *Mr Music* (50); *Anything Goes* (56); *The Joker Is Wild* (57); *Say One for Me* (59); *Let's Make Love* (60); *Robin and the Seven Hoods* (64); *Thoroughly Modern Millie* (67). Broadway shows: *Swingin' the Dream* (39); *Nellie Bly* (46); *Carnival in Flanders* (53); *Skyscraper* (65); *Walking Happy* (66).

WARREN, Harry (Salvatore Guaragne) Composer, b. 24 Dec 1893, Brooklyn, NY. While his only 'book' show was an unsuccessful version of *Lost Horizon* called *Shangri-La* (56), Warren must be regarded as one of the greatest composers of film songs, initially with Al Dubin in the Warner/Busby Berkeley era of the thirties, with Mack Gordon in 20th Century Fox's wartime extravaganzas, and with other lyricists in work for MGM in the forties and fifties. After a varied career as a carnival drummer, silent-movie pianist and song-plugger he wrote popular songs, and contributed numbers to Billy Rose revues. Darryl F. Zanuck brought him to Hollywood, where he remained permanently to write some sixty-six screen musicals. High spots among these were: the *Golddiggers* series; *Footlight Parade* (33); *42nd Street* (33); *Dames* (34); *Moulin Rouge* (34); *Wonder Bar* (34); *Go Into Your Dance* (35); *Mr Dodd Takes the Air* (37); *Going Places* (38); *Hard to Get* (38); *Honolulu* (39); *Naughty but Nice* (39); *Down Argentine Way* (40); *Tin Pan Alley* (40); *Sun Valley Serenade* (41); *That Night in Rio* (41); *Weekend in Havana* (41); *Iceland* (42); *Orchestra Wives* (42); *The Gang's All Here* (43); *Hello Frisco, Hello* (43); *Diamond Horseshoe* (45); *The Harvey Girls* (45); *Yolande and the Thief* (45); *Summer Holiday* (46); *The Barkleys of Broadway* (48); *Summer Stock* (50); *The Belle of New York* (52); *Just for You* (52).

WEILL, Kurt Composer, b. 2 March 1900, Dessau, East Germany; d. 3 Apr 1950. At ten Weill was accompanist at the court of the Duke of Anhalt, and at fifteen he was choral director at Dessau Opera House. He studied with Humperdinck and Busoni in Berlin and wrote his first opera at the age of twenty-four, his early work bearing a superficial resemblance to the sort of jazz he would have heard then. His big success was *Die Dreigroschenoper*, a 1928 version of *The Beggar's Opera* with text by Bertolt Brecht, which ran in Germany for over 4,000 performances. The new Nazi Party opposed their later work and in 1933 Weill fled to Paris. When he arrived on Broadway he rapidly assimilated the modern American style, and there is little trace of his Germanic pseudo-jazz writing in: *Johnny Johnson* (36); *Knickerbocker Holiday* (38); *Lady in the Dark* (41); *One Touch of Venus* (43); *The Firebrand of Florence* (45); *Street Scene* (47); *Love Life* (48); *Lost in the Stars* (49); or in his screen scores for: *The Goldwyn Follies* (38); *You and Me* (38); *Where Do We Go from Here?* (45). After his death his widow, Lotte Lenya, revived *The Threepenny Opera* in a 1954 off-Broadway production which ran for 2,707 performances, a record at that time.

WHITING, Richard A. Composer, b. 12 Nov 1891, Peoria, Ill; d. 10 Feb 1938. A self-taught pianist and failed vaudeville performer, Whiting joined Remick's as professional manager. After writing for revues and one musical, *Take a Chance* (32), he settled in Hollywood to write musicals including: *Monte Carlo* (30); *Paramount on Parade* (30); *Playboy of Paris* (30); *One Hour with You* (32); *Big Broadcast of 1936* (36); *Rhythm on the Range* (36); *Sing Baby Sing* (36); *Hollywood Hotel* (37); *Ready, Willing and Able* (37); *The Varsity Show* (37).

WILLSON, Meredith Composer, lyricist, author, conductor, b. 18 May 1902. Willson was fifty-five before he wrote his first Broadway show, but he had a long and distinguished career, from his days as principal flute with Sousa's band and the New York Philharmonic, through his duties in the AFRS in World War II, to his main career as a top-line radio conductor. Broadway scores: *The Music Man* (57); *The Unsinkable Molly Brown* (60); *Here's Love* (63).

WILSON, Sandy Composer, lyricist, author, b. 19 May 1924, Sale, Cheshire. Along with Julian Slade (qv) Wilson was responsible for the West End revival of musical comedy styles of previous decades. He never repeated the fantastic success of *The Boy Friend* (54), which went from little theatre to West End to wide screen, and which had more than mere 'camp' appeal. Other shows: *The Buccaneer* (55); *Valmouth* (58); *Call It Love* (60); *Divorce Me Darling* (65).

WODEHOUSE, Pelham Grenville (P.G.) Author, lyricist, b. 15 Oct 1881, Guildford, Surrey; d. 1976. Although Britain's best-selling humorous author, it is not generally known that P.G. Wodehouse was very much a part of Broadway in his early years, with his songs and libretti for shows by Friml, Gershwin, Porter and Romberg (qqv). His greatest achievement was his collaboration with Guy Bolton and Jerome Kern (qqv), beginning with the Princess Theater shows which established Kern. Musicals: *Miss Springtime* (16); *Have a Heart* (17); *Leave It to Jane* (17); *Miss 1917* (17); *Oh, Boy!* (17); *The Girl Behind the Gun* (18); *Oh, Lady, Lady!* (18); *Oh, My Dear!* (18); *The Riviera Girl* (18); *Kissing Time* (19); *Sally* (20); *The Golden Moth* (21); *The Cabaret Girl* (22); *The Beauty Prize* (23); *Sitting Pretty* (24); *Oh Kay!* (26); *The Nightingale* (27); *Show Boat* (27); *Rosalie* (28); *The Three Musketeers* (28); *Hearts and Diamonds* (30); *Anything Goes* (34).

WRIGHT and FORREST ROBERT CRAIG ('BOB') WRIGHT, b. 25 Sept 1914, Daytona Beach, Fla. GEORGE ('CHET') FORREST, b. 31 July 1915, Brooklyn, NY. Joint composers, lyricists and authors, Wright and Forrest first came together as boys. They have made a successful team, yet have seldom produced original musicals. Under a long-term MGM contract in the thirties they specialized in updating operetta scores for cinema consumption – for example, *Maytime* (37); *Sweethearts* (38); *Let Freedom Ring* (39); *Balalaika* (39); *The New Moon* (40); *I Married an Angel* (42). On Broadway they limited their activity to creating musical comedy scores by long-dead composers: *Song of Norway* (Grieg) (44); *Gypsy Lady* (Herbert) (46); *Magdalena* (Villa-Lobos) (48); *Kismet* (Borodin) (53); *Anya* (Rachmaninov) (65); *The Great Waltz* (Strauss) (70). *Kean* (61) was original but never achieved success.

YOUMANS, Vincent Composer, b. 27 Sept 1898, New York; d. 5 Apr 1946. The ill-health which cut short his career prevented Youmans from being an all-time great of popular music, but the work he did in a twelve-year span gave us enough fine songs to warrant his acceptance as a legendary figure. He began writing in the US Navy in 1916 while producing service shows. After the war his fellow song-plugger at Harms Inc was George Gershwin (qv), who helped him to a job as Victor Herbert's (qv) rehearsal pianist. His first show was a hit, and he worked steadily on Broadway in the twenties with: *A Night Out* (20); *Two Little Girls in Blue* (21); *Mary Jane McKane* (23); *Wildflower* (23); *No, No, Nanette* (25); *Oh Please* (26); *Hit the Deck* (27); *Rainbow* (28); *Great Day* (29); *Smiles* (30); *Take a Chance* (32); *Through the Years* (32). His only film score was the memorable *Flying Down to Rio* (33), prior to his permanent retirement in a TB sanatorium.

Musical Calendar 1866–1979

Purely for the sake of completeness, and to give some idea of the genesis of the modern (i.e. post-1919) musical as discussed throughout the book, the musical calendar is prefaced by a less comprehensively documented list of the earlier shows in New York and London.

Broadway		**London**
The Black Crook	1866	
Humpty Dumpty	1868	
	1871	*Thespis*
Evangeline	1874	
	1875	*Trial by Jury*
	1877	*The Sorcerer*
	1878	*HMS Pinafore*
The Brook; *The Pirates of Penzance*	1879	
	1881	*Patience*
	1882	*Iolanthe*
Adonis	1884	*Princess Ida*
	1885	*The Mikado*
The Little Tycoon	1887	*Ruddigore*
	1888	*The Yeoman of the Guard*
	1889	*The Gondoliers*
Castles in the Air; *Robin Hood*	1890	*Ivanhoe*
Wang	1891	
The Isle of Champagne; *The Knickerbockers*	1892	*Utopia Limited*
The Glassblowers; *A Trip to Chinatown*	1893	*A Gaiety Girl*
Prince Ananias; *Rob Roy*	1894	*Mirette*; *The Shop Girl*
Princess Bonnie; *The Wizard of the Nile*	1895	
El Capitan; *The Idol's Eye*	1896	*An Artist's Model*; *The Circus Girl*; *The Geisha*
The Belle of New York; *The Bride Elect*; *The Highwayman*; *Serenade*	1897	
The Fortune Teller	1898	*A Greek Slave*

A Gaiety Girl (1893). An artist's impression of (left to right) Blanche Massey, Grace Palotta, Florence Lloyd and Violet Robinson, used as programme cover for the well-remembered Prince of Wales Theatre musical comedy by Sidney Jones, Percy Greenbank and Owen Hall.

Broadway		London
The Belle of Bohemia; The Casino Girl	1900	*Floradora*
The Governor's Son; The Strollers	1901	*The Silver Slipper*
A Chinese Honeymoon; King Dodo	1902	*The Country Girl; Merrie England; Three Little Maids*
Babes in Toyland; A Guest of Honour; In Dahomey; The Prince of Pilsen; The Red Feather; The Runaways	1903	*The Cherry Girl; The Duchess of Danzig; The Earl and the Girl; My Lady Molly; The Schoolgirl*
Babette; It Happened in Nordland; Little Johnny Jones; Mr Wix of Wickham; Piff, Paff, Pouf; The Sho-Gun; Woodland	1904	*The Cingalee; Lady Madcap*
Fantana; The Ham Tree; Lifting the Lid; Mlle Modiste	1905	*The Blue Moon*
45 Minutes from Broadway; George Washington Jnr; A Parisian Model; The Red Mill; The Rich Mr Hoggenheimer	1906	*The Belle of Mayfair; The Dairymaids*
The Grand Mogul; The Honeymooners; The Merry Widow; The Talk of New York	1907	*The Girls of Gottenburg; Tom Jones*
Fifty Miles from Boston; Marcelle; Rose of Algeria; The Three Twins; A Waltz Dream; The Yankee Prince	1908	*The Belle of Brittany; Havana*
A Broken Doll; The Fair Co-ed; In Hayti; The Man Who Owns Broadway	1909	*The Arcadians; The Dollar Princess; Our Miss Gibbs*
Girlies; Madame Sherry; Naughty Marietta; The Old Town; The Social Whirl; The Summer Widowers	1910	*The Balkan Princess; Captain Kidd; The Girl in the Train; The Quaker Girl; The Slim Princess*
La Belle Paree; The Enchantress; The Happiest Night of His Life; The Hen Pecks; The Little Millionaire; The Pink Lady; Treemonisha; Vera Violetta	1911	*Castles in the Air; Peggy*
The Firefly; The Gipsy; The Lady of the Slipper; Oh, Oh, Delphine!; The Red Petticoat; Wall Street Whirl; The Whirl of Society	1912	*The Dancing Mistress; The Dancing Viennese; The Girl in the Taxi; The Sunshine Girl*
An American Maid; Her Little Highness; Honeymoon Express; High Jinks; Somewhere Else; The Sunshine Girl; Sweethearts	1913	*The Girl from Utah; Love and Laughter*
Chin Chin; The Crinoline Girl; The Madcap Duchess; 90 in the Shade; The Only Girl; Watch Your Step; When Claudia Smiles	1914	*After the Girl; Mam'selle Tra-La-La*
The Blue Paradise; Katinka; Nobody Home; The Peasant Girl; The Princess Pat; Ruggles of Red Gap; Stop! Look! Listen!; Very Good, Eddie	1915	*Betty; Bric-a-Brac; The Light Blues; Tina; Tonight's the Night*
Betty; The Century Girl; Flora Bella; Follow Me; The Girl from Brazil; Miss Springtime; Pom Pom; Robinson Crusoe Jnr; See America First; So Long, Letty; Sybil	1916	*Blighty; Chu Chin Chow; Follow the Crowd; The Happy Day; Houp-la; Seesaw; Theodore & Co; Toto; Young England*

Broadway		London
Eileen; *Going Up*; *Have a Heart*; *Hoop-la*; *Kitty Darlin'*; *Leave It to Jane*; *Love o' Mike*; *Maytime*; *The Melting of Molly*; *Miss 1917*; *My Lady's Glove*; *Oh, Boy!*; *Over the Top*; *You're in Love*	1917	*Arlette*; *The Better 'ole*; *The Boy*; *The Maid of the Mountains*; *Round the Map*; *Suzette*; *Yes, Uncle*
The Girl Behind the Gun; *Head over Heels*; *Ladies First*; *Listen Lester*; *Oh, Lady, Lady!*; *Oh, Look!*; *Oh, My Dear!*; *The Riviera Girl*; *Rockabye Baby*; *Sinbad*; *Somebody's Sweetheart*; *Sometime*; *Toot Toot*; *Yip, Yip, Yaphank*	1918	*Flora*; *The Lilac Domino*; *The Officers' Mess*

It is impracticable to list every musical ever performed in London and New York, many of which lasted only a matter of weeks (even nights in some cases), but an attempt has been made to list opening dates of and theatres used for all the principal 'book' musicals of any importance. Revues and foreign (i.e. non-English) operettas are excluded, as well as revivals. The productions listed are those of the original performances in the country of origin, dates in parentheses indicating transatlantic versions.

1919

Feb 3 *The Velvet Lady*
Feb 6 *Good Morning Judge* Shubert
Feb 17 *The Royal Vagabond* Cohan and Harris
March 24 *Tumble Inn* Selwyn
May 5 *She's a Good Fellow* Globe
May 12 *The Lady in Red* Lyric
May 26 *La, La Lucille* Henry Miller
June 7 *Lonely Romeo* Shubert
Oct 7 *Apple Blossoms* Globe
Nov 18 *Irene* Vanderbilt

Apr 19 *Monsieur Beaucaire* Princes
May 20 *Kissing Time* Winter Garden (NY, 1918)
Sept 13 *Who's Hooper?* Adelphi
Sept 17 *Afgar* Pavilion (NY, 1920)
Sept 27 *Baby Bunting* Shaftesbury

1920

Jan 5 *Always You*
Feb 2 *The Night Boat* Liberty
July 28 *Poor Little Ritz Girl*
Aug 17 *Tickle Me* Selwyn
Aug 31 *Sweetheart Shop* Knickerbocker
Sept 6 *Honeydew* Casino
Oct 5 *Tip-Top* Globe
Oct 18 *Mary* Knickerbocker (Queen's, London, 1921)
Dec 22 *Sally* New Amsterdam (Winter Garden, London, 10 Sept 1921)

Feb 3 *Pretty Peggy* Princes
Feb 12 *Wild Geese* Comedy
May 15 *A Southern Maid* Daly's
Sept 18 *A Night Out* Winter Garden

1921

May 3 *Two Little Girls in Blue* Cohan
May 10 *The Last Waltz* Century (Gaiety, London, 1922)
May 23 *Shuffle Along* 63rd Street
June 8 *The Broadway Whirl* Times Square
Aug 9 *Tangerine* Casino
Sept 29 *Blossom Time* Ambassador
Oct 4 *The Love Letter* Globe
Oct 6 *Bombo* Jolson
Nov 1 *Good Morning Dearie* Globe

March 12 *The Rebel Maid* Empire
Oct 5 *The Golden Moth* Adelphi

1922

Broadway		London	
Jan 13	*The Blue Kitten* Selwyn (Gaiety, London, 23 Dec 1925)	Feb 10	*Jenny* Empire
Feb 20	*For Goodness' Sake* Lyric (as *Stop Flirting* Shaftesbury, London, 30 May 1923)	Feb 21	*The Lady of the Rose* Daly's (as *Lady in Ermine* Ambassador, NY, 2 Oct 1922)
Feb 20	*The French Doll* Lyceum	Sept 6	*The Smith Family* Empire
Aug 22	*Daffy Dill*	Sept 19	*The Cabaret Girl* Winter Garden
Aug 28	*The Gingham Girl* Earl Carroll	Dec 8	*Battling Butler* New Oxford
Sept 1	*Molly Darling*	Dec 22	*Lilac Time* Lyric (*Blossom Time*, 1921)
Sept 4	*Sally, Irene and Mary* Casino		
Sept 19	*Orange Blossoms* Fulton		
Nov 6	*Up She Goes* Playhouse		
Nov 13	*Little Nellie Kelly* Liberty (New Oxford, London, 2 July 1923)		
Nov 28	*The Bunch and Judy* Globe		
Dec 4	*Our Nell* Nora Bayes		

1923

Broadway		London	
Jan 24	*Dancing Girl* Winter Garden	Apr 3	*The Rainbow* Empire
Feb 7	*Wildflower* Casino (Shaftesbury, London, 1926)	Sept 5	*The Beauty Prize* Winter Garden
May 21	*Aren't We All?* Gaiety	Sept 8	*Head Over Heels* Adelphi
June 19	*Helen of Troy, NY* Selwyn		
Aug 15	*Little Jessie James* Longacre		
Aug 28	*Little Miss Bluebeard* Lyceum (Wyndham's, London, Apr 1925)		
Sept 3	*Poppy* Apollo		
Nov 6	*Stepping Stones* Globe		
Dec 25	*Mary Jane McKane*		
Dec 31	*Kid Boots* Earl Carroll (Winter Garden, London, Feb 1926)		

1924

Broadway		London	
Jan 21	*Sweet Little Devil* Astor	May 12	*Toni* Shaftesbury
Jan 31	*Moonlight* Longacre	June 27	*The Street Singer* Lyric
Feb 19	*The Chiffon Girl* Lyric	Sept 11	*Primrose* Winter Garden
March	*Louie the XIV* Cosmopolitan		
May 18	*The Melody Man* Ritz		
May 19	*I'll Say She Is* Casino		
Aug 20	*The Dream Girl*		
Sept 1	*Top Hole*		
Sept 2	*Rose Marie* Imperial (Drury Lane, London, 20 March 1925)		
Sept 3	*Be Yourself*		
Sept 23	*Dear Sir* Times Square		
Aug 13	*No Other Girl* Morosco		
Oct 15	*The Firebrand*		
Nov 4	*Annie Dear* Times Square		
Dec 1	*Lady Be Good* Liberty (Empire, London, 14 Apr 1926)		
Dec 2	*The Student Prince* Jolson (His Majesty's, London, 3 Feb 1926)		
Dec 23	*Topsy and Eva* Sam H. Harris (Gaiety, London, 4 Oct 1928)		

1925

Broadway		London	
Jan	*Big Boy* Winter Garden	March 10	*Boodle* Empire
Jan 13	*The Love Song* Century	May 11	*No, No, Nanette* Palace (Globe, NY, 16 Sept)
March 2	*Sky High* Shubert	Aug 25	*Dear Little Billie* Shaftesbury
Apr 13	*Mercenary Mary* Longacre (Hippodrome, London, 7 Oct 1925)	Nov 11	*Betty in Mayfair* Adelphi
Apr 13	*Tell Me More* Gaiety (Winter Garden, London, 26 May 1925)		
Sept 8	*Captain Jinks*		

Broadway		London	
Sept 18	*Dearest Enemy* Knickerbocker		
Sept 21	*The Vagabond King* Casino (Winter Garden, London, Apr 1927)		
Sept 22	*Sunny* New Amsterdam (Hippodrome, London, 1926)		
Nov 2	*Princess Flavia* Century		
Nov 9	*Naughty Cinderella* Lyceum		
Dec 8	*The Cocoanuts* Lyric (Garrick, London, 20 March 1928)		
Dec 28	*Tip Toes* Liberty (Winter Garden, London, Apr 1926)		
Dec 30	*Song of the Flame* 44th Street		

1926

March 17	*The Girl Friend* Vanderbilt (Palace, London, Sept 1927)	Oct 21	*Princess Charming* Palace (NY, 1929)
Sept 6	*Castles in the Air* Selwyn (Shaftesbury, London, 29 June 1927)	Nov 17	*My Son John* Shaftesbury
Sept 8	*Queen High* Ambassador	Dec 1	*Lido Lady* Gaiety
Sept 20	*Honeymoon Lane* Knickerbocker		
Sept 20	*The Ramblers* Lyric		
Oct 12	*Criss Cross* Globe		
Nov 8	*Oh Kay!* Imperial (His Majesty's, London, 21 Sept 1927)		
Nov 30	*The Desert Song* Casino (Drury Lane, London, 7 Apr 1927)		
Dec 21	*Oh Please* Fulton		
Dec 27	*Peggy-Ann* Vanderbilt (Daly's, London, 27 July 1927)		
Dec 28	*Betsy* New Amsterdam		

1927

Jan	*The Nightingale* Jolson	Apr 27	*Lady Luck* Carlton
Feb 2	*Rio Rita* Ziegfeld (Prince Edward, London, 3 Apr 1930)		
Apr 25	*Hit the Deck* Belasco (Hippodrome, London, 3 Nov 1927)		
Sept 6	*Good News* 46th Street (Carlton, London, 15 Aug 1928)		
Sept 12	*My Maryland* Jolson		
Sept 26	*Manhattan Mary* Apollo		
Sept 26	*The Merry Malones* Erlanger		
Oct 3	*Yes Yes, Yvette* Harris		
Oct 10	*The Five O'Clock Girl* 44th Street (Hippodrome, London, 1929)		
Oct 16	*My Princess* Shubert		
Nov 3	*A Connecticut Yankee* Vanderbilt		
Nov 22	*Funny Face* Alvin (Princes, London, 8 Nov 1928)		
Nov 22	*Take the Air* Waldorf		
Nov 30	*Golden Dawn* Hammerstein		
Dec 27	*Show Boat* Ziegfeld (Drury Lane, London, 3 May 1928)		
Dec 29	*Lovely Lady* Sam H. Harris (Phoenix, London, 25 Feb 1932)		

1928

Jan 3	*She's My Baby* Globe	Feb 8	*The Yellow Mask* Carlton
Jan 10	*Rosalie* New Amsterdam	Apr 27	*Blue Eyes* Piccadilly
Feb 8	*Sunny Days* Imperial	June 5	*That's a Good Girl* Hippodrome
Feb 9	*Rain or Shine* George M. Cohan	Nov 14	*Lucky Girl* Shaftesbury
March 13	*The Three Musketeers* Lyric (Drury Lane, London, 28 March 1930)		

Broadway		London	
Apr 26	*Present Arms* Mansfield		
May 1	*Here's Howe*		
Sept 17	*Cross My Heart*		
Sept 19	*The New Moon* Imperial (Drury Lane, London, 4 Apr 1929)		
Sept 25	*Chee-Chee* Mansfield		
Sept 25	*Good Boy* Hammerstein		
Oct 1	*Billie* Erlanger		
Oct 8	*Paris* Music Box		
Oct 8	*Upsadaisy*		
Oct 10	*Hold Everything* Broadhurst (Palace, London, 1929)		
Oct 23	*Animal Crackers* 44th Street		
Nov 8	*Treasure Girl* Alvin		
Nov 21	*Rainbow* Gallo		
Dec 4	*Whoopee* New Amsterdam		
Dec 26	*Hello Daddy* Mansfield		

1929

Jan 9	*Follow Thru* 46th Street (Dominion, London, 3 Oct 1929)	Feb 11	*Mr Cinders* Adelphi
March	*Spring Is Here* Alvin	March 27	*Wake Up and Dream* Pavilion (Selwyn, NY, 30 Dec 1929)
July 2	*Show Girl* Ziegfeld	July 18	*Bitter Sweet* His Majesty's (Ziegfeld, NY, 5 Nov 1929)
Sept 3	*Sweet Adeline* Hammerstein	Nov 14	*Dear Love* Palace
Oct 17	*Great Day*		
Nov 11	*Heads Up* Alvin (Palace, London, 1930)		
Nov 26	*Sons O'Guns* Imperial (Hippodrome, London, 1930)		
Nov 27	*Fifty Million Frenchmen* Lyric		
Dec 25	*Top Speed* 46th Street		

1930

Jan 14	*Strike Up the Band* Times Square	Feb 20	*Here Comes the Bride* Piccadilly
Feb 18	*Simple Simon* Ziegfeld	March 26	*Damask Rose* Savoy
Feb 26	*Green Pastures*	Sept 17	*Follow a Star* Winter Garden
March 3	*Flying High* Apollo	Nov 19	*Little Tommy Tucker* Daly's
Sept 19	*Luana* Hammerstein	Dec 3	*Evergreen* Adelphi
Sept 20	*Nina Rosa* Majestic (Lyceum, London, 1931)	Dec 5	*Wonder Bar* Savoy (Nora Bayes, NY, 17 March 1931)
Sept 23	*Fine and Dandy* Erlanger		
Oct 7	*Brown Buddies* Liberty		
Oct 14	*Girl Crazy* Alvin		
Oct 15	*Three's a Crowd* Selwyn		
Nov 18	*Smiles* Ziegfeld		
Dec 8	*The New Yorkers* Moss's Broadway		
Dec 22	*Ballyhoo* Hammerstein (Comedy, London, 1932)		

1931

Jan 19	*You Said It* 46th Street	?	*The Good Companions* His Majesty's
Feb 10	*America's Sweetheart* Broadhurst	Jan 9	*Song of the Drum* Drury Lane
June 3	*The Band Wagon* New Amsterdam	Jan 20	*Blue Roses* Gaiety
Oct 13	*Everybody's Welcome* Shubert	March 5	*Stand Up and Sing* Hippodrome
Oct 15	*The Cat and the Fiddle* Globe (Palace, London, 4 March 1932)	Oct 8	*For the Love of Mike* Saville
Oct 27	*East Wind* Manhattan	Dec 23	*Hold My Hand* Gaiety
Nov 3	*Here Goes the Bride*		
Dec 26	*Of Thee I Sing* Music Box		

1932

Jan 18	*A Little Racketeer* 44th Street	June	*Tell Her the Truth* Saville (Cort, NY, 28 Oct 1932)
Jan 28	*Through the Years* Manhattan	June 6	*Out of the Bottle* Hippodrome
Feb 17	*Face the Music* New Amsterdam		
March 8	*Hot-Cha* Ziegfeld		

Broadway		London	
Sept 15	*Flying Colors* Imperial		
Nov 8	*Music in the Air* Alvin (His Majesty's, London, 19 May 1933)		
Nov 26	*Take a Chance* Apollo		
Nov 29	*The Gay Divorce* Ethel Barrymore (Palace, London, 2 Nov 1933)		

1933

Jan 20	*Pardon My English* Majestic	March 28	*He Wanted Adventure* Saville
Feb 14	*Melody* Casino	Oct 6	*Nymph Errant* Adelphi
March 4	*Strike Me Pink* Majestic	Nov 22	*That's a Pretty Thing* Daly's
Sept 8	*Murder at the Vanities* New Amsterdam		
Sept 25	*Hold Your Horses* Winter Garden		
Sept 30	*As Thousands Cheer* Music Box		
Oct 21	*Let 'em Eat Cake* Imperial		
Nov 7	*Here Goes the Bride*		
Nov 18	*Roberta* New Amsterdam		

1934

Jan 30	*All the King's Horses* Shubert (His Majesty's, London, as *Royal Exchange*, 6 Dec 1935)	Feb 1	*Mr Whittington* Hippodrome
		Feb 16	*Conversation Piece* His Majesty's (NY, 1934)
Sept 22	*The Great Waltz* Center	Apr 9	*Three Sisters* Drury Lane (Ethel Barrymore, NY, 21 Dec 1942)
Nov 15	*Say When* Imperial		
Nov 21	*Anything Goes* Alvin (Palace, London, 14 June 1935)	Sept 27	*Yes, Madam?* Hippodrome
		Dec 19	*Jill Darling* Saville
Nov 28	*Revenge with Music* New Amsterdam		

1935

Oct 10	*Porgy and Bess* Alvin (Stoll, London, 9 Oct 1952)	Feb 25	*Jack o' Diamonds* Gaiety
		May 2	*Glamorous Night* Drury Lane
Oct 12	*Jubilee* Imperial	May 4	*The Flying Trapeze* Alhambra
Nov 16	*Jumbo* Hippodrome	May 23	*The Gay Deceivers* Gaiety
Dec 5	*May Wine* St James	Oct 2	*Please Teacher* Hippodrome

1936

Apr 11	*On Your Toes* Imperial (Palace, London, 5 Feb 1937)	May 7	*Rise and Shine* Drury Lane
		Sept 11	*Careless Rapture* Drury Lane
Oct 29	*Red, Hot and Blue* Alvin	Sept 23	*Over She Goes* Saville
Nov 2	*Forbidden Melody* New Amsterdam	Dec 22	*Balalaika* Adelphi
Nov 19	*Johnny Johnson* 44th Street		

1937

Apr 14	*Babes in Arms* Shubert	Sept 1	*Crest of the Wave* Drury Lane
June 15	*The Cradle will Rock* Venice	Sept 16	*Going Greek* Gaiety
Sept 2	*Virginia* Center	Oct 14	*Hide and Seek* Hippodrome
Nov 29	*I'd Rather Be Right* Alvin	Dec 16	*Me and My Girl* Victoria Palace
Dec 1	*Hooray for What?* Winter Garden		

1938

May 16	*I Married an Angel* Shubert	March 16	*Operette* His Majesty's
Sept 21	*You Never Know* Winter Garden	June 8	*No Sky So Blue* Savoy
Oct 19	*Knickerbocker Holiday* Ethel Barrymore	June 9	*The Sun Never Sets* Drury Lane
		Nov 24	*Under Your Hat* Palace
Nov 9	*Leave It to Me* Imperial		
Nov 23	*The Boys from Syracuse* Alvin (Drury Lane, London, Nov 1963)		
Dec 1	*Great Lady* Majestic		
Dec 22	*Between the Devil* Imperial		

Broadway		London	

1939

Feb 9	*Stars in Your Eyes* Majestic	Jan 20	*Magyar Melody* Princes
March 23	*The Hot Mikado* Broadhurst	March 23	*The Dancing Years* Drury Lane
July 6	*Yokel Boy* Majestic	Aug 17	*Sitting Pretty* Princes
Oct 18	*Too Many Girls* Imperial		
Nov 17	*Very Warm for May* Alvin		
Nov 29	*Swingin' the Dream* Center		
Dec 6	*Dubarry Was a Lady* 46th Street (His Majesty's, London, 1942)		

1940

Apr 4	*Higher and Higher* Shubert		
May 23	*Keep Off the Grass*		
May 28	*Louisiana Purchase* Imperial		
Sept 11	*Hold On to Your Hats* Shubert		
Oct 25	*Cabin in the Sky* Martin Beck		
Oct 30	*Panama Hattie* 46th Street (Piccadilly, London, 4 Nov 1943)		
Dec 30	*Pal Joey* Ethel Barrymore (Princes, London, 31 March 1954)		

1941

Jan 5	*No for an Answer*		
Jan 23	*Lady in the Dark* Alvin		
Oct 1	*Best Foot Forward* Ethel Barrymore		
Oct 29	*Let's Face It* Imperial (Hippodrome, London, 19 Nov 1942)		
Oct 31	*High Kickers* Broadhurst		
Dec 25	*Banjo Eyes* Hollywood		
Dec	*Sunny River* St James (Piccadilly, London, 1943)		

1942

Jan 9	*The Lady Comes Across* Shubert	March 17	*Blossom Time* Lyric
June 2	*By Jupiter* Shubert	Apr 16	*Full Swing* Palace
July 4	*This Is the Army* Broadway (Palladium, London, 1943)	Aug 6	*Wild Rose* Princes

1943

Jan 7	*Something for the Boys* Alvin (Coliseum, London, 1944)	Feb	*Old Chelsea* Princes
March 31	*Oklahoma!* St James (Drury Lane, London, 30 Apr 1947)	June 17	*The Lisbon Story* Hippodrome
June 17	*Early to Bed* Broadhurst	Oct 26	*The Love Racket* Victoria Palace
Oct 7	*One Touch of Venus* Imperial	Sept 23	*Something in the Air* Palace
Nov 11	*What's Up?*	Nov 9	*Arc de Triomphe* Phoenix
Nov 20	*Winged Victory*		
Dec 2	*Carmen Jones* Broadway		

1944

Jan 13	*Jackpot*	Oct 2	*Jenny Jones* Hippodrome
Jan 28	*Mexican Hayride* Winter Garden		
Apr 8	*Follow the Girls* Century (His Majesty's, London, 1945)		
Aug 21	*Song of Norway* Imperial (Palace, London, 7 March 1946)		
Oct 5	*Bloomer Girl* Shubert		
Nov 16	*Sadie Thompson*		
Dec 7	*Seven Lively Arts* Ziegfeld		
Dec 28	*On the Town* Adelphi (London, 1963)		

Broadway		London	

1945

Jan 27	*Up in Central Park* Century	Apr 21	*Perchance to Dream* Hippodrome
March 22	*The Firebrand of Florence* Alvin		
Apr 19	*Carousel* Majestic (Drury Lane, London, 7 June 1950)		
Nov 10	*Are You With It?*		
Nov 22	*The Day Before Spring* National		
Dec 21	*Billion Dollar Baby* Alvin		

1946

Jan 21	*Nellie Bly*		
Feb 6	*Lute Song* Plymouth	July 17	*Big Ben* Adelphi
March 30	*St Louis Woman* Martin Beck	Aug 1	*Sweetheart Mine* Victoria
Sept 17	*Gypsy Lady*	Dec 19	*Pacific 1860* Drury Lane Palace
Apr 18	*Call Me Mister* National		
May 16	*Annie Get Your Gun* Imperial (Coliseum, London, 7 June 1947)		
May 31	*Around the World in Eighty Days* Adelphi		
Nov 4	*Park Avenue* Shubert		
Dec 26	*Beggars' Holiday*		

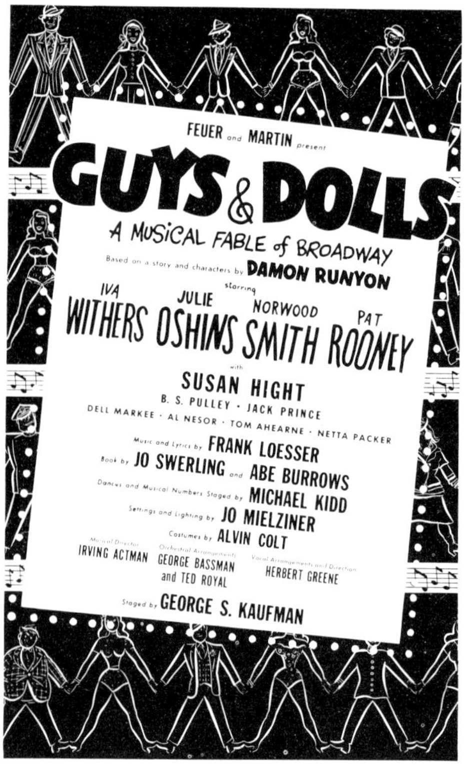

1947

Jan 9	*Street Scene* Adelphi	Apr 26	*Bless the Bride* Adelphi
Jan 10	*Finian's Rainbow* 46th Street (Palace, London, 21 Oct 1947)		
March 13	*Brigadoon* Ziegfeld (His Majesty's, London, 14 Apr 1949)		
Oct 9	*High Button Shoes* Century (Hippodrome, London, 1948)		
Oct 10	*Allegro* Majestic		

1948

Jan 29	*Look Ma, I'm Dancin'*	March 10	*Carissima* Palace
Oct 7	*Love Life* 46th Street	Sept 30	*The Kid from Stratford*
Oct 11	*Where's Charley?* St James (Palace, London, 1958)		
Nov 13	*As the Girls Go* Winter Garden		
Nov 29	*My Romance* Shubert		
Dec 30	*Kiss Me Kate* New Century (Coliseum, London, 8 May 1951)		

1949

Apr 7	*South Pacific* Majestic (Drury Lane, London, 1 Nov 1951)	March 25	*Belinda Fair*
July 15	*Miss Liberty* Imperial	June 22	*Her Excellency*
Oct 30	*Lost in the Stars* Music Box	July 15	*Tough at the Top* Adelphi
Oct 31	*Regina* 46th Street	Sept 15	*King's Rhapsody* Palace
Nov 25	*Texas, Li'l Darling*		
Dec 8	*Gentlemen Prefer Blondes* Ziegfeld (Princes, London, Aug 1962)		

1950

Feb 2	*Arms and the Girl*	July 7	*Ace of Clubs* Cambridge
Oct 12	*Call Me Madam* Imperial (Coliseum, London, 15 March 1952)	Oct 13	*Dear Miss Phoebe* Phoenix
Nov 24	*Guys and Dolls* 46th Street (Coliseum, London, 28 May 1953)	Nov 30	*Blue for a Boy* His Majesty's
Dec 21	*Out of This World* New Century		

1951

Broadway		London	
March 29	*The King and I* St James (Drury Lane, London, 8 Oct 1953)	Feb	*Gay's the Word* Saville
Apr 18	*Make a Wish*	Oct 17	*And so to Bed* New
Apr 19	*A Tree Grows in Brooklyn* Alvin	Oct 20	*Zip Goes a Million* Palace
May 14	*Flahooley*		
Nov 1	*Top Banana* Winter Garden		
Nov 12	*Paint Your Wagon* Shubert (His Majesty's, London, 1953)		

1952

Broadway		London	
June 25	*Wish You Were Here* Imperial (Casino, London, 10 Oct 1953)	Feb 18	*Bet Your Life* Hippodrome

1953

Broadway		London	
Feb 11	*Hazel Flagg*	Sept 25	*Love from Judy* Saville
Feb 25	*Wonderful Town* Winter Garden (Princes, London, 24 Feb 1955)		
May 7	*Can Can* Shubert (Coliseum, London, 14 Oct 1954)		
May 28	*Me and Juliet* Majestic		
Sept 8	*Carnival in Flanders*		
Dec 3	*Kismet* Ziegfeld (Stoll, London, 20 Apr 1955)		

1954

Broadway		London	
March 5	*The Girl in Pink Tights* Mark Hellinger	Jan 14	*The Boy Friend* Wyndham's (NY, 30 Sept 1954)
March 10	*The Threepenny Opera* Theater De Lys (Royal Court, London, Feb 1956)	Apr 3	*Wedding in Paris* Hippodrome
Apr 8	*By the Beautiful Sea* Majestic	June 10	*After the Ball* Globe
Apr 20	*Golden Apple* Alvin	July 25	*The Duenna* Westminster
May 13	*The Pajama Game* St James (as *The Pyjama Game*, Coliseum, London, 13 Oct 1955)	Aug 2	*The Water Gipsies* Winter Garden
Oct 20	*Peter Pan*	Aug 5	*Salad Days* Vaudeville
Nov 4	*Fanny* Majestic (Drury Lane, London, 15 Nov 1956)	Dec 22	*Happy Holiday* Palace
Dec 30	*House of Flowers* Alvin		

1955

Broadway		London	
Jan 27	*Plain and Fancy* Mark Hellinger (Drury Lane, London, 25 Jan 1956)	July 13	*Twenty Minutes South* St Martin's
Feb 24	*Silk Stockings* Imperial	July 14	*Wild Thyme* Duke of York's
May 5	*Damn Yankees* 46th Street (Coliseum, London, 28 March 1957)	Sept 8	*The Buccaneer* Lyric, Hammersmith
May 26	*Seventh Heaven*	Sept 13	*Romance in Candlelight*
Nov 30	*Pipe Dream* Shubert	Dec 15	*A Girl Called Jo* Piccadilly

1956

Broadway		London	
March 15	*My Fair Lady* Mark Hellinger (Drury Lane, London, 30 Apr 1958)	Feb 16	*Summer Song* Princess
March 22	*Mr Wonderful* Broadway	Dec 26	*Grab Me a Gondola* Lyric
May 3	*The Most Happy Fella* Imperial (Coliseum, London, 21 Apr 1961)	May 3	*Wild Grows the Heather* Hippodrome
Nov 15	*Li'l Abner* St James	July 17	*Oh, My Papa* Garrick
Nov 29	*Bells Are Ringing* Shubert (Coliseum, London, 14 Nov 1957)		

Broadway		London	
Dec 1	*Candide* Martin Beck (Saville, London, Apr 1959)		
Dec 6	*Happy Hunting* Majestic		

1957

Jan 23	*Body Beautiful*	Apr 17	*Harmony Close*
Apr 13	*Shinbone Alley*	June 6	*Free as Air* Savoy
May 14	*New Girl in Town* 46th Street		
Sept 26	*West Side Story* Winter Garden (Her Majesty's, London, 12 Dec 1958)		
Oct 31	*Jamaica* Imperial		
Dec 19	*The Music Man* Majestic (Adelphi, London, 16 March 1961)		

1958

Apr 3	*Say Darling* Anta	Apr 23	*Expresso Bongo* Saville
Feb 4	*Oh, Captain!* Alvin	July 17	*Irma la Douce* Lyric (NY, 1960)
Dec 1	*Flower Drum Song* St James (Palace, London, 24 March 1960)	Oct 2	*Valmouth* Lyric, Hammersmith
		Nov 13	*Chrysanthemum*
		Dec 18	*Cinderella* Coliseum

1959

Feb 5	*Redhead* 46th Street	Feb 17	*Fings Ain't Wot They Used t'Be* Theatre Royal, Stratford
March 9	*Juno* Winter Garden	May 27	*Marigold*
March 19	*First Impressions* Alvin	May 28	*Lock Up Your Daughters* Mermaid
Apr 24	*Destry Rides Again* Imperial	Sept 10	*The Crooked Mile* Cambridge
May 11	*Once Upon a Mattress* Phoenix (Adelphi, London, 1960)	Oct 19	*Make Me an Offer* Theatre Royal, Stratford
May 21	*Gypsy* Broadway (Piccadilly, London, May 1973)	Dec 17	*Aladdin* Coliseum
Oct 22	*Take Me Along* Shubert	Dec 26	*When in Rome* Adelphi
Nov 16	*The Sound of Music* Lunt-Fontanne (Palace, London, 18 May 1961)		
Nov 18	*Little Mary Sunshine* Orpheum		
Nov 23	*Fiorello* Broadhurst (Piccadilly, London, 1962)		
Dec 7	*Saratoga* Winter Garden		

1960

March 8	*Greenwillow* Alvin	March 17	*Follow That Girl* Vaudeville
Apr 14	*Bye Bye Birdie* Martin Beck (Her Majesty's, London, 25 June 1961)	May 5	*The Golden Touch* Piccadilly
May 3	*The Fantasticks* Sullivan St Playhouse	June 22	*Call It Love* Wyndham's
May 4	*Ernest in Love* Gramercy Arts	June 30	*Oliver!* New (Imperial, NY, 6 Jan 1963)
Oct 17	*Tenderloin* 46th Street	July 14	*Joie de Vivre* Queen's
Nov 3	*The Unsinkable Molly Brown* Winter Garden	Dec 20	*Hooray for Daisy* Lyric, Hammersmith
Dec 3	*Camelot* Majestic (Drury Lane, London, 19 Aug 1964)		
Dec 16	*Wildcat* Alvin		
Dec 26	*Do-Re-Mi* St James (Prince of Wales, London, Oct 1961)		

1961

March 4	*The Happiest Girl in the World*	May 4	*Belle* (*The Ballad of Dr Crippen*) Strand
Apr 13	*Carnival* Imperial (London, 1962)	July 20	*Stop the World, I Want to Get Off* Queens (NY, 3 Oct 1962)
Oct 3	*Milk and Honey* Martin Beck	Aug 3	*Wildest Dreams* Vaudeville
Oct 10	*How to Succeed in Business without Really Trying* 46th Street (Shaftesbury, London, March 1963)		

Broadway

Oct 12	*Let It Ride*
Oct 14	*Sail Away* (Savoy, London, June 1962)
Nov 2	*Kean* Broadway
Nov 18	*The Gay Life* Shubert
Dec 27	*Subways Are for Sleeping* St James

London

1962

Broadway

Jan 27	*Family Affair*
March 15	*No Strings* 54th Street (London, 1963)
March 19	*All-American*
March 22	*I Can Get It for You Wholesale* Shubert
May 8	*A Funny Thing Happened on the Way to the Forum* Alvin (Strand, London, Oct 1963)
Oct 20	*Mr President* St James
Nov 17	*Little Me* Lunt-Fontanne (Cambridge, London, 1964)

London

May 8	*Blitz* Adelphi
Nov 27	*Vanity Fair* Queen's

1963

Broadway

March 18	*Tovarich* Broadway
Apr 23	*She Loves Me* Eugene O'Neill (London, 1964)
Oct 3	*Here's Love* Shubert
Oct 17	*Jennie*
Oct 24	*110 in the Shade* Broadhurst (Palace, London, 1967)
Dec 8	*The Girl Who Came to Supper* Broadway

London

March 21	*Half a Sixpence* Cambridge (NY, 1965)
Apr 10	*Virtue in Danger* Mermaid
June 20	*Oh What a Lovely War!* Wyndham's
July 4	*Pickwick* Saville (NY, 1965)

1964

Broadway

Feb 16	Foxy Ziegfeld
Feb 27	*What Makes Sammy Run* 46th Street
March 20	*Cindy* (Fortune, London, 29 May 1968)
March 26	*Funny Girl* Winter Garden (Prince of Wales, London, 5 Apr 1966)
Apr 4	*Anyone Can Whistle* Majestic
Apr 7	*High Spirits* Alvin (Savoy, London, Nov 1964)
May 26	*Fade Out – Fade In* Mark Hellinger
June 16	*Hello Dolly* St James (Drury Lane, London, 2 Dec 1965)
Sept 22	*Fiddler on the Roof* Imperial (Her Majesty's, London, Feb 1967)
Oct 20	*Golden Boy* Majestic (London, 1965)
Oct 27	*Ben Franklin in Paris* Lunt–Fontanne
Dec 10	*The Yearling*
Dec 15	*I Had a Ball* Martin Beck

London

Aug 1	*Instant Marriage* Piccadilly
Sept 22	*Maggie May* Adelphi
Oct 20	*Robert and Elizabeth* Lyric
Dec 22	*Our Man Crichton* Shaftesbury

1965

Broadway

Feb 16	*Baker Street* Broadway
March 18	*Do I Hear a Waltz?* 46th Street
May 11	*Flora, the Red Menace* Alvin
May 16	*The Roar of the Greasepaint, the Smell of the Crowd* Shubert
May 22	*Man of La Mancha* Anta (Piccadilly, London, Apr 1968)
Oct 17	*On a Clear Day You Can See Forever* Mark Hellinger
Nov 10	*The Zulu and the Zayda* Cort
Nov 13	*Skyscraper* Lunt-Fontanne

London

Feb 1	*Divorce Me Darling* Globe
Aug 24	*Passion Flower Hotel* Prince of Wales
Dec 15	*Charlie Girl* Adelphi
Dec 20	*Twang!* Shaftesbury

Broadway		London	

1966

Jan 30	*Sweet Charity* Palace (Prince of Wales, London, Oct 1967)	May 31	*Come Spy with Me* Whitehall
March 29	*It's a Bird, It's a Plane, It's Superman* Alvin	Sept 22	*Jorrocks* New
May 24	*Mame* Winter Garden (Drury Lane, London, 20 Feb 1969)		
Oct 18	*The Apple Tree* Shubert		
Oct 25	*Autumn's Here* Bert Wheeler		
Nov 6	*The Man with a Load of Mischief* Jan Hus Playhouse (Comedy, London, 9 Dec 1968)		
Nov 20	*Cabaret* Imperial (Palace, London, 1967)		
Nov 26	*Walking Happy* Lunt-Fontanne		
Dec 5	*I Do, I Do* 46th Street (London, 1968)		

1967

March 7	*You're a Good Man, Charlie Brown* Theater 80, St Marks	July 27	*Annie* Westminster
Apr 11	*Ilya Darling* Mark Hellinger	Dec 5	*The Four Musketeers* Drury Lane
Apr 26	*Hallelujah Baby* Martin Beck		
Oct 23	*Henry, Sweet Henry* Palace		
Dec 7	*How Now, Dow-Jones* Lunt–Fontanne		

1968

Jan 7	*Have I Got One for You?* Theater 4	Nov 14	*Mr and Mrs* Palace
Jan 13	*Your Own Thing* Orpheum		
Jan 18	*The Happy Time* Broadway		
Jan 29	*Who's Who, Baby?* Players		
Feb 4	*Golden Rainbow* Shubert		
Apr 4	*The Education of Hyman Kaplan* Alvin		
Apr 10	*George M.* Palace		
Apr 29	*Hair* Biltmore (Shaftesbury, London, Sept 1968)		
Sept 26	*Grass Roots* Theater De Lys		
Nov 17	*Zorba* Imperial (Greenwich, London, Nov 1973)		
Dec 1	*Promises, Promises* Shubert (Prince of Wales, London, Oct 1969)		
Dec 5	*Jimmy Shine* Brooks Atkinson		
Dec 20	*Dames at Sea* Bouwerie Lane (Duchess, London, 1969)		

1969

Jan 22	*Celebration* Ambassador	Feb 27	*Two Cities* Palace
Jan 26	*Red, White and Maddox* Cort	Apr 16	*Anne of Green Gables* New
Feb 6	*Dear World* March 16 *1776* Mark Hellinger (London, 1970)	Apr 17	*Ann Veronica* Cambridge
		Apr 30	*Belle Starr* Palace
March 23	*Billy* Billy Rose	Nov 13	*Phil the Fluter* Palace
June 4	*Promenade* Promenade		
Sept 24	*Salvation* Jan Hus Playhouse		
Nov 5	*Rondelay* Hudson West		
Dec 2	*Buck White* George Abbott		
Dec 18	*Coco* Mark Hellinger		

1970

Jan 26	*The Last Sweet Days of Isaac* Eastside Playhouse	May 26	*Sing a Rude Song* Garrick
		July	*The Great Waltz* Drury Lane
Jan 28	*But Most of Us Cry at Movies* La Mama	Dec	*Catch My Soul* Roundhouse

Broadway		London	
Feb 8	*Exchange* Mercer-O'Casey		
Feb 26	*Georgy* Winter Garden		
March 12	*Operation Sidewinder* Beaumont		
March 15	*Purlie* Winter Garden		
March 18	*House of Leather* Ellen Stewart		
March 22	*Blood Red Roses* John Golden		
March 26	*Minnie's Boys* Imperial		
March 29	*Look to the Lilies* Lunt–Fontanne		
March 30	*Applause* Palace (Her Majesty's, London, 16 Nov 1972)		
Apr 13	*The Drunkard* 13th Street		
Apr 26	*Company* Alvin (Her Majesty's, London, Jan 1972)		
May 18	*The Me Nobody Knows* Orpheum		
Oct 19	*The Rothschilds* Lunt-Fontanne		
Nov 10	*Two by Two*		

1971

Jan 15	*Ari* Mark Hellinger	Oct 19	*Ambassador* Her Majesty's (Lunt-Fontanne, NY, 19 Nov 1972)
Feb 28	*The Survival of St Joan* Anderson		
Apr 4	*Follies* Winter Garden		
Apr 15	*70 Girls 70* Broadhurst		
May 17	*Godspell* Cherry Lane (Roundhouse, London, 17 Nov 1971)		
Oct 20	*Jesus Christ, Superstar* Mark Hellinger (Palace, London, 9 Aug 1972)		
Oct 21	*Ain't Supposed to Die a Natural Death* Ethel Barrymore		
Nov 4	*Wedding of Iphigenia* Public		
Dec	*Inner City* Ethel Barrymore		
Dec 1	*Two Gentlemen of Verona* (Phoenix, London, 26 Apr 1973)		

1972

Feb 14	*Grease* Martin Eden	May 3	*Gone with the Wind* Drury Lane
Apr 9	*Sugar* Majestic	May 9	*Tom Brown's Schooldays*
Apr 19	*Don't Bother Me, I Can't Cope* Edison	Aug 22	*Popkiss* Globe
May 16	*Don't Play Us Cheap* Ethel Barrymore	Aug 27	*Trelawney* Prince of Wales
Oct 23	*Pippin* Imperial (Her Majesty's, London, 1973)	Oct 5	*Costa Packet* Theatre Royal, Stratford
Nov 13	*Lysistrata* Brooks Atkinson	Nov 6	*I and Albert* Piccadilly
Nov 23	*Dr Selavy's Magic Theater* Mercer-O'Casey	Dec 20	*The Good Old, Bad Old Days* Prince of Wales
Dec 18	*Rainbow* Orpheum		

1973

Feb 6	*Shelter* John Golden	Feb 16	*Joseph and the Amazing Technicolour Dreamcoat* Albery
Feb 25	*A Little Night Music* Shubert (Adelphi, London, 1975)	July 24	*The Card* Queen's
March 18	*Seesaw* Uris		
May 13	*Cyrano* Palace		
May 19	*Smith* Eden		

1974

Apr 18	*Bordello* Queen's	July 11	*The Good Companions* Her Majesty's
May 1	*Billy* Drury Lane		

1975

Jan 5	*The Wiz* Majestic	Apr 22	*Jeeves*
Jan 7	*Shenandoah* Alvin	Apr 24	*The Black Mikado* Cambridge
Jan 27	*Pacific Overtures*		
March 19	*The Rocky Horror Show* (Royal Court, London, 1974)		
May 28	*The Magic Show* Cort		
June 3	*Chicago* 46th Street		
Oct 27	*Me and Bessie* Edison		

Broadway		**London**	

1976

March 2	*Bubbling Brown Sugar* Anta	March 18	*Mardi Gras* Prince of Wales
April 25	*Rex*	May 27	*Teeth 'n' Smiles* Wyndham's
	2 by 5 Village Gate	June 3	*Leave Him to Heaven* New London
June 2	*Godspell* Ambassador	June 8	*Liza of Lambeth* Shaftesbury
July 25	*A Chorus Line* Shubert (Drury Lane, London, 22 July 1976)	Aug 10	*T. Zee* Royal Court
Dec 20	*Music Is* St James		
Dec 22	*Your Arm's Too Short to Box with God* Lyceum		
Dec 26	*The Robber Bridegroom* Biltmore		

1977

Apr 17	*I Love My Wife* Ethel Barrymore (Prince of Wales, London, 6 Oct 1977)	Jan 8	*The Point* Mermaid
Apr 21	*Annie Alvin* (Victoria Palace, London, 3 May 1978)	Oct 12	*Maggie* Shaftesbury
June 1	*Beatlemania* Winter Garden	Dec 5	*Elvis* Astoria
		Dec 13	*The Magic Man* Mayfair

1978

Feb 19	*On the Twentieth Century* St James	Feb 2	*Privates on Parade* Piccadilly
March 9	*Runaways* Public/Cabaret	Mar 1	*Kings and Clowns* Phoenix
March 27	*Dancin* Broadhurst	Mar 28	*Travelling Music Show* Her Majesty's
Apr 17	*Best Little Whorehouse in Texas* Entermedia	Jun 21	*Evita* Prince Edward
May 9	*Ain't Misbehavin* Longacre	Oct 31	*Bar Mitzvah Boy* Her Majesty's
Nov 6	*I'm Getting my Act Together and Taking it on the Road* Circle in the Square	Nov 9	*Beyond the Rainbow* Adelphi
		Dec	*Troubadour* Cambridge

1979

Feb 6	*Tommy* Queens		
Apr	*Carmelina* St James		

Where Did That Song Come From?

Broadway and Hollywood have provided twentieth-century music with some of its finest and most durable 'evergreen' songs. Many of these have been in the popular repertoire for several decades and their origins have long been forgotten, as have the shows themselves in which they first appeared. It is hoped that this index will help resolve arguments on the subject which sometimes arise – even in the best-behaved circles – when *aficionados* get together. Problems of space preclude the listing of songs written especially for the many original screen musicals; but songs added to, or interpolated in, the film versions of stage musicals (in which they did not feature) are indicated by an asterisk. In these cases the date shown is that of the film, which may vary from that of the original stage production by a number of years.

Ace in the hole *Let's Face It*, 1941
Adelaide/Adelaide's lament *Guys and Dolls*, 1950
After the ball *A Trip to Chinatown*, 1893
After you, who? *The Gay Divorce*, 1932
Ah, sweet mystery of life *Naughty Marietta*, 1910
Ain't got no/I got life *Hair*, 1967
Ain't there anyone here for love? *Gentlemen Prefer Blondes*, 1953*
Alice blue gown *Irene*, 1919
Allah's holiday *Katinka*, 1915
All alone Monday *The Ramblers*, 1926
All at once you love her *Pipe Dream*, 1955
All er nothin' *Oklahoma!*, 1943
Allez-vous en *Can Can*, 1953
All I need is the girl *Gypsy*, 1959
All of you *Silk Stockings*, 1955
All the things you are *Very Warm for May*, 1939
All through the night *Anything Goes*, 1934
Almost like being in love *Brigadoon*, 1947
Alone together *Flying Colors*, 1932
Alone too long *By the Beautiful Sea*, 1954
Along with me *Call Me Mister*, 1946
Always true to you in my fashion *Kiss Me Kate*, 1948
America *West Side Story*, 1957
And this is my beloved *Kismet*, 1953
Angelus, The *Sweethearts*, 1913
Another opening, another show *Kiss Me Kate*, 1948
Any place I hang my hat is home *St Louis Woman*, 1946
Anything you can do *Annie Get Your Gun*, 1946
April showers *Bombo*, 1921
Aquarius *Hair*, 1967
As long as he needs me *Oliver!*, 1960
At long last love *You Never Know*, 1938
At the Balalaika *Balalaika*, 1936
Auf Wiedersehen *The Blue Paradise*, 1915
Avalon *Sinbad*, 1918

Babbitt and the bromide, The *Funny Face*, 1927
Bachelor gay, A *The Maid of the Mountains*, 1917
Bali ha'i *South Pacific*, 1949
Bambalina *Wildflower*, 1923
Baubles, bangles and beads *Kismet*, 1953
Beat out dat rhythm on a drum *Carmen Jones*, 1943
Before the parade passes by *Hello Dolly*, 1964
Begat, The *Finian's Rainbow*, 1947
Begin the beguine *Jubilee*, 1935
Belly up to the bar, boys *The Unsinkable Molly Brown*, 1960
Bess, you is my woman *Porgy and Bess*, 1935
Best thing for you, The *Call Me Madam*, 1950
Best things in life are free, The *Good News*, 1927
Better than a dream *Bells Are Ringing*, 1960*
Bewitched *Pal Joey*, 1940
Bianca *Kiss Me Kate*, 1948
Bidin' my time *Girl Crazy*, 1930
Big D *The Most Happy Fella*, 1956
Big spender *Sweet Charity*, 1966
Bill *Show Boat*, 1927
Bloody Mary *South Pacific*, 1949
Blow, Gabriel, blow *Anything Goes*, 1934
Blue heaven *see* Desert song
Blue room *The Girl Friend*, 1926
Blue skies *Betsy*, 1926
Body and soul *Three's a Crowd*, 1930
Bonjour Paris *Funny Face*, 1956*
Bowery, The *A Trip to Chinatown*, 1893
Boy, like that, A *West Side Story*, 1957
Break of day *Old Chelsea*, 1943
Brotherhood of man, The *How to Succeed in Business without Really Trying*, 1961
Brush up your Shakespeare *Kiss Me Kate*, 1948
Buckle down Winsocki *Best Foot Forward*, 1941
Bushel and a peck, A *Guys and Dolls*, 1950
Busy doing nothing *A Connecticut Yankee*, 1948*
But in the morning, no *Dubarry Was a Lady*, 1939
But not for me *Girl Crazy*, 1930
Button up your overcoat *Follow Thru*, 1929
Bye bye baby *Gentlemen Prefer Blondes*, 1949
By myself *Between the Devil*, 1938; *The Band Wagon*, 1953*
By Strauss *The Show Is On*, 1936

Cabaret *Cabaret*, 1966
California, here I come *Bombo*, 1921
Call of life, The *Bitter Sweet*, 1929
Call of the sea *No, No, Nanette*, 1925
Can't help lovin' that man *Show Boat*, 1927
Carefully taught *South Pacific*, 1949
Carousel in the park *Up in Central Park*, 1945
C'est magnifique *Can Can*, 1953
C'est moi *Camelot*, 1960
Cherry pies ought to be you *Out of This World*, 1950; *Aladdin*, 1959
Chloe *Sinbad*, 1918
Chop suey *Flower Drum Song*, 1958
Circus on parade, The *Jumbo*, 1935
Clap yo' hands *Oh Kay!*, 1926; *Funny Face*, 1956*
Climb ev'ry mountain *The Sound of Music*, 1959
Close *Rosalie*, 1937*
Close as pages in a book *Up in Central Park*, 1945
Cockeyed optimist, A *South Pacific*, 1949
Cocoanut sweet *Jamaica*, 1957
Colorado, my home *The Unsinkable Molly Brown*, 1960
Come along with me *Can Can*, 1953
Come back to me *On a Clear Day You Can See Forever*, 1965
Come boys *The Student Prince*, 1924
Comedy tonight *A Funny Thing Happened on the Way to the Forum*, 1962
Come rain or some shine *St Louis Woman*, 1946
Comes love *Yokel Boy*, 1939
Come to me, bend to me *Brigadoon*, 1947
Company way, The *How to Succeed in Business without Really Trying*, 1961
Consider yourself *Oliver!*, 1960
Continental, The *The Gay Divorce*, 1934*
Cool *West Side Story*, 1957
Cossack love song (Don't forget me) *The Song of the Flame*, 1925
Could it be you? *Something for the Boys*, 1943
Could you use me? *Girl Crazy*, 1930
Crazy rhythm *Here's Howe*, 1928

Cuddle up a little closer *The Three Twins*, 1908

Dance only with me *Say Darling*, 1958
Dancing *Hello Dolly*, 1964
Dancing in the dark *The Band Wagon*, 1931
Dancing on the ceiling *Evergreen*, 1930
Dancing time *The Cabaret Girl*, 1922
Dardanella *Afgar*, 1919
Dark music *Arc de Triomphe*, 1943
Darn that dream *Swingin' the Dream*, 1939
Dawn of love, The *The Firefly*, 1912
Day by day *Godspell*, 1971
Dearest love *Operette*, 1938
Dear friend *She Loves Me*, 1963
Dear little café *Bitter Sweet*, 1929
Deep in my heart, dear *The Student Prince*, 1924
Desert song, The (Blue heaven) *The Desert Song*, 1926
Diamonds are a girl's best friend *Gentlemen Prefer Blondes*, 1949
Dinah *Kid Boots*, 1923
Dis-donc, dis-donc *Irma la Douce*, 1958
Dites-moi *South Pacific*, 1949
Do, do, do *Oh Kay!* 1926
Do I hear a waltz? *Do I Hear a Waltz?*, 1965
Do I love you? *Dubarry Was a Lady*, 1939
Do I love you (because you're beautiful)? *Cinderella*, 1958
Doin' what comes naturally *Annie Get Your Gun*, 1946
Do it again *The French Doll*, 1922
Donkey serenade, The *The Firefly*, 1937*
Don't ever leave me *Sweet Adeline*, 1929
Don't let it bother you *The Gay Divorce*, 1934*
Don't marry me *Flower Drum Song*, 1958
Don't rain on my parade *Funny Girl*, 1964
Door of my dreams, The *Rose Marie*, 1924
Do-re-mi *The Sound of Music*, 1959
Down in the depths (on the 90th floor) *Red, Hot and Blue*, 1936
Drinking song *The Student Prince*, 1924
Drummer boy *Strike Up the Band*, 1940*
Drums in my heart *Through the Years*, 1932
Dulcinea *The Man of La Mancha*, 1965
D'ye love me? *Sunny*, 1925

Eadie was a lady *Take a Chance*, 1932
Easter parade *As Thousands Cheer*, 1933
Edelweiss *The Sound of Music*, 1959
Elizabeth *Wonder Bar*, 1930
Embraceable You *Girl Crazy*, 1930
Evelina *Bloomer Girl*, 1944
Everybody has the right to be wrong *Skyscraper*, 1965
Everybody ought to have a maid *A Funny Thing Happened on the Way to the Forum*, 1962
Everybody's got a home but me *Pipe Dream*, 1955
Every street's a boulevard in old New York *Hazel Flagg*, 1953
Everything I love *Let's Face It*, 1941
Everything I've got *By Jupiter*, 1942
Everything's coming up roses *Gypsy*, 1959
Every time we say goodbye *Seven Lively Arts*, 1944
Experiment *Nymph Errant*, 1933

Falling in love with love *The Boys from Syracuse*, 1938
Fancy our meeting *That's a Good Girl*, 1928
Fanny *Fanny*, 1954
Far away *Blitz*, 1962
Farmer and the cowman, The *Oklahoma*, 1943
Fascinating rhythm *Lady Be Good*, 1924; *Girl Crazy*, 1943*
Fate *Kismet*, 1953
Fated to be mated *Silk Stockings*, 1957*
Fellow needs a girl, A *Allegro*, 1947
Fidgety feet *Oh Kay!*, 1926
Fine and dandy *Fine and Dandy*, 1930
Fishermen of England, The *The Rebel Maid*, 1921
Flash! Bang! Wallop! *Half a Sixpence*, 1962
Fly home, little heart *King's Rhapsody*, 1949
Fold your wings *Glamorous Night*, 1935
Follow me *Camelot*, 1960
Food, glorious food *Oliver!*, 1960
Freddy and his fiddle *Song of Norway*, 1944
Friendship *Dubarry Was a Lady*, 1939
From this moment on *Out of This World*, 1950; *Kiss Me Kate*, 1953*
Fugue for tinhorns *Guys and Dolls*, 1950

Gaby glide, The *Vera Violetta*, 1911
Gay Parisienne *The Desert Song*, 1943*
Gee, Officer Krupke *West Side Story*, 1957
Gentleman is a dope, The *Allegro*, 1947
Get me to the church on time *My Fair Lady*, 1956
Get out of town *Leave It to Me*, 1938
Getting to know you *The King and I*, 1951
Giannina mia *The Firefly*, 1912
Girl of the moment *Lady in the Dark*, 1941
Girl on the magazine cover, The *Stop! Look! Listen!* 1915; *Follow the Crowd*, 1916
Girl that I marry, The *Annie Get Your Gun*, 1946
Give me your tired, your poor *Miss Liberty*, 1949
Glad to be unhappy *On Your Toes*, 1936
God bless America *This Is the Army*, 1944*
God's country *Hooray for What?*, 1937; *Babes in Arms*, 1939*
Golden days *The Student Prince*, 1924
Gonna build a mountain *Stop the World, I Want to Get Off*, 1961
Goodbye girls, I'm through *Chin Chin*, 1914
Good morning *Babes in Arms*, 1939*
Good morning starshine *Hair*, 1967
Good news *Good News*, 1927
Goodnight my someone *The Music Man*, 1957
Good things in life, The *The Good Old, Bad Old Days*, 1972
Got a date with an angel *For the Love of Mike*, 1931
Grant Avenue *Flower Drum Song*, 1958
Great day *Great Day*, 1929
Good news *Good News*, 1927
Green-up time *Love Life*, 1948
Growing pains *A Tree Grows in Brooklyn*, 1951
Guys and dolls *Guys and Dolls*, 1950
Gypsy love song *The Fortune Teller*, 1898

Half-of-it-dearie blues, The *Lady Be Good*, 1924
Hallelujah *Hit the Deck*, 1927
Happiness is a thing called Joe *Cabin in the Sky*, 1942*
Happy talk *South Pacific*, 1949
Happy to make your acquaintance *The Most Happy Fella*, 1956
Hare Krishna *Hair*, 1967
Have you met Miss Jones? *I'd Rather Be Right*, 1937
Heart *Damn Yankees*, 1955
Heather on the hill, The *Brigadoon*, 1947
Heat wave *As Thousands Cheer*, 1933
Hello, Dolly *Hello Dolly!*, 1964
Hello, my lover, goodbye *Here Goes the Bride*, 1933
Hello young lovers *The King and I*, 1951
He loves and she loves *Funny Face*, 1927
Here am I *Sweet Adeline*, 1929
Here in my arms *Dearest Enemy*, 1925; *Lido Lady*, 1926
Here's that rainy day *Carnival in Flanders*, 1953
Hernando's hideaway *The Pajama Game*, 1954
He's in love *Kismet*, 1953
He who loves and runs away *The Firefly*, 1912
Hey, good-lookin' *Something for the Boys*, 1943
Hey, look me over *Wildcat*, 1960
Hey there *The Pajama Game*, 1954

High and low *Here Comes the Bride*, 1930; *The Band Wagon*, 1931
Highwayman love *Perchance to Dream*, 1945
Hill of dreams *The Song of Norway*, 1944
His love makes me beautiful *Funny Girl*, 1964
Honey bun *South Pacific*, 1949
Honey in the honeycomb *Cabin in the Sky*, 1940
Hooray for Captain Spaulding *Animal Crackers*, 1928
Hostess with the mostes', The *Call Me Madam*, 1950
How are things in Glocca Morra? *Finian's Rainbow*, 1947
How can love survive? *The Sound of Music*, 1959
How could we be wrong? *Nymph Errant*, 1933
How do you speak to an angel? *Hazel Flagg*, 1953
How long has this been going on? *Rosalie*, 1928; *Funny Face*, 1956*
How lovely to be a woman *Bye Bye Birdie*, 1960
How to handle a woman *Camelot*, 1960
Huguette waltz *The Vagabond King*, 1925
Hymn to him, A *My Fair Lady*, 1956

I ain't down yet *The Unsinkable Molly Brown*, 1960
I ain't got nobody *Strike Up the Band*, 1940*
I am going to like it here *Flower Drum Song*, 1958
I am in love *Can Can*, 1953
I am loved *Out of This World*, 1950; *Aladdin*, 1959
I believe in you *How to Succeed in Business without Really Trying*, 1961
I cain't say no *Oklahoma!*, 1943
I can give you the starlight *The Dancing Years*, 1939
I can't sit down *Porgy and Bess*, 1935
I could be happy with you *The Boy Friend*, 1954
I could have danced all night *My Fair Lady*, 1956
I couldn't sleep a wink last night *Higher and Higher*, 1943*
I could write a book *Pal Joey*, 1940
I'd do anything *Oliver!*, 1960
I didn't know what time it was *Too Many Girls*, 1939; *Pal Joey*, 1957*
I don't know how to love him *Jesus Christ, Superstar*, 1971
I enjoy being a girl *Flower Drum Song*, 1958
I feel pretty *West Side Story*, 1957
If a girl isn't pretty *Funny Girl*, 1964
If ever I would leave you *Camelot*, 1960
If he walked into my life *Mame*, 1966
If I had my druthers *Li'l Abner*, 1956
If I love again *Hold Your Horses*, 1932
If I loved you *Carousel*, 1945
If I ruled the world *Pickwick*, 1963
If I were a bell *Guys and Dolls*, 1950
If I were a rich man *Fiddler on the Roof*, 1964
If love were all *Bitter Sweet*, 1929
If my friends could see me now *Sweet Charity*, 1966
If only he'd looked my way *Gay's the Word*, 1961
If there is someone lovelier than you *Revenge with Music*, 1934
If this isn't love *Finian's Rainbow*, 1947
If you stub your toe on the moon *A Connecticut Yankee*, 1948*
I get a kick out of you *Anything Goes*, 1934
I got it bad (and that ain't good) *Jump for Joy*, 1941
I got lost in his arms *Annie Get Your Gun*, 1946
I got plenty o' nuttin' *Porgy and Bess*, 1935
I got rhythm *Girl Crazy*, 1930
I got the sun in the morning *Annie Get Your Gun*, 1946
I guess I'll have to change my plan *The Band Wagon*, 1953*
I hate men *Kiss Me Kate*, 1948
I have a love *West Side Story*, 1957
I have confidence in me *The Sound of Music*, 1965*
I have dreamed *The King and I*, 1951
I just can't make my eyes behave *A Parisian Model*, 1906
I know that you know *Oh Please*, 1926; *Hit the Deck*, 1927
I leave my heart in an English garden *Dear Miss Phoebe*, 1950
I left my heart at the stage door canteen *This Is the Army*, 1942
I like to recognize the tune *Too Many Girls*, 1939
I'll be hard to handle *Roberta*, 1933
I'll buy you a star *A Tree Grows in Brooklyn*, 1951
I'll follow my secret heart *Conversation Piece*, 1934
I'll go home with Bonnie Jean *Brigadoon*, 1947
I'll know *Guys and Dolls*, 1950
I'll never be jealous again *The Pajama Game*, 1954
I'll never fall in love again *Promises, Promises*, 1968
I'll only miss her when I think of her *Skyscraper*, 1965
I'll say she does *Sinbad*, 1918
I'll see you again *Bitter Sweet*, 1929
Ilona *She Loves Me*, 1963
I love a piano *Stop! Look! Listen!* 1915; *Follow the Crowd*, 1916
I loved you once in silence *Camelot*, 1960
I love Louisa *The Band Wagon*, 1931
I love Paris *Can Can*, 1953
I loves you, Porgy *Porgy and Bess*, 1935
I love to cry at weddings *Sweet Charity*, 1966
I love you (Archer-Thompson) *Little Jessie James*, 1923
I love you (Cole Porter) *Mexican Hayride*, 1944
I love you (Grieg, adapted by Wright-Forrest) *The Song of Norway*, 1944
I'm a brass band *Sweet Charity*, 1966
I'm all smiles *The Yearling*, 1964
I'm always chasing rainbows *Oh, Look!*, 1918
I'm an Indian too *Annie Get Your Gun*, 1946
I married an angel *I Married an Angel*, 1938
I met a girl *Bells Are Ringing*, 1956
I'm falling in love with someone *Naughty Marietta*, 1910
I'm getting tired so I can sleep *This Is the Army*, 1942
I'm goin' south *Bombo*, 1921
I'm gonna wash that man right outa my hair *South Pacific*, 1949
I might fall back on you *Show Boat*, 1927
I'm in love with a wonderful guy *South Pacific*, 1949
I'm in love with Vienna *The Great Waltz*, 1934
I'm just wild about Harry *Shuffle Along*, 1921
I'm not at all in love *The Pajama Game*, 1954
I'm on a seesaw *Jill, Darling*, 1934
I'm on my way (Gershwin) *Porgy and Bess*, 1935
I'm on my way (Loewe-Lerner) *Paint Your Wagon*, 1951
Impossible dream, The *Man of La Mancha*, 1965
I'm the belle of New York *The Belle of New York*, 1897
I'm the greatest star *Funny Girl*, 1964
I'm unlucky at gambling *Fifty Million Frenchmen*, 1929
I'm yours *Simple Simon*, 1930
Indian love call *Rose Marie*, 1924
I never has seen snow *House of Flowers*, 1954
In my own little corner *Cinderella*, 1958
In our little den of iniquity *Pal Joey*, 1940
In the still of the night *Rosalie*, 1937*
I saw you first *Higher and Higher*, 1943*
I see your face before me *Between the Devil*, 1938
Isle of our dreams, The *The Red Mill*, 1906
Isn't it a pity? *Pardon My English*, 1933
I still get jealous *High Button Shoes*, 1947
I still see Elisa *Paint Your Wagon*, 1951
I still suits me *Show Boat*, 1936*
It *The Desert Song*, 1924
It ain't necessarily so *Porgy and Bess*, 1935
Italian street song *Naughty Marietta*, 1910
I talk to the trees *Paint Your Wagon*, 1951
It all depends on you *Big Boy*, 1925
It never entered my mind *Higher and Higher*, 1940
It only takes a moment *Hello Dolly*, 1964
It's a lovely day today *Call Me Madam*, 1950
It's a lovely day tomorrow *Louisiana Purchase*, 1940
It's alright with me *Can Can*, 1953
It's a musical world *The Good Old, Bad Old Days*, 1972
It's a perfect relationship *Bells Are Ringing*, 1956
It's de-lovely *Red, Hot and Blue*, 1936
It's got to be love *On Your Toes*, 1936
It's love *Wonderful Town*, 1953

It's never too late to fall in love *The Boy Friend*, 1954
It's only a paper moon *Take a Chance*, 1933*
It takes a woman *Hello Dolly*, 1964
I've come to wive it weathily in Padua *Kiss Me Kate*, 1948
I've got a crush on you *Treasure Girl*, 1928; *Strike Up the Band*, 1930
I've got five dollars *America's Sweetheart*, 1931
I've gotta be me *Golden Rainbow*, 1968
I've got to crow *Peter Pan*, 1954
I've grown accustomed to her face *My Fair Lady*, 1956
I've never been in love before *Guys and Dolls*, 1950
I've told every little star *Music in the Air*, 1932
I wanna be loved by you *Good Boy*, 1928
I wanna get married *Follow the Girls*, 1944
I want to be happy *No, No, Nanette*, 1925
I was never kissed before *Bless the Bride*, 1947
I whistle a happy tune *The King and I*, 1951
I wish I were in love again *Babes in Arms*, 1937
I wonder what became of me *St Louis Woman*, 1946
I wonder what the King is doing tonight *Camelot*, 1960
I won't dance *Three Sisters*, 1934; *Roberta*, 1935*

Jet song *West Side Story*, 1957
Joey, Joey, Joey *The Most Happy Fella*, 1956
Johnny one-note *Babes in Arms*, 1937
Joker, The *The Roar of the Greasepaint, the Smell of the Crowd*, 1965
Jubilation T. Cornpone *Li'l Abner*, 1956
June is bustin' out all over *Carousel*, 1945
Just a kiss apart *Gentlemen Prefer Blondes*, 1949
Just a memory *Manhattan Mary*, 1927
Just for a while *The Last Waltz*, 1921
Just imagine *Good News*, 1927
Just in time *Bells Are Ringing*, 1956
Just one of those things *Jubilee*, 1935; *Can Can*, 1960*
Just we two *The Student Prince*, 1924
Just you wait *My Fair Lady*, 1956

Ka-lu-a *Good Morning Dearie*, 1921; *The Cabaret Girl*, 1922
Kansas City *Oklahoma!*, 1943
Katie went to Haiti *Dubarry Was a Lady*, 1939
Keepin' myself for you *Hit the Deck*, 1927
Keep it gay *Me and Juliet*, 1953
Kids *Bye Bye Birdie*, 1960
Kiss in the dark, A *Orange Blossoms*, 1922
Kiss me again *Miss 1917*, 1917
Kiss waltz *The Pink Lady*, 1911
Knowing when to leave *Promises, Promises*, 1968

La belle Marguerite *Bless the Bride*, 1947
Ladies of the town *Bitter Sweet*, 1929
Lady is a tramp, The *Babes in Arms*, 1937; *Pal Joey*, 1957*
Lambeth walk, The *Me and My Girl*, 1937
Last time I saw Paris, The *Lady Be Good*, 1941*
Lazy afternoon *Golden Apple*, 1954
Leap year waltz *The Dancing Years*, 1939
Leave it to Jane *Leave It to Jane*, 1917
Legalize my name *St Louis Woman*, 1946
Let me entertain you *Gypsy*, 1959
Let's be buddies *Panama Hattie*, 1940
Let's begin *Roberta*, 1933
Let's do it *Paris*, 1928; *Can Can*, 1960*
Let's have another cup of coffee *Face the Music*, 1932
Let's kiss and make up *Funny Face*, 1927
Let's knock knees *The Gay Divorce*, 1934*
Let's not talk about love *Let's Face It*, 1941
Let's take an old-fashioned walk *Miss Liberty*, 1949
Let the sunshine in *Hair*, 1967

Lida Rose *The Music Man*, 1957
Life's full of consequence *Cabin in the Sky*, 1942*
Life upon the wicked stage *Show Boat*, 1927*
Little fish in a big pond, A *Miss Liberty*, 1949
Little girl blue *Jumbo*, 1935
Little girl from Little Rock, A *Gentlemen Prefer Blondes*, 1949
Little Nellie Kelly *Little Nellie Kelly*, 1922
Live and let live *Can Can*, 1953
Liza *Show Girl*, 1929
Lonely goatherd *The Sound of Music*, 1959
Lonely house *Street Scene*, 1947
Lonely town *On the Town*, 1944
Long before I knew you *Bells Are Ringing*, 1956
Look for the silver lining *Sally*, 1920
Looking for a boy *Tip Toes*, 1925
Look to the rainbow *Finian's Rainbow*, 1947
Lorelei *Pardon My English*, 1933
Lost in loveliness *The Girl in Pink Tights*, 1954
Lost in the stars *Lost in the Stars*, 1949
Lot of livin' to do, A *Bye Bye Birdie*, 1960
Louisiana hayride *Flying Colors*, 1932; *The Band Wagon*, 1953*
Love for sale *The New Yorkers*, 1930
Love I long for, The *Sadie Thompson*, 1944
Love in a home *Li'l Abner*, 1956
Love is my reason *Perchance to Dream*, 1945
Love is sweeping the country *Of Thee I Sing*, 1931
Lovelier than ever *Where's Charley?*, 1948
Love look away *Flower Drum Song*, 1958
Lovely *A Funny Thing Happened on the Way to the Forum*, 1962
Lovely night, A *Cinderella*, 1958
Lovely to look at *Roberta*, 1935*
Lovely way to spend an evening, A *Higher and Higher*, 1943*
Love makes the world go round *Carnival*, 1961
Love me or leave me *Whoopee*, 1928; *Simple Simon*, 1930
Love nest, The *Mary*, 1920
Lover come back to me *New Moon*, 1928
Love will find a way *The Maid of the Mountains*, 1917
Luck be a lady *Guys and Dolls*, 1950
Lucky in love *Good News*, 1927
Lucky to be me *On the Town*, 1944
Lusty month of May, The *Camelot*, 1960

Ma blushin' Rosie *Fiddle-De-Dee*, 1900
Mack the knife *The Threepenny Opera*, 1954
Maidens typical of France *Can Can*, 1953
Main Street *On the Town*, 1949*
Make a miracle *Where's Charley?*, 1948
Make believe *Show Boat*, 1927
Make someone happy *Do-Re-Mi*, 1960
Make the man love me *A Tree Grows in Brooklyn*, 1951
Makin' whoopee *Whoopee*, 1928
Malady in 4-F *Let's Face It*, 1941
Mame *Mame*, 1966
Mandy *Yip, Yip, Yaphank*, 1918; *This Is the Army*, 1942
Many a new day *Oklahoma!*, 1943
March of the musketeers *The Three Musketeers*, 1928
March of the Siamese children *The King and I*, 1951
March of the toys *Babes in Toyland*, 1903
Maria (Bernstein-Sondheim) *West Side Story*, 1957
Maria (Rodgers-Hammerstein) *The Sound of Music*, 1959
Maria (Schwartz-Dietz) *Revenge with Music*, 1934
Marianne *New Moon*, 1928
Marian the librarian *The Music Man*, 1957
Marriage-type love *Me and Juliet*, 1953
Marrying for love *Call Me Madam*, 1950
Mary *Forty-five Minutes from Broadway*, 1906
Matchmaker, matchmaker *Fiddler on the Roof*, 1964
Maybe *Oh Kay!*, 1926
Maybe this time *Cabaret*, 1972*

Memories of you *Shuffle Along*, 1921
Mine *Let 'em Eat Cake*, 1933
Miracle of miracles *Fiddler on the Roof*, 1964
Miss Marmelstein *I Can Get It for You Wholesale*, 1962
Mr Snow *Carousel*, 1945
Mr Wonderful *Mr Wonderful*, 1956
Money money *Cabaret*, 1966
Montmartre *Can Can*, 1953
Moonburn *Anything Goes*, 1936*
Moon-faced, starry-eyed *Street Scene*, 1947
Moonshine lullaby *Annie Get Your Gun*, 1946
More I cannot wish you *Guys and Dolls*, 1950
More than you know *Great Day*, 1929; *Hit the Deck*, 1955*
Most beautiful girl in the world, The *Jumbo*, 1935
Most gentlemen don't like love *Leave It to Me*, 1938
Mountain greenery *The Girl Friend*, 1927
Mountain high, valley low *Lute Song*, 1946
Music in May *Careless Rapture*, 1936
Music stopped, The *Higher and Higher*, 1943*
Music that makes me dance *Funny Girl*, 1964
Mutual admiration society *Happy Hunting*, 1956
My baby just cares for me *Whoopee*, 1928
My British buddy *This Is the Army*, 1943 (UK production)
My cup runneth over *I Do, I Do*, 1966
My darling, my darling *Where's Charley?*, 1948
My dearest dear *The Dancing Years*, 1939
My defences are down *Annie Get Your Gun*, 1946
My dream girl *Dream Girl*, 1924
My favourite things *The Sound of Music*, 1959
My funny valentine *Babes in Arms*, 1937; *Pal Joey*, 1957*
My girl back home *South Pacific*, 1958*
My heart and I (Hollander) *Anything Goes*, 1936*
My heart and I (Tauber) *Old Chelsea*, 1943
My heart belongs to Daddy *Leave It to Me*, 1938
My heart is so full of you *The Most Happy Fella*, 1956
My heart stood still *A Connecticut Yankee*, 1927
My life belongs to you *The Dancing Years*, 1939
My lord and master *The King and I*, 1951
My lucky star *Follow Thru*, 1929
My mammy *Sinbad*, 1918
My man's gone now *Porgy and Bess*, 1935
My one and only *Funny Face*, 1927
My romance *Jumbo*, 1935
My ship *Lady in the Dark*, 1941
My time of day *Guys and Dolls*, 1950

Namely you *Li'l Abner*, 1956
Neapolitan love song *The Princess Pat*, 1915
'Neath the southern moon *Naughty Marietta*, 1910
Necessity *Finian's Rainbow*, 1947
Needle in a haystack, A *The Gay Divorce*, 1934*
Never will I marry *Greenwillow*, 1960
New-fangled tango, A *Happy Hunting*, 1956
New sun in the sky *The Band Wagon*, 1931
New York, New York *On the Town*, 1944
Next time it happens, The *Pipe Dream*, 1955
Night and day *The Gay Divorce*, 1932
Night of my nights *Kismet*, 1953
Night song *Golden Boy*, 1964
Night waltz *A Little Night Music*, 1973
Night was made for love, The *The Cat and the Fiddle*, 1931
Nobody does it like me *Seesaw*, 1974
Nobody else but me *Show Boat*, 1946
Nobody's heart *By Jupiter*, 1942
No other love *Me and Juliet*, 1953
No strings *No Strings*, 1962
Not for all the rice in China *As Thousands Cheer*, 1933
Not since Nineveh *Kismet*, 1953
No way to stop it *The Sound of Music*, 1959

Ocarina, The *Call Me Madam*, 1950
O thee I sing *Of Thee I Sing*, 1931
Oh, Donna Clara *Wonder Bar*, 1930
Oh, how I hate to get up in the morning *Yip, Yip, Yaphank*, 1918; *This Is the Army*, 1942
Ohio *Wonderful Town*, 1953
Oh, lady be good *Lady Be Good*, 1924
Oh, what a beautiful morning *Oklahoma!*, 1943
Old devil moon *Finian's Rainbow*, 1947
Oldest established, The (permanent floating crap game) *Guys and Dolls*, 1950
Olive tree, The *Kismet*, 1953
Ol' man river *Show Boat*, 1927
On a clear day you can see forever *On a Clear Day You Can See Forever*, 1965
Once and for always *A Connecticut Yankee*, 1948*
Once-a-year day *The Pajama Game*, 1954
Once in a lifetime *Stop the World, I Want to Get Off*, 1961
Once in love with Amy *Where's Charley?*, 1948
Once upon a time *All-American*, 1962
One *A Chorus Line*, 1976
One alone *The Desert Song*, 1926
One flower *The Desert Song*, 1926
One hand, one heart *West Side Story*, 1957
One kiss *New Moon*, 1928
One last kiss *Bye Bye Birdie*, 1960
One life to live *Lady in the Dark*, 1941
Only another boy and girl *Seven Lively Arts*, 1944
Only a rose *The Vagabond King*, 1925
On the street where you live *My Fair Lady*, 1956
Ordinary couple, An *The Sound of Music*, 1959
Ordinary man, An *My Fair Lady*, 1956
Ordinary people *Zip Goes a Million*, 1951
Other generation, The *Flower Drum Song*, 1958
Other side of the tracks, The *Little Me*, 1962
Our language of love *Irma la Douce*, 1958
Our love affair *Strike Up the Band*, 1940*
Out of my dreams *Oklahoma!*, 1943
Outside of that I love you *Louisiana Purchase*, 1940
Over and over again *Jumbo*, 1935

Paradise for two, A *The Maid of the Mountains*, 1917
Paris loves lovers *Silk Stockings*, 1955
Party's over, The *Bells Are Ringing*, 1956
Pedro the fisherman *The Lisbon Story*, 1943
People *Funny Girl*, 1964
People tree, The *The Good Old, Bad Old Days*, 1972
People will say we're in love *Oklahoma!*, 1943
Physician, The *Nymph Errant*, 1933
Play a simple melody *Watch Your Step*, 1914
Pleasure of your company, The *The Good Companions*, 1974
Poor Pierrot *The Cat and the Fiddle*, 1931
Poppa won't you dance with me? *High Button Shoes*, 1947
Pore Jud is dead *Oklahoma!*, 1943
Pretty things *Rose Marie*, 1924
Primrose *The Dancing Years*, 1939
Princess of pure delight *Lady in the Dark*, 1941
Promises, promises *Promises, Promises*, 1968
Put on a happy face *Bye Bye Birdie*, 1960
Put on your Sunday clothes *Hello Dolly*, 1964
Puzzlement, A *The King and I*, 1951

Quiet Girl, A *Wonderful Town*, 1953

Racing with the clock *The Pajama Game*, 1954
Rain in Spain, The *My Fair Lady*, 1956
Razzle dazzle *Chicago*, 1975
Real American folk song, The *Ladies First*, 1918
Real live girl, A *Little Me*, 1962
Real nice clambake, A *Carousel*, 1945

Reuben, Reuben *A Trip to Chinatown*, 1893
Rhymes have I *Kismet*, 1953
Rhythm of life, The *Sweet Charity*, 1966
Ribbons down my back *Hello Dolly*, 1964
Rich man's frug *Sweet Charity*, 1966
Riding high *Red, Hot and Blue*, 1936; *Aladdin*, 1959
Riff song *The Desert Song*, 1926
Right as the rain *Bloomer Girl*, 1944
Rio Rita *Rio Rita*, 1927
Rise and shine *Take a Chance*, 1932
Road to paradise, The *Maytime*, 1917
Rockabye your baby with a Dixie melody *Sinbad*, 1918
Romance *The Desert Song*, 1926
Room in Bloomsbury, A *The Boy Friend*, 1954
Room without windows, A *What Makes Sammy Run?*, 1964
Rosalie *Rosalie*, 1937*
Rose Marie *Rose Marie*, 1924
Rose of England *Crest of the Wave*, 1937
Rosie *Bye Bye Birdie*, 1960
Roxie *Chicago*, 1975

Sadder but wiser girl, The *The Music Man*, 1957
Saga of Jenny, The *Lady in the Dark*, 1941
Sail away *Ace of Clubs*, 1950; *Sail Away*, 1961
Sam and Delilah *Girl Crazy*, 1930
Sands of time *Kismet*, 1953
Sawdust, spangles and dreams *Jumbo*, 1962*
Second-hand rose *Funny Girl*, 1968*
Send in the clowns *A Little Night Music*, 1973
September song *Knickerbocker Holiday*, 1938
Serenade *The Student Prince*, 1924
76 trombones *The Music Man*, 1957
Shall we dance? *The King and I*, 1951
Shalom *Milk and Honey*, 1961
Shanty town *Glamorous Night*, 1935
She did't say yes *The Cat and the Fiddle*, 1931
She loves me *She Loves Me*, 1963
She's my lovely *Hide and Seek*, 1937
Shine on your shoes, A *Flying Colors*, 1932; *The Band Wagon*, 1953*
Shine through my dreams *Glamorous Night*, 1935
Ship without a sail, A *Heads Up*, 1929
Shortest day in the year, The *The Boys from Syracuse*, 1938
Show me *My Fair Lady*, 1956
Simple joys of maidenhood, The *Camelot*, 1960
Sing for your supper *The Boys from Syracuse*, 1938
Siren's song *Leave It to Jane*, 1917
Sit down, you're rockin' the boat *Guys and Dolls*, 1950
Sixteen going on seventeen *The Sound of Music*, 1959
Slaughter on 10th Avenue *On Your Toes*, 1936
Sleepin' bee, A *House of Flowers*, 1954
Small talk *The Pajama Game*, 1954
Small world *Gypsy*, 1959
Smoke gets in your eyes *Roberta*, 1933
So far *Allegro*, 1947
Soft lights and sweet music *Face the Music*, 1932
Softly as in a morning sunrise *New Moon*, 1928
So in love *Kiss Me Kate*, 1948
Soliloquy (My boy Bill/My little girl) *Carousel*, 1945
Solomon *Nymph Errant*, 1933
So long, farewell *The Sound of Music*, 1959
So long, Mary *Forty-five Minutes from Broadway*, 1906
Some day *The Vagabond King*, 1925
Some day my heart will awake *King's Rhapsody*, 1949
Some day we shall meet again *The Lisbon Story*, 1943
Some enchanted evening *South Pacific*, 1949
Someone nice like you *Stop the World, I Want to Get Off*, 1961
Someone to watch over me *Oh Kay!*, 1926
Some people *Gypsy*, 1959
Something good *The Sound of Music*, 1965*

Opposite: **Godspell** (1971). Stephen Schwartz's rock-*religioso* opened at The Round House in London's suburbia in November 1971, moving to the West End two months later. David Essex (centre) played the leading role.

Something's coming *West Side Story*, 1957
Something sorta grandish *Finian's Rainbow*, 1947
Something to dance about *Call Me Madam*, 1950
Something to remember you by *Three's a Crowd*, 1930
Something wonderful *The King and I*, 1951
Sometimes I'm happy *Hit the Deck*, 1927
Somewhere *West Side Story*, 1957
Some wonderful sort of someone *Ladies First*, 1918; *The Lady in Red*, 1919
Song of love *Blossom Time*, 1921
Song of the Mounties *Rose Marie*, 1924
Song of the Rangers *Rio Rita*, 1927
Song of the vagabonds *The Vagabond King*, 1925
Song is you, The *Music in the Air*, 1932
Soon *Strike Up the Band*, 1930
Soon it's gonna rain *The Fantasticks*, 1960
Sound of music, The *The Sound of Music*, 1959
South America, take it away *Call Me Mister*, 1946
Speak low *One Touch of Venus*, 1943
Spread a little happiness *Mr Cinders* 1929
Spring is here *Spring Is Here*, 1929; *I Married an Angel*, 1938
Standing on the corner *The Most Happy Fella*, 1956
Stand up and fight *Carmen Jones*, 1943
Star light, star bright *The Wizard of the Nile*, 1895
Stately homes of England, The *Operette*, 1938
Steam heat *The Pajama Game*, 1954
Stereophonic sound *Silk Stockings*, 1956
Stouthearted men *New Moon*, 1928
Strange music *The Song of Norway*, 1944
Stranger in paradise *Kismet*, 1953
Strike another match *Wedding in Paris*, 1954
Strike up the band *Strike Up the Band*, 1930
Suddenly it's spring *Lady in the Dark*, 1944*
Sue me *Guys and Dolls*, 1950
Summertime *Porgy and Bess*, 1935
Summertime love *Greenwillow*, 1960
Sunday *Flower Drum Song*, 1958
Sunrise, sunset *Fiddler on the Roof*, 1964
Sunshine girl *New Girl in Town*, 1957
Supper time *As Thousands Cheer*, 1933
Surrey with the fringe on top, The *Oklahoma!*, 1943
Swanee *Sinbad*, 1918
Sweethearts *Sweethearts*, 1913
Sweet and lowdown *Tip Toes*, 1925
Sweet lady *Tangerine*, 1921
Sweetest sounds, The *No Strings*, 1962
'S wonderful *Funny Face*, 1927
Sympathy *The Firefly*, 1912

Take back your mink *Guys and Dolls*, 1950
Take it slow, Joe *Jamaica*, 1957
Take your girl *King's Rhapsody*, 1949
Taking a chance on love *Cabin in the Sky*, 1940
Talk to me baby *Foxy*, 1964
Tea for two *No, No, Nanette*, 1925
Tell me I'm forgiven *Wonder Bar*, 1930
Ten cents a dance *Simple Simon*, 1930
Ten minutes ago *Cinderella*, 1958
That certain feeling *Tip Toes*, 1925
That great come-and-get-it day *Finian's Rainbow*, 1947
That's entertainment *The Band Wagon*, 1953*
That terrific rainbow *Pal Joey*, 1940
Then you may take me to the fair *Camelot*, 1960
There are angels outside heaven *Old Chelsea*, 1943
There but for you go I *Brigadoon*, 1947

Opposite: **Cabaret** (1966). Joel Grey in one of his big numbers that helped earn *Cabaret* two awards as 'Best Musical of the Year'.

There is nothing like a dame *South Pacific*, 1949
There must be something better than love *Arms and the Girl*, 1950
There once was a man *The Pajama Game*, 1954
There's a boat that's leavin' soon for New York *Porgy and Bess*, 1935
There's a coach comin' in *Paint Your Wagon*, 1951
There's a great day coming manana *Hold On to Your Hats*, 1940
There's always tomorrow *Stand Up and Sing*, 1931
There's a small hotel *On Your Toes*, 1936; *Pal Joey*, 1957*
There's gotta be something better than this *Sweet Charity*, 1966
There's no business like show business *Annie Get Your Gun*, 1946
They call the wind Maria *Paint Your Wagon*, 1951
They didn't believe me *The Girl from Utah*, 1913; *Tonight's the Night*, 1915
They say it's wonderful *Annie Get Your Gun*, 1946
Thinking of you *The Five O'Clock Girl*, 1927
This can't be love *The Boys from Syracuse*, 1938; *Jumbo*, 1962*
This is my lovely day *Bless the Bride*, 1947
This is new *Lady in the Dark*, 1941
This is the life *Golden Boy*, 1964
This nearly was mine *South Pacific*, 1949
This time of the year *Finian's Rainbow*, 1947
Thou swell *A Connecticut Yankee*, 1927
Till the clouds roll by *Oh Boy!*, 1917
Till there was you *The Music Man*, 1957
Time on my hands *Smiles*, 1930
Together wherever we go *Gypsy*, 1959
Tokay *Bitter Sweet*, 1929
To keep my love alive *A Connecticut Yankee*, 1943
Tom, Dick and Harry *Kiss Me Kate*, 1948
Tomorrow mountain *Beggars' Holiday*, 1946
Tonight *West Side Story*, 1957
Too close for comfort *Mr Wonderful*, 1956
Too darn hot *Kiss Me Kate*, 1948
Too many rings around Rosie *No, No, Nanette*, 1925
Totem tom-tom *Rose Marie*, 1924
Touch of your hand, The *Roberta*, 1933
Tradition *Fiddler on the Roof*, 1964
Tramp, tramp, tramp *Naughty Marietta*, 1910
Treat me rough *Girl Crazy*, 1930
Tree in the Park, A *Peggy Ann*, 1926
Triplets *Between the Devil*, 1938; *The Band Wagon*, 1953*
Try to remember *The Fantasticks*, 1960
Tschaikowsky *Lady in the Dark*, 1941
Two ladies in the shade of de banana tree *House of Flowers*, 1954
Two little babes in the wood *Paris*, 1928
Two little bluebirds *Sunny*, 1925
Typically English *Stop the World, I Want to Get Off*, 1961

Varsity drag, The *Good News*, 1927
Very special day, A *Me and Juliet*, 1953
Violin began to play, A *King's Rhapsody*, 1949
Vitality *Gay's the Word*, 1951

Waiting for my dearie *Brigadoon*, 1947
Wait till you see her *By Jupiter*, 1942
Waltz of my heart *The Dancing Years*, 1939
Wand'rin' star *Paint Your Wagon*, 1951
Wanting you *New Moon*, 1928
Warm all over *The Most Happy Fella*, 1956
We kiss in a shadow *The King and I*, 1951
Well, did you evah? *Dubarry Was a Lady*, 1939
We'll gather lilacs *Perchance to Dream*, 1945
We must never say goodbye *The Lisbon Story*, 1943
We open in Venice *Kiss Me Kate*, 1948
We're having a baby *Banjo Eyes*, 1941
Were thine that special face *Kiss Me Kate*, 1948
We said we wouldn't look back *Salad Days*, 1954
We were so young *Sweet Adeline*, 1934*
What chance have I with love? *Louisiana Purchase*, 1940; *Call Me Madam*, 1953*
What did I have that I don't have? *On a Clear Day You Can See Forever*, 1965
What do I care for a dame? *Pal Joey*, 1957*
What do the simple folks do? *Camelot*, 1960
Whatever Lola wants *Damn Yankees*, 1955
What I did for love *A Chorus Line*, 1976
What is this thing called love? *Wake Up and Dream*, 1929
What kind of fool am I? *Stop the World, I Want to Get Off*, 1961
What's the use of wonderin'? *Carousel*, 1945
When a maid comes knocking at your heart *The Firefly*, 1912
When hearts are young *Lady in Ermine*, 1922
When I'm not near the girl I love *Finian's Rainbow*, 1947
When is sometime? *A Connecticut Yankee*, 1948*
When love goes wrong *Gentlemen Prefer Blondes*, 1953*
When she walks in the room *Up in Central Park*, 1945
When the children are asleep *Carousel*, 1945
When the idle poor become the idle rich *Finian's Rainbow*, 1947
When you're away *The Only Girl*, 1914
Where did the night go? *Wish You Were Here*, 1952
Where is love? *Oliver!*, 1960
Where is my Bess? *Porgy and Bess*, 1935
Where is the life that late I led? *Kiss Me Kate*, 1948
Where or when? *Babes in Arms*, 1937
Where's that rainbow? *Peggy Ann*, 1926
While the city sleeps *Golden Boy*, 1964
Whip-poor-will *Sally*, 1920
Who? *Sunny*, 1925
Who are you? *The Boys from Syracuse*, 1940*
Who can I turn to? *The Roar of the Greasepaint, the Smell of the Crowd*, 1965
Who cares? *Of Thee I Sing*, 1930
Who do you love, I hope? *Annie Get Your Gun*, 1946
Who knows? *Rosalie*, 1937*
Whose baby are you? *The Night Boat*, 1920
Why can't the English? *My Fair Lady*, 1956
Why can't you behave? *Kiss Me Kate*, 1948
Why did I choose you? *The Yearling*, 1964
Why do I love you? *Show Boat*, 1927
Why, oh why, oh wherefore? *Hit the Deck*, 1927
Why shouldn't I? *Jubilee*, 1935
Why was I born? *Sweet Adeline*, 1929
Wildflower *Wildflower*, 1923
Wild Rose *Sally*, 1920
Willkommen *Cabaret*, 1966
Will you remember? *Maytime*, 1917
Wings of sleep *The Dancing Years*, 1939
Wish you were here *Wish You Were Here*, 1952
With a little bit of luck *My Fair Lady*, 1956
With a song in my heart *Spring Is Here*, 1929
With my head in the clouds *This Is the Army*, 1942
Without a song *Great Day*, 1929
Without love (De Sylva-Brown-Henderson) *Flying High*, 1930
Without love (Porter) *Silk Stockings*, 1955
Without you *My Fair Lady*, 1956
Woman in love, A *Guys and Dolls*, 1955*
Woman is a sometime thing, A *Porgy and Bess*, 1935
Woman's prerogative, A *St Louis Woman*, 1946
Wonderful day like today, A *The Roar of the Greasepaint, the Smell of the Crowd*, 1965
Wouldn't it be luverly? *My Fair Lady*, 1956
Wrong note rag *Wonderful Town*, 1953
Wunderbar *Anything Goes*, 1934 (*as* Waltz down the aisle); *Kiss Me Kate*, 1948

Ya got trouble *The Music Man*, 1957

Yama-yama man *The Three Twins*, 1908
Yes I can *Golden Boy*, 1964
Yesterdays *Roberta*, 1933
You and the night and the music *Revenge with Music*, 1934
You are beautiful *Flower Drum Song*, 1958
You are love *Show Boat*, 1927
You are woman, I am man *Funny Girl*, 1964
You can count on me *On the Town*, 1949*
You can dance with any girl you please *No, No, Nanette*, 1925
You can't get a man with a gun *Annie Get Your Gun*, 1946
You'd be so nice to come home to *Something to Shout About*, 1943
You'd be surprised *Afgar*, 1919
You'd better love me *High Spirits*, 1964
You did it *My Fair Lady*, 1956
You do something to me *Fifty Million Frenchmen*, 1929; *Can Can*, 1960*
You have cast your shadow on the sea *The Boys from Syracuse*, 1938
You kissed me *Arms and the Girl*, 1950
You'll never get away from me *Gypsy*, 1959
You'll never walk alone *Carousel*, 1945
You mustn't kick it around *Pal Joey*, 1940
Young and foolish *Plain and Fancy*, 1955
Younger than springtime *South Pacific*, 1949
You're always in my arms *Rio Rita*, 1927
You're an old smoothie *Take a Chance*, 1932
You're a queer one, Julie Jordan *Carousel*, 1945
You're awful *On the Town*, 1949*
You're devastating *Roberta*, 1933
You're just in love *Call Me Madam*, 1950
You're my girl *High Button Shoes*, 1947
You're nearer *Too Many Girls*, 1940*
You're so sweet to remember *Winged Victory*, 1943
You're the cream in my coffee *Hold Everything*, 1928
You're the top *Anything Goes*, 1934
Your land and my land *My Maryland*, 1927
Yours sincerely *Spring Is Here*, 1929
You took advantage of me *Present Arms*, 1928; *On Your Toes*, 1954
You've got that thing *Fifty Million Frenchmen*, 1929
You've got to pick a pocket or two *Oliver!*, 1960

Zigeuner *Bitter Sweet*, 1929
Zip! *Pal Joey*, 1940

Plot Summaries

Below and on the pages following is a brief description of the musical shows from 1919, as listed in the Musical Calendar, with writing credits denoted as follows: m. = composer of the music, l. = lyricist, b. = librettist. Where applicable, the source of the musical – whether novel, play or film – is shown, the figure in parenthesis indicating the number of performances achieved in the original run. Normally this refers only to that in the country of origin, but where known the length of run of American shows in London, and vice versa, is included. The date is of the year of the original production. Asterisk (*) following number of performances designates 'as of May 31, 1977'.

Ace of Clubs Crime story. 1950. m.l.b. Noël Coward (short run).

Afgar International spectacular. 1919. m. Charles Cuvillier, l. Douglas Furber, b. Warton David, Fred Thompson. (2 years).

After the Ball Adapt of *Lady Windermere's Fan*. 1954. m.l.b. Noël Coward (188).

Ain't Supposed to Die a Natural Death Rock musical. 1971 m.l.b. Melvin Van Peebles (325).

Aladdin Fairy Tale. 1959. m.l. Cole Porter, b. S. J. Perelman.

All-American Patriotic tribute. 1962. m. Charles Strouse, l. Lee Adams (short-run).

Allegro Medical drama. 1947. m. Richard Rodgers l.b. Oscar Hammerstein II (315).

All The King's Horses Adapted from play *Carlo Rocco* by Lawrence Clarke and Max Giersberg. Film star and King change places. 1934. m. Edward A. Horan l.b. Frederick Herendeen (120).

Ambassador Adapt of Henry James's *The Ambassadors*. 1971. m. Don Gohman, l. Hal Hackaday, b. Don Ellinger, and Anne Marie Barlow (19).

America's Sweetheart Twenties' Hollywood. 1931. m. Richard Rodgers, l. Lorenz Hart, b. Herbert Fields (135).

And So to Bed Adapt from Pepys's *Diary*. 1951. m.l. Vivian Ellis, b. J. B. Fagan (323).

Animal Crackers Marx Brothers romp, with Groucho as Captain Spaulding. Vaguely involves a stolen painting at a Long Island house party, but plot merely an excuse for by-play for the Brothers and Margaret Dumont. 1928. m. Harry Ruby, l. Bert Kalmar, b. George S. Kaufman, Morrie Ryskind (191).

Anne of Green Gables Adolescents' classic. 1969. m.l.b. Norman Campbell, Donald Harron.

Annie London Romance. 1967. (243 perfs).

Annie Musical version of the comic strip Little Orphan Annie. Annie vanquishes the wicked head of the orphanage. Included is the character Daddy Warbucks as her parent surrogate. 1977. m. Charles Strouse. l. Martin Charnin. b. Thomas Meehan (44)*.

Annie Dear Romantic Comedy. 1924. m. Sigmund Romberg, l. Clifford Grey, b. Clare Kummer.

Annie Get Your Gun Backwoods girl Annie Oakley becomes beautiful shooting star of Buffalo Bill's Wild West Show, falls in love with rival Frank Butler, and settles for family life. 1946. m. Irving Berlin, b. Herbert and Dorothy Fields (1,147 USA, 1,304 GB).

Ann Veronica H. G. Wells romance. 1969. m. Cyril Ornadel (short run).

Anyone Can Whistle Comedy-drama. 1965. m.l. Stephen Sondheim, b. Arthur Laurents (9).

Anything Goes Shipboard romance of hero torn between heiress and night-club singer, complicated by English noble suitor. Secondary plot involves Public Enemy No 13, disappointed with his low rating. 1934. m.l. Cole Porter, b. Guy Bolton, P. G. Wodehouse, Howard Lindsay and Russell Crouse (420 USA, 261 GB).

Applause Film *All About Eve*. 1970. m. Charles Strouse, l. Lee Adams, b. Betty Comden and Adolph Green (896 USA, 11 months GB).

Apple Blossoms American operetta. 1919. m. Fritz Kreisler and Victor Jacobi, l.b. William le Baron (256).

Apple Tree, The Three feminine plays. 1966. m. Jerry Bock, l. Sheldon Harnick, b. Jerome Coopersmith (463).

Arc de Triomphe Romantic drama. 1943. m.b. Ivor Novello, l. Christopher Hassall.

Aren't We All? Musical comedy. 1923.

Are You with It? Forties musical. 1945. m. Harry Revel, l. Arnold B. Howitt.

Ari Musical *Exodus*. 1971. m. Walt Smith, l.b. Leon Uris.

Arms and the Girl Adapt of *The Pursuit of Happiness*. 1950. m. Morton Gould, l.b. Herbert and Dorothy Fields (134).

Around the World in Eighty Days Verne/Welles/. 1946. m.l. Cole Porter, b. Orson Welles (75).

As the Girls Go Political comedy. 1948. m. Jimmy McHugh, l. Harold Adamson, b. William Ross (420).

As Thousands Cheer Satirical revue. 1933. m.l. Irving Berlin, b. Moss Hart (400).

Autumn's Here Adapt of *The Legend of Sleepy Hollow*. 1966.

Babes in Arms Archetypal putting-on-a-show-in-the-barn musical. Children of vaudeville parents, left at home while their parents are on the road, solve their emotional and financial problems thus. 1937. m.b. Richard Rodgers, l.b. Lorenz Hart (289).

Baby Bunting Farcical comedy. 1919. m.l. Nat D. Ayer, l. Clifford Grey, b. Fred Thompson and Warton David.

Baker Street Featuring Sherlock Holmes. 1965. m.l. Raymond Jessell and Marion Grudeff, b. Jerome Coopersmith (311).

Balalaika Romance in pre-revolutionary Russia between Cossack officer and beautiful singer, with reunion twenty years later in Paris. 1936. m. George Posford and Bernard Grun, b.l. Eric Maschwitz (570).

Ballyhoo Musical comedy. 1930. m. Louis Alter, l.b. Oscar Hammerstein II, E. Y. Harburg and Harry Ruskin (68).

Band Wagon, The Basically a revue, generally regarded as the finest of the genre, which later became two successful 'book' musicals on the screen. The last, and best, vehicle for Fred and Adele Astaire. 1931. m. Arthur Schwartz, l.b. Howard Dietz, b. George S. Kaufman (260).

Banjo Eyes Adapt of *Three Men on a Horse*. 1941. m. Vernon Duke, l. Harold Adamson and John Latouche, b. Joe Quillan and Izzy Elinson (126).

Bar Mitzvah Boy Jewish family comedy set around a young man's coming-of-age, adapted by Jack Rosenthal from his own play. 1978. m. Jule Styne, l. Don Black (77).

Battling Butler Musical play. 1922. m. Philip Braham, l. Douglas Furber, b. Austin Melford and Stanley Brightman.

Beauty Prize Romantic comedy. 1923. m. Jerome Kern, l.b. P. G. Wodehouse and George Grossmith (212).

Beggars' Holiday Musical fantasy. 1947. m. Duke Ellington, l. John Latouche.

Belinda Fair Period romance. 1949. m. Jack Strachey, l.b. Eric Maschwitz.

Belle (or) *The Ballad of Dr Crippen* Period melodrama. 1961. m. Monty Norman.

Belle Starr Western adventure. 1969.

Bells Are Ringing Girl who runs telephone answering service becomes involved in her clients' problems, defeats gambling syndicate, and in helping playwright finds her own destiny. 1956. m. Jule Styne, l.b. Betty Comden and Adolph Green (924).

Ben Franklin in Paris American history. 1964. m. Mark Sandrich Jnr, l. Sidney Michaels (6 months).

Best Foot Forward Campus frolic in which a student invites a glamorous movie actress to the college prom, nearly loses his own girl, almost gets expelled, but all comes right in the end. As always. 1941. m. Hugh Martin, l. Ralph Blane, b. John Cecil Holm (326).

Betsy Ziegfeld flop. 1926. m. Richard Rodgers, l. Lorenz Hart, b. Irving Caesar and David Freedman (39).

Betty in Mayfair Adapt of *Lilies of the Field*. 1925. m. Harold Fraser-Simpson, l. Harry Graham.

Between the Devil Musical comedy. 1938. m. Arthur Schwartz, l.b. Howard Dietz (93).

Bet Your Life Sporting comedy. 1952.

Beyond The Rainbow Italian comedy from David Forrest's *After Me, The Deluge* 1978. m. Armando Trovaioli, l. Leslie Bricusse, b. Pietro Garinei, Sandro Giovanni, David Forrest (50 to Jan 1979).

Be Yourself Romantic comedy. 1924. m. Lewis E. Geusler, l. Ira Gershwin, l.b. George S. Kaufman and Marc Connolly (93).

Big Ben London life. 1946. m. Vivian Ellis, l.b. A. P. Herbert (172).

Big Boy Allegedly a horse-racing comedy with Al Jolson as a blackface jockey. But the plot, as in so many Jolson shows, sometimes went astray when the star sent the cast home and did his solo act. 1925. m. James F. Hanley and Joseph Meyer, l.b. Harold Atteridge and B. G. de Sylva.

Billie Anticlimactic Cohan. 1928. m.l.b. George M. Cohan.

Billion Dollar Baby Roaring twenties. 1945. m. Morton Gould, l.b. Betty Comden and Adolph Green (220).

Billy Adapt of *Billy Budd*. USA, 1969. m.l. Ron Dante and Gene Allan, b. Stephen Glassman (2 years).

Billy. Adapt of *Billy Liar*. GB. 1974. m. John Barry, l. Don Black, b. Keith Waterhouse.

Bitter Sweet Grand Old Lady looks back on her life in Vienna in the 1880s, her romance with a penniless singing teacher who died in a duel, and her marriage to a marquis. 1929. m.l.b. Noël Coward (697 GB, 151 USA).

Black Mikado, The All-black version of *The Mikado*. 1975. m. Arthur Sullivan, l.b. W. S. Gilbert.

Bless the Bride Romantic musical. 1947. m. Vivian Ellis, l.b. A. P. Herbet (836).

Blitz! Wartime London. 1962. m.l.b. Lionel Bart.

Blood Red Roses Transatlantic romance. 1970. m. Michael Valenti, l.b. John Lewin.

Bloomer Girl Biographical saga. 1944. m. Harold Arlen, l.b. E. Y. Harburg (654).

Blossom Time (also *Lilac Time*) Apocryphal biography of Franz Schubert and the broken love-affair which allegedly caused the incompleteness of the 'Unfinished' Symphony. Songs based on his music. 1921, 1922, 1942. m. Franz Schubert adapt Sigmund Romberg and G. H. Clutsom, l.b. Rodney Ackland, Dorothy Donnelly and Adrian Ross (1921: 592, 1922: 626).

Blue Eyes Romantic musical. 1928. m. Jerome Kern, l.b. Guy Belton and Graham John (276).

Blue for a Boy Farcical comedy. 1950. m. Harry Parr-Davies, l. Harold Purcell, b. Austin Melford.

Blue Kitten, The Twenties operetta. 1922. m. Rudolf Friml, l.b. Otto Habach, Greatrex Newman and William Cary Duncan.

Blue Roses Romantic comedy. 1931. m. Vivian Ellis, l.b. Desmond Carter, b. Caswell Garth (54).

Body Beautiful Glamour musical. 1957. m. Jerry Bock, l. Sheldon Harnick, b. Joseph Stein (2 months).

Bombo Frail story of Christopher Columbus and his blackface helper (Al Jolson) buying Manhattan from the Indians. Joly took as many liberties with this script as the story did with historical fact. 1921. m. Sigmund Romberg, l.b. Harold Attrridge and B. G. de Sylva (219).

Boodle Musical comedy. 1925. m. Herman Darewski and Philip Braham, l. Douglas Furber, b. Sydney Blow, Douglas Hoare.

Bordello Toulouse-Lautrec. 1974.

Boy Friend, The Twenties pastiche. 1954. m.l.b. Sandy Wilson (2,078 GB, 485 USA).

Boys from Syracuse, The Shakespeare's *Comedy of Errors*, still set in Ancient Greece, with the complications of two sets of twins expressed in modern vernacular with sophisticated Rodgers score. 1938. m. Richard Rodgers, l. Lorenz Hart, b. George Abbott (235 USA, 100 GB).

Brigadoon Two Americans discover a village in the Scottish Highlands that, under a magic spell, comes back for one day every hundred years. True love between past and present characters conquers all. 1947. m. Frederick Loewe, l.b. Alan Jay Lerner (581).

Broadway Whirl Spectacular musical. 1921. m. Harry Tierney, l.b. Joseph McCarthy and B. G. de Sylva.

Brown Buddies All Negro musical. 1930. m. Joe Jordan, l. Millard Thomas, b. Carl Rickman (113).

Buccaneer, The Newspaper story. 1955. m.l.b. Sandy Wilson (short run).

Buck White Boxing story. 1969. m.l.b. Oscar Brown Jnr, b. Joseph Dolan Tuotti.

Bunch and Judy, The Flimsy comedy. 1922. m. Jerome Kern, l.b. Anne Caldwell, b. Hugh Ford (65).

But Most of Us Cry at Movies Rock musical. 1970. m.l.b. Bruce Kirle.

Bye Bye Birdie Generation gap problems surveyed light-heartedly in satire on rock and roll and the publicity surrounding Elvis Presley's induction into US Army, guyed by 'Birdie' character. 1960. m. Charles Strouse, l. Lee Adams, b. Michael Stewart (607 USA, 8 months GB).

By Jupiter Greeks versus Amazons. 1942. m.b. Richard Rodgers, l.b. Lorenz Hart (427).

By the Beautiful Sea Menopausal romance. 1954. m. Arthur Schwartz, l.b. Herbert and Dorothy Fields (270).

Cabaret John Van Druten's *I Am a Camera* based on Christopher Isherwood's stories of pre-war Berlin, the rise of the Nazis, and the music and life of a second-rate cabaret. 1966. m. John Kander, l. Fred Ebb, b. Joe Masteroff (1,166 USA, 316 GB).

Cabaret Girl, The Romantic comedy. 1922. m. Jerome Kern, l.b. P. G. Wodehouse, Geo. Grossmith and Anne Caldwell (361).

Cabin in the Sky Emissaries of De Lawd and the Devil compete for the soul of a trouble-prone, downtrodden Negro. Tempted by seductress he is saved by his faithful wife. 1940. m. Vernon Duke, l. John Latouche and Ted Fetter, b. Lynn Root (156).

Call It Love Musical romance. 1960. m.l.b. Sandy Wilson (short run).

Call Me Madam Lady Ambassador to small European state (based on Mrs. Perle Mesta of Luxembourg) sorts out the romantic problems of the younger generation – and her own. 1950. m.l. Irving Berlin, b. Howard Lindsay and Russell Crouse (644).

Call Me Mister Readjustment of US soldiers facing post-war demobilization problems, comparing army and civilian life in revue-type numbers. 1946. m.l. Harold Rome, b. Arnold Auerbach and Arnold B. Horwitt (734).

Camelot From T. H. White's *The Once and Future King*. Glamorized adventures of the mythical King Arthur, Queen Guinevere, Sir Lancelot and the Knights of the Round Table. 1960. m. Frederick Loewe, l.b. Alan Jay Lerner (873 USA, 518 GB).

Can Can Turn-of-the-century Paris, in which a staid judge appointed to investigate the iniquitous can-can at a Montmartre café loses his dignity and falls for the attractive café owner. 1953 m.l. Cole Porter, b. Abe Burrows (892).

Candide Adapt. from Voltaire novel about hero whose vicissitudes force him to reject his former tutor's philosophy of eternal optimism. 1956. m. Leonard Bernstein l. Richard Wilbur, Dorothy Parker, John Latouche. b. Lilliam Hellman (73).

Captain Jinks Twenties comedy. 1925. m. Lewis E. Geusler, l. Ira Gershwin, l.b. B. G. de Sylva (107).

Card, The Period comedy. 1973. m. Tony Hatch, l. Jackie Trent (4 months).

Careless Rapture English operetta. 1936. m.b. Ivor Novello, l. Christopher Hassall (10 months).

Carissima Musical romance. 1947. m. Hans May, l.b. Eric Maschwitz (466).

Carmen Jones Bizet's *Carmen* updated to wartime America for an all-black cast. Toreador became a boxer, hero a GI, and seductress Carmen a war worker in a parachute factory. 1943. m. Georges Bizet, l.b. Oscar Hammerstein II (502).

Carnival Film *Lili* 1961. m.l. Bob Merrill, b. Michael Stewart (719).

Carousel Ferenc Molnár's *Liliom* moved from Hungary to New England. Carnival barker marries mill-girl, dies in disgrace, but is allowed to return to earth to redeem his soul. 1945. m. Richard Rodgers, l.b. Oscar Hammerstein II (899).

Castles in the Air Musical romance. 1927. m. Percy Wenrich, l.b. Raymond W. Peck.

Cat and the Fiddle, The Popular music versus classical in European locale. Popular writer (she) and operatic composer (he) turns mutual personal and musical dislike into mutual affection. 1931. m. Jerome Kern, l.b. Otto Harbach (395).

Catch My Soul Rock *Othello*. 1970. (5 months).

Celebration Fantastic masque. 1969. m. Harvey Schmidt, l.b. Tom Jones (109).

Charlie Girl Romantic comedy. 1966. m. David Heneker (2,202).

Chee-Chee Oriental fable. 1928. m. Richard Rodgers, l. Lorenz Hart, b. Herbert Fields (31).

Chicago Adapt of Maurice Dallas Watkins's *Roxie Hart*. 1975. m. John Kander, l. Fred Ebb.

Chiffon Girl Musical romance. 1924. m.l. Monte Carlo and Alma M. Sanders.

Chorus Line, A Backstage drama that strips the gloss from show business by revealing the heartaches of auditions for chorus members. 1975. m. Marvin Hamlisch l. Edward Kleban b. Nicholas Dante and James Kirkwood (855)*.

Chrysanthemum Light comedy. 1958. m. Robb Stewart (short run).

Cinderella Fairy story. 1958. m. Richard Rodgers, l.b. Oscar Hammerstein II.

Cindy Modern *Cinderella*. 1964. m.l. Johnny Brandon, b. Joe Sauter and Mike Sawyer.

Coco Chanel biography. 1960. m. Andre Previn, l.b. Alan Jay Lerner.

Cocoanuts, The Usual Marx Brothers mayhem, in nominal plot, regarding a Florida hotel during the twenties real-estate boom, which would vary from night to night. 1925. m.l. Irving Berlin, b. George S. Kaufman and Morrie Ryskind (276).

Come Spy with Me Musical farce. 1966. m.l. Bryan Blackburn (468).

Company Marriage analysis. 1970. m.l. Stephen Sondheim, b. George Furth (705).

Connecticut Yankee, A Mark Twain's *A Connecticut Yankee in King Arthur's Court*. Modern youth, transported back in time, brings the twentieth century to Camelot. 1927. m. Richard Rodgers, l. Lorenz Hart, b. Herbert Fields (418).

Conversation Piece Sophisticated comedy. 1934. m.l.b. Noël Coward (177 GB, 55 USA).

Costa Packet Holiday mood. 1972. m.l. Lionel Bart, b. Frank Norman (68).

Cradle Will Rock, The Political tract. 1937. m.l.b. Marc Blitzstein (108).

Crest of the Wave Romantic play. 1937. m.b. Ivor Novello, l. Christopher Hassall.

Criss Cross Vaudevillian comedy. 1926. m. Jerome Kern, l.b. Otto Harbach and Anne Caldwell (206).

Crooked Mile, The London comedy. 1959. m.l. Peter Greenwell, b. Peter Wildeblood.

Cross My Heart Romantic comedy. 1928. m. Harry Tierney, l. Joseph McCarthy, b. David Kusell.

Cyrano Rostrand's *Cyrano de Bergerac*. 1973. m. Michael J. Lewis, l.b. Anthony Burgess.

Daffy Dill Musical comedy. 1922. m. Herbert Stothart, l. Oscar Hammerstein II.

Damask Rose Chopin-based operetta, 1930. m.l.b. G. H. Clutsam, b. Robert Courtneidge.

Dames at Sea. Thirties satire. 1968. m. Jim Wise, l.b. George Hamish and Robin Miller (575).

Damn Yankees From Douglas Wallop's *The Year the Yankees Lost the Pennant*. Middle-aged baseball fan sells his soul to the Devil to become a young ball star. 1955. m. Richard Adler, l. Jerry Ross, b. George Abbott and Douglas Wallop (1,019).

Dancing Girl Routine musical. 1923. Various contributors, composers and lyricists.

Dancing Years, The Romance of composer and leading lady in middle European country, moving through the years to the rise of the Nazi Party. 1939. m.b. Ivor Novello, l. Christopher Hassall (969).

Day before Spring, The Marital breakdown. 1945. m. Frederick Loewe, l. b. Alan Jay Lerner (165).

Dean Biography of actor James Dean. 1977 (flop).

Dearest Enemy American War of Independence. 1925. m. Richard Rodgers, l. Lorenz Hart, b. Herbert Fields (286).

Dear Love Musical farce. 1929. m. Jack Waller, Joseph Tunbridge and Haydn Wood.

Dear Miss Phoebe Period musical. 1950. m. Harry Parr-Davies, l.b. Christopher Hassall.

Dear Sir Musical comedy. 1924. m. Jerome Kern, l.b. Howard Deitz.

Dear World Adapt of *The Madwoman of Chaillot*. 1969. m.l. Jerry Herman (4 months).

Desert Song, The Operetta set in Morocco. Governor's son has dual identity as leader of rebels, and heroine loves them both in turn without realizing they are the same man. 1926. m. Sigmund Romberg, l.b. Otto Harbach, Oscar Hammerstein II and Frank Mandell (465 USA, 432 GB).

Destry Rides Again From the film. 1959. m.l. Harold Rome, b. Leonard Gershe (473).

Divorce Me Darling Sequel to *The Boy Friend*. 1965. m.l.b. Sandy Wilson (87).

Doctor Selavy's Magic Theatre Rock musical. 1972. m. Stanley Silverman, l. Tom Hendry, b. Richard Foreman (144).

Do I Hear a Waltz? Adapt of *The Time of the Cuckoo*. 1965. m. Richard Rodgers, l. Stephen Sondheim, b. Arthur Laurents (220).

Don't Bother Me, I can't Cope Seventies generation. 1972. m.l. Micki Grant, b. Vinnette Carroll (1,065).

Don't Play Us Cheap Rock musical. 1972. m.l.b. Melvin Van Peebles (164).

Do-Re-Mi Jukebox racketeers. 1960. m. Jule Styne, l. Adolph Green and Betty Comden, b. Garson Kanin (400 USA, 4 months GB).

Dream Girl, The Romantic operetta. 1924. m. Victor Herbert, l.b. Riola Johnson Young and Harold Atteridge.

Drunkard, The Old-time melodrama. 1970. m.l. Barry Mainlow, b. Bro Herrod.

Dubarry Was a Lady Night-club owner dreams he is Louis XV and his girl friend is Dubarry. Bedroom farce making great play on incongruity of modern slang in a period of French elegance. 1939. m.l. Cole Porter, b. Herbert Fields and B. G. de Sylva (408).

Duenna, The Sheridan play. 1954. m.l. Julian Slade, b. Dorothy Reynolds (134).

Early to Bed Light-hearted musical. 1943. m.l. Fats Waller, l.b. George Marion Jnr.

East Wind Oriental romance. 1931. m. Sigmund Romberg, l.b. Oscar Hammerstein II, b. Frank Mandel (23).

Education of Hyman Kaplan From Leo Rosten stories. 1968. m.l. Oscar Brand and Paul Nassau, b. B. B. Zavin.

Elvis Musical tribute to rock star Elvis Presley. 1977. Various m. & l.

Ernest in Love Adapt of *The Importance of Being Earnest*. 1960. m. Lee Pockriss, l. Anne Crosswell.

Evergreen Musical romance. 1930. m. Richard Rodgers, l. Lorenz Hart, b. Benn Levy.

Everybody's Welcome Greenwich Village romance from Frances Goodrich & Albert Hackett play *Up Pops The Devil*. 1931. m. Sammy Fain, l. Irving Kahal, b. Lambert Carroll (139).

Evita Story of Eva Peron and her effect on Argentina's modern history. 1978. m.b. Andrew Lloyd Webber, l.b. Tim Rice (226 to end of 1978).

Exchange 'Pop' musical. 1970. m.l.b. Mike Brandt, Michael Knight and Robert Lowery.

Expresso Bongo Satirical exposé of late fifties pop-music scene. Fast talking promoter hitches his wagon to a rising rock star, who becomes involved with older woman. 1958. m. David Heneker and Monty Norman, l.b. Julian More, b. Wolf Mankowitz

Face the Music Depression satire. 1932. m.l. Irving Berlin, b. Moss Hart (165).

Fade Out Fade In Hollywood satire. 1964. m. Jule Styne, l.b. Betty Comden and Adolph Green (271).

Family Affair Domestic comedy. 1962. m. John Kander b. William Goldman and James Goldman (5 months).

Fanny From Marcel Pagnol's film trilogy *Marius, Cesar*, and *Fanny*, about Marseilles waterfront life. Older man marries pregnant woman, brings up her son as his own. On his death she returns to her first love. m.l. Harold Rome, b. S. N. Behrman and Joshua Logan (888).

Fantasticks, The Adapt from Edmond Rostand's play *Les Romantiques*. Neighbours try to bring their children together by keeping them romantically apart. 1960 m. Harvey Schmidt l.b. Tom Jones (7,115)*.

Fiddler on the Roof From Scholem Aleichem's stories. Persecution of Russian Jews in early twentieth century, allied to meticulous description of community and family life and Jewish traditions. 1964. m. Jerry Bock, l. Sheldon Harnick, b. Joseph Stein (3,242 USA, 2,030 GB).

Fifty Million Frenchmen Parisian romance, satirising the attitudes of Americans in France. Main theme concerns rich young man pretending to be poor so small-town girl will love him for himself alone. 1929. m. Cole Porter, b. Herbert Fields (254).

Fine and Dandy Slapstick comedy. 1930. m. Kay Swift, l. Paul James, b. Donald Ogden Stewart (255).

Fings Ain't Wot They Used t'Be Cockney comedy. 1959. m.l. Lionel Bart, b. Frank Norman (2 years).

Finian's Rainbow Fantasy with political overtones. Elderly Irishman steals leprechaun's crock of gold, plants it in America. Leprechaun follows, and the magic crock finally grants everyone's wishes. 1947. m. Burton Lane, l.b. E. Y. Harbur, b. Fred Said (725).

Fiorello! Musical biography of Mayor Fiorello La Guardia, his rise from poor lawyer, through Congress, and, via his opposition to Tammany Hall politics, to New York's highest office. 1959. m. Jerry Bock. l. Sheldon Harnick. b. George Abbott, Jerome Weidman (796).

Firebrand, The/Firebrand of Florence, The From Edwin Justis Meyer play. 1924. m. Robert Russell Bennett and Maurice Nitke, l. Ira Gershwin 287; 1945. m. Kurt Weill, l.b. Ira Gershwin (43).

First Impressions Adapt of *Pride and Prejudice*. 1959. m. Glenn Paxton, l. Robert Goldman, b. Abe Burrows.

Five O'Clock Girl Factory romance. 1927. m. Harry Ruby, l. Bert Kalmar, b. Guy Bolton and Fred Thompson (280).

Flora, the Red Menace Communist satire. 1965. m. John Kander, l. Fred Ebb, b. George Abbott and Robert Russell (87).

Flower Drum Song San Francisco Chinatown romance, pointing the different attitudes of the older and younger generations of Chinese towards marriage and their whole way of life. 1958. m. Richard Rodgers, l.b. Oscar Hammerstein II (601 USA, 14 months GB).

Flying Colours Revue-type musical. 1932. m. Arthur Schwartz, l.b. Howard Dietz (188).

Flying High Aeronautical comedy. Juvenile lead wins air race and the girl. Comic support breaks air record by accident and becomes a hero. 1930. m.l. De Sylva, Brown and Henderson, b. John McGowan and B. G. de Sylva (357).

Flying Trapeze, The Musical comedy, 1935. m. Ralph Benatzky, l.b. Douglas Furber.

Follies Showgirls' reunion. 1971. m.l. Stephen Sondheim, b. James Goldman (521).

Follow a Star Musical comedy. 1930. m. Vivian Ellis, l.b. Douglas Furber, b. Dion Titheradge (118).

Follow That Girl London romance. 1960. m.l.b. Julian Slade and Dorothy Reynolds.

Follow the Girls Wartime comedy. 1944. m. Phil Charig, l. Milton Pascal, b. Guy Bolton and Fred Thompson (882).

Follow Thru (Through) Twenties youth comedy set in a country club. Man hunting heroine chases shy hero, with subsidiary romance between golf champion and lady contender. 1929. m. De Sylva, Brown and Henderson, b. B. G. de Sylva and Lawrence Schwab (403 USA, 148 GB).

Forbidden Melody European romance based on King Carol of Roumania. 1936. m. Sigmund Romberg, l.b. Otto Harbach (32).

For Goodness' Sake (*Stop Flirting* in *UK*) Romantic comedy. 1922. m. William Daly and George Gershwin, l. Arthur Jackson and Ira Gershwin, b. Fred Jackson (103 USA, 418 GB).

For the Love of Mike Musical farce. 1931. m. Jack Waller and Joseph Tunbridge, l. Clifford Grey and Sonnie Miller, b. H. F. Maltby (239).

Four Musketeers From Alexandre Dumas. 1967. m. Laurie Johnson.

Foxy Modern comedy. 1964. m. Robert Emmett Dolan, l. Johnny Mercer (2 months).

Free as Air Holiday romance. 1957. m.l.b. Julian Slade and Dorothy Reynolds.

French Doll, The Musical comedy. 1922. m. George Gershwin, l.b. B. G. de Sylva (120).

Full Swing Musical comedy. 1942. m. George Posford, l.b. Arthur Macrae and Archie Menzies.

Funny Face Gershwin songs bolster a thin plot about incompetent thieves trying to steal jewels belonging to heroine, who is also persuading her boy friend to steal them from her guardian. 1927. m. George Gershwin l. Ira Gershwin, b. Paul Gerard Smith and Fred Thompson (250 USA, 263 GB).

Funny Girl Biography of Follies star Fanny Brice, told in flashback; her rise to fame from the back streets, attempt to make marriage to a gambler work at cost of her career, and subsequent return to the stage. 1964. m. Jule Styne, l. Bob Merrill, b. Isobel Lennart (1,348 USA, 109 GB).

Funny Thing Happened on the Way to the Forum, A Roman farce based on plays by Plautus. Broad comedy treatment given to thin story of slave trying to buy his freedom by finding his master a courtesan. 1962. m.l. Stephen Sondheim, b. Burt Shevelove and Larry Gelbart (964 USA, 762 GB).

Gay Deceivers Musical comedy. 1935.

Gay Divorce, The Marital complications in which heroine seeking divorce mistakes hero, already in love at first sight, as professional correspondent. 1932. m.l. Cole Porter, b. Dwight Taylor, Kenneth Webb and Samuel Hoffenstein (248 USA, 108 GB).

Gay Life, The Musical romance, 1961. m. Arthur Schwartz, l.b. Howard Dietz.

Gay's The Word Showbiz comedy. 1951. m. Ivor Novello, l.b. Alan Melville.

Gentlemen Prefer Blondes From Anita Loos book about the Roaring Twenties. Two not-so-dumb showgirls on a trip to France set out to entrap a couple of millionaires. 1949. m. Jule Styne, l. Leo Robin, b. Joseph Fields and Anita Loos (740 USA, 7 months GB).

George M Cohan biography. 1968. m.l. George M. Cohan, b. Michael Stewart, John and Fran Pascal (427).

Georgy Film *Georgy Girl*. 1970. m. George Fischoff. l. Carole Bayer, l. Tom Mackiewicz.

Gingham Girl Greenwich Village romance. 1922. m. Albert von Tilzer, l. Neville Fleeson, b. Dan Kussell (322).

Girl Called Jo, A Adapt of *Little Women*. 1955. (short run).

Girl Crazy Playboy sent to small town by his father to escape the high life, turns the small town into a high-life centre, but is redeemed by the love of the local postmistress. 1930. m. George Gershwin, l. Ira Gershwin, b. Guy Bolton and John McGowan (272).

Girl Friend, The Amateur cyclist defeats the efforts of gambling syndicate to fix the result of a six-day cycle race, wins it himself and, naturally, gets the girl. 1926. m. Richard Rodgers, l. Lorenz Hart, b. Herbert Fields (409 USA, 421 GB).

Girl in Pink Tights, The Period piece. 1954. m. Sigmund Romberg, l. Leo Robin, b. Joseph Fields and Jerome Chodorov (115).

Girl Who Came to Supper, The Adapt of *The Sleeping Prince*. 1963. m.l. Noël Coward, b. Terence Rattigan.

Glamorous Night Ruritanian romance. 1935. m.b. Ivor Novello, l. Christopher Hassall.

Godspell Rock religion. 1971. m.l. Stephen Schwartz, b. John-Michael Tabelak (2,100)†.

Going Greek Musical comedy. 1937. m.l. Sammy Lerner, Al Goodhart and Al Hoffman, b. Guy Bolton, Douglas Furber and Fred Thompson.

Golden Apple, The Classical satire. 1954. m. Jerome Moross, l.b. John Latanche (125).

Golden Boy From Odets play. 1964. m. Charles Strouse, l. Lee Adams, B. Clifford Odets and William Gibson (568).

Golden Dawn Basically operetta, derived from a World War I story and set in Africa, with secondary love interest featuring Australian prisoner of war. 1927. m. Herbert Stothart, Robert Stolz and Emmerich Kalman, l.b. Oscar Hammerstein II and Otto Harbach (184).

†as of May 31, 1976; it has continued since June 2, 1976, on Broadway and is still running (413).

Golden Moth, The Musical play. 1921. m. Ivor Novello, l.b. P. G. Wodehouse and Fred Thompson.

Golden Rainbow Film *A Hole in the Head*. 1968. m.l. Walter Marks, b. Ernest Kinoy (383).

Golden Touch, The Greek holiday setting. 1960. l.b. Julian More (short run).

Gone with the Wind From the Margaret Mitchell novel. 1972. m.l. Harold Rome (11 months GB).

Good Boy Rustics in Manhattan. 1928. m. Harry Ruby and Herbert Stothart, l. Bert Kalmar, b. Otto Harbach, Oscar Hammerstein II and Henry Myers (253).

Good Companions, The Adapt of J. B. Priestley story about touring theatrical company, its trials and tribulations, and personal relationships. 1931. m. Richard Addinsell, l. Harry Graham and Frank Eyton, b. J. B. Priestley; 1974. m. André Previn, l. Johnny Mercer, b. Ronald Harwood.

Good Morning Dearie Shopgirl romance. 1921. m. Jerome Kern, l.b. Anne Caldwell (347).

Good Morning Judge Musical comedy. 1919. m. George Gershwin, l.b. Irving Caesar and Al Bryan (140).

Good News Twenties collegiate romp, set on a campus where football is more important than academic learning. Hero passes exams, wins position on team, helps win big game, and gets girl. 1927. m.l. De Sylva, Brown and Henderson, b. B. G. de Sylva and Lawrence Schwab (557).

Good Old, Bad Old Days, The Musical optimism. 1972. m.l.b. Leslie Bricusse and Anthony Newley (1 year).

Grab Me a Gondola Musical romance. 1956. (20 months).

Grease Rock nostalgia. 1972. m.l.b. Jim Jacobs and Warren Casey (2,179)*.

Great Day Musical comedy. 1929. m. Vincent Youmans, l. Billy Rose and Edward Eliscu, b. William Cary Duncan (36).

Great Lady Costume sex comedy-drama. 1938. m. Frederick Loewe, l.b. Earle Crooker, b. Lowell Brentano (20).

Great Waltz, The Lavish spectacular based on music of the Strauss family. Fictitious details embroidered true story of the conflict between Johann I and II for title of Vienna's 'Waltz King'. 1934. l. Desmond Carter, b. Moss Hart (297).

Green Pastures Roark Bradford's *Ol' Man Adam and His Chillun*. 1930. m.l. Trad., b. Marc Connolly (640).

Greenwillow Adapt of B. J. Chute's novel set in a small town. 1960. m.l.b. Frank Loesser, b. Lesser Samuels (95).

Guys and Dolls Adapt of Damon Runyon's *The Idylls of Sarah Brown*. Broadway gambler who later loves Salvation Army girl, wins a bet by taking her to Havana, and brings in all his fellow-gamblers to save the mission. 1950. m.l. Frank Loesser. b. Jo Scoerling, Abe Burrows (1,200).

Gypsy Biography of Gypsy Rose Lee (from her book). Domineering stage mother concentrates her efforts on making sister June a star, but Rose finally becomes America's No 1 strip artiste. 1959. m. Jule Styne, l. Stephen Sondheim, b. Arthur Laurents (702).

Gypsy Lady Musical romance. 1946. m. Victor Herbert, adapt l.b. Robert Wright and Chet Forrest.

Hair Rock musical. 1968. m. Galt MacDermot, l.b. James Rado and Jerome Ragni (1,705 USA, 1,999 GB).

Half a Sixpence Adapt of H. G. Wells's *Kipps*. Small-town draper becomes a success, yearns for rich girl, but eventually finds happiness with a girl in his own class. 1963. m.l. David Heneker, b. Beverley Cross (511 USA, 677 GB).

Hallelujah Baby Black showbiz. 1967. m. Jule Styne, l. Betty Comden and Adolph Green, b. Arthur Laurents (293).

Happiest Girl in the World, The Adapt of Aristophanes' *Lysistrata*. 1961. l. E. Y. Harburg, b. Fred Saidy (96).

Happy End Translation of Brecht's 1929 satire in which love triumphs in a light-hearted plot about pre-Prohibition Chicago involving a den of gangsters led by a mysterious woman known as 'The Fly'. 1977. m. Kurt Weill (29)*.

Happy Holiday Broad comedy. 1954. m. George Posford, l.b. Eric Maschwitz.

Happy Hunting *Nouveau riche* manhunt. 1956. m. Harold Carr, l. Matt Dubey. b. Howard Lindsay and Russell Crouse (408).

Happy Time, The R. L. Fontaine book and movie. 1968. m. John Kander, l. Fred Ebb, b. N. Richard Nash (285).

Harmony Close London suburbia. 1957.

Have I Got One for You? From *Thumbelina*. 1968. m.l.b. Jerry Blatt, b. Lonnie Bustein.

Hazel Flagg Film *Nothing Sacred*. 1953. m. Jule Styne, l. Bob Hilliard.

Head Over Heels Musical comedy. 1923. m. Harold Fraser-Simpson, l. Adrian Rose and Harry Graham, b. Seymour Hicks.

Heads Up Comedy romance. 1929. m. Richard Rodgers, l. Lorenz Hart, b. John McGowan and Paul Gerard Smith (144).

Hearts and Diamonds Musical farce. 1930. m. Max Darewski and Bruno Grainchtadten, l. Graham John, b. P. G. Wodehouse and Laurie Wylie.

Helen of Troy NY Business satire. 1923. m. Harry Ruby, l. Bert Kalmar, b. Marc Connolly and George S. Kaufman (191).

Hello Daddy Adapt of the German farce *The High Cost of Living*. 1928. m. Jimmy McHugh, l. Dorothy Fields, b. Herbert Fields (198).

Hello Dolly Adapt of Thornton Wilder's *The Matchmaker*. Professional matchmaker hired to promote romance between parsimonious storekeeper and gown shopowner contrives to keep him for herself. 1964. m.l. Jerry Herman, b. Michael Stewart (2,844 USA, 794 GB).

Here Comes the Bride Romantic complications. 1930. m. Arthur Schwartz, l. Howard Dietz and Desmond Carter, b. R. P. Weston and Bert Lee.

Here Goes the Bride Comedy romance. 1933. m. Johnny Green. l. Edward Heyman. b. Peter Arno (7).

Here's Howe Musical comedy. 1928. m. Joseph Meyer and Roger Wolfe Kahn, l. Irving Caesar.

Here's Love Film *Miracle on 34th Street*. 1963. m.l.b. Meredith Willson (334).

Her Excellency Romantic comedy. 1949. m. Harry Parr-Davies.

He Wanted Adventure Adapt of Walter Hackett's *Ambrose Applejohn's Adventure*. 1933. m. Jack Waller and Joseph Tunbridge, l. Clifford Grey, b. R. P. Weston and Bert Lee (152).

Hide and Seek Romantic comedy. 1937. m. Vivian Ellis, Sammy Lerner, Al Goodhart and Al Hoffman, l.b. Douglas Furber, b. Guy Bolton and Fred Thompson (204).

High Button Shoes From the Stephen Longstreet novel. 1947. m. Jule Styne, l. Sammy Cahn, b. George Abbott (727).

Higher and Higher Domestic staff of a New York mansion pool their resources to pass off the parlourmaid as a débutante. Subsidiary plot concerns fortune hunter after the rich daughter of the house. 1940. m. Richard Rodgers, l. Lorenz Hart, b. Joshua Logan and Gladys Hurlbut.

High Kickers Nostalgic musical. 1941. m. Harry Ruby, l.b. Bert Kalmar and George Jessel.

High Spirits Adapt of Noël Coward's *Blithe Spirit*. 1964. m.b. Hugh Martin, l.b. Timothy Gray (365 USA, 2 months GB).

Hit the Deck Adapt of Hubert Osborne's play *Shore Leave*. Sailor and café owner fall in love, but he leaves when she becomes rich. She follows him and agrees to give away her money – to their first child. 1927. m. Vincent Youmans, l. Clifford Grey, Leo Robin and Irving Caesar, b. Herbert Fields (352).

Hold Everything Combination of broad comedy, sporting satire and romance. Society girl comes between boxer and his girl, but true love survives when his girl conspires to make him win championship. 1928. m. De Sylva, Brown and Henderson, b. B. G. de Sylva, John McGowan (413).

Hold My Hand Romantic comedy. 1931. m. Noel Gay, l. Desmond Carter, b. Stanley Lupino.

Hold On to Your Hats Western comedy. 1940. m. Burton Lane. l. E. Y. Harburg. b. Guy Bolton, Matt Brooks and Eddie Davis (158).

Hold Your Horses Hansom cab driver becomes Mayor of New York. 1933. m. Robert Russell Bennett, l. Owen Murphy, Robert A. Simon, b. Russel Crouse, Corey Ford from their play (88).

Honeymoon Lane Small-town romance in which hero dreams that his fiancée becomes a star. All ends happily back in their simple cottage, and working side by side in the pickle factory. 1926. m. James F. Hanley, l.b. Eddie Dowling, l. Hubert Reynolds and Henry Creamer (364).

Hooray for Daisy Bovine comedy. 1960. m. Julian Slade, l.b. Dorothy Reynolds.

Hooray for What? Anti-war burlesque. 1937. m. Harold Arlen, l. E. Y. Harburg, b. Howard Lindsay and Russell Crouse (200).

Hot-Cha Musical comedy. 1932. m. Ray Henderson, l.b. Lew Brown, b. Mark Hellinger (119).

Hot Mikado Jazz *Mikado*. 1939. m. Arthur Sullivan, l. W. S. Gilbert (85).

House of Flowers Set in Caribbean brothel. 1954. m. Harold Arlen, l.b. Truman Capote (165).

House of Leather Rock musical. 1970. m.l. Dale F. Menten, l.b. Frederick Gaines.

How Now Dow-Jones? Musical comedy. 1967. m. Elmer Bernstein, l. Carolyn Leigh (6 months).

How to Succeed in Business without Really Trying From the Shepherd Mead novel. Big-business satire in which window cleaner of office buildings bluffs his way to chairman of the board. 1961. m.l. Frank Loesser, b. Abe Burrows, Jack Weinstock and Willie Gilbert (1,417 USA, 520 GB).

I and Albert Featuring Queen Victoria. 1972. m. Charles Strouse, l. Lee Adams, b. Jay Allen (120).

I Can Get It for You Wholesale From the Jerome Weidman novel. 1962. m.l. Harold Rowe, b. Jerome Weidman (301).

I Do, I Do Adapt of Jan de Hartog's *Fourposter*. 1966. m. Harvey Schmidt, l.b. Tom Jones (560).

I'd Rather Be Right Presidential satire. 1937. m. Richard Rodgers, l. Lorenz Hart, b. George S. Kaufman and Moss Hart (290).

I Had a Ball Musical comedy. 1965. m. Stan Freeman, l. Jack Lawrence (6 months)

I'll Say She Is Marx Brothers' first show. 1924. m. Tom Johnstone, l.b. Will B. Johnstone (2 years).

I Love My Wife Two New Jersey couples decide to take a fling at an orgy. 1977. m. Cy Coleman, l.b. Michael Stewart (52)*.

Ilya Darling Adapt of *Never on Sunday*. 1967. m. Manos Hadjidakis, l. Joe Darion, b. Jules Dassin (318).

I Married an Angel John Vaszary fantasy. Nobleman tires of mortal women and marries an angel. Her lack of human vices proves too much, but it ends happily when she acquires some. 1938. m. Richard Rodgers, l. Lorenz Hart, b. Joshua Logan (338).

Inner City Ghetto problems theme. 1971. m. Helen Miller, l.b. Eve Merriam (97).

Instant Marriage Contemporary romance. 1964. (366).

Irene Archetypal shopgirl romance. She meets rich man, becomes fashion model, conquers the élite on Long Island, makes her employer famous, marries the rich man and lives happily ever after. 1919. m. Harry Tierney, l. Joseph McCarthy, b. James Montgomery (670).

Irma la Douce From the Alexandre Breffort book. Offbeat romance between Parisian prostitute and the nice young policeman who becomes her protector – in the nicest possible way of course. 1958. m. Marguerite Monnot, l.b. David Heneker, Monty Norman and Julian More (524).

It's a Bird, It's a Plane, It's Superman Comic strip theme. 1966. m. Charles Strouse, l. Lee Adams, b. David Newan and Robert Benton (75).

Jack o' Diamonds Musical comedy. 1935. m. Noel Gay, l.b. Clifford Grey, b. H. F. Maltby.

Jackpot Musical romance. 1944. m. Vernon Duke, l. Howard Dietz (short run).

Jamaica Caribbean romance. 1957. m. Harold Arlen, l.b. E. Y. Harburg, b. Fred Saidy (557).

Jeeves Wodehouse stories. 1975. m. Andrew Lloyd-Webber, l.b. Alan Ayckbourne (short run).

Jennie Laurette Taylor biography. 1963. m. Arthur Schwartz, l.b. Howard Dietz.

Jenny Jones Romantic comedy. 1944. m. Harry Parr-Davies, l. Harold Purcell, b. Ronald Gow.

Jesus Christ Superstar Rock musical translating the New Testament into contemporary terms, with modern costumes and settings. 1971. m. Andrew Lloyd-Webber, l.b. Tim Rice (720).

Jill Darling Musical romance. 1934. m. Vivian Ellis, l. Desmond Carter, b. Marriott Edgar (242).

Jimmy Shine Rock musical. 1968. m.l. John Sebastian, b. Murray Schisgal.

Johnny Johnson Anti-war propaganda. 1936. m. Kurt Weill, l.b. Paul Green (68).

Joie de Vivre Adapt of Terence Rattigan's *French Without Tears*. 1960. m. Robert Stolz (4).

Jorrocks Featuring the huntin' set. 1966. m. David Heneker (181).

Joseph and the Amazing Technicolor Dreamcoat Rock religion. 1973. m. Andrew Lloyd-Webber, l. Tim Rice, b. Ray Galton and Alan Simpson.

Jubilee Royalty satire. 1935. m.l. Cole Porter, b. Moss Hart (169).

Jumbo Billy Rose spectacular which turned the Hippodrome into a circus. Romeo and Juliet romance between offspring of rival circus owners is secondary to publicist's efforts to save circus from bankruptcy. 1935. m. Richard Rodgers, l. Lorenz Hart, b. Ben Hecht and Charles McArthur (233).

Jump for Joy Jazz musical. 1941. m. Duke Ellington, l. Paul Francis Webster, Sid Kuller and Hal Borne.

Juno Adapt of Sean O'Casey's *Juno and the Paycock*. 1959. m.l. Marc Blitzstein, b. Joseph Stein.

Kean Theatrical biography. 1961. m.l.b. Robert Wright and Chet Forrest (short run).

Keep Off the Grass Musical comedy. 1940. m. Jimmy McHugh, l. Al Dubin, l.b. Howard Dietz.

Kid Boots Golfing comedy featuring a caddy who is also a part-time bootlegger, crooked golf instructor and general know-all who takes care of the juvenile leads' romantic problems. 1923. m. Harry Tierney, l. Joseph McCarthy, b. Otto Harbach and William Anthony McGuire (479 USA, 163 GB).

King and I, The Adapt of Margaret Landon's *Anna and the King of Siam*. English governess at Siamese court tries to bring Western civilization to despotic ruler and, unsuccessfully, to aid young lovers. 1951. m. Richard Rodgers, l.b. Oscar Hammerstein II (1,246).

Kings & Clowns Historical comedy-drama. 1978. m.l.b. Leslie Bricusse (4 mths).

King's Rhapsody Ruritanian romance. 1949. m.b. Ivor Novello, l. Christopher Hassall (839).

Kismet Edward Knoblock play in exotic setting with Borodin music. Beggar poet becomes Emir of Baghdad for one day, overthrows wicked Wazir, and sees his own daughter betrothed to the Caliph. 1953. m. Borodin adapt Robert Wright and Chet Forrest, b. Charles Lederer and Luther Davis (583 USA, 648 GB).

Kissing Time Romantic musical. 1919. m. Ivan Caryll, l. Irving Caesar, b. Guy Bolton and P. G. Wodehouse (430).

Kiss Me Kate Road company presenting *The Taming of the Shrew* find that Shakespeare's plot is paralleled in their own private situations. Divorced leading man and lady come back together again. 1948. m.l. Cole Porter, b. Sam and Bella Spewack (1,077).

Knickerbocker Holiday Based on *Father Knickerbocker's History of New York* by Washington Irving, one of the characters portrayed in the story of New Amsterdam in 1647 and its governor Peter Stuyvesant. 1938. m. Kurt Weill, l.b. Maxwell Anderson (168).

Lady Be Good Brother-and-sister dancing act falls on hard times, but, after various complicated situations involving a rich heiress and fradulent claims to an inheritance, all comes out as it should. 1924. m. George Gershwin, l. Ira Gershwin, b. Guy Bolton and Fred Thompson (330 USA, 326 GB).

Lady Do Small-town romance. 1927. m. Abel Baer, l. Sam Lewis and Joe Young, b. Jack McLelland and Albert Cowles.

Lady in Ermine (*Lady of the Rose* in UK). Operetta set in Italy in Napoleonic times includes flashback in which a portrait comes to life and shows how history repeats itself. 1922. m. Sigmund Romberg and Al Goodman, l. Cyrus Wood, b. Frederick Lonsdale (232).

Lady in Red, The Musical comedy. 1919. m. George Gershwin, l. Lou Paley and Schuyler Greene (48).

Lady in the Dark Magazine editress undergoing psychiatric treatment has glamorous fantasies based on mundane real-life situations. They help resolve her doubts and problems, leading to a happy ending. 1941. m. Kurt Weill, l. Ira Gershwin, b. Moss Hart (388).

Lady Luck Musical farce. 1927. m. Jack Strachey and Richard Rodgers. l. Desmond Carter, Lorenz Hart, b. Firth Shephard and William Cary Duncan. Greatrex Newman (324).

La, La Lucille Bedroom farce. 1919. m. George Gershwin, l. Arthur Jackson, B. G. de Sylva, Lou Paley and Irving Caesar, b. Fred Jackson (104).

Last Sweet Days of Isaac, The Two-part rock musical. 1970. m. Nancy Ford, l.b. Gretchen Cryer (465).

Last Waltz, The Romantic operetta. 1921. m. Oscar Straus, l.b. Harold Atteridge, Robert Evett and Reginald Arkell.

Leave Him to Heaven Rock era play. 1976. Songs interpolated. b. Ken Lee (short run).

Leave It to Me Communist satire. 1938. m.l. Cole Porter, b. Sam and Bella Spewack (307).

Let 'Em Eat Cake Political satire. 1933. m. George Gershwin, l. Ira Gershwin, b. George S. Kaufman and Morrie Ryskind (90).

Let It Ride Musical comedy. 1961. m.l. Jay Livingston and Ray Evans.

Let's Face It Adapt from the 1925 play *The Cradle Snatchers*, updated to World War II. Lonely wives 'adopt' three GI's from nearby army camp, leading to inevitable complications. 1941. m.l. Cole Porter, b. Herbert and Dorothy Fields (547).

Lido Lady Holiday romance. 1926. m. Richard Rodgers, m.b. Harry Ruby, l. Lorenz Hart, l.b. Bert Kalmar, b. Ronald Jeans and Guy Bolton.

Li'l Abner Based on Al Capp's comic-strip characters. Combination of satire and hayseed comedy as inhabitants of Dogpatch unite to defeat politicians and big business. 1956. m. Gene de Paul, l. Johnny Mercer, b. Norman Panama and Melvin Frank (693).

Lilac Time see *Blossom Time*

Lisbon Story, The Espionage, intrigue and romance in wartime in Europe's neutral port. 1943. m. Harry Parr-Davies, l.b. Harold Purcell.

Little Jessie James Romantic comedy. 1923. m. Harry Archer, l. Harlan Thompson (385).

Little Mary Sunshine Satire on operetta. 1959. m.l.b. Rick Besoyan (1,143).

Little Me From the Patrick Dennis book. 1962. m. Cy Coleman, l. Carolyn Leigh, b. Neil Simon (257 USA, 334 GB).

Little Miss Bluebeard Musical comedy. 1922. (175).

Little Nellie Kelly New York Irish policeman loses his wife in childbirth, brings up daughter (heroine plays both roles), the darling of the force who resolves old feuds. 1922. m.l.b. George M. Cohan.

Little Night Music, A Adapt of Ingmar Bergman's *Smiles of a Summer Night*. Operetta-type treatment of turn-of-the-century infidelities and other marital complications. 1973. m.l. Stephen Sondheim, b. Hugh Wheeler (600).

Little Racketeer, A Comedy about tomboy who wants to be Public Enemy No. 1, from German play by F. Kalbfuss & P. Wilde. 1932. m. Haskell Brown, l. Edward Eliscu, b. Harry Clarke (48).

Little Tommy Tucker Musical comedy. 1930. m. Vivian Ellis, l.b. Desmond Carter, b. Caswell Garth, Bert Lee and R. P. Weston (86).

Lock Up Your Daughters Adapt of Henry Fielding's *Rape Upon Rape*. 1959. m. Laurie Johnson, l. Lionel Bart, b. Bernard Miles.

Lonely Romeo Musical farce, 1919. m. R. H. Bowers, m.l. M. M. Franklin, l. Robert B. Smith, b. Harry B. Smith.

Look Ma, I'm Dancin' Country comedy. 1948. m.l. Hugh Martin, b. Jerome Lawrence.

Lost in the Stars Adapt of Alan Paton's *Cry The Beloved Country*. 1949. m. Kurt Weill, l.b. Maxwell Anderson (273).

Louie the XIV Musical farce. 1924. m. Sigmund Romberg, l.b. Arthur Wimperis and Clifford Grey (79).

Louisiana Purchase Political-business comedy. Senator sets up investigation of shady New Orleans company, whose lawyer tries to compromise him to buy his silence. Virtue triumphs. 1940. m.l. Irving Berlin, b. Morrie Ryskind and B. G. de Sylva (444).

Love from Judy Adapt of *Daddy Long Legs*. 1953. m.l. Hugh Martin, l. Timothy Grey, b. Eric Maschwitz (584).

Love Letter, The Romantic comedy. 1921. m. Victor Jacobi, l.b. William le Baron (31).

Love Life American history. 1948. m. Kurt Weill, l.b. Alan Jay Lerner (252).

Lovely Lady Adapt of the French play *Dejeuner de Soleil*. 1927. m. Dave Stamper and Harold Levey, l.b. Cyrus Wood, b. Gladys Unger (164).

Love Racket, The Musical farce. 1943. m. Noel Gay, l. Frank Eyton. b. Stanley Lupino.

Luana South Seas romance from play *Bird Of Paradise* by Richard Walton Tully. 1930. m. Rudolf Friml, l. J. Keirn Brennan, b. Howard Emmett Rogers (21).

Lucky Girl Adapt of Reginald Berkeley's *Mr. Abdullah*. 1928. m. Phil Charig, l.b. Douglas Furber, b. R. P. Weston and Bert Lee.

Lute Song Adapt of the Oriental fantasy *Pi-Pa-Ki*. 1946. m. Raymond Scott, l. Bernard Hanighen, b. Sidney Howard (385).

Lysistrata From Aristophanes. 1972. m.l. Peter Link, b. Michael Cacoyannis (8).

Maggie Musical adaptation of J. M. Barrie's *What Every Woman Knows*. 1977. m.l.b. Michael Wild (46 weeks).

Maggie May Liverpool saga. 1964. m.l.b. Lionel Bart (499).

Magic Man, The 'Magical' musical comedy. 1978. m.l.b. Barbara & Anthony Damato (3 weeks).

Magic Show Modern-day fairy tale about a shy young musician and his hypnotic feats of magic, which are generously performed on stage. 1975. m.l. Stephen Schwartz, b. Bob Randall (1,253)*.

Magyar Melody Operetta-ish romance. 1939. m. George Posford, l.b. Eric Maschwitz.

Make a Wish Adapt of Ferenc Molnár's *The Good Fairy*. 1951. m. Hugh Martin, l. Timothy Gray, b. Abe Burrows.

Make Me an Offer Set in Cockney markets. 1959. m.l. David Heneker, b. Wolf Mankowitz.

Mame Adapt of Patrick Dennis's *Auntie Mame*. Boy is brought up by eccentric aunt in her own madcap life-style. She climaxes her guardianship by steering him from the wrong girl to the right one. 1966. m.l. Jerry Herman, b. Jerome Lawrence and Robert E. Lee (1,508).

Manhattan Mary Musical comedy. 1927. m.l. De Sylva, Brown and Henderson, b. B. G. de Sylva.

Man of La Mancha Author Miguel Cervantes, in prison for a tax offence, is to be tried by his fellow-prisoners. He relates his own story of Don Quixote, becoming the knight himself, as his defence. 1965. m. Mitch Leigh, l. Joe Darion, b. Dale Wasserman (2,330).

Man with a Load of Mischief, The Adapt from Ashley Dukes's play. 1966. m.l. John Clifton, b.l. Ben Tarver (200).

Mardi Gras New Orleans story. 1976. m.l. Ken Howard and Alan Blaikley, b. Melvyn Bragg (short run).

Marigold Musical romance. 1959. l.b. Alan Melville.

Mary Kansas romance. 1920. m. Lewis A. Hirsch, l.b. Otto Harbach and Frank Mandel (219).

Mary Jane McKane Musical comedy. 1923. m. Vincent Youmans and Herbert Stothart, l.b. Oscar Hammerstein II.

May Wine Adapt of Wallace Smith and Erich von Stroheim's *The Happy Alienist*. 1935. m. Sigmund Romberg, l. Oscar Hammerstein II, b. Frank Mandel (213).

Me and Bessie Black musical. 1975.

Me and Juliet Backstage drama. 1953. m. Richard Rodgers, l.b. Oscar Hammerstein II (358).

Me and My Girl Cockney comedy. 1937. m. Noel Gay, l.b. Douglas Furber, b. Arthur Rose (1,046).

Melody European romance over half a century in time. 1933. m. Sigmund Romberg, l. Irving Caesar, b. Edward Childs Carpenter (79).

Melody Man, The Songwriting comedy. 1924. m.b. Richard Rodgers, l.b. Lorenz Hart, b. Herbert Fields (overall credit to Herbert Richard Lorenz) (short run).

Me, Nobody Knows, The Ghetto parables. 1970. m. Gary William Freedman, l. Will Holt, b. Herb Shapiro and Stephen M. Joseph (587).

Mercenary Mary Musical romance. 1925. m. Con Conrad and William Friedlander, l. Irving Caesar, l. Isabel Leighton and William Friedlander.

Merry Malones, The Cohan revival. 1927. m.l.b. George M. Cohan.

Mexican Hayride Mike Todd spectacular. American on the run in Mexico becomes guest of the government through a misunderstanding. American official falls for lady bullfighter, falsely believed to be crook's accomplice. 1944. m.l. Cole Porter, b. Herbert and Dorothy Fields (481).

Milk and Honey Romantic and ethnic problems of American visitors and residents in an Israeli kibbutz, with a bitter sweet denouement. 1961. m.l. Jerry Herman, b. Don Appell (543).

Minnie's Boys Marx Brothers biography. 1970. m. Larry Grossman, l. Hal Hackady, b. Arthur Marx and Robert Fisher.

Miss Liberty New York 1885. 1949. m.l. Irving Berlin, b. Robert Sherwood (308).

Mr and Mrs Adapt of the film *Brief Encounter*. 1968. m.l.b. Noël Coward (short run).

Mr Cinders Musical romance. 1929. m. Vivian Ellis and Richard Meyers, l.b. Clifford Grey, b. Greatrex Newman (528).

Mr. President Political comedy-drama. 1962. m.l. Irving Berlin, b. Howard Lindsay and Russell Crouse (265).

Mr Whittington Musical comedy. 1933. m. Johnny Green and Jack Waller.

Mr. Wonderful Small time cabaret entertainer has qualms about trying for Broadway stardom but – as this slender thread was tailor-made for Sammy Davis Jr – he finally makes it. 1956. m. Jerry Bock, l. Larry Holfcenor and George Weiss, b. Will Glickman, Joseph Stein (383).

Molly Darling Musical romance. 1922. m. Milton Schwarzwald, l. Ira Gershwin, l.b. Otto Harbach, b. William Cary Duncan (101).

Monsieur Beaucaire Operetta from Booth Tarkington. 1919. m. Andre Messager, l. Adrian Ross, b. Frederick Lonsdale (221).

Moonlight Musical comedy. 1923. m. Con Conrad and William Friedlander, l.b. William le Baron.

Most Happy Fella, The Adapt from Sidney Howard play *They Knew What They Wanted*. Ageing Napa Valley winegrower sends mail-order bride his young foreman's photograph; after romantic complications she realises his true worth. 1956. m.l.b. Frank Loesser (676).

Murder At The Vanities Usual Earl Carroll Vanities decked out with backstage murder plot to try and revive a fading genre. 1933. *Songs* Victor Young & Ned Washington, John Jacob Loeb & Paul Francis Webster, Johnny Green & Edward Heyman, Herman Hupfield, b. Earl Carroll, Rufus King, Eugene Conrad (207).

Music In The Air Sweethearts from a Bavarian village travel to Munich to arrange publication of song, become involved in the theatrical world, but realize their happiness lies at home. 1932. m. Jerome Kern, l.b. Oscar Hammerstein II (342).

Music Is Musical divertissement. 1976. m. Richard Adler, l. Will Holt, b. George Abbott.

Music Man Confidence trickster comes to Iowa to trick the locals into buying band instruments and uniforms, but falls for the town librarian and 'goes straight' as the town bandleader. 1957. m.l.b. Meredith Willson (1,375 USA, 395 GB).

My Fair Lady George Bernard Shaw's *Pygmalion* presented intact, with fine songs integrated into the story of the Cockney flower girl turned into a lady by professor of phonetics, who belatedly recognizes her quality. 1956. m. Frederick Loewe, l.b. Alan Jay Lerner (2,717 USA, 2, 281 GB).

My Maryland American operetta. 1927. m. Sigmund Romberg, l.b. Dorothy Donnelly.

My Princess Operetta romance. 1927. m. Sigmund Romberg, l.b. Dorothy Donnelly.

My Romance Adapt of Edward Sheldon's *Romance*. 1948. m. Sigmund Romberg (short run).

My Son John Musical comedy. 1926. m. Oscar Straus and Vivian Ellis, l. Harry Graham and Desmond Carter, b. Graham John.

Naughty Cinderella Romantic musical. 1925. m.l.b. Henri Christine, Ray Goetz, A. L. Keith and Lee Sterling.

Nellie Bly Musical comedy. 1946. m. Jimmy Van Heusen, l. Johnny Burke.

New Girl in Town Adapt of Eugene O'Neill's *Anna Christie*. 1957. m.l. Bob Merrill, b. George Abbott (431).

New Moon, The Operetta based on life of French revolutionary Robert Mission in late eighteenth century. Being shipped from New Orleans back to France, he inspires a mutiny, and settles with his love on his own island. 1928. m. Sigmund Romberg, l.b. Oscar Hammerstein II, Frank Mandel and Lawrence Schwab (509).

New Yorkers, The Sophisticated musical. 1930. m.l. Cole Porter, b. Herbert Fields (168).

Night Boat, The Musical romance. 1920. m. Jerome Kern, l.b. Anne Caldwell.

Nightingale, The Jenny Lind biography. 1927. l.b. P. G. Wodehouse, b. Guy Bolton.

Night Out, A Musical comedy. 1920. m. Melville Gideon and Cole Porter, l. Clifford Grey, b. George Grossmith and Arthur Miller (311).

Nina Rosa Operetta romance. 1930. m. Sigmund Romberg, l. Irving Caesar, b. Otto Harbach (137).

No for an Answer Political drama. 1941. m.l.b. Marc Blitzstein.

No, No Nanette Flimsy musical which succeeded for its songs rather than for thin plot about a businessman who likes helping girls, and his flighty daughter, Nanette, who is finally reunited with her fiancé. 1925. m. Vincent Youmans, l. Irving Caesar, l.b. Otto Harbach, b. Frank Mandel (321 USA, 665 GB).

No Other Girl Musical comedy. 1924. m. Harry Ruby, l.b. B Kalmar.

No Strings Interracial romance. 1962. m.l. Richard Rodgers, b. Samuel Taylor (580).

Nymph Errant Adapt from the James Laver novel. Romantic comedy. 1933. m.l. Cole Porter, b. Romney Brent (154).

Of Thee I Sing Political satire. 1931. m. George Gershwin, l. Ira Gershwin and Morrie Ryskind (441).

Oh Captain! Film *The Captain's Paradise*. 1958. m. Jay Livingston, l. Roy Evans.

Oh Kay! Long Island romance. 1926. m. George Gershwin, l. Ira Gershwin and Howard Dietz, b. Guy Bolton and P. G. Wodehouse (256).

Oh My Papa Swiss musical. 1956. m. Paul Burkhard.

Oh, Please! Musical comedy. 1926. m. Vincent Youmans, l.b. Otto Harbach and Anne Caldwell.

Oh What a Lovely War! Black comedy in the form of an anti-war satire, illustrated by jingoism and false sentiment of songs of the two world wars. 1963. Interpolated songs (501).

Oklahoma! Adapt of Lynn Riggs's play *Green Grow the Lilacs*. Turn-of-the-century Western taking a light-hearted view of the differences between farmers and cowmen before the territory became a state. 1943. m. Richard Rodgers, l.b. Oscar Hammerstein II (2,212 USA, 1,543 GB).

Old Chelsea Period musical. 1943. m. Richard Tauber and Bernard Grun, l. Fred Tysh, l.b. Walter Ellis.

Oliver! Adapt of Dickens's *Oliver Twist*. Orphan, after various tribulations, is kidnapped and brought up to be a pickpocket in nineteenth-century London. Principal action is with gang of urchins, also subsidiary romance between villain and the girl he kills. 1960. m.l.b. Lionel Bart (2,618 GB, 774 USA).

On a Clear Day You Can See Forever Psychiatric fantasy in which patient relives previous existences. Psychiatrist loves one of her past incarnations, but finally realizes they belong together in the present. 1965. m. Burton Lane, l.b. Alan Jay Lerner (280).

Once Upon a Mattress Adapt of Hans Andersen's *Princess and the Pea*. 1959. m. Mary Rodgers, l. Marshall Baren, b. Dean Fuller and Jay Thompson (460 USA, 39 GB).

110 in the Shade Adapt of the film/play *The Rainmaker*. 1963. m. Harvey Schmidt, l. Tom Jones, b. Richard Nash (331 USA, 101 GB).

One Touch of Venus Adapt of Anstey's *The Painted Venus*. Young man accidentally brings a statue of Venus to life and falls in love with her, causing complications with his own fiancée. 1943. m. Kurt Weill, l.b. Ogden Nash, b. S. J. Perelman (567).

On the Town Adapt from the Leonard Bernstein–Jerome Robbins ballet *Fancy Free*. Three sailors on one day's leave in New York see the town and find their girls. 1944. m. Leonard Bernstein, l.b. Betty Comden and Adolph Green (463).

On Your Toes Son of vaudevillians helps moribund ballet company by presenting and starring in a jazz ballet (*Slaughter on 10th Avenue*) which is, naturally, a great success. 1936. m.b. Richard Rodgers, l.b. Lorenz Hart, b. George Abbott (315).

Operation Sidewinder Rock musical. 1970. m.l.b. Sam Shepard.

Operette Backstage musical. 1938. m.l.b. Noël Coward (4 months).

Orange Blossoms American operetta. 1922. m. Victor Herbert, l. B. G. de Sylva.

Our Man Crichton Adapt of James Barrie's *The Admirable Crichton*. 1964. m. Dave Lee, l. Herbert Kretzmer (6 months).

Our Nell Musical comedy. 1922. m. George Gershwin and William Daly, l.b. Brian Hooker, b. A. E. Thomas (40).

Out of the Bottle Romantic musical. 1932. m. Oscar Levant and Vivian Ellis, l.b. Clifford Grey, b. Fred Thompson (106).

Out of This World Greek legend. 1950. m.l. Cole Porter, b. Dwight Taylor and Reginald Lawrence (157).

Over She Goes Musical farce. 1936. m. Billy Mayerl, b. Stanley Lupino (248).

Pacific 1860 South Seas romance. 1946. m.l.b. Noël Coward (4 months).

Pacific Overtures Oriental musical. 1976. m.l. Stephen Sondheim.

Paint Your Wagon One girl among seven hundred men in a Gold Rush town. The strike peters out but the town, named after and owned by her father, now becomes a farming community. 1951. m. Frederick Loewe, l.b. Alan Jay Lerner (289).

Pajama Game Adapt from Richard Bissell's book *7½ Cents* about Union problems in a pajama factory. Worker falls in love with supervisor, and after misunderstandings, and exposing crooked proprietor, they come together. 1954. m. Richard Adler, l. Jerry Ross, b. George Abbott and Richard Bissell (1,063 USA, 17 months GB).

Pal Joey Adapt from John O'Hara's book of short stories. Small-time night-club performer rejects honest girl for rich woman who sets him up in business. When she tires of him he is left alone. 1940. m. Richard Rodgers, l. Lorenz Hart, b. John O'Hara (374).

Panama Hattie Loud and vulgar bar proprietor in Panama loves US diplomat and finally wins over his daughter and himself when she defeats a plot to blow up the Panama Canal. 1940. m.l. Cole Porter, b. Herbert Fields and B. G. de Sylva (501).

Pardon My English Unsuccessful comedy. 1933. m. George Gershwin, l. Ira Gershwin, b. Herbert Fields (46).

Paris Parisian musical comedy. 1928. m.l. Cole Porter, b. Martin Brown (195).

Park Avenue Sophisticated musical. 1946. m. Arthur Schwartz, l. Ira Gershwin, b. George S. Kaufman and Nunnally Johnson (72).

Passion Flower Hotel Adolescent comedy. 1965. m. John Barry, l. Trevor Peacock, b. Wolf Mankowitz.

Peggy Ann Psychological fantasy, adapt from Edgar Smith's *Tillie's Nightmare*. 1926. m. Richard Rodgers, l. Lorenz Hart, b. Herbert Fields (333).

Perchance to Dream Ruritanian operetta. 1945. m.b. Ivor Novello, l. Christopher Hassall (1,022).

Peter Pan Adapt of favourite James Barrie fantasy. 1954. m. Leonard Bernstein, Jule Styne, l. Betty Comden, Adolph Green, Carolyn Leigh and Mark Charlap.

Phil the Fluter Songwriter biography. 1969.

Pickwick Adapt of Dickens's *Pickwick Papers*. 1963. m. Cyril Ornadel, l. Leslie Bricusse, b. Wolf Mankowitz (19 months).

Pipe Dream Adapt of John Steinbeck's *Sweet Thursday*. 1955. m. Richard Rodgers, l.b. Oscar Hammerstein II (246).

Pippin Illusionary fantasy contrived to tell the story of Emperor Charlemagne's son and his search for the meaning of life. 1972. m.l. Stephen Schwartz b. Roger O'Hirson (1928)*.

Plain and Fancy Centred on Pennsylvania Amish sect. 1955. m. Albert Hague, l. Arnold B. Howitt, b. Joseph Stein and William Glickman (461).

Please Teacher Musical comedy. 1935. m. Jack Waller and Joseph Tunbridge, l.b. R. P. Weston, Bert Lee and K. R. G. Browne.

Point, The Modern fantasy. 1977. m.l.b. Harry Nilsson, adapt Ron Pember, Bernard Miles (2 months).

Poor Little Ritz Girl Musical comedy. 1920. m. Sigmund Romberg and Richard Rodgers, l. Lorenz Hart and Alex Gerber, b. Lew Fields, H. M. Stillman and George Campbell.

Popkiss Adapt of the farce *Rookery Nook*. 1972. m. David Heneker and John Addison, l.b. Michael Ashton (63).

Poppy Ward of a medicine man at a county fair, falls in love with a rich man. Con-man presents his ward as a missing heiress to claim an inheritance – and she really is! 1923. m. Arthur Samuels, John Egan and Stephen Jones, l. Dorothy Donnelly and Howard Dietz (328).

Porgy and Bess Adapt of DuBose and Dorothy Heward's *Porgy*. In a Negro community in South Carolina crippled Porgy loves Bess. After she is enticed to New York by drug peddler, he goes to search for her. 1935. m. George Gershwin, l. Ira Gershwin, l.b. DuBose and Heyward (124).

Present Arms Musical play. Marine private poses as captain to impress English lady, but is discovered and court-martialled. Finally triumphs over a German pineapple farmer by saving lives in a shipwreck. 1928. m. Richard Rodgers, l. Lorenz Hart, b. Herbert Fields (155).

Pretty Peggy Musical romance. 1920. m. A. Emmett Adams, l.b. Arthur Rose and Charles Austin (168).

Primrose Musical comedy. 1924. m. George Gershwin, l. Ira Gershwin and Desmond Carter, b. George Grossmith and Guy Bolton (255).

Princess Charming Romantic operetta. 1926. m. Albert Sirmay, l. Arthur Swanstrom (362).

Princess Flavia Romantic operetta. 1925. m. Sigmund Romberg.

Privates On Parade Wartime tribulations of an Army concert party in the Middle East. 1978. m. Denis King, l.b. Peter Nichols (208).

Promenade Contemporary satire. 1969. m. Al Carmines, l.b. Maria Irene Fornes (259).

Promises, Promises Adapt from Billy Wilder and I. A. L. Diamond film *The Apartment*. Ambitious company man loans his apartment for his superiors' extra-marital assignations. m. Burt Bacharach, l. Hal David, b. Neil Simon (1281).

Purlie Black satire. 1970. m. Gary Geld, l.b. Peter Udell, b. Philip Rose and Ossie Davis (689).

Queen High Slight story concerns business partners who gamble for sole rights to the business. Loser must serve as the other's butler. Subsidiary romance between their children. 1926. m. Lewis E. Gensler, l.b. B. G. de Sylva and Howard Deitz (378).

Rainbow, The Romantic comedy. 1923. m. George Gershwin, l. Clifford Grey, b. Albert de Courville, Edgar Wallace and Noël Scott (113).

Rainbow Folk-influenced operetta that predated *Oklahoma!* and *Paint Your Wagon*. Army scout breaks out of prison where he is held on a murder charge, joins the Gold Rush of '49 and finds a happy ending. 1928. m. Vincent Youmans, l.b. Oscar Hammerstein II, Laurence Stallings and Edward Eliscu (30).

Rainbow Rock musical. 1972. m.l.b. James Rado, b. Ted Rado.

Rain or Shine Circus comedy. 1928. m. Milton Ager and Owen Murphy, l. Jack Yellen, b. James Gleason and Maurice Marks (356).

Ramblers, The Broad comedy combining various elements of spiritualism, movie-making, crime fiction and Westerns. 1926. m. Harry Ruby, l.b. Bert Kalmar, b. Guy Bolton (289).

Rebel Maid, The British operetta. 1921. m. Montague Phillips, l. Gerald Dalton, b. Alexander M. Thompson.

Redhead Period murder mystery. m. Albert Hague, l.b. Dorothy Fields, b. Herbert Fields, Sidney Sheldon and David Shaw (452).

Red, Hot and Blue Vaudeville comedy. 1936. m.l. Cole Porter, b. Howard Lindsay and Russell Crouse (183).

Red, White and Maddox 'Pop' musical. 1969. m.l. Don Tucker, b. Jay Broad.

Regina Deep South drama. Adapt from Lillian Hellman's *Little Foxes*. 1949. m.l.b. Marc Blitzstein (56).

Revenge with Music Adapt of *The Three Cornered Hat*. 1934. m. Arthur Schwartz, l.b. Howard Dietz (158).

Rex 1976. m. Richard Rodgers, l. Sheldon Harnick (3 weeks).

Rio Rita Mexican romance-adventure, with the Texas Rangers hunting a bandit beside the Rio Grande, who may or may not be

Above: **Company** (1970). The entire cast on stage at the Alvin Theater, New York, in Stephen Sondheim's marital musical.

Below: **Coco** (1969). Katherine Hepburn starred as Coco Chanel in the musical biography of the queen of fashion.

the heroine's brother. 1927. m. Harry Tierney, l. Joseph McCarthy, b. Guy Bolton and Fred Thompson (494).

Roar of the Greasepaint, The Smell of the Crowd, The Show-biz story. 1965. m.b. Leslie Bricusse, l.b. Anthony Newley (3 weeks).

Roberta Adapt of Alice Duer Miller's *Gowns by Roberta*. Footballer inherits a gown-shop, makes it a success and falls in love with the designer, who turns out to be a Russian princess. 1933. m. Jerome Kern, l.b. Otto Harbach (295).

Robert and Elizabeth Musical version of *The Barretts of Wimpole Street*. 1964. m. Ron Grainer, l. Ronald Millar (957).

Rocky Horror Show, The Rock satire. 1974. m.l.b. Richard O'Brien. (3 weeks USA).

Romance in Candlelight Musical romance. 1955. m.l. Sam Coslow (short run).

Rondelay Adapt from Arthur Schnitzler's story and film *La Ronde*. 1969. m. Hal Jordan, l.b. Jerry Douglas.

Rosalie Operetta based on romance between West Point officer and Ruritanian princess, begun in her country, carried on in America, and brought to a happy ending when she becomes a commoner. 1928. m. George Gershwin and Sigmund Romberg, l. Ira Gershwin and P. G. Wodehouse, b. Guy Bolton and William Anthony Maguire (335).

Rose Marie Hotel singer loves a trapper falsely accused of murder by villain who wants her for himself. Canadian Mounted Police sergeant clears it all up and finds real killer. 1924. m. Rudolf Friml and Herbert Stothart, l.b. Otto Harbach and Oscar Hammerstein II (557 USA, 851 GB).

Rothschilds, The Adapt from Frederic Morton book about the banking family. 1970. m. Jerry Bock, l. Sheldon Harnick, b. Sherman Yellen (507).

Royal Vagabond, The Musical comedy. 1919. m. Harry Tierney and George M. Cohan, l. Joseph McCarthy and Cohan, b. William Cary Duncan and Cohan.

Sadie Thompson Adapt of Somerset Maugham's *Rain*. 1944. m. Vernon Duke, l.b. Howard Dietz (2 months).

Sail Away Shipboard romance. 1961. m.l.b. Noël Coward (167 USA, 252 GB).

St. Louis Woman Black racing driver. Adapt from Bontemps book *God Sends Sunday*. 1946. m. Harold Arlen, l. Johnny Mercer, b. Countee Cullen and Arna Bontemps (113).

Salad Days Musical comedy. 1954. m.l. Julian Slade, l.b. Dorothy Reynolds (2,329).

Sally Variation on the shopgirl theme, as dishwasher pretends to be a Russian dancer at Long Island party, becomes a Follies star and marries a rich man. 1920. m. Jerome Kern, l. B. G. de Sylva and Clifford Grey, b. P. G. Wodehouse and Guy Bolton (570 USA, 387 GB).

Sally, Irene and Mary Small-town girl goes to New York, becomes a star. Rich man wants to marry her, but she goes back to her small-town boy friend. 1922. m. J. Fred Coots, l. Raymond Klages, l.b. Eddie Dowling and Cyrus D. Wood (318).

Salvation Anti-religious rock. 1969. m.l.b. Peter Link and C. C. Courtney (239).

Saratoga Adapt of Edna Ferber's *Saratoga Trunk*, the story of a gambler and Creole girl. 1959. m. Harold Arlen, l. Johnny Mercer, b. Morton da Costa (short run).

Say Darling Adapt from the Richard Bissell book about the making of *The Pajama Game*. 1958. m. Jule Styne, l. Betty Comden and Adolph Green, b. Abe Burrows, Marion and Richard Bissell.

Say When Comedy romance. 1934. m. Ray Henderson, l. Ted Koehler and Raymond Klages, b. Jack McGowan (76).

Secret Life of Walter Mitty, The Adapt of the James Thurber story about a milksop's fantasies. 1964. m.l. Leon Carr and Earl Shuman.

Seesaw Adapt from William Gibson's romantic comedy *Two for the Seesaw*. 1973. m. Cy Coleman, l. Dorothy Fields, b. Michael Bennett.

Seven Lively Arts Revue-type musical. 1944. m.l. Cole Porter, b. Moss Hart, George S. Kaufman, Ben Hecht, Robert Pirosh, Joseph Schrank and Charles Sherman (183).

1776 American history, detailing the activities of the members of the Continental Congress in the months leading up to the Declaration of Independence. 1969. m.l. Sherman Edwards, b. Peter Stone (1,217).

Seventh Heaven Remake of film. 1955. m. Victor Young, l. Stella Unger.

70 Girls 70 Adapt of Peter Coke's *Breath of Spring*, a story about geriatric shoplifters. 1971. m. John Kander, l.b. Fred Ebb, b. Norman Martin.

She Loves Me Adapt of Miklos Lazslo's play *Parfumerie*, a Hungarian shop romance. 1963. m. Jerry Bock, l. Sheldon Harnick, b. Joe Masteroff (301).

Shelter Rock musical. 1973. m. Nancy Ford, l.b. Gretchen Cryer (31).

Shenandoah Story of a Virginia pacifist's family during the Civil War. 1975. m. Gary Geld, l. Peter Udell, b. James Lee Barrett, Peter Udell, Philip Rose (973)*.

She's a Good Fellow Romantic comedy. 1919. m. Jerome Kern, l.b. Anne Caldwell.

She's My Baby Musical comedy. 1928. m. Richard Rodgers, l. Lorenz Hart, b. Bert Kalmar, Harry Ruby and Roy Bolton (2 months).

Shinbone Alley Adapt of *Archie and Mehitabel*. 1957. m. George Kleinsinger, l.b. Joe Darion and Mel Brooks.

Show Boat Adapt of Edna Ferber's novel, the story of a gambler who joins riverboat theatrical company, marries the star, resumes his gambling, but returns for a happy ending. 1927. m. Jerome Kern, l.b. Oscar Hammerstein II and P. G. Wodehouse (572 USA, 350 GB).

Show Girl Backstage musical, adapted from J. P. McEvoy's novel. 1924. m. George Gershwin, l. Ira Gershwin and Gus Kahn, b. William Anthony Maguire (111).

Shuffle Along Election comedy-revue. 1921. m.l. Eubie Blake and Noble Sissle, b. F. E. Miller and Aubrey Lyle (504).

Silk Stockings From film *Ninotchka*. American theatrical agent and Paris in the spring combine to melt a Soviet female emissary who finally discovers that West is Best. 1955. m.l. Cole Porter, b. George S. Kaufman, Abe Burrows and Leueen McGrath (477).

Simple Simon Daydreamer's fantasies. 1930. m. Richard Rodgers, l. Lorenz Hart, b. Guy Bolton and Ed Wynn (135).

Sing a Rude Song Marie Lloyd biography. 1970. m. Ron Grainer, l.b. Caryl Brahms and Ned Sherrin.

Sky High Comedy-revue. 1925. m. Victor Herbert and Hal Dyson, l. Clifford Grey, l.b. Harold Atteridge.

Skyscraper Adapt from Elmer Rice's *Dream Girl*, a daydreamers romance. 1965. m. Jimmy Van Heusen, l. Sammy Cahn, b. Peter Stone (241).

Smiles Musical comedy. 1930. m. Vincent Youmans, l. Harold Adamson, Clifford Grey and Mack Gordon, b. Ring Lardner and William Anthony McGuire (68).

Smith Romantic comedy. 1973. m.l.b. Matt Dubay and Dean Fuller, b. Tony Hendra.

Smith Family, The Musical comedy. 1922. m.l. Nat D. Ayer, l.b. Clifford Grey, b. Stanley Logan and Philip Page.

Something for the Boys Wartime comedy. Three heirs inherit house near air-base which they turn into a billet for airmen's wives. 1943. m.l. Cole Porter, b. Herbert and Dorothy Fields (422).

Song of Norway Adapt of Homer Curran's play, in the form of an operetta based on fictionalized episodes in the life of the composer Grieg, his romances and marriage. 1944. m. Edvard Grieg adapt Robert Wright and Chet Forrest, b. Milton Lazarus (860 USA, 526 GB).

Song of the Drum Musical drama. 1931. m. Herman Finck and Vivian Ellis, l. Desmond Carter, b. Guy Bolton and Fred Thompson (131).

Song of the Flame Operetta in *echt*-Russian style with story of peasants versus nobility leading to happy ending in Paris. 1925. m. George Gershwin and Herbert Stothart, l.b. Otto Harbach and Oscar Hammerstein II (219).

Sons o' Guns Wartime comedy. 1929. m. J. Fred Coots, l. Arthur Swanstrom and Benny Davis, b. Fred Thompson and Jack Donahue (295).

Sound of Music, The Story of the Trapp Family Singers from the book by Maria Trapp. Novice leaves convent to be governess to large family, marries their father, and uses their singing act as a cover to escape from the Nazis. 1959. m. Richard Rodgers, l. Oscar Hammerstein II, b. Howard Lindsay and Russell Crouse (1,442 USA, 2,385 GB).

Opposite above: **Jesus Christ, Superstar.** Rice and Lloyd Webber's rock version of the Bible began in London as a record album, opened on stage in Broadway in 1971 and returned to London in triumph the following year.

Opposite below: **Oliver.** Clive Revill as Fagin and Georgia Brown as Nancy in the 1963 production at the Imperial Theater, New York.

Southern Maid British operetta. 1920. m. Harold Fraser-Simpson and Ivor Novello, l.b. Dion Clayton Calthrop and Harry Graham.

South Pacific Adapt of James Mitchener's *Tales of the South Pacific* into World War II musical drama, principally concerning two romances hindered by racial prejudice inherent in small-town Americans. 1949. m. Richard Rodgers, l.b. Oscar Hammerstein II, b. Joshua Logan (1,925 USA, 2 years GB).

Spring is Here Musical romance. 1929. m. Richard Rodgers, l. Lorenz Hart, b. Owen Davis (3 months).

Stag Movie Seventies musical. 1971. m. Jacques Urbont, l.b. David Newburge.

Stars in Your Eyes Musical comedy. 1939. m. Arthur Schwartz, l. Dorothy Fields, b. J. P. McEvoy (127).

Stepping Stones Modern Red Riding Hood story. 1923. m. Jerome Kern, l.b. Anne Caldwell, b. R. H. Burnside.

Stop the World, I Want to Get Off Satirical view of life through the experiences of an average Little Man overwhelmed by circumstances. 1961. m.b. Leslie Bricusse, l.b. Anthony Newley (555).

Street Scene Urban drama adapt from Elmer Rice's play. 1947. m. Kurt Weill, l.b. Langston Hughes, b. Elmer Rice (148).

Street Singer, The Musical romance. 1924. m. Harold Fraser-Simpson, l. Ivy St. Helier, b. Frederick Lonsdale and Cyrus D. Wood (360).

Strike Me Pink Vaudevillian-style comedy located in an amusement park. 1933. m.b. Ray Henderson, l. Lew Brown (105).

Strike Up the Band Anti-war satire. USA declares war on Switzerland over the price of cheese, and American soldiers find life more comfortable in a non-existent war than back home in the Depression. 1930. m. George Gershwin, l. Ira Gershwin, b. Morrie Ryskind and George S. Kaufman (191).

Student Prince, The Operetta set in Mittel-Europa. Prince goes anonymously to Heidelberg University, falls in love with a waitress, but on becoming King must put his duty first. 1924. m. Sigmund Romberg, l.b. Dorothy Donnelly (608).

Subways Are for Sleeping Musical romance. 1961. m. Jule Styne, l.b. Betty Comden and Adolph Green.

Sugar Twenties comedy from Billy Wilder and I. A. L. Diamond's film *Some Like It Hot*. 1972. m. Jule Styne, l. Bob Merrill, b. Peter Stone (505).

Summer Song Period musical. 1956. m. Anton Dvorak, l.b. Eric Mashwitz.

Sunny Post-World War I romance between ex-soldier and circus performer in England. 1925. m. Jerome Kern, l.b. Oscar Hammerstein II and Otto Harbach (517).

Sunny Days Musical comedy. 1928. m. Jean Schwartz, l.b. Clifford Grey and William Cary Duncan.

Sunny River Modern operetta. 1942. m. Sigmund Romberg, l.b. Oscar Hammerstein II (6 weeks).

Survival of St. Joan, The Rock musical. 1971. m. Hank and Gary Ruffin, l.b. James Lineberger.

Sweet Adeline Musical comedy of the nineties. Beer-garden singer becomes a star, and after several romantic involvements marries her co-star. 1929. m. Jerome Kern, l.b. Oscar Hammerstein II (234).

Sweet Charity From Federico Fellini's film *Nights of Cabiria*, the story of a dance-hall girl who dreams of a better life with a steady young man, but because of his innate prejudice against her way of life the man she finds leaves her alone again. 1966. m. Cy Coleman, l. Dorothy Fields, b. Neil Simon (608 USA, 484 GB).

Sweetheart Mine Cockney romance. 1946. m. Noel Gay, l. Frank Eyton.

Sweetheart Shop, The Musical romance. 1920. l.b. Anne Caldwell (55).

Sweet Little Devil Musical comedy. 1924. m. George Gershwin, l. B. G. de Sylva, Frank Mandel and Lawrence Schwab (120).

Swingin' the Dream Adapt of *A Midsummer Night's Dream*. 1939. m. Jimmy Van Heusen, l. Eddie de Lange, b. Gilbert Seldes and Eric Charrell (13).

Take a Chance College graduate anxious to get on Broadway stages a show, running foul of crooks promoting a singer who falls for him. 1932. m. Vincent Youmans, Richard Whiting and Nacio Herb Brown, l.b. B. G. de Sylva and Lawrence Schwab, b. Sid Silvers (243).

Take Me Along Period comedy adapt from Eugene O'Neill's *Ah, Wilderness*. 1959. m.l. Robert Merrill, b. Joseph Stein and Robert Russell (448).

Take the Air Vaudevillian comedy. 1927. m. Dave Stamper, J. Russell Robinson and Willard Robison, l. Gene Buck, b. Anne Caldwell (206).

Tangerine South Sea romance. 1921. m. Frank Crumit, Monte Carlo and Dave Zoob, l. Howard Johnson and Alma Sanders, b. Guy Bolton and Philip Bartholomae (337).

Teeth 'n' Smiles Rock musical. 1976. Interpolated rock songs, b. David Hare (short run).

Tell Her the Truth Adapt of James Montgomery's *Nothing But the Truth*. 1932. m. Jack Waller and Joseph Tunbridge, l.b. R. P. Weston and Bert Lee (234 GB, 11 USA).

Tell Me More Musical comedy. 1925. m. George Gershwin, l. Ira Gershwin and B. G. de Sylva, b. Fred Thompson and William K. Wells (100 USA, 263 GB).

Tenderloin Adapt of Samuel Hopkins Adams's novel set in the Naughty Nineties. 1960. m. Jerry Bock, l. Sheldon Harnick, b. George Abbot and Jerome Weidman (216).

Texas Li'l Darlin' Western musical. 1949. m. Robert Emmett Dolan, l. Johnny Mercer.

That's a Good Girl Musical romance. 1928. m. Phil Charig and Joseph Meyer, l. Douglas Furber, Desmond Carter and Ira Gershwin, b. Donald Furber (363).

That's a Pretty Thing Musical farce. 1933. m. Noel Gay, l. Desmond Carter, b. Stanley Lupino.

This Is the Army Army show, 1942. m.l. Irving Berlin, b. Jimmy Shirl and James McColl.

Three Musketeers Adapt of the Alexandre Dumas novel. 1928. m. Rudolf Friml, l. Clifford Grey and P. G. Wodehouse, b. William Anthony Maguire (319).

Threepenny Opera, The From Weill's *Der Dreigroschenoper* (4,000 performances in Berlin, 1928), John Gay's *Beggar's Opera* updated to satirize and criticize pre-war Berlin. 1954. m. Kurt Weill, l.b. Marc Blitzstein from German of Bertolt Brecht (2,707 USA, 140 GB).

Three's a Crowd Revue-type musical. 1930. m. Arthur Schwartz and Burton Lane, l. Howard Dietz, b. Dietz, Fred Allen, Groucho Marx, Cory Ford and Lawrence Schwab (272).

Three Sisters Musical comedy. 1934. m. Jerome Kern, l.b. Oscar Hammerstein II (6 weeks).

Through the Years Tender romance, adapt from Jane Cowl's *Smiling Through*. 1932. m. Vincent Youmans, l. Edward Heyman, b. Brian Hooker (20).

Tickle Me Hollywood comedy. 1920. m. Herbert Stothart, l.b. Otto Harbach, Oscar Hammerstein II and Frank Mandel.

Tip Toes Story of how dancer wins millionaire. 1925. m. George Gershwin, l. Ira Gershwin, b. Fred Thompson and Guy Bolton.

Tip Top Comedy operetta. 1920. m. Ivan Caryll, b. R. H. Burnside.

Tom Brown's Schooldays Adapt of the classic novel by Thomas Hughes. 1972.

Tommy 'Rock Opera' about deaf, dumb and blind boy who becomes pinball champion. m.b. Andrew Lloyd Webber. l.b. Tim Rice (Feb 1979, no perfs. rec.).

Too Many Girls Campus comedy about college, in which girls outnumber boys by ten to one, finding difficulty in fielding a football team. 1939. m. Richard Rodgers, l. Lorenz Hart, b. George Marion Jr. (249).

Top Banana Television burlesque. 1951. m.l. Johnny Mercer, b. Hy Kraft (350).

Top Hole Musical comedy. 1924. m. Jay Gorney and Lewis E. Gensler, l. Ira Gershwin and Russell Bennett, b.m. Owen Murphy.

Top Speed Flimsy romantic comedy in which two American businessmen engineer their way into a big Canadian hotel in pursuit of a millionaire's daughter. 1929. m. Harry Ruby, l. Bert Kalmar, b. Guy Bolton (102).

Topsy and Eva Musical comedy. 1924. b. Catherine Cushing.

Tough at the Top Musical romance. 1949. m. Vivian Ellis, l.b. A. P. Herbert (154).

Tovarich European comedy. 1963. m. Lee Pockriss, l.b. Anne Croswell.

Travelling Music Show Backstage vaudeville story. 1978. b.l.m. Leslie Bricusse and Anthony Newley (112).

Treasure Girl Twenties treasure-hunt. 1928. m. George Gershwin, l. Ira Gershwin, b. Fred Thompson and Vincent Lawrence (68).

Tree Grows in Brooklyn, A Adapt of Betty Smith's novel, a period drama. 1951. m. Arthur Schwartz, l. Dorothy Fields, b. George Abbott and Betty Smith (270).

Trelawney Adapt of Pinero's *Trelawney of the Wells*. 1972. m. Julian Slade, l.b. Aubrey Woods.

Tumble Inn Musical comedy. 1919. m. Rudolf Friml, l.b. Otto Harbach.

Twang! Robin Hood. 1964. m.l.b. Lionel Bart (43).

Twenty Minutes South Suburban comedy. 1955. m.l. Peter Greenwell, b. Maurice Browning.

Two by Two Adapt of Clifford Odets's *The Flowering Peach*, Noah's Ark theme. 1970. m. Richard Rodgers, l. Martin Charnin, b. Peter Stone (1 year).

Two Cities Adapt of Dickens's *A Tale of Two Cities*. 1969. m.l.b. Jeff and Jerry Wayne (short run).

Two Gentlemen of Verona Rock Shakespeare. 1971. m. Galt McDermott, l.b. John Guare and Mel Shapiro. (627).

Two Little Girls in Blue Twins' romances. 1921. m. Paul Lannin and Vincent Youmans, l. Ira Gershwin (as Arthur Francis), b. Fred Jackson (226).

T. Zee Rock musical. 1976. m.l.b. Richard O'Brien (short run).

Under Your Hat Holiday comedy. 1938. m.l. Vivian Ellis, b. Arthur Macrae, Jack Hulbert and Archie Menzies (512).

Unsinkable Molly Brown Western adventure-romance. Saloon singer strikes it rich but fails to gain acceptance by local society, even after European triumph. Highspot is *Titanic* sinking. 1960. m.l. Meredith Willson, b. Richard Morris (532).

Up in Central Park New York in the 1870s. Newspaper man dedicated to the downfall of Boss Tweed's Tammany Hall political machine falls in love with daughter of a Tweed supporter. 1945. m. Sigmund Romberg, l.b. Herbert and Dorothy Fields (504).

Upsadaisy Musical comedy. 1928. m. Lewis E. Gensler, l.b. Clifford Grey and Robert A. Simon.

Up She Goes Domestic comedy adapt from Frank Craven's play *Too Many Cooks*. 1922. m. Harry Tierney, l. Joseph McCarthy, b. Frank Craven (256).

Vagabond King, The Adapt of J. H. McCarthy's *If I Were King*, the story of vagabond-poet François Villon who becomes King of France for a day, and of his beggar friends who defeat a revolution. 1925. m. Rudolf Friml, l.b. W. H. Post, and Brian Hooker (511 USA, 480 GB).

Valmouth Seaside romance adapt from Ronald Firbank's story. 1958. m.l. Sandy Wilson, b. Ronald Firbank (3 months).

Velvet Lady American operetta. 1919. m. Victor Herbert, l.b. Henry Blossom and Eddie Dowling.

Very Warm for May Musical romance. 1939. m. Jerome Kern, l.b. Oscar Hammerstein II (59).

Virginia American romance. 1937. m. Arthur Schwartz, l. Al Stillman, l.b. Lawrence Stallings, b. Owen Davis (60).

Virtue in Danger Adapt of Vanbrugh's *The Relapse*, a period comedy. 1963. m. James Bernard, l. Paul Dehn.

Wake Up and Dream Sophisticated musical. 1929. m.l. Cole Porter, b. John Hastings Turner (263 GB, 136 USA).

Walking Happy Comedy romance. 1966. m. Jimmy Van Heusen, l. Sammy Cahn.

Water Gipsies, The Adapt from A. P. Herbert's book about British canal life. 1954. m. Vivian Ellis, l.b. A. P. Herbert (138).

Wedding in Paris Middle-aged and young love. 1954. m. Hans May.

Wedding of Iphigenia, The From Euripides set in Ancient Greece. 1971. m.b. Peter Link, l.b. Gretchen Cryer, b. Doug Dyer (139).

West Side Story The Romeo and Juliet story transferred to New York slums, and the conflict between native Americans and Puerto Rican immigrants. 1957. m. Leonard Bernstein, l. Stephen Sondheim, b. Arthur Laurents (732 USA, 1,040 GB).

What Makes Sammy Run? Hollywood exposé, adapt from Budd Schulberg's book. 1964. m.l. Ervin Drake, b. Stuart and Budd Schulberg (540).

What's Up? Flop comedy. 1943. m. Frederick Loewe, l.b. Alan Jay Lerner (63).

When in Rome Holiday comedy. 1959. m.l. Miller and Cramer.

Where's Charley? Adapt of Brandon Thomas's play *Charley's Aunt*. Oxford undergraduates need a chaperone for their lady visitors. One of them impersonates his own aunt from Brazil, with complications when real aunt arrives. 1948. m.l. Frank Loesser, b. George Abbot (792).

Whoopee Adapt of Owen Davis's play *The Nervous Wreck* about hypochondriac on rest-cure in the West who is shaken out of his troubles by adventures with sheriff, girl and Indians. 1928. m. Walter Donaldson, l. Gus Kahn, b. William Anthony McGuire (379).

Who's Hooper? Romantic comedy. 1919. m. Howard Talbot and Ivor Novello, l.b. Clifford Grey.

Who's Who, Baby? Off-broadway musical. 1968. m.l. Johnny Brandon, b. Gerald Frank.

Wildcat Story revolving round 1912 oil strike. 1960. m. Cy Coleman, l. Carolyn Leigh, b. N. Richard Nash (171).

Wildest Dreams Light comedy. 1961. m. Julian Slade, l.b. Dorothy Reynolds.

Wildflower Rags-to-riches theme. 1923. m. Vincent Youmans and Herbert Stothart, l.b. Oscar Hammerstein II and Otto Harbach (477).

Wild Geese Comedy operetta. 1920. m.l.b. Charles Cuvillier, l.b. Ronald Jeans.

Wild Grows the Heather Scottish romance. 1956. (short run).

Wild Rose American operetta. 1926. m. Rudolf Friml, l.b. Otto Harbach and Oscar Hammerstein II.

Wild Thyme Musical romance. 1955. m.l. Donald Swann, b. Philip Guard (short run).

Winged Victory Tribute to the American Army Air Corps performed by service personnel, which included many future stars. 1943. m. David Rose, b. Moss Hart (212).

Wish You Were Here Adapt of Kober's *Having Wonderful Time*, a summer-camp romance. 1952. m.l. Harold Rome, b. Arthur Kober and Joshua Logan (598).

The Wiz Black version of the film *The Wizard of Oz*, adapted from Frank Baum's classic fantasy. 1975. m.l. Charlie Small (972)*.

Wonder Bar Usual Al Jolson one-man show based on nominal story about a Parisian restaurant-night club owned by the star. Previous British production based on original German show was more orthodox. 1930/1. m. Robert Katscher and Rowland Leigh, l. Irving Caesar (210 GB, 76 USA).

Wonderful Town Adapt of Joseph Fields's and Jerome Chodorov's play *My Sister Eileen*, centred on Greenwich Village life. 1953. m. Leonard Bernstein, l. Betty Comden and Adolph Green, b. Fields and Chodorov (559).

Yearling, The Story of a boy and a fawn. 1964. m. Michael Leonard, l.b. Herbert Martin (1 performance).

Yellow Mask, The Musical play. 1928. m. Vernon Duke, l. Desmond Carter, b. Edgar Wallace (218).

Yes, Madam Musical farce adapt from K. R. G. Browne's novel. 1934. m. Jack Waller and Joseph Tunbridge, l.b. R. P. Weston and Bert Lee.

Yes, Yes, Yvette Musical comedy. 1927. m. Phil Charig, Peter de Rose, Stephen O. Jones, Harold Orlob and Joseph Meyer, l. Irving Caesar, b. William Cary Duncan (40).

Yokel Boy Hollywood hillbillies. 1939. m.l. Charles Tobias, Al Sherman and Sam Stept, l.b. Lew Brown (208).

You Never Know Continental romance, adapt from Rowland Leigh's *By Candlelight*. 1938. m.l. Cole Porter, b. Rowland Leigh.

Your Arm's Too Short to Box with God Rock religion. 1976. m.l. Alex Bradford and Micki Grant, b. Vinnette Carroll.

You're a Good Man, Charlie Brown Based on the *Peanuts* cartoon characters of Charles M. Schultz. 1967. m.l. Clark Gesner, b. John Gordon (1,597).

Your Own Thing Adapt from *Twelfth Night*, updated Shakespeare. 1968. m.l. Hal Hester and Danny Apolinar, b. Donald Driver (933).

Yours Truly Musical comedy. 1927. m. Raymond Hubbell, l.b. Anne Caldwell.

You Said It Romantic comedy. 1931. m. Harold Arlen, l.b. Sid Silvers and Jack Yellen (192).

Zip Goes a Million Adapt from the play *Brewster's Millions*. 1951. m. George Posford, l.b. Eric Maschwitz.

Zorba Adapt of Nikos Kazantzaki's novel and film *Zorba the Greek*. 1968. m. John Kander, l. Fred Ebb, b. Joseph Stein (305).

Zulu and the Zayda m.l. Harold Rome (5 months)

Long Runs
On and Off-Broadway

On Broadway

Fiddler on the Roof/3,242
Hello Dolly/2,844
My Fair Lady/2,717
Man of La Mancha/2,328
Oklahoma!/2,212
Grease/2,179
Pippin/1,928
South Pacific/1,925
Hair/1,750
Mame/1,508
The Sound of Music/1,443
How to Succeed in Business without Really Trying/1,417
The Music Man/1,375
Funny Girl/1,348
Oh! Calcutta!/1,314
Promises, Promises/1,281
The Magic Show/1,253
The King and I/1,246
1776/1,217
Guys and Dolls/1,200
Cabaret/1,165
Annie Get Your Gun/1,147
Kiss Me Kate/1,077
Don't Bother Me, I Can't Cope/1,065
The Pajama Game/1,063
Damn Yankees/1,019
Shenandoah/973
The Wiz/972
A Funny Thing Happened on the Way to the Forum/964
Bells Are Ringing/924
Applause/896
Can Can/892
Carousel/890
Fanny/888
Follow the Girls/882
Camelot/873
Song of Norway/860
A Chorus Line/855
Fiorello!/795
Where's Charley/792
Oliver!/774
Gentlemen Prefer Blondes/740
Call Me Mister/734
West Side Story/732
High Button Shoes/727
Finian's Rainbow/725
Jesus Christ Superstar/720
Carnival/719
Company/705
Gypsy/702
Li'l Abner/693
Purlie/688
The Most Happy Fella/676
Irene/670
Bloomer Girl/654
Call Me Madam/644
The Green Pastures/640
Two Gentlemen of Verona/627
The Student Prince/608
Sweet Charity/608
Bye Bye Birdie/607
Flower Drum Song/600
A Little Night Music/600
Wish You Were Here/598
Blossom Time/592
The Me Nobody Knows/586
Kismet/583
Brigadoon/583
No Strings/580
Show Boat/572
Sally/570
Golden Boy/568
One Touch of Venus/567
I Do, I Do/560
Wonderful Town/559
Rose Marie/557
Jamaica/555
Stop the World, I Want to Get Off/555
Floradora/553
Good News/551
Let's Face It/547
Milk and Honey/543
What Makes Sammy Run?/540
The Unsinkable Molly Brown/532
Irma la Douce/524
Follies/521
Sunny/517
Half a Sixpence/511
The Vagabond King/511
The New Moon/509
The Rothschilds/507
Sugar/505
Shuffle Along/504
Up in Central Park/504
Carmen Jones/503
Panama Hattie/501

Off-Broadway

*The Fantasticks/7,115
The Threepenny Opera/2,707
**Godspell/2,100
You're a Good Man Charlie Brown/1,897

*as of May 31, 1977, and still running.
**until May 31, 1976 only; it opened on Broadway June 2, 1976 and is still running (413).

Filmography

An alphabetical list of filmed stage musicals indicating (a) date of original stage production (b) film producing company (c) film copyright date and (d) where applicable, change of title for the film version.

Animal Crackers (28) Paramount 1930
Annie Get Your Gun (46) MGM 1949
Anything Goes (34) Paramount 1936, 1956
Are You with It? (45) Universal 1948
Babes in Arms (37) MGM 1939
Balalaika (36) MGM 1939
The Band Wagon (31) MGM 1953
Bells Are Ringing (56) MGM 1960
Best Foot Forward (41) MGM 1943
Be Yourself (24) United Artists 1930
Big Boy (25) Warner 1930
Bitter Sweet (29) MGM 1940
Blossom Time (21) BIP 1934
The Boy Friend (54) MGM 1971
The Boys from Syracuse (38) Universal 1940
Brigadoon (47) MGM 1955
Bye Bye Birdie (60) Columbia 1963
Cabaret (66) Allied Artists 1972
Cabin in the Sky (40) MGM 1942
Call Me Madam (50) 20th Century Fox 1953
Call Me Mister (46) 20th Century Fox 1951
Camelot (60) Warner/Seven Arts 1967
Can Can (53) 20th Century Fox 1960
Carmen Jones (43) 20th Century Fox 1954
Carousel (45) 20th Century Fox 1956
The Cat and the Fiddle (31) MGM 1934
The Cocoanuts (25) Paramount 1929
A Connecticut Yankee (27) Paramount 1948 (*A Yankee at King Arthur's Court* in UK)
Damn Yankees (55) Warner 1958 (*What Lola Wants* in UK)
The Dancing Years (39) ABC c. 1950
The Desert Song (26) Warner 1929, 1943, 1952
Dubarry Was a Lady (39) MGM 1943
Evergreen (30) Gaumont-British 1935
Expresso Bongo (58) 1959
Fanny (54) 1961
Fiddler on the Roof (64) Mirisch/United Artists 1971
Fifty Million Frenchmen (29) Warner 1931
Finian's Rainbow (47) Warner/Seven Arts 1968
The Firefly (12) MGM 1937
Flower Drum Song (58) Universal 1961
Flying High (30) MGM 1931
Follow Thru (29) Paramount 1930
Funny Face (27) Paramount 1956
Funny Girl (64) Columbia 1968
A Funny Thing Happened on the Way to the Forum (62) United Artists 1967
The Gay Divorce (32) RKO 1934 (*The Gay Divorcée*)
Gentlemen Prefer Blondes (49) 20th Century Fox 1953
Gipsy Love (12) MGM 1930 (*The Rogue Song*)
Girl Crazy (30) Radio 1932, MGM 1943, 1966* (*When the Boys Meet the Girls*)*
The Girl Friend (26) Columbia 1935
Godspell (71) Columbia 1973
Golden Dawn (27) Warner 1930
The Good Companions (31) 1933
Good News (27) MGM 1930, 1947
The Great Waltz (34, 70) MGM 1938, 1972
Green Pastures (30) Warner 1936
Guys and Dolls (50) Goldwyn/MGM 1955
Gypsy (59) Warner 1962
Half a Sixpence (63) Paramount 1967
Hazel Flagg (53) Paramount 1954 (*Living It Up*)
Heads Up (29) Paramount 1930
Hello Dolly (64) 20th Century Fox 1969

Higher and Higher (40) RKO 1943
Hit the Deck (27) Radio 1929, MGM 1955
Hold Everything (28) Warner 1930
Honeymoon Lane (26) Paramount 1931
How to Succeed in Business without Really Trying (61) Mirisch/United Artists 1966
I Married an Angel (38) MGM 1942
Irene (19) RKO 1940
Irma la Douce (58) United Artists 1963
Jesus Christ, Superstar (71) Universal 1973
Jumbo (35) MGM 1962 (*Billy Rose's Jumbo*)
Kid Boots (23) Paramount 1926
The King and I (51) 20th Century Fox 1956
King's Rhapsody (49) Wilcox 1956
Kismet (53) MGM 1955
Kiss Me Kate (48) MGM 1953
Knickerbocker Holiday (38) United Artists 1944
Lady Be Good (24) MGM 1941
The Lady in Ermine (22) 1st National 1930 (*Bride of the Regiment*), 20th Century Fox 1948 (*That Lady in Ermine*)
Lady in the Dark (41) Paramount 1943
Let's Face It (41) Paramount 1943
Li'l Abner (56) Paramount 1959
The Lisbon Story (43) British National 1945
Little Johnny Jones (04) National 1930
Little Nellie Kelly (22) MGM 1940
A Little Night Music (73) scheduled for 1977
Louisiana Purchase (40) Paramount 1941
Mlle Modiste (05) 1st National (*Toast of the Legion*)
Mame (66) Warner 1974
Manhattan Mary (27) Paramount 1930 (*Follow the Leader*)
Man of La Mancha (65) United Artists 1972
Maytime (17) MGM 1937
Me and My Girl (37) 1939 (*The Lambeth Walk*)
The Melody Man (24) Columbia 1930
Mexican Hayride (44) Universal 1948
Music in the Air (32) Fox 1934
The Music Man (57) Warner 1962
My Fair Lady (56) Warner 1964
Naughty Marietta (10) MGM 1935
The New Moon (28) MGM 1930, 1940
No, No, Nanette (25) 1st National 1930, RKO 1940, Warner 1950* (*Tea for Two*)*
Oh What a Lovely War! (63) 1969
Oklahoma! (43) Magna 1955
Oliver! (60) Columbia 1968
On a Clear Day You Can See Forever (65) Paramount 1969
One Touch of Venus (43) Universal 1948
On the Town (44) MGM 1949
On Your Toes (36) 1st National 1939
Paint Your Wagon (51) Paramount 1969
The Pajama Game (54) Warner 1957
Pal Joey (40) Columbia 1957
Panama Hattie (40) MGM 1942
Paris (28) 1st National 1929
Poppy (23) Paramount 1936
Porgy and Bess (35) Goldwyn/Columbia 1959
Present Arms (28) Radio 1930 (*Leathernecking*)
Queen High (26) Paramount 1930
Rainbow (28) Warner 1930 (*Song of the West*)
The Ramblers (26) RKO 1930 (*Cuckoos*)
Red, Hot and Blue (36) Paramount 1949
Rio Rita (27) Radio 1929, MGM 1942
Rise and Shine (36) 20th Century Fox 1941
Roberta (33) RKO 1934, MGM 1952* (*Lovely to Look At*)*
The Rocky Horror Show (74) 20th Century Fox/Rank 1975
Rosalie (28) MGM 1937
Rose Marie (24) MGM 1935, 1954
Sally (20) 1st National 1929
Sally, Irene and Mary (22) 20th Century Fox 1937
1776 (69) Columbia 1971
Show Boat (27) Universal 1929, 1936, MGM 1951
Silk Stockings (55) MGM 1956
So Long, Letty (1916) Warner 1930
Something for the Boys (43) 20th Century Fox 1944
Song of Norway (44) ABC 1970
Song of the Flame (25) 1st National 1930
The Sound of Music (59) 20th Century Fox 1965
South Pacific (49) 20th Century Fox 1958
Spring Is Here (29) 1st National 1930
Stop the World, I Want to Get Off (61) 1966
Strike Me Pink (33) Goldwyn/United Artists 1935
Strike Up the Band (30) MGM 1940
The Student Prince (24) MGM 1954
Sunny (25) 1st National 1930, RKO 1941
Sweet Adeline (29) Warner 1934
Sweet Charity (66) Universal 1968
Sweethearts (13) MGM 1938
Take a Chance (32) Paramount 1933
That's a Good Girl (28) 1933
This Is the Army (42) Warner 1943
The Threepenny Opera (28, 54) Embassy/Paramount 1964
Too Many Girls (39) RKO 1940
Top Banana (51) Justman-Popkin 1953 (filmed 'live' for limited distribution and television)
Top Speed (29) 1st National 1930
Under Your Hat (38) British Lion 1940
The Unsinkable Molly Brown (60) MGM 1964
Up in Central Park (45) Universal 1948
The Vagabond King (25) Paramount 1930, 1956
Very Warm for May (39) MGM 1943 (*Broadway Rhythm*)
Waltz Dream (07) Paramount 1931 (*The Smiling Lieutenant*)
West Side Story (57) Mirisch/United Artists 1961
Where's Charley? (48) Warner 1952
Whoopee (28) Goldwyn/United Artists 1930
Winged Victory (43) 20th Century Fox 1944
Wonder Bar (30) 1st National 1934

For the greater part of the 1960s this sign was a permanent part of the decor of Cambridge Circus in London's West End.

Discography

Record Label Abbreviations

Ang	Angel	Mer	Mercury
AoC	Ace of Clubs	MFP	Music for Pleasure
AoH	Ace of Hearts	Mon	Monmouth-Evergreen
Ari	Arista	Mot	Motown
Atl	Atlantic	Para	Paramount
Bru	Brunswick	Parl	Parlophone
Bud	Buddah	Phi	Philips
Cam	Camden	Pol	Polydor
Cap	Capitol	Pro	Probe
Col	Columbia	Pro 3	Project 3
Cor	Coral	Ron	Rondolette
Dec	Decca	Stan	Standard
Ele	Elektra	Star	Starline
Emb EMB	CBS/Embassy	U-A	United Artists
Emb NR	Ember	Ver	Verve
Enc	Encore	Vic	Victrola
Fon	Fontana	War	Warner Brothers
Lon	London	Wld	World Records

This discography can only be of academic interest, since the record industry, with its volatile nature, will have rendered it out of date almost before publication. 'Vintage' recordings such as 'Original Cast' and soundtrack albums tend to be reissued so often, as labels change hands, that it is not practicable to do more than list the most recent reissues. If an album has not been reissued it is highly unlikely that the original is still available; it is therefore suggested that the discography be taken as a starting-point rather than as a permanent and definitive list. Only *original* 'Original Cast' recordings are listed; there are no revivals or studio-made 'cover versions' of well-known shows included. That would take another book. Three types of recording are listed, classified as follows:

(B) Original Broadway cast recording
(L) Original London cast recording
(F) Film soundtrack recording

American record numbers are denoted by **bold** type; British numbers are in regular type.

A guide to the abbreviated names of record labels is given at the top of the page.

After the Ball (L) Phi BBL-7005
Allegro (B) **RCA LSO-1099**
All-American (B) **Col AKOS-2160**
Annie Get Your Gun (B) **Dec 79018**/Cor CRL-1074 (L) Col SEG-7711 (F) **MGM SES-42-ST**/MGM 2353032
Anyone Can Whistle (B) **Col S-32608**
Anything Goes (L) Wld SHB-26 (F) **Dec 8318**/Bru LAT-8118
Applause (B) **ABC OC-11**/Pro SPB-1055
Apple Tree, The (B) **Col KOS-3020**
Arc de Triomphe (L) Wld SH-216
Band Wagon, The (B) **RCA LPV-565**/RCA LSA-3082 (F) **MGM SES-44-ST**/MGM 2353091
Beauty Prize The, (L) Wld SHB-34
Belle (or *The Ballad of Dr Crippen*) (L) Dec SKL-4136
Bells Are Ringing (B) **Col OS-2006**/Phi BBL-7201 (F) **Cap SW-1435**/Wld T-707
Billy (L) CBS-70133
Bless the Bride (L) Wld SH-228
Blitz! (L) HMV CSD-1441
Bloomer Girl (B) **Dec 8015**
Boy Friend, The (L) MFP 1206 (F) Col SCXA-9251
Bravo Giovanni (B) **Col KOS-2200**
Brigadoon (B) **RCA LSO-1001** (F) **MGM SES-50-ST**/MGM 2353065
Bye Bye Birdie (B) **Col KOS-2025**/Fon SCFL-137 (L) **Mer 17000**/Phi SABL-205 (F) **RCA LSO-1081**/RCA SF-7580
Cabaret (B) **Col KOS-3040** (L) Emb EMB-31026 (F) **ABC DS-752**/ABC ABCL-5019
Cabaret Girl, The (L) Wld SHB-34
Call Me Madam (B) **Dec DL-8035**/Bru LA-8539 (L) Col 33SX-1002 (F) **Dec DL-5465**/AoH AH-137
Call Me Mister (B) Bru LA-8523
Camelot (B) **Col S-32602**/CBS 70009 (L) HMV CSD-1559 (F) **War 1712**/War WS-1712
Can Can (B) **Cap S-452**/Enc ENC-117 (L) Parl PMD-1017 (F) **Cap SM-1301**/Wld T-746
Candide (B) **Col OS-2350**/Phi BBL-7305
Card, The (L) Pye NSPL-18408
Careless Rapture (L) Wld SHB-23
Carmen Jones (B) **Dec 9021**/Bru LAT-8057 (F) **RCA LM-1881**/RCA AHL1-0046
Carnival (B) **MGM S-3946-OC**/MGM C-918 (L) HMV CSD-1476
Carousel (B) **Dec 79020**/Cor CPS-13 (L) Col SED-5536 (F) **Cap SW-694**/Cap SLCT-6105
Celebration (B) **Cap SW-198**
Charlie Girl (L) CBS 62627
Chicago (B) **Ari 9005**
Chorus Line, A (B) **Col PS-33581**/CBS 70142
Company (B) **Col OS-3550**
Crest of the Wave (L) Wld SH-216
Cyrano (B) **A & M 3702**
Dames at Sea (B) **Col OS-3330** (L) CBS 70063
Damn Yankees (B) **RCA LOC-1021**/HMV CLP-1108 (F) **RCA LSO-1047**/RCA RD-27103
Dancing Years, The (L) Wld SHB-23
Dear World (B) **Col ABOS-3260**
Destry Rides Again (B) **Dec 79075**
Do I Hear a Waltz? (B) **Col AKOS-2770**
Don't Bother Me, I Can't Cope (B) **Pol 6013**
Do-Re-Mi (B) **RCA LSOD-2002**/RCA SF-5107 (L) Dec SKL-4145
Ernest in Love (B) **Col OS-2027**
Expresso Bongo (L) Pye NPL-18016
Family Affair, A (B) **U-A 5099**
Fanny (B) **RCA LOC-1015**
Fantasticks, The (B) **MGM S-3872-OC**/MGM C-871
Fiddler on the Roof (B) **RCA LSO-1093**/RCA SF-7843 (L) **Col SX-30742**/Emb EMB-31210 (F) **U-A 10900**
Fings Ain't Wot They Used t'Be (L) Dec SKL-4092
Finian's Rainbow (B) **Col CS-2080**/Phi BBL-7466 (F) **War BS-2550**/War WFS-2550
Fiorello! (B) **Cap SWAO-1321**/Cap SW-1321
First Impressions (B) **Col AOS-2014**
Flower Drum Song (B) **Col OS-2009**/Phi SABL-145 (L) **Ang S-35886**/HMV CSD-1359 (F) **MCA 2069**/Bru LAT-8392
Follies (B) **Cap SO-761**
Four Musketeers, The (L) Phi SAL-3655
Funny Face (L) **Mon MES-7037**/Wld SH-144 (F) **Ver MGV-15001**/HMV CLP-1119

Funny Girl (B) **Cap STAO-2059**/Cap SW-2059 (F) **Col BOS-3220**/CBS 70044
Funny Thing Happened on the Way to the Forum, A (B) **Cap SW-1717**/Emb NR-5039 (L) HMV CSD-1518 (F) **U-A LA-284-G**/U-A SULP-1153
Gay Divorce, The (L) Wld SHB-26 (F) EMI EMC-101
Gay Life (B) **Cap SWAO-1560**
Gay's the Word (L) Wld SH-216
Gentlemen Prefer Blondes (B) **Col OS-2310**/CBS 62087 (L) HMV CSD-1464 (F) MGM 2353067
George M. (B) **Col KOS-3200**
Girl in Pink Tights, The (B) **Col OL-4890**
Glamorous Night (L) Wld SHB-23
Godspell (B) **Ari 4001**/Bell SBLL-146 (L) Bell SBLL-203 (F) **Ari 4005**/Bell SBLL-223
Golden Apple (B) **Ele 5000**
Golden Boy (B) Cap SW-2124
Gone with the Wind (L) Col SCXA-9252
Good Companions, The (L) EMI EMC-3042
Good News (F) **MGM SES-49-ST**/MGM 2353038
Good Old, Bad Old Days, The (L) EMI EMA-751
Grease (B) **MGM ISE-34-OC**
Guys and Dolls (B) **Dec 79023**/Cor CRL-1072
Gypsy (B) **Col OS-2017**/Emb EMB-31025 (L) **RCA LBLI-5004**/RCA SER-5686 (F) **War SB-1480**/War WS8120
Hair (B) **RCA LSO-1115**/RCA INTS-1133 (L) Pol 583043
Half a Sixpence (L) Dec SKL-4521 (F) RCA SB-6735
Happiest Girl in the World, The (B) **Col KOS-2050**
Hello Dolly (B) **RCA LSOD-1087** (L) RCA SF-7768 (F) **20th Cent 102**/Pye NSPH-28501
Here's Love (B) **Col KOS-2400**
High Spirits (L) Pye NSPL-83022
Hit the Deck (F) **MGM 3163**/MGM 2353090
House of Flowers (B) **Col COS-2320**
How to Succeed in Business without Really Trying (B) **RCA LSO-1066** (L) RCA SF-7564 (F) U-A SULP-1162
I Can Get It for You Wholesale (B) **Col AKOS-2180**
I Do, I Do (B) **RCA LSO-1128** (L) RCA SF-7938
Inner City (B) **RCA LSO-1171**
Irma la Douce (B) **Col OS-2029** (L) Phi BBL7274
It's a Bird, It's a Plane, It's Superman (B) **Col AKOS-2970**
Jeeves (L) MCA MCF-2726
Jesus Christ, Superstar (B) **MCA 5000** (L) MCA MDKS-8008 (F) **MCA 11000**/MDKS-8012/3
Jorrocks (L) HMV CSD-3591
Joseph and the Technicolour Dreamcoat (L) MCA MCF-2544
Kean (B) **Col KOS-2120**
King and I, The (B) **Dec 79008**/Cor CDL-8026 (L) Phi BBL-7002 (F) **Cap SW-740**/Cap SLCT-6108
King's Rhapsody (L) Wld SHB-23 (F) Par GEP-8553
Kismet (B) **Col OS-2060**/Phi BBL-7023 (F) **MGM 3281**/MGM 2353057
Kiss Me Kate (B) **Col OS-2300**/Phi BBL-7232 (L) Wld SHB-26 (F) **MGM SES-44-ST**/MGM 2353062
Kwamina (B) **Cap SW-1645**
Lady Be Good (L) **Mon MES-7036**/Wld SH-124
Lady in the Dark (B) **RCA LPV-503**/Vic VIC-1225
Let It Ride (B) **RCA LSO-1064**
Li'l Abner (B) **Col OL-5150** (F) **Col OS-2021**/Phi SBBL-565
Little Mary Sunshine (B) **Cap SWAO-1240**/Cap SW-1240
Little Me (B) **RCA LSO-1078** (L) Wld T-789
Little Night Music, A (B) **Col KS-32265**/Emb EMB-31153 (L) **RCA LRL-5090**/RCA LRL1-5090
Liza of Lambeth (L) CBS 70148
Lock Up Your Daughters (L) Dec SKL-4070
Lost in the Stars (B) **Dec 8028**
Lute Song (B) **Dec 8030**/AoH AH-129
Maggie May (L) Dec SKL-4643
Magic Show, The (B) **Ari 9003**
Make Me an Offer (L) HMV CSD-1295
Mame (B) **Col KOS-3000**/CBS 70051 (F) War K56035
Man of La Mancha (B) **MCA 2018**/MCA MUPS-5466 (L) **MCA 10010**/MUCS-123/4 (F) U-A UAG-29422
Mardi Gras (L) EMI EMC-3123
Me Nobody Knows, The (B) **Atl S-1566**
Milk and Honey (B) **RCA LSO-1065**
Minnie's Boys (B) **Pro 3 TS-6002**
Miss Liberty (B) **Col OL-4220**
Mr President (B) **Col KOS-2270**
Mr Wonderful (B) Bru LAT-8184
Most Happy Fella, The (B) **Col OS-2330**/Phi BBL-7374 (L) **Ang S-35887**/HMV CSD-1306
Music Man, The (B) **Cap SW-990**/Wld T-732 (L) **Sta 10039**/HMV CLP-1444 (F) **War BS-1459**/War WS8066
My Fair Lady (B) **Col PS-2015**/Phi RBL-1000 (L) CBS 70005 (F) **Col PS-2600**/CBS 70000
Nervous Set, The (B) **Col OS-2018**
New Girl in Town (B) **RCA LSO-1027**
No Strings (B) **Cap 01695**/SW-1695 (L) Dec SKL-4576
Nymph Errant (L) Wld SHB-26
Oh Boy! (Oh Joy!) (L) Wld SHB-34
Oh, Captain! (B) **Col OL-5280**
Oh Kay! (L) **Mon MES-7043**
Oh What a Lovely War! (L) Dec SPA-27 (F) ABC ABCL-5072
Oklahoma! (B) **Dec 79017**/Cor CRL-1069 (L) HMV 7EP-7023 (F) **Cap SWA-595**/Cap SLCT-6100
Oliver! (B) **RCA LSOD-2004** (L) **Dec SPA-30**/Dec SPA-30 (F) **RCA COSD-5501**/RCA SB-6777
On a Clear Day You Can See Forever (B) **RCA LSOD-2006** (F) **Col AS-30086**/CBS 70075
Once Upon a Mattress (B) **MCA 2079**/Lon HAR-2286
110 in the Shade (B) **RCA LOS-1085**/RCA SF-7841
On the Town (B) **Dec 8030**/AoH AH-129
Out of This World (B) **Col OL-4390**
Pacific Overtures (B) **RCA ARL1-1367**/RCA ARL1-1367
Paint Your Wagon (B) **RCA LOC-1006**/HMV CLP-1005 (F) **Para 1001**/ABC ABCL-5073
Pajama Game, The (B) **Col OL-4840**/Phi BBL7050 (L) HMV CLP-1062 (F) **Col OL-5210**/Phi BBL-7197
Pal Joey (B) **Col OL-4364**/Phi BBL-7213 (F) **Cap SM-912-E**/Cap VMP-1005
Perchance to Dream (L) AoC ACL-1112
Pickwick (L) Phi 6382070
Pippin (B) **Mot 6-760**/Mot STMA-8014
Plain and Fancy (B) **Cap W-603**/Cap LCT-6102
Porgy and Bess (B) **Dec DL-79024**/Cor CRL-1085 (F) **Col OS-2016**/CBS 70007
Prince and the Pauper (B) Lon SHU-8201
Promises, Promises (B) **U-A 9902**
Redhead (B) **RCA LSO-1048**
Rex (B) **RCA ABL1-1683**
Roar of the Greasepaint, The (B) **RCA LOS-1109**
Robert and Elizabeth (L) HMV CSD-1575
Rocky Horror Show, The (B) Ode ODE-77026 (L) UK UKAL-1015 (F) Ode ODE-78332
Rose Marie (L) Wld SHB-37 (F) **MGM 3769**/MGM 2353077
Rothschilds, The (B) **Col S-30337**
Sail Away (B) **Cap SWAO-1643**/Cap SW-1643 (L) **Stan 10027**/HMV CSD-1445
Salad Days (L) Emb EMB-31046
Sally (L) Wld SHB-34
Salvation (B) Cap E-ST-337
Secret Life of Walter Mitty, The (B) **Col AOS-2720**
Seesaw (B) **Bud 95006**
1776 (B) **Col BOS-3310**/CBS 70071 (L) Col SCX-6424
She Loves Me (B) **MGM 4118-OC**/MGM CS-6077 (L) HMV CSD-1546
Show Boat (L) Wld SH-240 (F) **MGM SES-42-ST**/MGM 2353045
Silk Stockings (B) **RCA LSO-1102** (F) **MGM SES-51-ST**/MGM 2353034

Song of Norway (B) **Dec 79019** (F) Pro SPB-1017
Sound of Music, The (B) **Col KOS-2020**/CBS 70008 (L) **Stan 10044**/Star SRS-5003 (F) **RCA LSOD-2005**/RCA SB-6616
South Pacific (B) **Col OS-2040**/CBS 70019 (L) Col SEG-7688 (F) **RCA LSO-1032**/RCA SB-2011
Stop the World, I Want to Get Off (L) **Lon 88001**/Dec SKL-4142
Street Scene (B) **Col OL-4139**
Student Prince, The (F) **RCA LSC-2339**/RCA LSB-4107
Subways Are for Sleeping (B) **Col AOS-2130**
Sugar (B) **U-A 9905**
Summer Song (L) Wing WL-1172
Sunny (L) Wld SH-240
Sweet Charity (B) **Col KOS-2900** (L) CBS 70035 (F) MCA MUCS-133
Take Me Along (B) **RCA LSO-1050**
Tenderloin (B) **Cap SWAO-1492**/Cap SW-1492
Theodore & Co (L) Wld SHB-34
Threepenny Opera, The (F) **RCA LSO-1086**
Tom Brown's Schooldays (L) Dec SKL-5137
Tree Grows in Brooklyn, A (B) **Col OL-4405**/Phi BBL-7206
Trelawney (L) Dec SKL-5144
Two Gentlemen of Verona (B) **ABC 1001**/Pro PBSP-114 (L) Pol 2394110
Unsinkable Molly Brown, The (B) **Cap SW-2152** (F) **MGM 4232**
Vagabond King, The (L) Wld SHB-37
Valmouth (L) Pye NSPL-18029
Water Gipsies, The (L) Wld SH-228
West Side Story (B) **Col S-32603**/Emb EMB-31027 (L) **Ron 856** (F) **Col OS-2070**/CBS 70006
Where's Charley? (L) Col 33SX-1085
Whoop-Up (B) **MGM S-3745**
Wildcat (B) **RCA LSO-1060**
Wildflower (L) **Mon MES-7052**
Wish You Were Here (B) **Cam 621**
Wiz, The (B) **Atl 18137**
Wonderful Town (B) **Dec 79010**/Bru LAT-8058 (L) Col SEG-7569
You're a Good Man, Charlie Brown (B) **MGM ISE-9-OC**/MGM CS-8045
Your Own Thing (B) RCA SF-7972
Zorba (B) **Cap SO-118**

Bibliography

Anobile, Richard J., and Marx, Groucho, *The Marx Brothers Scrapbook*. New York: Darien House, 1973; London: W.H. Allen, 1973.
Astaire, Fred, *Steps in Time*. New York: Harper, 1959; London: Heinemann, 1960.
Atkinson, Brooks, *Broadway*. London: Cassell, 1971.
Burton, Jack, *The Blue Book of Broadway Musicals*. New York: Century House, 1952.
——, *The Blue Book of Hollywood Musicals*. New York: Century House, 1953.
Cahn, Sammy, *I Should Care*. London: W.H. Allen, 1975.
Cantor, Eddie, and Ardmore, Jane Kesner, *Take My Life*. New York: Doubleday, 1957.
Croce, Arlene, *The Fred Astaire and Ginger Rogers Book*. New York: Galahad, 1972.
Duke, Vernon, *Passport to Paris*. Boston, Mass: Little, Brown, 1955.
Eells, George, *Cole Porter*. London: W.H. Allen, 1967.
Ewen, David, *A Journey to Greatness*. London: W.H. Allen, 1956.
——, *New Complete Book of the American Musical Theater*. New York: Henry Holt, 1976.
——, *The Story of the American Musical Theater*. Philadelphia, Pa: Chilton, 1961.
Farnol, Lynn, Group Inc, *ASCAP Biographical Dictionary*. New York: ASCAP, 1966.
Frank, Gerold, *Judy*. London: W.H. Allen, 1975.
Freedland, Michael, *Jolson*. New York: Stein & Day, 1972; London: W.H. Allen, 1973.
——, *Irving Berlin*. New York and London: W.H. Allen, 1974.
Gammond, Peter, and Clayton, Peter, *A Guide to Popular Music*. London: Phoenix House, 1960.
Green, Stanley, *The World of Musical Comedy*. New York: Ziff-Davis, 1960.
——, *The Rodgers and Hammerstein Story*. New York: John Day; London: W.H. Allen, 1963.
Green, Stanley, and Goldblatt, Burt, *Starring Fred Astaire*. New York and London: W.H. Allen, 1974
Heppner, Sam, *Cockie*. London: Leslie Frewin, 1969.
Hirschhorn, Clive, *Gene Kelly*. London: W.H. Allen, 1974.
Hubler, Richard G., *The Cole Porter Story*. New York: World, 1965.
Jablonski, Edward, and Stewart, Lawrence D., *The Gershwin Years*. London: Robson, 1974.
Jay, Dave, *The Irving Berlin Songography*. New York: Arlington House, 1969.
Kerr, Walter, *Pieces at Eight*. London: Max Reinhardt, 1958.
Kimball, Robert, and Simons, Alfred, *The Gershwins*. London: Jonathan Cape, 1974.
Kimball, Robert, and Gill, Brendan, *Cole*. London: Michael Joseph, 1971.
Kobal, John, *Gotta Sing, Gotta Dance*. New York and London: Paul Hamlyn, 1970.
Lewine, Richard, and Simons, Alfred, *Encyclopedia of Theater Music*. New York: Random House, 1961.
McVay, Douglas, *The Musical Film*. London: Zwemmer, 1967; New York: Barnes, 1967.
Mander, Raymond, and Mitchenson, Joe, *Musical Comedy – A Story in Pictures*. London: Peter Davies, 1970.
——, *Revue – A Story in Pictures*. London: Peter Davies, 1971.
——, *The Theatres of London*. London: New English Library, 1975.
Martin, David, *The Films of Busby Berkeley*. San Francisco, Calif: David Martin, 1965.
May, Robin, *A Companion to the Theatre*. London: Lutterworth Press, 1973.
Melville, Alan, *Merely Melville*. London: Hodder & Stoughton, 1970.
Merman, Ethel, *Don't Call Me Madam*. London: W. H. Allen, 1955.
Mordden, Ethan, *Better Foot Forward: The History of American Musical Theater*. New York: Grossman, 1976.

Morella, Joe, and Epstein, Edward, *Judy*. London: Leslie Frewin, 1969.
——, *The Amazing Careers of Bob Hope*. London: W.H. Allen, 1974.
Morley, Sheridan, *A Talent to Amuse*. London: Heinemann, 1969.
Moshier, W. Franklyn, *The Alice Faye Movie Book*. Harrisburg, Pa: Stackpole, 1974.
Noble, Peter, *Ivor Novello: Man of the Theatre*. London: Falcon Press, 1951.
Payne, Robert, *Gershwin*. London: Robert Hale, 1962.
Richards, Dick, *Ginger: Salute to a Star*. Brighton, Sussex: Clifton Books, 1969.
Roth, Lilian, with Frank, Gerold, and Connelly, Mike, *I'll Cry Tomorrow*. New York: Frederick Fell, 1954.
Rust, Brian, *The Complete Entertainment Discography*. New York: Arlington House, 1973.
Shapiro, Nat, *Popular Music: An Annotated Index of American Popular Songs*. New York: Adrian Press, 1964, 1965, 1967, 1968, 1969.
Shaw, Arnold, *Sinatra*. London: W.H. Allen, 1968.
Silvers, Phil, and Saffron, Robert, *The Man Who Was Bilko*. New York and London: W.H. Allen, 1974.
Smith, Cecil, *Musical Comedy in America*. New York: Theatre Art Books, 1950.
Springer, John, *All Talking, All Singing, All Dancing*. New York: Citadel Press, 1966.
Stambler, Irwin, *Encyclopedia of Popular Music*. New York: St Martin's Press, 1965.
——, *Encyclopedia of Pop, Rock and Soul*. New York: St Martins' Press, 1975.
Taylor, Deems, *Some Enchanted Evenings*. New York: Harper, 1953.
Taylor, John Russell, and Jackson, Arthur, *The Hollywood Musical*. London: Secker & Warburg, 1971; New York: McGraw-Hill, 1971.
Tynan, Kenneth, *Curtains*. London: Longmans, Green, 1961.
Vallance, Tom, *The American Musical*. London: Zwemmer, 1970; New York: Barnes, 1970.
Wilder, Alec, *American Popular Song: The Great Innovators 1900–1950*. New York and London: Oxford University Press, 1972 and 1973.
Wilk, Max, *They're Playing Our Song*. London: W.H. Allen, 1974.
Wilson, Earl, *The Show Business Nobody Knows*. New York and London: W.H. Allen, 1972.

Acknowledgments

The publisher would like to thank the following for permission to reproduce photographs in this book:

Black-and-white:
The author: 114, 116t, 118, 119, 120, 124, 125, 128; by courtesy of the Victoria & Albert Museum: 16tl; Jos. Abeles Studio: 8, 12, 13, 59, 60, 62t, 62b, 63r, 64, 65, 71, 72, 77, 79, 81, 83, 84, 85; ASCAP: 20b, 135, 141, 147; Camera Press Ltd: 76r, 199; Donald Cooper: 106, National Film Archives: 108, 109, 110b, 129, 130t, 130b, 131, 132t, 132b, 133; Zoe Dominic: 74-5; Fred Fehl: 10, 11, 42, 45, 47t and b, 49, 50, 52, 54, 55, 58l, 58r, 61, 66, 67, 148; Kobal Collection: 110t, 112tl, 112bl, 112tr, 112br, 113, 115t, 115b, 116b, 117t, 134t, 134b; by courtesy of the Library of Congress, Washington: 143, 157; Mander and Mitchenson Theatre Collection: 16tr, 16b, 20t, 21t, 23, 28b, 33, 37, 38b, 46, 48l and r, 51, 53, 54l, 56, 63r, 73, 91, 93t, 93b, 94, 97t, 98r, 100l, 100r, 102t, 102b, 152, 160; NYPLL: 14, 19, 21b, 22, 24, 25l, 25r, 26t, 28t, 29t, 29b, 30, 31, 32, 34, 38t, 39, 40; Radio Times Hulton Picture Library: 26b, 90, 92, 95l, 97, 98l, 101, 137; Rex Features: 103t, 104; Mick Rock: 80; Houston Rogers: 96, 99, 103b; Reg Wilson: 105, 107; Harvard University Theatre Collection/photo Angus McBean: 44, 95r, 101.

Colour
Jos. Abeles Studio: 35t, 69, 87, 88, 175, 191tb, 192; Kobal Collection 122, 139t; Houston Rogers: 35b; Maunder and Mitchenson Theatre Collection: 36tlrb; Reg Wilson: 70, 121, 139, 140, 192t; Rex Features: 174; Victoria and Albert Museum: 17tb, 18tb

Index

The numbers in italics refer to illustrations.